HISTORY OF
United States Naval Operations
IN WORLD WAR II

★

VOLUME TEN

The Atlantic Battle Won
May 1943–*May* 1945

From a painting by Cdr. Albert K. Murray USNR

Admiral Royal E. Ingersoll USN

HISTORY OF UNITED STATES NAVAL
OPERATIONS IN WORLD WAR II

VOLUME X

The Atlantic
Battle Won

May 1943–*May* 1945

BY SAMUEL ELIOT MORISON

WITH AN INTRODUCTION BY
Robert Love

NAVAL INSTITUTE PRESS
Annapolis, Maryland

This book was brought to publication with the generous assistance of Marguerite and Gerry Lenfest.

Naval Institute Press
291 Wood Road
Annapolis, MD 21402

First Naval Institute Press paperback edition published 2011
New Introduction © 2011 by the United States Naval Institute.

Library of Congress Cataloging-in-Publication Data
Morison, Samuel Eliot, 1887–1976.
    History of United States naval operations in World War II / Samuel Eliot Morison.
        v. cm.
    Originally published: Boston : Little, Brown, 1947–62.
    Includes bibliographical references and index.
    Contents: v. 1. The Battle of the Atlantic, 1939–1943 — v. 2. Operations in North African waters, October 1942–June 1943 — v. 3. The Rising Sun in the Pacific, 1931–April 1942 — v. 4. Coral Sea, Midway and Submarine Actions, May 1942–August 1942 — v. 5. The Struggle for Guadalcanal, August 1942–February 1943 — v. 6. Breaking the Bismarcks Barrier, 22 July 1942–1 May 1944 — v. 7. Aleutians, Gilberts and Marshalls, June 1942–April 1944 — v. 8. New Guinea and the Marianas, March 1944–August 1944 — v. 9. Sicily-Salerno-Anzio, January 1943–June 1944 — v. 10 The Atlantic Battle Won, May 1943–May 1945 — v. 11 The Invasion of France and Germany, 1944–1945 — v. 12 Leyte, June 1944–January 1945.
    ISBN 978-1-59114-547-9 (v. 1 : alk. paper) — ISBN 978-1-59114-548-6 (v. 2 : alk. paper) — ISBN 978-1-59114-549-3 (v. 3 : alk. paper) — ISBN 978-1-59114-550-9 (v. 4 : alk. paper) — ISBN 978-1-59114-551-6 (v. 5 : alk. paper) — ISBN 978-1-59114-552-3 (v. 6 : alk. paper) — ISBN 978-1-59114-553-0 (v. 7 : alk. paper) — ISBN 978-1-59114-554-7 (v. 8 : alk. paper) — ISBN 978-1-59114-575-2 (v. 9 : alk. paper) — ISBN 978-1-59114-576-9 (v. 10 : alk. paper) — ISBN 978-1-59114-577-6 (v. 11 : alk. paper) — ISBN 978-1-59114-535-6 (v. 12 : alk. paper) 1. World War, 1939-1945—Naval operations, American. I. Title.
    D773.M6 2010
    940.54'5973—dc22   2009052288

Printed in the United States of America on acid-free paper

19 18 17 16 15 14 13 12 11   9 8 7 6 5 4 3 2 1

First printing

To

The Memory of

JONAS HOWARD INGRAM

1886–1952

Admiral, United States Navy

. . . The only course for us to pursue is to revert to the ancient practice of convoy. This will be a purely offensive measure, because if we concentrate our shipping into convoys and protect it with our naval forces we will thereby force the enemy . . . to encounter naval forces . . . which are a great danger to the submarine.

— REAR ADMIRAL SIMS to Secretary Daniels
28 June 1917 (Victory at Sea p. 388)

You were right about the predominant place which submarine warfare should have in our plans. There is no question in my mind but that the German submarine menace is the most dangerous thing we have to face in our efforts at victory over Hitler.

— SECRETARY KNOX to Admiral Stark
27 November 1942

The "tonnage war" is the main task for the submariners, probably the decisive contribution of submarines to winning the war. This war on merchant shipping must be carried out where the greatest successes can be achieved with the smallest losses.

— GROSSADMIRAL DOENITZ in B.d.U. War Diary
31 December 1942

Tough as the submarine situation is I feel there is no cause for discouragement, though God knows there is none for congratulating ourselves. However, we will win this struggle.

— ADMIRAL STARK to Admiral King
24 April 1943

Preface

VOLUME X is the continuation of Volume I of this series, entitled *The Battle of the Atlantic, September 1939–May 1943*, which appeared in 1947, and in a new and revised edition in 1954.

The Battle of the Atlantic in the period covered by this volume includes only one surface action, that of the sinking of *Scharnhorst*. Many amphibious operations have already been related in Volumes II and IX; the account of those in the invasion of France has been postponed to Volume XI. Consequently the theme of this book is the war on enemy submarines.

Antisubmarine warfare in the Atlantic is perhaps the most absorbing and interesting aspect of naval warfare in World War II. It was unremitting, subject to constant ups and downs, and fought on three levels — on the surface of the ocean, under the sea, and in the air; a war fought by scientists, inventors, naval construction and ordnance experts, as well as by sailors and aviators. In this conflict the United States Navy, Coast Guard, and Merchant Marine, the Royal Canadian Navy and Air Force, the Royal Navy and Air Force, and the British Merchant Navy were closely integrated. It was an exceedingly complicated war, fascinating to technicians and professional sailormen; but exceedingly difficult to narrate in the scope of two volumes. I cannot neglect the superb work performed in this theater by our Allied Navies and Air Forces, although it is obviously impossible to relate them in the same detail as our own. And in all areas of Anglo-Canadian responsibility, such as the Northern Transatlantic and North Russian convoy routes and the Indian Ocean, a large number of American merchant ships with United States Naval Armed Guards participated.

First drafts of Chapters II–IV, VI, VIII–X were written between 1944 and 1946. At that time, my assistants were Lieutenant Commander Henry Salomon USNR, who visited Recife, Bermuda and other bases in search of information, Lieutenant Commander Henry D. Reck USNR, who visited the Mediterranean theater, Chief Yeoman Donald R. Martin USNR, and Wave Yeoman 1st Class Antha E. Card. The last two, as civilians, are still with me. Mr. Martin compiled the task organizations in the Appendices and Miss Card did some valuable text revision as well as accurately typing my frequently rewritten and corrected drafts.

In 1950 I obtained the services of Lieutenant Philip K. Lundeberg USNR, one of the three officers who survived the sinking of *Frederick C. Davis* by *U-546*. Mr. Lundeberg performed several laborious tasks such as combing the records in the Division of Naval History for every significant antisubmarine action in which the United States Navy participated, and comparing these with captured German documents to determine which U-boat did what, and how the German submarines were deployed. He prepared a very detailed and accurate ms., "American Antisubmarine Operations in the Atlantic May 1943–May 1945," about four times the length of the present volume. This, indexed by Mr. Martin and Mr. Roger Pineau, will be deposited in the Division of Naval History, Navy Department, and will be an indispensable source of information for future historians of the United States Navy.

Beginning in 1953 Mr. Pineau, who has been assisting me since 1947, has done the most thorough research possible for anyone to do on very many questions that came up. Rear Admiral Bern Anderson (Ret.) who has been assisting me since he took a Ph.D. at Harvard after the war, did the spadework for Chapters V and XIV, besides bringing his long naval experience, historical training and passion for accuracy to bear on almost every action that has been described. Yeoman 1st Class Roger F. Schofield also helped with the typing.

In addition, I have obtained oral information from scores of United States and British naval officers who participated in the Atlantic war. Rear Admiral Roger Bellairs of the Historical Section of the Admiralty and members of his staff placed their historical records at my disposal, read my draft of this volume, and made numerous suggestions and corrections. Captain Stephen W. Roskill RN, who is writing the volumes on "The War at Sea" for the overall British War History, performed the same service for this volume and allowed me to read an advance typescript of his volume which covers in part the same period. Konteradmiral Eberhard Godt, formerly the operations officer of Grossadmiral

Doenitz, and Dr. Jürgen Rohwer of Frankfort-on-Main, who is writing the history of the U-boats, have given me valuable information orally and in writing. And I have received constant support, welcome advice and much information from successive Chiefs of Naval Operations, Secretaries and Assistant Secretaries of the Navy, and from Rear Admiral John B. Heffernan, Director of Naval History. Miss Loretta Mac-Crindle, head of the Historical Records Branch, has been unfailingly patient and helpful. The charts were prepared in the drafting room of the United States Naval War College under the direction of Mr. John Lawton and drafted by Mr. Joseph A. Domingoes Jr. and Mr. Frederick J. Wagner.

My beloved wife, Priscilla B. Morison, who has accompanied me on research missions to Washington, London and Germany, has been of assistance in ways too numerous to mention.

My own limited experience of escort-of-convoy began in 1942 when I was a temporary member of the staff of Captain Heffernan, Comdesron 13, in U.S.S. *Buck*. Late in 1944 I crossed the Atlantic again as a temporary member of the staff of Captain W. A. P. Martin when escorting a convoy in U.S.C.G.C. *Campbell*. Brief as these experiences were, they gave me an insight into the constant and unremitting vigilance required in antisubmarine warfare that could never be acquired from books. Many of my shipmates were lost in the war. Others too have since departed to the place where brave sailormen go. They became my warm friends; I have done my best to fulfill their expectations, and those of our shipmates who survived.

In order to avoid an excessive number of footnotes, I shall here describe the principal sources which have been drawn upon for this volume.

1. *Action Reports and other Primary Records, in Division of Naval History, Navy Department*

Action Reports of task force and task group commanders, of squadron and division commanders, of C.O.s of individual ships and pilots of individual aircraft. Those by the pilots are called "Aircraft A/S Action Reports." Thus, for every important antisubmarine attack by an Escort Carrier Group there are Action Reports by the task group commander, the screen commander, the air group commander, the C.O. of each ship, and the pilot of each plane which participated.

War Diaries of task force commanders, of shore commands such as Eastern Sea Frontier and Fourth Fleet, and of individual ships.

Convoy Files of Convoy and Routing Section, Tenth Fleet, in Division of Naval History. Indispensable for the histories of convoys.

Interviews about important actions with officers concerned, on tape-recordings or microfilm, in the same Division of Naval History.

Tenth Fleet Antisubmarine Incidents, several thousand in number, compiled at Tenth Fleet headquarters from every reported attack on or by an enemy submarine, no matter how insignificant.

2. *Reference Works and Compilation of Facts*

Chief of Naval Operations *German, Japanese, and Italian Submarine Losses World War II* (1946), commonly known as "The Yellow Book." This joint work of the Admiralty and C.N.O. Assessment of Damage Committees, compiled and printed immediately after the war, gives the date, position, and agent of every enemy submarine sunk during the war. It is on the whole very accurate and I have referred to it only on occasions when it is in error.

U.S. Fleet Antisubmarine Warfare Bulletin, published monthly from June 1943 to June 1945 inclusive. Familiarly known during the war as "The Yellow Peril," this restricted periodical contains a large variety of information.

Administrative History of the Atlantic Fleet, 11 volumes, by a variety of authors. Bound typescripts deposited in the Division of Naval History. Particularly useful are Vol. I on Cinclant, Vol. XI on Fourth Fleet, and an unnumbered first draft called "History of the Antisubmarine Measures Division of Tenth Fleet." Cominch Headquarters compiled in May 1945 a similar "History of Convoy and Routing," a most useful compendium of convoy information.

C. M. Sternhell & A. M. Thorndike, *Antisubmarine Warfare in World War II* (Ops. Evaluation Group Report No. 51, Washington 1946). A valuable analysis by two men of science.

A number of naval commands and ships compiled their own *War Histories.*

3. *"Survivor" Documents*

Office of Naval Intelligence *Summaries of Interrogations* of (1) survivors of sunk American merchant vessels; (2) survivors of sunk or captured enemy submarines.

Naval Armed Guard Reports by C.O.s or senior survivors, in the form of letters to Vice Chief of Naval Operations, Armed Guard files, Division of Naval History.

A separate collection of pamphlets called the "250 Series," with the general title *Post Mortems on Enemy Submarines,* issued by the Office of Naval Intelligence during the war.

4. *United States Army Air Force Documents*

Assistant Chief of Air Staff Intelligence Historical Division *The Antisubmarine Command,* a 307-pp. typescript prepared in April 1945.

Three Historical Essays relating to Army Antisubmarine Activities prepared by 1st Lt. Henry Grattan USA, April 1944.

These two are indispensable for presenting the A.A.F. point of view on antisubmarine warfare and for the claims and achievements of the Army A/S Command. Both in Army Air Force Archives, Washington.

The Official History of the South Atlantic Division Army Air Forces Air Transport Command (2 vols., 1945) is one of several such command histories that contain items relevant to naval history.

5. *British Admiralty Documents*

These are very numerous and most important for the Atlantic War.

6. *German Documents*

Ms. "Befehlshaber der Untersee-Booten Kriegstagebuch"; the English translation abbreviated as B.d.U. War Diary. The official day-by-day record kept by the staff of Grossadmiral Doenitz. A comprehensive, reliable, and indispensable source for German naval strategy and movements of U-boats.

War Diaries of individual U-boat commands, especially of Fuehrer der U-Booten, Norwegen *(F.d.U. Norway)* for Arctic operations, and *F.d.U. Italy* for the Mediterranean.

War Diaries of individual U-boats. Microfilms of over a thousand, captured at the close of the war, are in the Tambach Collection, Division of Naval History. The originals are in London.

Karl Doenitz "The Conduct of the War at Sea," dictated to General Jodl in 1945; translation published by Navy Department.

Office of Naval Intelligence *Fuehrer Conferences on Matters Dealing with the German Navy, 1939–1945* (7 vols., Washington 1946–1947). Also printed in *Brassey's Naval Annual 1948* with introduction by Rear Admiral H. G. Thursfield RN.

7. *Published Books and Articles*

Besides the leading and well-known works by Fleet Admiral King and Walter Whitehill, Sir Winston Churchill, Admiral of the Fleet Viscount Cunningham, Hon. Henry L. Stimson and McGeorge Bundy, and by Dr. J. Phinney Baxter, the following are useful in greater or less degree: —

British Admiralty *The Battle of the Atlantic* (London 1946), 104 pp.

Kurt Assmann *Deutsche Schicksalsjahre* (Wiesbaden 1950). The first serious attempt to present the war as a whole to the German people, by a leading German naval historian.

Rear Admiral R. M. Bellairs RN "Historical Survey of Trade Defense since 1914," *Journal* of the Royal United Service Institution XCIV (1954) 359–77.

Rear Admiral W. S. Chalmers *Max Horton and the Western Approaches* (London 1954). Best account of the antisubmarine war from the British point of view.

W. F. Craven and J. L. Cate *The Army Air Forces in World War.* Vol. II (Chicago 1949) contains a good account of A.A.F. antisubmarine activities.

Wolfgang Frank *The Sea Wolves* (London 1954); a partial translation of his *Die Wölfe und der Admiral, der Roman der U-Boote* (Hamburg 1953). Best popular German account of the U-boats but unreliable as to details.

Rear Admiral D. V. Gallery *Clear the Decks!* (1951). By the C.O. of *Guadalcanal.*

Erich Gröner *Die Schiffe der Deutschen Kriegsmarine u. Luftwaffe 1939–45* (Munich 1954), the best reference book on the German Navy.

Rear Admiral Emory S. Land *The U.S. Merchant Marine at War* (1946).

Frederick C. Lane *Ships for Victory, A History of Shipbuilding under the U.S. Maritime Commission in World War II* (1951).

Denis Richards and Hilary St. G. Saunders *Royal Air Force 1939–1945,* Vol. II *The Fight Avails;* Vol. III *The Fight is Won* (by Saunders only); both London 1954. This work presents the thesis of the still unpublished "Despatch" by Air Chief Marshal Sir John Slessor.

Herbert Rosinski "Strategy and Propaganda in German Naval Thought," *Brassey's Naval Annual 1945,* 125–56.

Captain S. W. Roskill RN *The War at Sea,* Vol. I *The Defensive* (London 1954). This, first of three volumes on the Maritime War in the official *United Kingdom Military Series* edited by J. R. M. Butler, includes the years 1939–1941 only. Volume II will continue the story through May 1943.

Vizeadmiral Friedrich Ruge *Der Seekrieg 1939–1945* (Stuttgart 1954). The best general account of the Naval War from the German side that has yet appeared.

Gilbert N. Tucker *The Naval Service of Canada, Its Official History* (2 vols., Ottawa 1952). The third and operational volume of this series is Joseph Schull *The Far Distant Ships* (Ottawa 1950).

D. E. G. Wemyss *Walker's Groups in the Western Approaches* (Liverpool 1948). Spirited account of the work of Captain Frederick J. Walker, the Royal Navy's No. 1 U-boat killer.

This volume is dedicated to the memory of Admiral Jonas H. Ingram, Commander Fourth Fleet and subsequently Commander in Chief

Atlantic Fleet. Burly, colorful and aggressive, "Jonas" was one of the most popular flag officers in the Navy. Always mindful of the officers and men in his command, he won their affection and complete loyalty by praising where praise was due, and by stimulating the indolent or the unsuccessful to do better. He refused to be guided by precedent and protocol, yet became an excellent unofficial ambassador to Brazil; and, more than any other fleet commander, he used the services of antisubmarine scientists attached to his staff.

SAMUEL E. MORISON

WASHINGTON, D.C.
July 1955

Contents

List of Illustrations

Borie's Last Battle:
- U.S.S. *Borie*, damaged while successfully fighting two submarines, being sunk after abandonment
- Lieutenant Hutchins of *Borie* receives a citation from Admiral Ingersoll

A Fighting Patrol Craft and Her Skipper:
- U.S.S. *PC-565*
- Lieutenant Flynn observes scene of battle

Admiral John H. Hoover USN

Vice Admiral Jonas H. Ingram USN

U-848 under Attack by Liberators from Ascension Island

Two Mediterranean Escort Ships:
- U.S.S. *Niblack*
- U.S.C.G.C. *Campbell* with a GUS convoy

Two Escort Commanders in the Mediterranean:
- Captain Charles C. Hartman USN
- Captain Adelbert F. Converse USN

U-boat Fighters:
- U.S.S. *Buckley*
- U.S.S. *Barry* after being hit by an acoustic torpedo

"Captain Dan" and His Prize:
- Boarding party securing *U-505*
- Captain Gallery on deck of "Can Do!"

Fleet Air Wing Seven:
- Commodore William H. Hamilton USN
- Crew of Liberator to which *U-249* surrendered welcomed ashore

U.S.S. *Bogue* and One of Her Victims:
- *U-1229*, with snorkel raised, under attack by aircraft of VC-42
- U.S.S. *Bogue*

*(All photographs not otherwise described are Official
United States Navy)*

List of Charts

Abbreviations

Officers' ranks and bluejackets' ratings are those contemporaneous with the event. Officers and men named will be presumed to be of the United States Navy unless it is otherwise stated; officers of the Naval Reserve are designated USNR. Other service abbreviations are USA, United States Army; USCG, United States Coast Guard; USMC, United States Marine Corps; RAF, Royal Air Force; RCN, Royal Canadian Navy; RN, Royal Navy; RNR, Royal Naxy Reserve; RNVR, Royal Navy Volunteer Reserve.

A.A.F. — United States Army Air Force

Asdevlant — Antisubmarine Development Detachment Atlantic Fleet

ASV — Airborne Microwave Search Radar

A/SW — Antisubmarine Warfare

Asworg — Antisubmarine Warfare Operational Research Group

Bu — Bureau; Buord — Bureau of Ordnance; Bupers — Bureau of Naval Personnel

C.C.S. — Combined Chiefs of Staff

C.I.C. — Combat Information Center

Chop — Change of Operational Control; Chop Line — meridian where control passes from one command to another.

Cinclant — Commander in Chief, Atlantic Fleet; Cincmed — Commander in Chief, Mediterranean; Cincwa — Commander in Chief, Western Approaches

Com — Commander; Comdesron — Commander Destroyer Squadron

Cominch — Commander in Chief, United States Fleet

C.N.O. — Chief of Naval Operations

C.O. — Commanding Officer

CTF — Commander Task Force; CTG — Commander Task Group

CVE — Escort Aircraft Carrier

DC — Depth Charge

DD — Destroyer; DE — Destroyer Escort

Fairwing — Fleet Air Wing; Patwing — Patrol Wing

F.B.I. — Federal Bureau of Investigation

Fido — a homing torpedo used by aircraft

FXR — Foxer gear, a device to explode enemy acoustic torpedoes
HF/DF — pronounced "Huff-Duff" — High-Frequency Direction-Finder
H.M.C.S. — His Majesty's Canadian Ship
H.M.S. — His Majesty's Ship; H.N.M.S. — Her Netherlands Majesty's Ship
I.F.F. — Identification, Friend or Foe
J.C.S. — Joint Chiefs of Staff
LR — Long Range; VLR — Very Long Range; SR — Short Range Planes
MAD — Magnetic Airborne Detector
Momp — Mid-ocean Meeting Point; Westomp — West-ocean Meeting
    Point
M/V — Merchant Vessel
N.A.S. — Naval Air Station
N.O.B. — Naval Operating Base
O.N.I. — Office of Naval Intelligence
O.T.C. — Officer in Tactical Command
PC — 173-foot Patrol Craft
P.O.W. — Prisoner of War
PT — Motor Torpedo Boat
SC — 110-foot Submarine Chaser
Secnav — Secretary of the Navy
SS — Submarine; S.S. — Steamship
TBS (Talk Between Ships) — Voice Radio
TF — Task Force; TG — Task Group; TU — Task Unit
U.S.C.G.C. — United States Coast Guard Cutter
USSBS — United States Strategic Bombing Survey
V.C.N.O. — Vice Chief of Naval Operations
VB, VC, VF, VT — Bomber, Composite, Fighter, and Torpedo Squadrons
    of Aircraft
YMS — Motor Minesweeper

Aircraft designations (numerals in parentheses indicate
number of engines)

United States Army Air Force

A-29 — Hudson light bomber (2)
B-17 — Flying Fortress heavy bomber (4); B-24 — Liberator heavy bomber
    (4); B-25 — Mitchell medium bomber (2); B-26 — Marauder medium
    bomber (2)
B-18 — Bolo medium bomber (2)

P-39 — Bell Airacobra fighter (1)

United States Navy

F4F-4 — Wildcat (Grumman) fighter plane (1); FM-1 — Same (Eastern)
PB2Y-3 — Coronado patrol bomber seaplane (4)
PB4Y-1 — Navy equivalent to Army B-24 Liberator (4)
PBM-3 — Mariner patrol bomber seaplane (2)
PBY-5 — Catalina patrol bomber seaplane (2). 5A is amphibious
PV-1 — Ventura medium bomber (2)
SBD-5 — Dauntless dive-bomber (1)
TBF-1 — Avenger (Grumman) torpedo-bomber (1); TBM-3 — same
    (Eastern)

Royal Navy and Air Force

Beaufighter — Bristol fighter (2)
Halifax — Handley-Page heavy bomber (4)
Hudson — Lockheed light bomber (2)
Hurricane — Hawker fighter-bomber (1)
Lancaster — Avro heavy bomber (4)
Martlet — Fighter (1), equivalent to U.S.N. Wildcat
Spitfire — Vickers-Armstrong fighter (1)
Sunderland — Short patrol bomber seaplane (4)
Swordfish — Carrier-based biplane (1)
Wellington — Vickers-Armstrong medium bomber (2)
Whitley — Armstrong-Whitworth medium bomber (2)

Luftwaffe

Blohm & Voss-138 — Patrol bomber (3)
Do-217 — Dornier heavy bomber (2)
FW-190 — Focke-Wulf fighter (1)
FW-200 — Focke-Wulf heavy bomber (4)
He-111 — Heinkel medium bomber (2)
Ju-88 — Junkers medium bomber (2)
Me-109 — Messerschmitt fighter (1)

Introduction

The *Atlantic Battle Won, May 1943–May 1945,* is the tenth volume in Samuel Eliot Morison's magisterial "semiofficial" *History of United States Naval Operations in World War II.* It appeared on the bookshelves in 1956, slightly more than a decade after the struggle ended with Germany's capitulation. Unlike volume 1, *The Battle of the Atlantic, 1939–1943,* this volume was informed not only by documentary sources staggering in their quantity — especially the masterful summation by the distinguished naval historian Philip K. Lundeberg entitled "American Antisubmarine Operations in the Atlantic May 1943–May 1945." Rather, this tenth volume was also informed by a handful of important memoirs, including those of Fleet Admiral Ernest J. King, General of the Air Force Henry H. "Hap" Arnold, Fleet Admiral William D. Leahy, and British Prime Minister Winston Churchill. And it was informed by other British and American official histories, the most important being Stephen Roskill's *The War at Sea* and Wesley Frank Craven and James Lea Cate's *The Army Air Forces in World War II.*[1]

Our understanding of the conflict depicted in *The Atlantic Battle Won* was enhanced by a rich historiography that modified, amplified, and, on occasion, corrected Morison's findings. The first substantive chapter, for instance, dealt with the establishment of the wartime U.S. Tenth Fleet, which concentrated the command of all U.S. Navy antisubmarine activities under Admiral King as commander in chief, U.S. Fleet (CominCh)

---

[1]Memiors of the wartime joint chiefs of staff include Ernest J. King and Walter M. Whitehill, *Fleet Admiral King: A Naval Record* (New York: W. W. Norton, 1952); Henry H. Arnold, *Global Mission* (New York: Harper, 1949); William D. Leahy, *I Was There: The Personal Story of the Chief of Staff to Presidents Roosevelt and Truman* (New York: Whittlesey House, 1950). The most important official histories available to Morison before the publication of *The Battle of the Atlantic Won* were the first three volumes of Stephen Roskill, *The War at Sea* (4 vols.; London HMSO, 1954–1960). Also valuable was Wesley Frank Craven and James Lea Cate, eds., *The Army Air Forces in World War II* (7 vols.; Chicago: University of Chicago, 1948–1958).

and chief of naval operations. One of King's assistant chiefs of staff, Rear
Adm. Francis "Frog" Low, directed daily operations. Navy leaders por-
trayed this at the time as a major organizational step taken in the struggle, and Morison followed this line; the popular historian and sometime
naval intelligence figure Ladislas Farago did likewise in his more
detailed account, *The Tenth Fleet*, and as an early biographer of King.[2]
Other treatments were equally accepting.[3] However, Admiral Low would
later remark that the reorganization was hardly profound and merely
formalized and publicized arrangements already in place. In addition, a
careful examination indicates that the major effect of establishing the
Tenth Fleet was to strengthen CominCh's Convoy and Routing unit,
already a formidable and responsible bureaucracy, and to fend off the
aggrandizing encroachments of Secretary of War Henry Stimson.

Complicating the issue was the ongoing concurrent tussle between
Admiral King and the Army chief of staff, Gen. George C. Marshall,
and other War Department officials over the possession, command, and
operation of long-range, land-based bombers against the U-boats,
which Morison also dealt with in chapter II. Morison treated the dispute as one between Admiral King and Secretary of War Stimson, an
approach followed by several successive accounts, most notably
Montgomery Meigs in the well-documented but weakly argued *Slide
Rules and Submarines*.[4] Marshall's principal biographer, sometime U.S.
Army official historian Forrest C. Pogue, largely ignored the military
questions at hand and instead used the ruckus to demonstrate his
hero's alleged balance and reasonableness.[5] Revisiting the issue in a
superior account, historian Jeffrey Barlow settled the issue in favor of

---

[2]Ladislas Farago, *The Tenth Fleet* (Chicago: Ivan Obolensky, 1962); and Thomas
Buell, *Master of Sea Power: A Biography of Fleet Admiral Ernest J. King* (Boston: Little,
Brown, 1980).

[3]See, for instance, Robert Love, *History of the U.S. Navy*, vol. II: *1942–1991*
(Harrisburg, PA: Stackpole Books, 1992), 110.

[4]Montgomery C. Meigs, *Slide Rules and Submarines: American Scientists and
Subsurface Warfare in World War II* (Washington, D.C.: Government Printing Office,
1990).

[5]Forrest C. Pogue, *The Organizer of Victory*, vol. III of *George C. Marshall* (4 vols.;
New York: Viking Press, 1963–1981). Stimson's biographers evidence little under-
standing of the issues. See, for instance, Godfrey Hodgson, *The Colonel: The Life and
Wars of Henry Stimson, 1867–1950* (New York: Knopf, 1990).

the Navy Department.[6] This aspect of the intra-American effort should best be viewed as one feature of the lengthy drive by the generals of the U.S. Army Air Forces for institutional independence and authority over air policy and operations and the rugged resistance of generations of Navy leaders.

Morison's account of "New Antisubmarine Ships and Aircraft" generated a better informed but less contentious historiography. Aircraft carrier building and operations spurred more interest among naval historians than escorting destroyers, destroyer escorts, frigates, or corvettes. Covering both building policy and technical history, Norman Friedman's exacting account covers both destroyer and destroyer escort types in considerable detail.[7] Ships' histories vary considerably in quality and documentation, but one of the best is Bruce Franklin's account of U.S. Navy destroyer escorts in the Battle of the Atlantic.[8] Friedman and Franklin concur that the destroyer escort proved a more rugged and versatile vessel than expected and saw good service not only against the U-boats but also in the struggle in the Pacific against Japan.[9] As for the escort carriers, the account by the able and prolific air historian William Y'Blood set a high standard.[10] Morison's account of the contribution of airships was amplified in a lively account by Gordon J. Vaeth.[11]

Morison made the important point that victory in the Battle of the Atlantic was an Allied success requiring close policy, strategic,

[6]Jeffrey G. Barlow, "The Views of Stimson and Knox on Atlantic Strategy and Planning," in Timothy J. Runyan and Jan M. Copes, eds., *To Die Gallantly: The Battle of the Atlantic* (Boulder, CO: Westview Press, 1994), 22–37.

[7]Norman Friedman, *U.S. Destroyers: An Illustrated Design History* (Annapolis, MD: Naval Institute Press, 2003).

[8]Bruce H. Franklin, *The Buckley-class Destroyer Escorts* (Annapolis, MD: Naval Institute Press, 1999). An older memoir of operations at sea from the Royal Navy perspective remains informative. See Denys A. Rayner, *Escort: The Battle of the Atlantic* (Annapolis, MD: Naval Institute Press, 1999).

[9]A balanced popular account was provided by Lewis M. Andrews, *Tempest, Fire, and Foe: Destroyer Escorts in World War II and the Men Who Manned Them* (Charleston, SC:, Narwhal Press, 1999).

[10]William T. Y'Blood, *Hunter-Killer: U.S. Escort Carriers in the Battle of the Atlantic* (Annapolis, MD: Naval Institute Press, 1983).

[11]Gordon J. Vaeth, *Blimps and U-Boats: U.S. Navy Airships in the Battle of the Atlantic* (Annapolis, MD: Naval Institute Press, 1992).

operational, and often-tactical cooperation. By contrast with Morison's first volume — which dealt with the prewar and early war years — in this concluding account he makes little reference to President Roosevelt. After Admiral King thwarted, in 1942, an attempt to establish a unified Atlantic theater under Royal Navy command, London mostly accepted a more collaborative relationship with both the Americans and Canadians during the last three years of the conflict. The complex questions of the disposition and deployment of American-built escorts and aircraft did not abate, however, remaining contentious even after the critical Atlantic Convoy Conference naval summit in Washington in March 1943.[12] In particular, the distribution of American naval shipping, aircraft, weapons, and ordnance to the British, Canadian, and other Allied navies under the Lend Lease Act needs further study. The Royal Canadian Navy's building policy and operations were explained in authoritative detail by Marc Milner.[13] Donald E. Graves provided a more recent overview.[14]

A signal aspect of *The Atlantic Battle Won* is Morison's attention to naval and air basing, an important topic that often eluded the interest of World War II–era historians. More concerned with getting the story straight than in positing broad interpretations in his naval histories and other works, Morison eschewed an overarching thesis about basing and strategy in the age of steam, which was largely left to geopolitical analysts.[15] Base histories abound, however, the most comprehensive being Paolo Coletta's important *United States Navy and Marine Corps Bases*.[16]

[12]For an attempt to place these issues in the larger context of World War II–era policy and strategy, see Robert W. Love, *History of the U.S. Navy*, vol. II: *1942–1991* (Harrisburg, PA: Stackpole Books, 1992), chapter 5.

[13]Marc Milner, *Corvettes of the Royal Canadian Navy, 1939–1945* (St. Catharines, ON: Vanwell Publishing, 1993). Operations were explored in Marc Milner, *The U-Boat Hunters: The Royal Canadian Navy and the Offensive against Germany's Submarines* (Annapolis, MD: Naval Institute Press, 1994).

[14]Donald E. Graves, *In Peril on the Sea: The Royal Canadian Navy and the Battle of the Atlantic* (Toronto: Canadian Naval Memorial Trust by R. Brass Studio, 2003).

[15]The most important work along this line is Robert E. Harkavy, *Strategic Basing and the Great Powers* (London: Routledge, 2007).

[16]Paolo E. Coletta, *United States Navy and Marine Corps Bases, Domestic* (Westport, CT: Greenwood Press, 1985); and *United States Navy and Marine Corps Bases, Overseas* (Westport, CT: Greenwood Press, 1985).

One of the best of dozens of local histories that incorporated the development of the city and the naval establishment was Thomas C. Parramore's account of Norfolk, Virginia.[17] And an important examination of the role of one major port may be found in Joseph F. Meany's study of wartime New York.[18]

As might have been expected, Morison's brief and early account of the "German Underwater Fleet" in the second half of the war was followed by a more spirited historiography. Inasmuch as Hitler — perhaps the laziest major war leader of the twentieth century — devoted little attention to naval policy or operations, his most astute biographers barely mentioned the subjects.[19] The tangle of Germany's interservice rivalries and prewar and wartime naval policy and operations was explained in a biography of the service's first commander-in-chief, Grand Admiral Erich Raeder.[20] His better known and more controversial successor, Grand Admiral Karl Donitz, was the subject of a somewhat older, less well documented, and less convincing life.[21] By contrast with Morison's summary, both of these accounts emphasize the early commitment of the German naval leaders to Nazi ideology and to Hitler personally and the zealousness of the U-boat crews in general, the latter observation made in a seminal study by Timothy Mulligan.[22] The best first-person account by a U-boat commander remains that of Peter E. Cremer.[23]

---

[17]Thomas C. Parramore, *Norfolk: The First Four Centuries* (Charlottesville: University Press of Virginia, 1994).

[18]Joseph F. Meany Jr., "Port in a Storm: The Port of New York," in Timothy J. Runyan and Jan M. Copes, eds., *To Die Gallantly: The Battle of the Atlantic* (Boulder, CO: Westview Press, 1994), 282–94

[19]See, for instance, Ian Kershaw, *Hitler: 1936–1945, Nemesis* (New York: Penguin Press, 2000).

[20]A superb account dealing not only with Raeder but also broader German naval policy is Keith W. Bird, *Erich Raeder: Admiral of the Third Reich* (Annapolis, MD: Naval Institute Press, 2006).

[21]The most complete biography remains Peter Padfield, *Donitz: The Last Fuhrer: Portrait of a Nazi War Leader* (New York: Harper and Row, 1984). Akin to most British accounts of wartime German leaders, it exudes an unnecessary and uncomfortable anti-German bias.

[22]Timothy Mulligan, *Neither Sharks Nor Wolves: The Men of Nazi Germany's U-Boat Arm, 1939–1945* (Annapolis, MD: Naval Institute Press, 1999).

[23]Peter E. Cremer, *U-Boat Commander: A Periscope View of the Battle of the Atlantic* (Annapolis, MD: Naval Institute Press, 1984).

Still, Morison's treatment of the German side after the spring of
1943 seems inadequate. For one thing, Donitz's "tonnage warfare" was
less a strategy than an objective, one based on a profoundly flawed and
misinformed understanding of Allied naval and merchant shipbuilding
resources and potential, as well as a lack of appreciation of the possible (indeed, likely) opposing defensive and offensive countermeasures.
The latter, quite surprising considering the success of the Allied fleets
against German "unrestricted submarine warfare" during World War I,
served as testimony not only to the weakness of Berlin's economic
intelligence but also to the prism of Nazi ideology that distorted
analysis. While the coalition opposing German naval efforts possessed
operational intelligence far superior to the Germans' understanding of
their enemy's political economy, the Allies' conservative, and unwar-
ranted, habit of exaggerating Axis industrial resources and output
clearly served their cause better than the gross underestimates guiding
Berlin's policies. Although the cataclysmic consequences of underesti-
mating their enemies was a central theme of most interwar German
histories of World War I, Donitz's "tonnage warfare" took scant account
of this abiding economic reality, explained by historian Adam Tooze.[24]
Akin to so many World War II–era German military exertions, the U-
boat offensive against commerce proceeded on the assumption that
doing the same thing but merely doing it better than the last time,
against mostly the same obstacles, would somehow achieve success.

The principal shortcoming of *The Atlantic Battle Won* was the absence
of any discussion of the use or importance of Ultra intelligence on the
naval operations, or any conclusions as to the importance of codebreak-
ing and evasive routing to the outcome.[25] The German side was ably
chronicled by the distinguished naval historian Jurgen Rohwer.[26] The

[24]Adam J. Tooze, *Wages of Destruction: The Making and Breaking of the Nazi Economy*
(New York: Allen Lane, 2006).
[25]The first scholarly papers on Ultra and the Battle of the Atlantic were delivered
at the 1977 Naval History Symposium sponsored by the History Department of the
United States Naval Academy. See Robert W. Love Jr., ed., *Changing Interpretations and
New Sources in Naval History* (New York: Garland, 1980), chapters 34–36.
[26]Jurgen Rohwer, *The Critical Convoy Battles of March 1943: The Battle for
HX.229/SC122* (Annapolis, MD: Naval Institute Press, 1977). Also see the relevant
chapters of Jurgen Rohwer, *Axis Submarine Successes of World War Two: German, Italian,*

Allied story was somewhat more complex.[27] A considerable fraction of the official British history of intelligence in World War II was devoted to the Battle of the Atlantic, although the account was not cross-checked with the well-informed historians at the Admiralty and thus contains serious errors. Seminal scholarship by David Syrett brought American participation into view.[28] Phyllis Soybel explained the early efforts between the Navy Department and the British Admiralty to coordinate Anglo-American naval intelligence and the attendant difficulties.[29] The most important synthesis regarding Ultra and the Battle of the Atlantic was provided by the able historian W. J. R. Gardner.[30] And a brief tribute to the work of Commander Roger Winn, RN, of the Admiralty's Submarine Tracking Room and Commander Kenneth Knowles, USNR, who handled Ultra for Admiral King, included significant details about their critical transatlantic partnership.[31] Morison was, however, aware of the importance of high-frequency direction finding (Huff-Duff), a topic ably treated by Kathleen B. Williams.[32]

While the historiography of the U.S. Navy's participation in the Battle of the Atlantic both amplified and corrected Morison's account, his two volumes on the struggle established the essential narrative and identified most of the key features followed by his scholarly legatees. This was an extraordinary accomplishment and a major contribution to the understanding of American naval history and to the general knowledge of one of mankind's most lethal conflicts.

ROBERT LOVE

and Japanese Submarine Successes, 1939–1945 (Annapolis, MD: Naval Institute Press, 1999).

[27]F. H. Hinsley, *British Intelligence in the Second World War: Its Influence on Strategy and Operations* (4 vols.; New York: Cambridge University Press, 1979–88).

[28]David Syrett, *The Defeat of the German U-Boats: The Battle of the Atlantic* (Columbia: University of South Carolina Press, 1994); and David Syrett, *U-Boat Situations and Trends, 1941–1945* (Aldershot, Hants, UK: Ashgate, 1998).

[29]Phyllis L. Soybel, *A Necessary Relationship: The Development of Anglo-American Cooperation in Naval Intelligence* (Westport, CT: Praeger, 2005).

[30]W. J. R. Gardner, *Decoding History: The Battle of the Atlantic and Ultra* (Annapolis, MD: Naval Institute Press, 1999).

[31]David Kohnen, *Commanders Winn and Knowles: Winning the U-Boat War with Intelligence, 1939–1945* (Krakow: Enigma Press, 1999).

[32]Kathleen B. Williams, *Secret Weapon: U.S. High-Frequency Direction Finding in the Battle of the Atlantic* (Annapolis, MD: Naval Institute Press, 1996).

The Atlantic Battle Won
May 1943–May 1945

CHAPTER I

Introduction[1]

September 1939–April 1943

THE CONTROL of Atlantic sea lanes during World War II, insuring the safe, regular and frequent passage of ships, was but one link in the chain of forces and events that led to victory over the Axis. And it was the central, vital link, without which the chain would have fallen into two dangling parts, shackled only at each end, neither strong enough to resist disaster and defeat.[2]

The challenge to Anglo-American and Anglo-American-Russian shipping by the weaker German Navy offers a classic example of the futility of *guerre de course* (commerce raiding), and the triumph of the balanced fleet. Our Battle of the Atlantic is the best example in modern history of the value of strong sea and air power, skillfully and courageously applied.

This battle opened with a bang on 3 September 1939, when *U–30*, in defiance of treaties to which Germany was a party, torpedoed and sank the unarmed and unescorted British passenger steamship *Athenia*. Before long, "no holds were barred," except what humanity and fear of reprisal dictated.

Although World War II in the Atlantic soon took on the same character as had World War I, neither side was prepared for it. At the outbreak, Germany had only 46 U-boats ready for combat, and not more than four were then being built monthly. The British and Canadian Navies were very short of destroyers and other ships suitable for escort-of-convoy, and had no air arm other than a few

[1] Based largely on my Vol. I and on Capt. S. W. Roskill RN *The War at Sea* Vol. I (1954) *The Defensive* (through 1941) and Volume II which I have been privileged to read in typescript.
[2] A paraphrase of Capt. A. T. Mahan *The Influence of Sea Power Upon History* (1906 ed.) pp. 225–26.

hundred carrier-based planes. The French Navy seems to have been unprepared for anything except watching the Italian Fleet. Coastal Command of the Royal Air Force, charged with protecting shipping in the narrow seas, had few aircraft suitable for antisubmarine operations. Disregarding the great lesson of World War I, that well-escorted convoys are the best means of protecting merchant vessels and of attracting enemy submarines to positions where they can be successfully attacked, the Admiralty dissipated part of its meager surface forces "to hunt enemy submarines in the vast ocean spaces." [3] It also had to deal with German surface raiders, with the Luftwaffe, which began to attack coastal shipping in 1940, and with magnetic and delayed-action mines planted in the Thames estuary and off East Coast harbors. Merchant shipping around the British Isles lost heavily. And although transatlantic convoys at this period were seldom attacked, and the Royal Navy smashed a distant raiding unit of the German Fleet off the River Plate, it lost H.M.S. *Royal Oak, Courageous, Glorious* and other valuable ships to enemy torpedo and gunfire attack. [4]

The outbreak of war in Europe found the American government and people more neutrality-minded than at any period of their history since 1870. The general feeling that we had been "had" in the last war was implemented by the Neutrality Acts. These forbade American ships to enter war zones and required the belligerents to obtain American supplies by "cash and carry." Although the general attitude toward Hitler and his Reich was hostile and the great majority of the people hoped that the Allies would win, they assumed that the French Army and British Navy combined could defeat Germany with no other assistance.

These sentiments and opinions were rudely dispelled by events

[3] Roskill I 10. Coastal had other duties as well: — reconnaissance of German surface warships, and air cover of waters between Scotland and Greenland.

[4] Surface raiders cost the British, Allied and Neutral merchant marines 86 ships of 524,967 tons by the end of 1940, 84 ships of 428,350 tons in 1941. Merchant ship losses to submarine attack were 585 ships of 2,607,314 tons in 1939–40; 432 ships of 2,171,754 tons in 1941. Total Allied and Neutral M/V losses to enemy aircraft were 202 ships of 583,023 tons in 1939–40; 371 ships of 1,017,422 tons in 1941. Total losses to mines in 1939–40 were 280 ships of 772,586 tons in 1939–40; 111 ships of 230,842 tons in 1941. Tables in Roskill I 615–16.

in the spring and summer of 1940. First neutral Denmark and Norway, then Belgium and Holland, were occupied by the Germans. The British Army, forced to retire from the Continent, was evacuated from Dunkirk in an operation that reflects the highest credit on the Royal Navy.[5] France, beaten to her knees in a blitz campaign, signed a humiliating capitulation in June; Mussolini, eager for his share of the loot, came in on Hitler's side. The Axis now commanded the coastline of continental Europe from the North Cape southward, and would soon take over the Ægean as well; only the Iberian nations were shakily neutral. As soon as Hitler had eliminated France from the war and occupied all parts of that country which appeared to be useful, he attempted to "soften up" England in preparation for invasion by air-bombing. At the same time the U-boats, which hitherto had confined their efforts largely to British coastal waters and their approaches, began to base on Brest and the Biscayan ports of France. Thence they moved into mid-Atlantic and to the bulge of Africa, employing new "wolf-pack" tactics against convoys. And the Royal Navy had only enough escorts to cover convoys up to 400 miles west of Ireland.

The impact of these events wrought a gradual evolution of American policy and public opinion toward participation in the war. The first "two-ocean Navy" acts were passed in June and July 1940. The National Defense Research Committee of scientists was set up; its members concluded that, thanks to radar and the Spitfire fighter plane, England would defeat the bombing blitz. President Roosevelt and Mr. Mackenzie King, Prime Minister of Canada, met in August 1940 to discuss hemisphere defense, and shortly after signed a mutual defense pact. The exchange of British naval base sites in the Caribbean for 50 American destroyers was agreed to on 2 September. Lend-lease, the most radical "short of war" step, became law on 11 March 1941. During the same month, high-level Anglo-American naval and military staff discussions were

[5] Roskill I 213–40, 603. No fewer than 848 ships and small craft (of which 235 were lost) were employed to evacuate 338,226 troops from Dunkirk; total evacuations from France amounted to 558,032 men.

held in Washington, and the basic strategy of the war, if and when
the United States entered it, was determined. In May American
forces occupied Greenland. The British and Canadian navies now
had enough escort vessels to protect transatlantic convoys all the
way across. In July United States forces began to relieve the British
in Iceland, whose air bases were a tremendous help in convoy coverage, and the United States Navy began to escort convoys thither.
In June 1941, Hitler shelved his plans for invading Britain and
swung his armies against Russia, to which President Roosevelt and
Congress promptly extended the benefit of lend-lease. In August
the President and the Prime Minister met at Argentia in Newfoundland to discuss high strategy. On 4 September a U-boat tried unsuccessfully to sink U.S.S. *Greer*, and shortly after, escort groups
of the U.S. Navy, commanded by such officers as Captains Mor-
ton L. Deyo, F. D. Kirtland and L. Hewlett Thébaud, began to
escort transatlantic convoys as far as a Mid-ocean Meeting Point
("Momp"), where they were relieved by British escort groups. On
one of these convoys, 31 October 1941, U.S.S. *Reuben James* was
sunk by a U-boat.

During "their finest hour," the years 1940–41, when they had to
face Fascist fury unaided, the British were exceedingly hard-
pressed both in the Mediterranean and in home waters, since the
eastern and southern shores of the North Sea were in enemy hands.
In order to protect the East Coast of the United Kingdom, minesweeping had to be almost continuous; [6] and over the North Sea
the air war was unremitting.

Hitler, faithful to his strategy of concentrating on one enemy at
a time, chose to ignore the increasing amount of assistance that the
United States was giving to Britain,[7] but reckoned without his
Oriental ally, Japan. The Roosevelt administration and the American Army and Navy hoped to avoid a war with Japan at least until

[6] From the outbreak of the war to Sept. 1942 the British operated 804 minesweepers in home waters and lost 140 of them. Down to 31 Dec. 1942, 102,157 ships
sailed in British East Coast convoys, with a loss of only 205. Data from Lt. Cdr.
D. W. Waters RN.
[7] Nevertheless, five U.S. merchant ships and one destroyer were sunk by German submarines, mines or aircraft before the German declaration of war.

the spring, when they would be better prepared; but Japan decided to eliminate the Pacific Fleet and on 7 December 1941 attacked Pearl Harbor. Hitler promptly declared war on the United States, and Mussolini followed. America was now at war with Germany, Italy and Japan, and allied with the British Commonwealth of Nations.

President Roosevelt appointed Admiral Ernest J. King Commander in Chief United States Fleet (Cominch) on 20 December; [8] and Admiral Royal E. Ingersoll relieved him as Commander in Chief Atlantic Fleet (Cinclant) on 1 January 1942. A deceptive quiet descended over the northern transatlantic convoy route, because the U-boats were being deployed in the Mediterranean and toward the Eastern Sea Frontier of the United States.

Hitler decided on the day following his declaration of war to attack American coastal shipping. One month later the U-boats began to strike. Very little had been done to prepare for their visitation. Mine fields had been planted off the Capes of the Chesapeake and certain harbors had been protected by antisubmarine nets; but no new convoys were organized because all available planes and escort vessels were employed in patrol, and none could be spared from transatlantic and transpacific convoys. The antisubmarine air patrol, by April 1942, had been built up to only 170 aircraft, mostly of very short range, based between Bangor and Jacksonville. The result of this lack of defensive measures was devastating. The German Navy, by keeping an average of a dozen U-boats constantly in the Eastern Sea Frontier, relieving them every two weeks and refueling them from tanker submarines stationed 300 miles east of Bermuda, pulled off one of the greatest merchant-ship massacres in history during the first four months of 1942. In round numbers, German submarines sank 82 merchant ships of 491,000 gross tons in the Eastern Sea Frontier, together with 55 ships of 337,000 tons in the Bermuda Area,[9] during January, February, March and April.

[8] Also Chief of Naval Operations (C.N.O.) from 26 Mar. 1942. See brief biography in Vol. I 51-2, 115.
[9] For chart of these and other ocean areas see Appendix I. For statistics see Vol. I 413.

None of these ships were in convoy and very few, as yet, had been furnished with Naval Armed Guards. During the same four months only 14 U-boats and 5 Italian submarines were sunk (three of the Germans by United States forces); and 80 new ones were added to the underwater fleet.

As early as February 1942 the U-boats began to move into the Gulf Sea Frontier (the Gulf of Mexico, the Yucatan Channel and western Cuban waters), and into the Caribbean Sea Frontier which included the rest of that sea except the waters off the Panama Canal. Between 1 March and 1 July the U-boats knocked off another 160 to 170 ships in these two areas, with tonnage approximating 870,-000. June of 1942 was all-time high for the U-boats and low for the Allies. In the Gulf and Caribbean, off the Panama Canal, and in the eastern approaches to the Caribbean, 69 ships of 365,115 tons were sunk by submarines. In the entire Atlantic, the Arctic and the Mediterranean, 121 ships of 613,750 tons were lost.

It was a fairly desperate situation. The British were beginning to lose confidence in the ability of the United States Navy to protect merchant ships in home waters, and the South American republics began to wonder whether their big neighbor was strong enough to beat Hitler. So large a proportion of the sunken ships were tankers that severe rationing of domestic fuel had to be imposed, and the supply of military fuel oil to Europe and the Pacific was threatened.

Both Navies recognized early in the war that normal naval training was not enough to qualify sailors to hunt and kill submarines; special training was required not only in tactics, but in radar, sonar, depth-charging, air-bombing, and the use of a variety of weapons. The nature of the antisubmarine war, the boredom of long and unrewarding patrols (only one U-boat sunk by the Royal Navy and two by the United States Navy in June 1942), meant that the best specialists easily went stale and needed refresher-training. On the British side Admirals Sir Percy Noble and Sir Max Horton, successive Commanders in Chief of the vital Western Approaches, were strong advocates of special training schools as, on the American side, were Admirals King and Ingersoll and Secretary Frank

Knox. These training units, whether British or American, were freely opened to members of the other navies; and the United States schools took care of the Latin American and other navies as well.[10]

Most important of all means and measures taken by the United States to fight the U-boats,[11] was the extension of convoys coastwise from Halifax to Key West, across the Caribbean to the Panama Canal and Trinidad, and finally to Brazil. Not until mid-May 1942 were there collected enough destroyers, patrol craft and converted yachts to provide escort-of-convoy southward. Trans-Caribbean convoys started in July, with the aid of several Canadian corvettes and air cover spliced out by a squadron of Hudsons of R.A.F. Coastal Command. An interlocking system of local and express convoys was established in August; and in October 1942 this network was extended to the principal ports of northern Brazil. The result proved that Admiral King and others who believed in convoying, as the best method of protecting merchant vessels, were right. Between 1 July and 7 December 1942, only 39 vessels were sunk out of 527 coastal and Caribbean convoys, comprising 9064 ships.

But the Germans were still building U-boats faster than the British and the Americans could sink them. United States forces sank 12 and the British and Canadians sank 46 enemy submarines in the last six months of 1942; but in the same period the Germans completed 121 new boats.

In September 1942, the northern transatlantic convoys, when outside the range of air cover, began again to suffer. Losses in these convoys continued at the average rate of 26 ships of 155,000 tons per month until the end of the year. In early 1943 the rate was accelerated, rising to an all-time high of 49 ships of 295,970 tons in March. And in that stormy winter, between 1 November and 31 March, Allied and neutral merchant ship losses by marine casualty

[10] Chalmers *Max Horton and the Western Approaches;* and summary in Admiral Sir Frederic Dreyer RN *The Sea Heritage* (1955) 412. For the U.S.N. schools see Vol. I chap. x. In the Subchaser School at Miami 360 officers and 1374 enlisted men were trained for 14 different Allied navies in 1942-43.
[11] For details see Vol. I chaps. x and xi.

alone reached the unprecedented figure of 166 vessels and 347,852 tons.[12] Nevertheless, the great convoys which brought a United States Army across the Atlantic to assault French Morocco on 8 November 1942 (Operation TORCH) arrived undetected and uninjured. Unfortunately the U-boats then moved into waters between Casablanca and Algiers, inflicting severe losses on empty unescorted transports but also suffering heavily themselves.

It was far from clear then, but clear enough now, that by the end of April 1943 the Germans had lost the strategic initiative in the Atlantic war, as in the war as a whole. They had lost 55 U-boats (and the Italians 8 submarines) since the beginning of the year, and had built only 83. The curve of new construction of Allied merchant shipping definitely passed above that of merchant ship losses in December 1942, and the two curves were diverging.[18] And there was no consolation for the Axis in the Pacific. Japan lost her initiative in the Battle of Midway on 4 June 1942; the United States-Australia-New Zealand lifeline was now secured. Guadalcanal fell into American hands in February 1943, and in April the great forward surge of American sea and air power, which within a year would clear the Bismarcks barrier and sweep the enemy from the Central Pacific islands, was about to begin.

In high command circles in England and the United States, the almost desperate feelings of mid-1942 were now replaced by sober confidence of eventual victory. Operation HUSKY (Sicily), the first invasion of enemy territory in Europe, was impending. The Allied navies had kept the ships sailing; they were getting the troops and matériel across; the lifegiving fuel oil was flowing to every theater of war from the Caribbean or the Persian Gulf; strategic materials from South America, Africa and India were reaching arms and munitions factories.[14] But the central and vital problem of killing U-boats or preventing them from getting to sea had not been solved. In the more vital trade routes there were not enough escort

[12] Vol. I 337. These last figures are world-wide; 92 of the ships were lost in the Atlantic.
[18] See graph in Vol. I 404.
[14] For table of average number of ships at sea, see Vol. I 405.

vessels per convoy to permit some to peel off and aggressively hunt the snarling wolf-packs. More and stronger escorts, better organization on the American side, more lethal weapons, more long-range bombers fitted for and trained in antisubmarine tactics, better training and, above all, hunter-killer groups built around escort carriers were wanted, before the Western Allies could seize the strategic initiative in the Atlantic war.

The story of that great offensive, in which old ships and new, increasing numbers of aircraft and improved weapons were employed, is the theme of this volume; and although the turning point had been passed by the end of May 1943, it was by no means a foregone conclusion that it would not turn again.[15] First one side would obtain an advantage with a new weapon or tactics; then the other would produce a new device or defensive weapon to counteract it. And always there was the bright expectation for the Germans, and apprehension for the Allies, that new and stronger types of U-boats or other secret weapons would burst forth like monstrous messengers from Mars, to sweep Allied shipping from the sea.

There has been nothing in modern history like this "war of groping and drowning, of ambuscade and stratagem, of science and seamanship," as Mr. Churchill once described it. By sheer weight of resources and numbers, and (let us not forget) by intelligent employment of scientists as well as sailors, the Allies should have won, and did win; but as long as the war continued one never knew what the morrow might bring forth.

As one experienced escort commander remarked to this writer, "Anything can happen in this war." And almost everything imaginable did — acoustic torpedoes, guided missiles, the hedgehog, the snorkel and microwave radar. But nuclear fission was first demonstrated on unfortunate Hiroshima.

[15] On 5 June 1943 the Secretary of the Navy wrote to Admiral Stark in London, "I am very much concerned over the extent to which the British, especially Alexander and Churchill, are talking about submarine activities. Already the more optimistic in this country are assuming that the battle with the submarine is won."

CHAPTER II
Tenth Fleet
March–September 1943

1. *American and British Antisubmarine Commands*

MORE than any other phase of the naval war, antisubmarine warfare required a tremendous expenditure of brains, energy, and money in organization, research, new weapons, devices and training methods, and something must be said about them if we are to understand how the Allies won the Battle of the Atlantic. Taking our departure from Tenth Fleet, set up in May 1943 to direct antisubmarine warfare, we shall describe the new antisubmarine ships, and the new training and technical developments in the United States, take a brief look at the enemy fleet, and then proceed to operations.

Organization comes first. In September 1942, Air Chief Marshal Sir Philip Joubert of the R.A.F. Coastal Command "proposed a single supreme control for the whole anti–U-boat war, with a central planning staff to coördinate the separate and often conflicting policies of the British, Canadian and American naval and air authorities." [1] Two months later Captain L. Hewlett Thébaud, United States naval control officer at Londonderry, urged that Great Britain and the United States set up a combined general staff under a single admiral, with complete operational authority over British and American escorts, convoys, and all antisubmarine warfare.

[1] Denis Richards & Hilary St. G. Saunders *Royal Air Force 1939–1945* II (1954) 107.

Several officers on the staff of Admiral Harold R. Stark, commanding United States Naval Forces Europe, urged the same thing. A
second memorandum from Captain Thébaud pointed out that,
while the conduct of the German underwater fleet had been flexible, the antisubmarine operations of the Western Allies had been
rigid.

That was the crux of the matter. So long as antisubmarine warfare was decentralized and parceled out among sea frontiers, naval
districts, and fleet commanders, as well as divided among the United
States, the United Kingdom, Canada and Brazil, it was hopeless to
expect great progress.

Nevertheless the proposed remedy, a Supreme Commander Atlantic Theater, was too drastic. That sort of thing was working
well under Admiral Nimitz in the Pacific and under General Mac-
Arthur in the Southwest Pacific, but in both theaters the prepon-
derance of Allied forces was American. Here, with two equal
Allies, the American of greater potential strength and the Anglo-
Canadian of longer experience, a supreme command was politically
impracticable. The Western Approaches to the British Isles was the
most vulnerable area in the British Empire, upon the protection of
which the people depended for their very existence; and the Royal
Navy and Air Force had driven German submarines out of it before
the United States entered the war. Hence no important American
suggested that the United Kingdom abdicate supreme responsibility
over the Western Approaches, and no British government could
have faced the public on such an issue. Similarly, President Roosevelt could not contemplate turning over responsibility for the
support and supply of the United States Army overseas to an Eng-

[EXPLANATORY NOTE]

Charts show sinkings of merchant ships as the U-boat war expanded across the Atlantic. Isolated crosses denote sinkings of individual ships, as a rule. Close-order crosses show the areas of concentrated
sinkings.

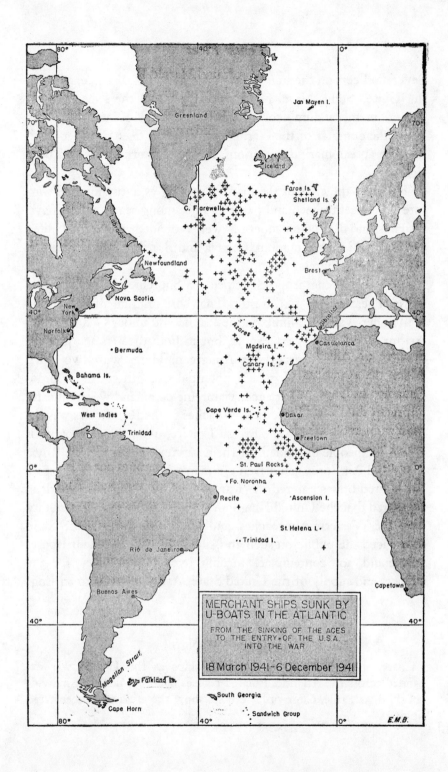

MERCHANT SHIPS SUNK BY
U-BOATS IN THE ATLANTIC

FROM THE SINKING OF THE ACES
TO THE ENTRY OF THE U.S.A.
INTO THE WAR

18 March 1941 - 6 December 1941

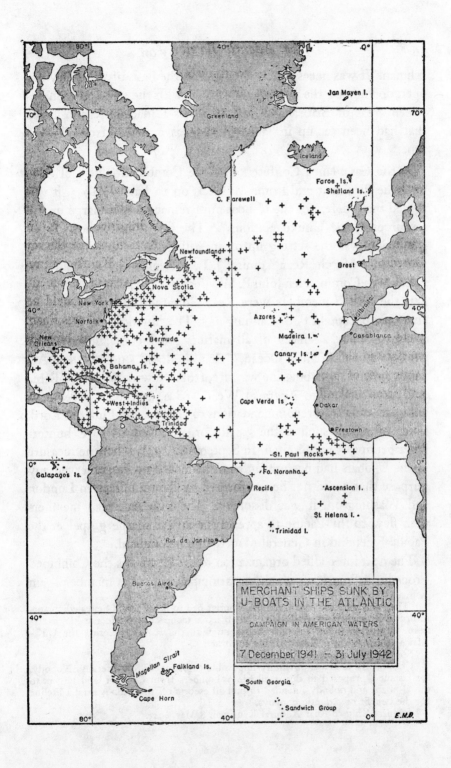

MERCHANT SHIPS SUNK BY
U-BOATS IN THE ATLANTIC

CAMPAIGN IN AMERICAN WATERS

7 December 1941 — 31 July 1942

lishman.[2] It was necessary to continue on the basis of voluntary co-operation among the nations concerned, with the same division between areas of British and United States–Canadian responsibility that had been set up in January 1942, as modified from time to time.[3]

In the Casablanca Conference of the Combined Chiefs of Staff with the President and Prime Minister, on 19 January 1943, it was agreed that "defeat of the U-boat must remain a first charge on the resources of the United Nations."[4] The first improvement in organization was the setting up of an Allied Antisubmarine Survey Board on 8 March. Rear Admiral J. L. ("Reggie") Kauffman presided, with Commander John P. W. Vest, a naval aviator, as a member; the British members were Rear Admiral J. M. Mansfield RN and Group Captain P. S. Canning RAF. The functions of this Board were to "make a survey of all matters relating to antisubmarine warfare in the Atlantic Ocean."[5] It visited and studied every Atlantic base of antisubmarine warfare, from Newfoundland to Bahia and from Iceland to Accra in West Africa, and made several intelligent and useful recommendations to C.N.O. and First Sea Lord, some of which, such as the speedy organization of CVE hunter-killer groups, were adopted. In September 1943, when the measure of the U-boats had been taken and this board no longer served any purpose that could not be performed by liaison officers in London and Washington, it was dissolved. The two American members then flew to the Pacific to spread the antisubmarine gospel in the Pacific Fleet and in General MacArthur's command.

The next inter-allied organization to be set up was the Combined Procedures Board, of which the principal American member again

---

[2] That was why the Moroccan Sea Frontier had to be a United States command, in order to protect the arrival of United States troop convoys in the Mediterranean. It was an inconvenient arrangement, with the R.A.F. covering the U.K.–Africa convoys from Gibraltar, but it worked.
[3] See Atlantic Chart in Appendix I.
[4] Cf. Vol. IX 5. It was obviously impossible to carry this out literally. Nobody, for instance, proposed to divert all heavy bombers from German land targets to the U-boats, and nobody intended to pull all escorts off the U.S.–Australia lifeline for the benefit of Atlantic convoys.
[5] Admiral King to Rear Admiral Kauffman 8 Mar. 1943.

was Vest, recently promoted captain. The duty of this board was to devise a single system of signals and procedures for the three navies engaged in antisubmarine warfare. Naturally there had grown up between the American and the British Navies a great divergence in command, tactics, gunnery, signaling and other communications; it was desirable to reduce these to a single system. The Board met at St. John's, Newfoundland, in June 1943, but reported that the problem was too complicated to be solved under the stress of war. Differences in procedure were too numerous; and as the United States frequently had to transfer destroyers and other antisubmarine ships from the Atlantic to the Pacific Fleet, and vice versa, it would be too confusing to adopt different procedures for the two oceans. So this effort came to naught, and the only possible solution was the one already adopted at the March 1943 Convoy Conference (to be mentioned shortly) — to do away with mixed escorts on specific convoy routes, so that each Navy could use its own procedures without confusion.[6]

British policy in antisubmarine warfare stemmed from the Anti-U-boat Subcommittee of the War Cabinet, formed in November 1942. This committee determined the allocation of ships, aircraft and matériel. Prime Minister, First Lord of the Admiralty (Mr. A. V. Alexander), First Sea Lord (Admiral of the Fleet Sir Dudley Pound), Commander in Chief Coastal Command R.A.F. (Air Chief Marshal Sir Philip Joubert, relieved by Air Vice Marshal John Slessor in February 1943), and a number of important min-

---

[6] There was a tendency in the R.N. to regard U.S.N. procedures as "immature," and in the U.S.N. to regard those of the R.N. as "obsolete." One difference, for instance, that could never be resolved, was that of escort command. The U.S.N. insisted on having in every escort group an escort commander (generally a Comdesdiv) who had no other duties. The R.N. preferred to use the senior C.O. of an escort vessel. Another difference was the optimum size of a convoy. The statement in Hilary St. G. Saunders *Royal Air Force 1939-45* II (1954) 37-8, to the effect that the A/S Survey and the Combined Procedures Boards were virtually sabotaged by the U.S.N. because "Admiral King and his staff did not view the Battle of the Atlantic in the same light as General Marshall viewed the invasion of Europe in 1944," is without foundation (see also note at end of this chapter). Admiral King adopted several recommendations of the Survey Board; but, for reasons stated in the text, he believed that combined procedures could not be worked out in war time.

isters, admirals, air marshals and civilian scientists were members of this committee. The roving U.S. Ambassador (Hon. W. Averell Harriman) and Commander United States Naval Forces Europe (Admiral Harold R. Stark) attended sessions, expressed their views freely, and kept President Roosevelt and Admiral King informed.

Control of antisubmarine warfare, as distinct from policy, always rested in the Admiralty. Without going into the intricacies, it will suffice to say that the most important commands for antisubmarine warfare were Commander in Chief Western Approaches ("Cincwa"), Admiral Sir Max Horton; and Commander in Chief Coastal Command, which was the branch of the Royal Air Force engaged in defending shipping from submarine and air attack. "Coastal" had been placed under Admiralty operational control in April 1941; and, although Sir John Slessor states in his official "Despatch" that this arrangement was little more than a "polite fiction," the Admiralty certainly did not so regard it. Admiralty, Coastal and Army operated in very close coöperation through subordinate Area Combined Headquarters; one at Liverpool for the Western Approaches, one at Rosneath for the Northern Transit Area, one near Plymouth for the Channel and Bay of Biscay, and one at Gibraltar for waters near the Strait. At each of these Area Combined Headquarters a flag officer of the Royal Navy, a general officer of the British Army and an air vice marshal of the R.A.F. sat side by side, and worked closely together in a spirit of harmony and understanding. Every morning, a secret telephone conference between Western Approaches headquarters at Liverpool, Coastal Command headquarters north of London, and the U-boat Intelligence department of the Admiralty decided what convoys needed air protection, and made the necessary aircraft dispositions.[7]

Not everyone in England was satisfied with this loose organization. Sir Stafford Cripps, leader of the House of Commons and minister of aircraft production, recommended to Mr. Churchill on 30 November 1942 that he place an officer "of very high naval rank

[7] Saunders III 40. This was in accordance with the procedure known as "Stipple" adopted by Slessor in May 1943, which meant concentrating air cover over those convoys only that were likely to be attacked by submarines.

in sole charge" of British antisubmarine operations. The Prime Minister turned him down, flat. "The sea war is all one," he replied on 12 December. "To try to take out one particular aspect of the sea war and place it under a separate authority for all purposes would, I am sure, cause an immense amount of friction and confusion. . . . Such an organism as you propose would cut across all existing arrangements and disturb all existing loyalties. . . . It is always tempting in time of stress to set up a local dictatorship, but it is very easy thereby to rupture the constitution." [8]

Admiral King agreed with the Prime Minister, but was far from complacent about the organization of antisubmarine warfare on the American side. His first problem, however, was to reach a working agreement with the British and Canadian navies on the operation of convoys.

On 1 March 1943, just as the midwinter U-boat blitz in the Atlantic was mounting to a climax, the Atlantic Convoy Conference, planned at Casablanca, met in Washington. Admiral Sir Percy Noble, Vice Admiral Sir Henry R. Moore (Vice Chief of the Naval Staff) and Rear Admiral V. G. Brodeur RCN of the Canadian Joint Staff, were there; the Royal Air Force and the United States Army Air Force Antisubmarine Command were represented. Admiral King in his opening address expressed his faith in convoys, not only as the best means of protecting shipping but as the most attractive bait for U-boats. He declared that hunter-killer groups would be desirable if "used directly in connection with the convoy routes," but not to hunt "needles in a haystack," and that in view of the shortage of suitable warships antisubmarine warfare for the present "must concern itself primarily with the escort of convoy." [9] In turning over the chairmanship to his chief of staff, Vice Admiral Richard S. Edwards, he gave this parting injunction: "A ship saved is worth two built. Think it over!"

In meetings that extended over twelve days the Atlantic Convoy

[8] Churchill *The Second World War* IV 913–14.
[9] Atlantic Convoy Conference, minutes 1st meeting 12 Mar. 1943. There is a detailed account of the Conference in G. N. Tucker *The Naval Service of Canada* II 409–17.

Conference made several recommendations which the Combined Chiefs of Staff adopted. First, and most important, it was agreed that the British and Canadian Navies should take complete charge of the northern transatlantic convoys, except for the short leg between Halifax and Boston or New York. This was done in part as a move toward simplification, in part to give the growing Canadian Navy the greater responsibility that it desired, and in part to release the few United States escort vessels then employed on that route,[10] for other convoys for which the United States Navy was responsible — such as the Caribbean, the tanker convoys to Britain, and the Central Atlantic convoys to Gibraltar and Casablanca.

In order to implement this decision the R.A.F. antisubmarine squadrons then operating from Quonset and Trinidad, and the Canadian corvettes then doing convoy duty in the Caribbean were released, and Canada set up a Northwest Atlantic Command to exercise full control over northern transatlantic convoys west of long. 47° W, to which the "chop line" was shifted from long. 40° W. Rear Admiral L. W. Murray RCN was appointed to this command.

Other important innovations that stemmed from this Conference were the setting up of new convoy "cycles" or timetables, increasing the strength of long-range aircraft in Newfoundland for convoy support to 48 units immediately, with more to come; [11] extending the high-frequency direction-finder (HF/DF) network, and the employment of escort carrier groups (the first to be organized around U.S.S. *Bogue*), as soon as available.[12]

Each country, however, was to unify antisubmarine warfare in its own way.

[10] At that time, the proportions of escorts on northern transatlantic convoys was as follows: R.N. 50%, R.C.N. 46%, U.S.N. 4%. When two U.S. carrier groups were supporting these convoys in the summer of 1943, the U.S.N. had virtually replaced all the units that it had withdrawn.

[11] The J.C.S. on 29 March directed that 140 LR or VLR planes (80 Army, 60 Navy) be sent to Newfoundland and Iceland by 1 July.

[12] Neither the land-based A/S planes nor the escort carrier groups were to revert from U.S.N. to Admiralty control, or vice versa, when they crossed the chop line.

2. *Tenth Fleet Emerges, April–May*

On 6 April 1943 Admiral King took a step toward unification of American antisubmarine warfare by appointing Rear Admiral Francis S. Low [13] his assistant chief of staff for antisubmarine warfare. Low promptly set himself to study the large and confusing mass of British and American antisubmarine literature. An "Appreciation of the Antisubmarine Situation" that he submitted to King on 20 April began by declaring, "The prosaic answer to the problem is *enough* escorts *and* aircraft, recognition of fundamentals, and pressure to make them work." He laid equal stress on training as a prime requisite for victory. And, besides detailed recommendations, he called for reorganization. After this memorandum had been approved by Admiral King, the Combined Chiefs of Staff on 30 April recommended that each Allied nation adopt a centralized control of antisubmarine warfare and coöperate closely with the others in the study and integration of antisubmarine effort.

While Washington was making this gingerly approach to reorganization, U-boats continued to destroy merchant shipping. From the beginning of 1943 losses rose steadily to 627,000 tons in March. And, although the figures for April declined over 50 per cent, Admiral King was now convinced that a fleet organization for antisubmarine warfare was a military necessity. Admiral Low modestly suggested on 25 April that all units and sections recently placed under his control be shifted to Admiral Royal E. Ingersoll, Commander in Chief Atlantic Fleet and one of the most capable and experienced senior officers of the Navy.

This proposal was rejected by Admiral King, for several good

[13] Born Albany 1894, Naval Academy '15, served in submarines in World War I and later engaged in submarine and torpedo research. On the staff of Rear Admiral M. M. Taylor, Commander Control Force and Submarine Divisions Atlantic Fleet, 1923; Naval War College 1926; staff duty with Subron 5 and C.O. *Paul Jones* 1932–35; Comsubdiv 13, 1937; on Admiral King's staff from Dec. 1940 to Aug. 1942. Commanded *Wichita* in Operation TORCH, and at the battle of Rennell Island (see Vol. V chap. xv). Chief of Staff Tenth Fleet 20 May 1943 to Jan. 1945 when he took command of Crudiv 16, participating in the Okinawa invasion. Comdespac 1945; Comserpac 1947; D.C.N.O. (Logistics) 1950; Com Western Sea Frontier 1953.

reasons in which Admiral Ingersoll cordially acquiesced: (1) Anti-submarine warfare needed a commander of the highest rank who could establish the proper liaison and coördination with the British Admiralty and who could resist "overhead interference" by the President and Prime Minister, both prone to act on sudden inspirations.[14] (2) The organization should operate in the Pacific and wherever submarines could penetrate, not merely in the Atlantic. (3) Admiral Ingersoll's headquarters were afloat and had to remain afloat for proper supervision of his various duties, and he wanted no responsibility for Eastern Sea Frontier. (4) The antisubmarine organization needed fleet status, even if it had no vessels of its own, in order to use fleet communication channels.

On 1 May 1943 Admiral King formally submitted this statement to the Joint Chiefs of Staff: —

It is arranged [15] to set up immediately in the Navy Department an antisubmarine command to be known as the Tenth Fleet.

The headquarters of the Tenth Fleet will consist of all existing antisubmarine activities of U.S. Fleet headquarters, which will be transferred intact to the Commander Tenth Fleet.[16] Such additional officers will be assigned to the Tenth Fleet as are necessary for its function, in the same manner as any other major command. In addition, a research-statistical analysis group will be set up composed of civilian scientists, headed by Dr. Vannevar Bush.

The Commander Tenth Fleet is to exercise direct control over all

---

[14] A bad instance of this occurred in March 1943. Mr. Churchill persuaded Harry Hopkins that the R.N. concept of optimum size of transatlantic convoys (about double that of the U.S.N.) was right, and Hopkins on his return to Washington persuaded President Roosevelt, without consulting anyone, to sign an order to double the HX convoy then being assembled at New York. Admiral King immediately protested, and the order was rescinded; but not before one HX convoy thus increased had sailed and had been badly hit by U-boats. Vice Admiral Wilson Brown "Aide to Four Presidents" in *American Heritage* Magazine Feb. 1955 p. 87; Admiral Stark to Admiral King 13 Apr. 1943.

[15] Note well the verb. Admiral King believed that he had sufficient authority to do this without the permission of the J.C.S.

[16] The Antisubmarine Warfare Unit of the Atlantic Fleet at Boston, then under Cdr. Thomas L. Lewis, the Antisubmarine Measures Unit of Cominch Readiness Div., then under Capt. Wilder D. Baker, the Antisubmarine Warfare Operational Research Group ("Asworg"), then under Dr. Philip M. Morse of M.I.T., and the Convoy and Routing Group of Cominch, then under Rear Admiral Martin K. Metcalf, had been placed under Admiral Low's direction in April before Tenth Fleet was created.

Atlantic Sea Frontiers, using sea frontier commanders as task force commanders. He is to control allocation of antisubmarine forces to all commands in the Atlantic, including the Atlantic Fleet, and is to re-allocate forces from time to time, as the situation requires. In order to insure quick and effective action to meet the needs of the changing antisubmarine situation, the Commander Tenth Fleet is to be given control of all LR and VLR aircraft, and certain groups of units of auxiliary carriers, escort ships and submarines which he will allocate to reënforce task forces which need help, or to employment as "killer groups" under his operational direction in appropriate circumstances.[17]

Admiral King decided to add this command to his many other responsibilities. He became Commander Tenth Fleet himself, but made Admiral Low his chief of staff for that fleet. On 18 May he issued a dispatch that, effective on the 20th, "There is established the Tenth Fleet . . . under direct command of Cominch, to exercise unity of control over U.S. antisubmarine operations in that part of the Atlantic under U.S. strategic control." [18]

The basic directive had been issued the previous day. It declared that the functions of Tenth Fleet were destruction of enemy submarines, protection of Allied and neutral merchant shipping, control of convoys and shipping, and control and correlation of antisubmarine training and matériel development. It concluded with this paragraph, typical of Admiral King's wisdom and way of doing things:

It is to be noted that the foregoing contemplates no measure calculated to effect an instantaneous cure. It is my belief, however, that improvement in the present situation will result if all officers in the chain of command require that fundamentals be *learned* and *applied*.[19]

There was a good deal of mystery about the Tenth Fleet. The word did not get about generally even within the Navy until Cominch made a general announcement on 29 July.[20]

---

[17] *Fleet Admiral King* p. 463.
[18] "First Draft Narrative History Cominch HQ" p. 167. See chart in Appendix I, below, for the boundary between U.S. and British areas of strategic responsibility and Vol. I 320n for exact description of it.
[19] Cominch–C.N.O. Ser. 01550 19 May 1943. Summarized in "First Draft Narrative."
[20] As late as mid-July an officer who had an important responsibility in the

Tenth Fleet was organized as follows:

1. *Operations Division* — Captain William D. Sample. This Division handled sea frontier forces and escort groups, and all units of the Naval Air Arm assigned to antisubmarine work. "Operations" used the Atlantic section of Cominch's Combat Intelligence Division, directed by Commander Kenneth A. Knowles. Its plotting room served as clearinghouse for U-boat Intelligence, including the high-frequency direction-finder network.[21]

2. *Anti-Submarine Measures Division* — Captain John M. Haines (later relieved by Captain H. C. Fitz). This Division, divided into air and surface sections, was charged with the correlation of antisubmarine research, matériel development, and training. It included "Asworg," the Antisubmarine Warfare Operational Research Group, whose analysis of the statistics of antisubmarine warfare was essential. In June 1943 it began the monthly issue of the secret *U.S. Fleet Anti-Submarine Bulletin,* commonly known as the "Yellow Peril."

3. *Convoy and Routing Division* — Rear Admiral M. K. Metcalf. This highly efficient division, taken over intact from Cominch headquarters, had already devised the remarkable interlocking convoy system.[22]

4. *Civilian Scientific Council* — Dr. John T. Tate, chairman.

5. *The Air Anti-Submarine Development Unit Atlantic Fleet (Airsdevlant)*, details of which will be found in Chapter IV.

The reader may well ask, What did this leave for Admiral Ingersoll to do? Actually, Cinclant had a continuing influence in antisubmarine warfare. Tenth Fleet used ships of the Atlantic Fleet, which was under Admiral Ingersoll's command. Cinclant, not Com-

---

antisubmarine war, then stationed in Boston, asked the writer, who was about to go to Washington, "to find out what the hell this Tenth Fleet is" and to let him know.

[21] For HF/DF see Vol. I 226–28. The network is also described in Navy Dept. press releases of 2 and 12 Jan. 1946. Admiral Sir Max Horton RN maintained a similar control center for the Western Approaches at Liverpool, with which Commander Knowles freely and constantly exchanged information.

[22] See Vol. I 260–5.

mander Tenth Fleet, issued operational orders to escort groups starting from the United States; and Admiral Ingersoll was a genius at working out escort-group timetables. He had direct communication with Cominch headquarters by teletype at every Atlantic port, and frequently visited Admiral King in person. He was particularly energetic and effective in organizing and instructing the escort carrier groups. Hating publicity, Ingersoll worked quietly and unobtrusively; but he was one of the principal architects of Allied victory over the U-boat.

Admiral Harold R. Stark [23] was also a very important figure in the antisubmarine setup. Accustomed to dealing with the British since early in World War I, he had had a distinguished career in the Navy, culminating in the office of Chief of Naval Operations in 1939. When President Roosevelt decided to make Admiral King C.N.O. as well as Cominch, he appointed Admiral Stark Commander United States Naval Forces Europe ("Comnaveu"), with headquarters in London. As such he was the leading liaison between the two navies. Admiral Stark's correspondence during the war, which I have been privileged to read, and which should one day be published, proves him to have been a keen diplomatist, a firm though courteous champion of the United States Navy in England, an equally tactful interpreter of the Royal Navy to us, and an intelligent and far-seeing naval strategist.

Tenth Fleet was a typical brainchild of Admiral King who (in contrast to President Roosevelt) believed in using existing units rather than creating new ones, and whose capacity for responsibility was immense. It was essentially a reshuffle and regrouping of units rather than one of the new creations that pullulated in wartime Washington. As such it was an improvement over the previous system of incoherent and haphazard units that had grown up to meet specific needs. Rear Admiral Low, a tough, conscientious, intelligent, and hardworking officer, was a perfect *alter ego* to Admiral King, who did not have the time to give this branch of warfare

[23] For brief biography to 1940 see Vol. I 39*n*. C.N.O. from 2 Aug. 1939 to midMarch 1942 when designated Comnaveu; relieved 15 Aug. 1945; retired 1 April 1946.

the detailed attention it required. "Frog" Low ruled with an iron hand, but he had the respect of his subordinates, who were never allowed to doubt what he wanted, and were never let down.

3. *The Navy–Air Force "Horse Trade," August–September* [24]

No place was provided in Tenth Fleet for the Army Antisubmarine Air Command, which had been playing an important rôle in antisubmarine operations since June 1942. In March 1943 the War Department, "fortified by a comprehensive and extremely able report" prepared by the distinguished physicist Dr. Edward L. Bowles, "began a final effort to win for Army aircraft the autonomy and full naval coöperation needed for a prosecution of offensive operations." [25] That effort, which in essence meant the Army Air Force Antisubmarine Command's assuming the place in the American setup that the Army thought that the Royal Air Force Coastal Command had in the British, was frustrated by the failure of Army and Navy to agree on principles of command, or on antisubmarine tactics.

The Navy system of command is functional; the commander of an operation or a mission uses any necessary weapons or forces, whether they be ground troops, ships, tanks or planes. The Army Air Force system, natural enough for a separate corps within the Army that was straining to become a separate force like the R.A.F., was to make the criterion weapons rather than functions or missions. [26] In the Army, only Air Force officers were allowed to use

[24] This controversy is told from the Air Force point of view in W. F. Craven and James L. Cate *The Army Air Forces in World War II* (1949) II 402–11; and in Henry L. Stimson and McGeorge Bundy *On Active Service in Peace and War* (1948) II 508–18. Short account from Navy point of view in King & Whitehill *Fleet Admiral King* (1952) pp. 463–70. My account is based on the Marshall–King correspondence, a copy of which is preserved in Navy files, and on a number of personal interviews.

[25] Stimson & Bundy II 512. By "offensive operations" the authors mean the reverse of protecting convoys.

[26] The Marine Corps is a separate Corps within the Navy, but the Marines have never boggled at Navy overall command in an operation in which they jointly

a plane or give orders to one. General Arnold wished that Navy planes engaged in antisubmarine warfare might be combined with Army planes under an Air Force general and subjected to Army methods of command. That made it difficult to find a place for the A.A.F. under Tenth Fleet.

As General Marshall and Admiral King talked it over and wrote notes to one another, their area of disagreement narrowed. The Admiral agreed that an Air Force general officer be appointed air commander of Tenth Fleet, provided his successor were a Naval Air admiral. The General conceded that no reorganization of naval command in the Atlantic was required. Then everything broke off, owing to disagreement on antisubmarine tactics.

This disagreement had existed since the beginning of the war. Admiral King, like the British Admiralty, insisted that the primary function of aircraft in antisubmarine war was to support convoys, and that the chances of their sinking submarines were increased if they operated around convoys. The Army Air Force labeled this concept "purely defensive." Its slogan was "Search, Strike, Sink!" [27] By frequently shouting "Let's take the offensive!" it converted many people who had not given the subject much study or thought. At the Atlantic Convoy Conference in March 1943, Dr. Bowles submitted a comprehensive report as a counterblast to Admiral King, stating, among other things, that "Convoying was at best a most inefficient procedure" and that aircraft could be used much more effectively "in carrying the attack to the enemy wherever he may be found." [28] In other words, land-based planes should not be

---

took part. If the Army system had prevailed, a Navy amphibious force commander in the Pacific would have had to go through the Commandant of the Marine Corps at Washington before ordering Marines to do anything different from the operation plan.

[27] H. H. Arnold *Global Mission* pp. 362–64. The General probably got this idea from Sir Philip Joubert, who in 1947 said: "For two years I fought for acceptance of the principle of offensive air action as opposed to defensive close escorting. . . . It was always my desire that we should act offensively, find and kill the submarine wherever it was operating." (*Journal* of Royal United Services Inst. XCII (1947) p. 212.) Sir John Slessor, however, seems to have been converted to the Navy point of view.

[28] Quoted in J.C.S. ms. War History chap. iv "Aircraft and Submarines" 31. See also on this subject my Vol. I 143.

used to support convoys but be organized in "offensive" missions to pursue U-boats over the illimitable ocean.

Even thoughtful naval officers were becoming impatient with the infrequent sinking of submarines. Captain Dudley W. Knox warned Admiral Stark in January 1943 that, unless hunter-killer groups were organized, the numbers of U-boats might so increase as to overwhelm convoys. Captain Richard W. Bates advocated escort carrier groups capable of maintaining round-the-clock patrols, to sweep the convoy lanes and kill submarines.[29] That, it should be said, is exactly what Admirals King and Pound intended to do as soon as they could procure the necessary ships and aircraft.

So much for the background. At the TRIDENT conference in May 1943, King asked Arnold to send to Newfoundland an echelon of B-24s which had recently operated from Bermuda, in order to strengthen air support of northern transatlantic convoys. The General sent it to Gander airport about 1 June, but ordered the squadron commander to engage only in "offensive" search and attack (or words to that effect), definitely forbidding him to cover convoys. Admiral King, apprised of this, observed that these aircraft were of no use to the Navy if they could not assist in escort-of-convoy. That was "the straw that broke the camel's back." [30]

The breakdown came during a conference between General Arnold, Lieutenant General McNarney, Rear Admiral John S. McCain and Captain M. B. Gardner, on 10 June 1943. The two air generals declared they had always been reluctant to take up antisubmarine warfare in the first place and would be glad to withdraw as soon as naval planes were ready to take over the duties of the Army antisubmarine bombers. Captain Gardner suggested that the Army turn over its antisubmarine-equipped Liberators to the Navy in return for an equal number of unmodified B-24s from Navy account. General Arnold agreed; and Admiral King promptly wrote to General Marshall, "This is a solution that I was preparing to propose

[29] To Sec. Operational Proposal Board 30 Mar. 1943.
[30] From an officer then close to Admiral King. This echelon belonged to the squadron which had refused to take orders from naval commanders at Bermuda, as related in *Fleet Admiral King* p. 464.

and I trust that you will recommend approval to the Secretary of War. . . . The Navy will be prepared to take over all antisubmarine air operations by 1 September 1943." [31] The agreement was formally accepted by the War and Navy Departments on 9 July.

Such was the famous "horse trade" between the Navy and the Army Air Force. Each party was relieved at so simple and friendly a solution to a long controversy. Both sides got what they wanted; the Navy assumed complete responsibility for land-based antisubmarine air operations, and the Army Air Force "really wanted to turn it over to the Navy and let them do their own work."

Air Vice Marshal Slessor, the energetic head of Coastal Command, was begging for big bombers to be used in the Bay of Biscay offensive, alleging that many of these units were being held without profitable employment in the United States or Newfoundland pending a decision. [32] Mr. Churchill, distressed at the possible hiatus involved in the "trade," wrote to Mr. Stimson on 22 July that he "earnestly" hoped that the two Army squadrons then operating under Coastal Command would continue to do so "until the Navy squadrons are fully trained and available to relieve them." [33] That they did; the last two were relieved in October and November 1943.

In conclusion, we should never forget that the Army Air Force came to the Navy's assistance at a critical moment and stood by until the Navy was ready to take over all land-based aspects of antisubmarine warfare; that it helped to protect convoys, contributed to the technique of this branch of warfare, and disposed of twelve U-boats, besides assisting in the destruction of several others.

NOTES ON THE NAVY–AIR FORCE CONTROVERSY

Certain statements in Stimson & Bundy *On Active Service* II 508–18 require specific comment or correction.

[31] Capt. Gardner to Admiral King 10 June 1943, and King to Marshall 14 June.
[32] Discussion in *Journal* of Royal United Services Inst. May 1947 pp. 214–5.
[33] Arnold *Global Mission* p. 363.

1. "Admiral King's [officers] were primarily concerned with the Pacific. With rare exceptions, antisubmarine warfare received only the partial attention of first-rate officers, while actual operations were left to commanders not always chosen from the top drawer" (p. 515). I disagree with this *in toto,* and the slur on the American escort commanders is undeserved. No man was more completely loyal to the "beat Germany first" strategic decision than Admiral King. He was deeply and constantly concerned with the antisubmarine war.

2. As regards Coastal Command, it is estimated (p. 510) that Coastal was free to wage "a direct offensive on U-boats" and only incidentally had anything to do with convoys. Coastal's first duty in antisubmarine warfare was to afford air escort and support to convoys; it was free to go all-out after U-boats *not* threatening a convoy only if planes were available.

3. The U.S. Navy "insisted on assigning planes to the command of individual sea frontier commanders, thus effectively preventing the concentrated use of air power against the points particularly threatened by U-boats" (p. 511). There is a good deal of truth in this; these conditions were not remedied until after the "horse trade" was completed, in September 1943. (See Chapter XI.) But, even within sea frontier headquarters, it often took hours for the Navy commander to clear a request for the use of Army planes. One such instance which came to this writer's attention occurred in the summer of 1942. A surfaced U-boat appeared in Casco Bay, but before the local district commander could get orders for Army bombers based a few miles distant to join the hunt, the submarine had put out to sea and disappeared.

4. It is assumed that a unified Army command of antisubmarine air would automatically bring "flexibility," so that, for instance, when Doenitz shifted his offensive from the Eastern Sea Frontier to the Caribbean, squadrons of antisubmarine planes would follow immediately. But the logistic difficulties of transferring planes from continental to insular bases are exactly the same for Army as for Navy aircraft; nor would the political pressure from Congressmen, mayors of coastal cities, etc., to secure aircraft for coastal protection have been any less if the planes wore different markings.

5. "King did not immediately reject" (p. 513) the Army proposal to place all land-based air in Tenth Fleet under an Army Air Officer. (Craven & Cate II 405 make the same mistake.) Actually King accepted the proposal, including the nomination of Major General Willis H. Hale USA of the VII A.A.F., then in the Pacific, who had had experience

directing over-water air operations. The failure to agree came about as I have related in the text.

6. "In November, 1943, two months later than it had at first promised, the Navy assumed full responsibility for the work" (p. 513). The transfer was 90 per cent complete in September when promised, and on 6 October A.A.F. Headquarters so reported. (Craven and Cate II 409.) The delay was caused by Mr. Churchill's desire to keep the 479th and 480th Groups of the U.S.A.A.F. at work under R.A.F. Coastal, in England and West Africa, until fully trained Navy Liberator squadrons could relieve them. The one was relieved in October and the other in November.

7. "The Air Forces, strongly supported by Stimson and Marshall, believed that antisubmarine air operations *must* be coördinated and directed by an aggressive air commander like Air Marshal Slessor of the British Coastal Command, subject only to the most general guidance of his naval superior. Admiral King believed this concept to be wholly mistaken and insisted that air operations must be directly controlled in each area by the local naval commander" (p. 513). The statement about the two contrasting conceptions is correct; but the assumption that every R.A.F. squadron commander had to await Slessor's orders before he could cover a convoy is unfounded. Commander Coastal determined air strategy in conjunction with the Admiralty; Area Combined Headquarters handled operations. The British system was much closer to what Admiral King established than what Mr. Secretary Stimson desired.

The essence of the matter is that General Arnold and Mr. Stimson wished to apply their incorrect notions of the British command system and antisubmarine tactics in an area stretching from Newfoundland to Brazil, so different from the British Isles that even a correct application of the British system would have been a mistake.

CHAPTER III

New Antisubmarine Ships and Aircraft

1. *The Destroyer Escorts*

"THE NAVY did not obtain adequate means to deal with the U-boat until late in 1943." Such was the sober conclusion of Admiral King after the war was over.[1] Foremost of the means that he had in mind were ships suitable for escort of convoy.

By April 1943 the 173-foot steel-hulled patrol craft (PC) and the 110-foot wooden-hulled subchaser (SC) were coming out in fair quantities, but the PCs were of slight use and the SCs were of none as escorts for blue-water convoys. The subchasers were not even fast enough to catch a surfaced U-boat, nor powerful enough to fight it if they did. The patrol craft were useful in the inter-locking coastal convoy system; even there, they had to be spliced with converted yachts, minesweepers, and small Coast Guard cutters. No 180-foot PCEs, the patrol craft especially designed for escort work, were then ready to operate.[2]

President Roosevelt initiated the destroyer escort program as early as June 1940, when he proposed to Frank Knox, Secretary of the Navy, that orders for two experimental DEs of 750 to 900 tons each be placed with a shipbuilding company.[3] Congressional au-

[1] *Fleet Admiral King* p. 448.
[2] See Vol. I of this History pp. 229–31, and table on p. 235 which shows number of each type of vessel available for antisubmarine warfare "on hand" in June 1943. The list includes 306 SCs, 35 DEs and 17 CVEs; but "on hand" does not mean that they had had their shakedown and were ready to operate.
[3] Records in the Bureau of Ships, especially two memos by Capt. L. B. McBride, endorsed by Chief of Bureau of Ships and presented to the Undersecretary of the Navy 15 Apr. 1943. These documents prove that President Roosevelt, far from being an obstructionist in the DE program, as charged in *Fleet Admiral King* pp. 445–48, was one of its earliest advocates.

thorization for building these and possibly more was provided under an appropriation of $50,000,000 for "patrol, escort, and miscel-
laneous craft" in the last of the "two-ocean Navy" acts, that of 19
July 1940.[4] The Bureau of Ships produced its first plan for a DE on
24 August, and four additional plans in the fall of that year, but
none met the approval of the General Board of the Navy. They ob-
jected largely on the ground of expense; Buships estimated that a
775-ton DE with adequate depth-charge and antiaircraft armament
would cost $4,700,000, not much less than a 1630-ton destroyer,
which would be the better all-round fighting ship. This computa-
tion convinced everyone from the President down, and in January
1941 it was decided to build "repeater" destroyers of the *Benson*
class. These amply proved their value in World War II, but the DE
program was shelved for many months.

Captain Edward L. Cochrane, an outstanding naval architect,
was responsible for the revival. On a visit to England in 1940–1941
on behalf of Buships to study the design and performance of British escort types, he had been impressed by the "Hunt" class 900-
ton destroyer, then unique for speed (27.5 knots), seaworthiness,
and the excellence of antiaircraft and antisubmarine armament.
Captain Cochrane then worked up a new design for a 1085-ton destroyer escort which could be built for a little over half the cost of
a *Benson* class destroyer. During the first six months of 1941 Rear
Admiral Samuel M. Robinson, Chief of the Bureau of Ships, tried
in vain to "sell" this design to the General Board of the Navy and
to Admirals King and Stark.

It is one of the ironies of American naval history that the United
States Navy obtained its first destroyer escorts by building them
for England's Royal Navy, and then taking them away. Our first
DE program was a back-handed gift to ourselves through lend-
lease.

Congress passed the first Lend-lease Act on 11 March 1941. In
June the Admiralty presented an urgent request for the construction of a hundred 1500-ton escort vessels, to counter the wider

[4] *U.S. Statutes at Large* **LIV** Part I 780.

range of German submarine operations that followed the fall of France. Rear Admiral J. W. S. Dorling RN, then the Admiralty supply representative in Washington, found Captain Cochrane's design acceptable; and Admiral Stark, then Chief of Naval Operations, approved building twenty escort vessels for Britain on 29 July. Within a month President Roosevelt stepped up the total to fifty. The contracts for these were not awarded until November, and under normal peacetime shipbuilding methods the vessels could hardly have been completed before the summer of 1943.

The Pearl Harbor attack brought about vast expansion and acceleration of naval construction. On 18 January 1942 the President recommended the "1799" Program,[5] so called because it provided for building 1799 ships and small craft for the Royal Navy. As passed, the bill provided that any of these vessels could be taken over by the United States Navy before completion; and of the destroyer escorts constructed under that program no fewer than 195 were destined to fly the Stars and Stripes rather than the White Ensign.

The entire list follows on page 35.

Successive United States naval building programs by August 1943 authorized over one thousand DEs. But before these programs were completed, the U-boat menace had so declined that 442 were canceled and only 520 were completed. In all, 420 were commissioned; but only 373, including the 195 taken over under the "1799" Program, actually saw duty as DEs during hostilities.[6]

So much for the authorization; production is a very different story. Secretary Knox, on 26 February 1943, remarked to this writer that the DE program had been "all bitched up from the beginning" — which was correct. The original estimate for completing DEs, 32 months, had been cut down to 15 months after Pearl Harbor, when "round the clock" work regardless of expense became the rule in American shipyards. Yet by 2 June 1943, 16 to 18

---

[5] Public Law No. 440, approved 6 Feb. 1942.

[6] C.N.O. "Combatant Shipbuilding 1 Jan. 1942 to July 1 1946." Of the remaining units, 47 were converted to destroyer transports (APDs) before or after commissioning.

months after the first keels had been laid, only 42 had been launched, and very few commissioned.

Superior priorities for other classes of warships were responsible for most of the delay. The ravages of U-boats along the Atlantic coast in 1942 brought construction of PCs and SCs into first place.

"1799" EMERGENCY CONSTRUCTION PROGRAM [7]

		Number Authorized	Number taken by U.S. Navy to Aug. 1943
DE	Destroyer Escorts	250	195
AM	Minesweepers	48	12
YMS	Motor Minesweepers	150	80
PCE	180-foot Patrol Craft, Escort	150	59
LST	Landing Ship, Tank	300	0
LSD	Landing Ship, Dock	10	0
LCT	Landing Craft, Tank	300	0
LCP	Higgins Landing Craft	500	0
Salvage Vessels, Harbor Craft, Rescue Tugs, Motor Launches, Crash Boats		91	35
	Total	1799	381

Most serious was "triple-A priority" granted to landing and beaching craft for Operation SLEDGEHAMMER, the proposed cross-channel invasion of France in 1942, which never came off. In the autumn of 1942, President Roosevelt directed Admiral King to give top priority to the completion of 260 destroyer escorts. But requirements for steel, labor, and machinery for "letter craft" (LSTs, LCTs, and so on) were so excessive that Buships had to reduce by half the turbine horsepower of 183 destroyer escorts. Thus, about one third of the new type were unable to make over twenty-one knots.

Spurred on by Under Secretary Forrestal, five navy yards and a dozen private shipbuilders put DE construction on a mass produc-

[7] Column one from "1799 Construction Program," a document shown to the writer by Admiral Reeves in 1942; column two from Admiralty Supply Representative (Admiral Dorling) "New Construction Program August 1943" p. 31.

tion basis in February 1943, and 260 were commissioned by 5 December.[8] In many units the planned steam-turbine engines had to be replaced by diesel, owing to shortage of steel and machine tools. None were ready for escort duty before June of 1943.

The DEs, as completed, fall into these three main classes: —

	SHORT HULL	LONG HULL I	LONG HULL II
	(*Original British design*)	(*U.S. design, some for R.N.*)	(*U.S. design, all for U.S.N.*)
Length	289 feet	306 feet	306 feet
Standard displacement	1,150 tons	1,200–1,450 tons	1,275 tons
Propulsion	diesel electric	diesel, diesel elec. or turbo elec.	geared steam turbine
Speed	20 knots	21 knots	24 knots
Range at 12 knots	6,600 miles	6,000 miles	12,000 miles
Torpedo tubes	none	three 21″	three 21″
Guns and Depth Charges	three 3″50 DP several 40-mm and 20-mm machine guns 8 or 9 single and one multiple (hedgehog) DC projector in each	three 3″50 DP	two 5″38 DP

DEs have a high reserve buoyancy and freeboard, good compartmentation, a minimum of equipment and plenty of working space. When they finally did come out they were the merchant convoys' "answer to prayer" and an excellent screen for escort carriers. Commanded and officered by the more salty reservists who had served early in the war as junior officers in destroyers and patrol craft and chasers,[9] they justified the wisdom of their designers and planners.

A less important escort type was the frigate (PF), 69 of which were contracted for by the Maritime Commission in December 1942 on oral instructions from the President. The design was based on that of two Canadian-built frigates which were turned over to the United States and named *Asheville* and *Natchez*. About 100 of this type were completed in 1944. They were never popular because they were almost unbearably hot below decks in the tropics.[10]

[8] Rear Admiral Cochrane statement in N.Y. *Times* 9 Dec. 1943.
[9] Total ship's complement for all three classes, about 180 officers and men.
[10] Frederic C. Lane *Ships for Victory* (1951) pp. 614–17. Frigates were named

2. *The Escort Carriers* [11]

There was a similar and even more complicated situation in building the escort carrier (CVE), smallest class of airplane carrier, capable of carrying about 24 operating planes and steaming up to 18.5 knots.

The earliest airplane carrier in any navy was H.M.S. *Argus*, converted from an Italian passenger liner in 1916; first in the United States Navy was *Langley*, converted from collier *Jupiter* in 1922. The small type then went into abeyance, while the American, British, and Japanese navies converted battle cruiser hulls to big carriers such as *Lexington, Saratoga, Furious, Glorious* and *Akagi*. Between wars the carrier was generally regarded as part of the scouting forces for major fleet operations. Admiral William V. Pratt, when Chief of Naval Operations, showed an interest in its potentialities for antisubmarine warfare, and Admiral J. M. Reeves, C. in C. U.S. Fleet in 1934–36, predicted that convoys could not be protected from enemy aircraft and submarines without carrier-borne air protection.

On 13 December 1940, Rear Admiral William F. Halsey, Commander Aircraft Battle Force, drew Admiral Stark's attention to the fact that a declaration of war would require immediate deployment of the six fleet carriers then available, with disastrous effect on the training of naval aviators and the transport of planes to overseas bases. To remedy this "woefully weak" situation, Halsey urged immediate procurement of "suitable merchant vessels and their earli-

---

after towns and small cities. They were 303 ft. long, displaced 1430 tons, were propelled at 19 knots by twin-screw reciprocating engines; armament was three 3"50, ten 20-mm and four DC throwers. Since the war they have been redesignated Patrol Escorts; *Mitscher* class Destroyer Leaders have been designated Frigates. Twenty-one of the original frigates were transferred to Great Britain under Lend-Lease; in the R.N. they were known as "Colony" class Frigates.

[11] Designated AVG (Auxiliary Aircraft Vessel) 5 Feb. 1941, ACV (Auxiliary Aircraft Carrier) 20 Aug. 1942, and CVE (Aircraft Carrier, Escort) 15 July 1943. (Documents in the Bureau of Ships: "Evolution of the Escort Carrier" in *O.N.I. Weekly* IV (Apr. 1945) 1309–17, 1397–1406.) For British developments see Roskill I 476–79.

est conversion to auxiliary aircraft carriers," specifying speed and flight deck requirements to give them an adequate landing platform. One week later, President Roosevelt recommended to Admiral Stark that 15-knot merchant ship hulls be fitted with short flight decks to accommodate autogiros or a few planes with low landing speeds.

The Royal Navy, whose problem at this time was convoy defense against enemy bombers and U-boats, was making a similar experiment. An old seaplane tender and three merchant ships were fitted with catapults. Each of these C.A.M. (Catapult Assisted Merchant) ships, as they were called, carried one or two Hurricanes which proved to be moderately successful in coping with German FW–200s, then homing in U-boats on convoys.[12] A more radical step was the conversion of a German prize ship to a full-fledged escort carrier – H.M.S. *Audacity* – completed in June 1941. She was torpedoed and sunk in a battle between U-boats and a Gibraltar–U.K. convoy in December 1941, but not until her planes and the surface escort had destroyed five submarines. The lesson, not lost on either Navy, was to skip the stopgaps and build escort carriers.

Already the United States Navy had converted its first escort carrier, *Long Island*, from the 10,000-ton S.S. *Mormacmail*. Initiated in January 1941, the conversion was so vigorously pushed by President Roosevelt that *Long Island* was delivered on 2 June. And three months earlier, in March 1941, the General Board had approved the conversion of an unspecified number of C–3 and other merchant hulls to escort carriers.

The Royal Navy, now paying dearly for its peacetime surrender of naval aviation to the R.A.F., turned to the United States to build escort carriers under Lend-lease. On 29 April 1941 the Admiralty requested that we convert six C–3 merchant hulls to "fighter carriers" for convoy protection. One week later the conversion of S.S. *Mormacland* to H.M.S. *Archer* was begun, and by mid-November it was completed. In the meantime, conversion had been

[12] Roskill I 477.

started on five more C–3 hulls, of which one became U.S.S. *Charger*, and the other four, H.M.S. *Avenger, Biter, Dasher* and *Tracker*, all except the last diesel-powered.

These "Woolworth carriers," as they were nicknamed, were regarded as very poor jobs by the Admiralty, which promptly sent them into British shipyards for extensive alterations.[18] But they paved the way for a tremendous American escort carrier program.

After the Pearl Harbor attack almost every branch of the United States Navy began to cast covetous eyes on Maritime Commission C–3 hulls, with a view to converting them to various urgently needed types such as transports, tenders, repair ships and escort carriers. The Auxiliary Vessels Board of the Navy had the ungrateful task of dividing a very thin pie among a mob of hungry boys, and the Maritime Commission was reluctant to release any pie to divide. They had a colossal number of merchantmen to construct, and did not wish to delay that program. The United States was up against hard facts — shortage of strategic materials, shortage of

---

[18] This and later "reconversions" in the U.K. were the occasion of a warm controversy between the U.S.N. and Royal Navy. The latter pointed to the sinking of H.M.S. *Avenger* by one torpedo hit on 15 Nov. 1942, leaving only 17 survivors, and the sinking of H.M.S. *Dasher* in the Clyde on 27 Mar. 1943, by a gasoline explosion, with a loss of 378 lives, as justification for radical alterations in the fuel system. The R.N. Director of Naval Construction regarded American-built CVEs as unstable by British standards and added 1200 to 2000 tons' ballast to each one. This had to be done because the R.N. refused to follow the U.S.N. practice of filling empty fuel tanks with salt water for ballast. The Antisubmarine Survey Board on 27 Aug. 1943 pointed out that the delay of 24 to 30 weeks between delivery of CVEs to the R.N. and the date of their becoming operational was "not considered acceptable," and recommended that "failing a drastic reduction in this delay, consideration be given to the U.S.N. manning some of the next 7 CVEs allocated to Britain with a view to a higher proportion of these vessels being employed on A/S operations with the minimum of delay." The C.C.S. adopted these suggestions 10 Sept., agreeing that "all possible steps should be taken to obviate the present delay in making British-manned CVEs operational." In this writer's opinion, the British failed to make best use of American-built CVEs, owing largely to the basic conditions under which they operated. They were not commanded by naval air officers, since none of sufficient seniority were available. Their Swordfish planes were too vulnerable for antisubmarine work. The R.N., short of manpower, provided so few ratings for deck crews (about 20 as compared with 80 in the U.S. CVEs) that landing and recovery were very slow; and, owing to lack of repair facilities on board, the CVEs spent a long time in dockyards between operations. But the British CVE operations improved greatly during 1943–44, as we shall see.

ships, shortage of everything; only the higher command could decide who would get what first.

In view of the intense competition for C–3 hulls, the Auxiliary Vessels Board decided in December 1941 to convert to escort carriers four fleet oilers of the *Cimarron* class. *Sangamon, Suwannee, Chenango* and *Santee* were completed in time to take part in Operation TORCH in November 1942. They proved so effective, not only in antisubmarine patrol but in covering amphibious operations, that the first three were sent to reinforce the carrier-starved Pacific Fleet. *Santee*, attached to the South Atlantic Force (later Fourth Fleet) on 10 March 1943, helped to track down and destroy German blockade runner *Kota Nopan*.[14] And she supported United States–Gibraltar convoys from mid-June to the close of 1943, as we shall see in due course. This *Sangamon* class fought through the Pacific war, sharing the glory of that Thermopylae of "jeep carriers," the Battle off Samar.

In December 1941, the Maritime Commission released twenty C–3 steam-powered freighter hulls, under construction on the West Coast, for conversion to CVEs. Ten became the escort carrier class [15] in which *Bogue, Card, Core, Croatan* and *Block Island* made enviable records as submarine hunters; the other ten were converted for the Royal Navy.[16] Their flight decks were 42 feet shorter than those of the *Sangamon* class.

Admiral Reeves's committee of the Joint Munitions Assignment Board voted for 15 additional C–3 conversions on 2 April 1942, and a contract for 20 more was given to West Coast yards on 1 May. Before completion it was decided to turn these over to the Royal Navy,[17] while the United States Navy kept all the newer "Kaiser" class.

14 See Vol. I 384–85.
15 Sometimes called the *Bogue*, sometimes the *Prince William* class.
16 H.M.S. *Attacker, Hunter, Battler, Chaser, Fencer, Stalker, Pursuer, Striker, Searcher, Ravager.*
17 H.M.S. *Ameer, Begum, Nabob*, etc. In all, 38 converted C–3 escort carriers were transferred to Britain.

Throughout the period of these conversions, Captain Cochrane and other naval architects in the Bureau of Ships were endeavoring to standardize escort carrier design and to incorporate longer flight decks and better compartmentation. Just as plans for an improved *Bogue* class were being drafted, Mr. Henry J. Kaiser, the West Coast shipbuilder, breezed into the picture. Armed with a sketch of a proposed "airplane transport vessel," he burst into the Bureau of Ships on 2 June 1942, offering to build 30 or more CVEs within six months, provided the Navy did not interfere with the design. Buships naturally turned him down; it was unprecedented for the Navy to finance, arm, equip and operate a fleet of ships privately designed [18] and privately built by a shipyard which had no previous experience in naval construction. But Mr. Kaiser appealed higher. President Roosevelt ordered the Navy and the Maritime Commission to negotiate with him, and before the end of June he got his contract. He agreed to build 50 to 55 escort carriers on the Maritime Commission's fast transport (P–1 type) hulls, with reciprocating steam engines capable of turning up 20 knots; the first five to be delivered in February 1943. He did not, however, obtain the complete contract that he demanded. He had to concede that the design be developed and the building supervised by the Maritime Commission, through which Buships and Buaër were able to prevent mistakes and obtain some of the positive features required of a man-of-war. *Casablanca*, first of these "jeep carriers" or "baby flat-tops," was not actually commissioned until July 1943. Almost every vessel of the Kaiser class was assigned to the Pacific Fleet — important exceptions being U.S.S. *Guadalcanal* and *Mission Bay*.

As soon as the *Bogue* class CVEs were ready for sea and air groups trained, they were employed — as President Roosevelt and Admiral King had long anticipated — to support transatlantic convoys. We shall hear much of their operations in subsequent chapters.

Characteristics of the two main classes were as follows: —

[18] The naval architect George G. Sharp drafted the working drawings.

	Bogue	Kaiser
Length	492 feet	512 feet
Standard displacement	14,200 tons	10,000 tons
Propulsion	Geared turbine	Twin-screw reciprocating
Speed	17 knots	19 knots
Range at 15 knots	26,300 miles	10,200 miles
Armament	Two 5″/38 DP	One 5″/38 DP
	10 40-mm AA twins	8 40-mm AA twins
	27 20-mm AA	20 20-mm AA
Aircraft	16 fighters and 12 torpedo-bombers	

3. *Antisubmarine Aircraft*

Parallel to Tenth Fleet was the command of Air Force Atlantic Fleet, "Comairlant." In March 1943 Rear Admiral Bellinger, who had grown up with naval aviation, was appointed to this command. "Pat" Bellinger had piloted seaplane NC–1 on its flight from Newfoundland to the Azores in 1919, had commanded aircraft carriers and patrol wings in the Pacific, and served as Admiral King's deputy chief of staff for air.[19] His was an administrative and type command. The Naval Air Arm remained under operational control of the Atlantic Fleet, but Admiral Bellinger's thirty years' experience as a naval aviator had a most beneficial influence on the air aspect of convoy coverage and antisubmarine warfare.

It was not enough to train pilots in antisubmarine warfare; more and better planes were needed. One of the difficulties in trans-

[19] Patrick N. L. Bellinger, born South Carolina 1885, Naval Academy '07; service in battleships until 1912, when after a brief submarine command he was assigned to aviation duty and helped to establish the first naval aviation training center at Pensacola. Piloted the first United States plane to come under enemy fire at Vera Cruz, 1914. Made the first catapult test and set a new record for seaplane altitude of 10,000 ft. in 1915, and first night seaplane flight, 1917. Commanded N.A.S. Hampton Roads during World War I. Joined Buaër at its first organization, 1921. Various aviation duties; Assistant Naval Attaché, Rome, 1928. C.O. aircraft tender *Wright* 1931, carrier *Langley* 1932–33, carrier *Ranger* 1936; N.O.B. Norfolk 1938–40, when promoted Rear Admiral and appointed Com Patwing Two at Honolulu. Deputy Chief of Staff for Air to Cominch Aug. 1942. Comairlant 20 Mar. 1943–Feb. 1946; retired 1947.

oceanic convoy cover was the want of air support in certain regions, or during foul weather. A great effort was made in mid-1943 to fill these holes by basing more long-range and very-long-range planes in Newfoundland and Iceland, by escort carrier groups, and by acquiring an air base in the Azores.

VLR planes included the modified Liberator,[20] Coronado (PB2Y-3) and others with a cruising range of over 2000 nautical miles. That meant that they were capable of remaining four hours on station a thousand miles from base. The combined United States Air Forces had 78 such planes available for antisubmarine work in the Atlantic in mid-April 1943, when and if modified. But immediate requirements were 260, and it was planned to have an additional 208 ready by 1 January 1944.

LR (long-range) planes included unmodified Liberators, Flying Fortresses (B-17s), Catalinas (PBYs), Mariners (PBMs), Venturas (PV-1s) and others with a cruising range of 1200 to 2000 nautical miles, which meant an operational radius of 400 to 600 miles from base. Army and Navy together had 482 of these on hand 15 April and planned to have an additional 114 ready by 1944.[21] .

The table (page 44) shows the approximate state of this arm during the last week of May 1943.

American aircraft production had now so increased that the Navy in the second half of 1943 was able to relieve both the Army Air Force and Civil Air Patrol from antisubmarine duties.[22] By the end of 1943 practically all aircraft in the United States strategic

---

[20] Army designation B-24; Navy designation PB4Y. Liberators had to have some of their armor and gun turrets removed and bigger gas tanks added before they could qualify as VLR. Most of them sent to England were not so modified, as LR was enough for Bay of Biscay patrol and the R.A.F. hoped to use them eventually for bombing Germany.

[21] C.C.S. "Measures for Combating Submarine Menace" Annex H to Appendix C. The less important MR (medium-range) planes included A-29s, B-18s, B-25s, and others with a range of up to 1200 nautical miles, or operational radius up to 400 miles. Of these, 649 were on hand, which was some 50 more than were required. The SR (short-range) included all types not mentioned above. They were practically useless for A/S warfare but were used in harbor patrol.

[22] See Chapter II, and Vol. I 276–81 for Civil Air Patrol. At the same time the Coastal Picket Patrol (see Vol. I 268–76) was taken over by the Coast Guard, and various other stopgaps and amateur efforts were liquidated or turned into other forms of service.

area that were engaged in antisubmarine work had come under United States Navy command. The exceptions were the Royal Canadian Air Force and a few Army squadrons which remained in Guiana and Ascension Island into 1944.

OPERATIONAL AIRCRAFT ENGAGED IN ANTISUBMARINE
WARFARE IN ATLANTIC [23]

	U.S. Navy Air Arm				U.S. Army Air Force			R.A.F. and R.C.A.F.		
	BLIMPS	VLR	LR	MR	VLR	LR	MR	VLR	LR	MR
Iceland	—	—	9	—	—	—	—	12	—	18
Greenland	—	—	5	1	—	—	8	—	—	8
Newfoundland, Nova Scotia	—	6	23	—	24	15	—	13	86	50
East. Sea Frontier	24	15	36	3	15	—	65	—	—	—
Gulf Sea Frontier	9	—	10	2	5	—	32	—	—	—
Carib. Sea Frontier:										
Guantanamo	1	—	16	—	—	—	6	—	—	—
Trinidad	2	—	18	—	—	—	32	—	—	—
Curaçao-Aruba	—	—	—	—	—	—	25	—	—	—
San Juan	—	—	8	—	—	—	8	—	—	—
Bermuda	—	8	8	—	—	—	—	—	—	—
Brazil and Guianas	—	—	35	—	—	—	—	—	—	—
Ascension I.	—	—	—	—	—	—	5	—	—	—
Moroccan Sea Frontier	—	—	23	—	15	—	—	—	—	—
Gibraltar	—	—	—	—	—	—	—	—	25	36
United Kingdom	—	—	—	—	—	—	—	216	139	15

The extreme scope of land-based air coverage over transatlantic convoys had now been extended to a radius of 900 miles from Newfoundland, 500 miles from Iceland, and 900 miles from the British Isles. But there was still a big "black pit" around the Azores with no air protection except what could be afforded by escort carrier groups – a very big exception, as we shall see.

[23] *U.S. Fleet A/S Bulletin* June 1943 pp. 16–17. Lt. Cdr. D. W. Waters RN points out that owing to the tendency of both countries to consider all Liberators VLR even if not so modified, this table is inexact in that column, and that the only really VlR planes able to help northern transatlantic convoys in mid-ocean in May 1943 were the B–24s of the R.A.F. and R.C.A.F. based on Iceland.

Negotiations looking toward the use of the Azores for Allied airfields [24] had been going on since May 1941, when a planned occupation of the islands by United States Marines and the British Army was called off because the Portuguese government refused to permit it. Dr. Salazar, the effective ruler of Portugal, like Dr. De Valera of Eire, having decided to keep his country neutral, refused to grant any concession to the United States which might give Germany an excuse to retaliate. Unlike De Valera, he was willing to honor his country's ancient ties with England, which were anterior by several centuries to the modern (though seldom respected) international law of neutrality. Consequently the Foreign Office took charge of the negotiations; but it was not until 12 October 1943 that Mr. Churchill was able to announce that the use of Lagens Field in Terceira had been accorded to Great Britain only. The first R.A.F. planes, including 30 B–17s and 9 Hudsons, flew in there that month.

So far, so good; but the 6000-foot strip at Lagens Field was insufficient for VLR planes and could be extended only with American help. On the last day of 1943, with Dr. Salazar's permission, an American airfield survey party, disguised as employees of a private concern, arrived at Terceira. On 6 January 1944, Admiral King set up a command called United States Naval Forces Azores (Comnavzor) "to administer United States Naval affairs in this area and specifically to provide a service point for Naval Air Transport, antisubmarine operations, and later, upon arrival of these planes, to insure their satisfactory performance under operational control of the R.A.F." The first commander, Captain William G. Tomlinson, on being briefed in Washington before his departure, was asked by Vice Admiral Edwards, "Now do you understand the Azores situation? . . . If you do, you are the only one in the Navy who does!"

[24] J.C.S. ms. War History chap. v, "Diplomacy and Military Command in the Battle of the Atlantic"; Cordell Hull *Memoirs* II (1948) 1339–44; Ministério dos Negócios Estrangeiros *Documentos relativos aos Acordos entre Portugal, Inglaterra e Estados da América para a Concessão de Facilidades nos Açores* (Lisbon 1946) pp. 35–42; Comnavzor (Capt. W. G. Tomlinson) War Diary 1944–45; see also Vol. I 66–67.

Nevertheless, Liberty ships and LSTs were allowed to land men and matériel, work was started on a naval camp at Lagens, and Seabees began to construct unloading slips for LSTs at Praia Bay, Terceira. The Lisbon government was then pressed to allow United States aircraft to operate from Lagens under R.A.F. Coastal Command, as others were doing in England; this was conceded in July 1944, when six Liberators of Fleet Air Wing Nine arrived at Terceira to fly antisubmarine patrol under British command. The Portuguese government permitted them to operate only on condition that they display British as well as American insignia.

In the meantime, events in Europe and the Far East had persuaded Dr. Salazar to grant the United States an air base in the island of Santa Maria, southernmost of the Azores. Portugal wanted American help to recover its half of Timor from the Japanese, and the State Department claimed that it needed an Azorean base for staging aircraft to the Indies! So the Santa Maria field was built by American Seabees and virtually completed by 1 May 1944.

It is too bad that Portugal did not see fit to make these concessions earlier; United States escort carrier groups, as we shall see, had to bear the brunt of "scouring" waters around the Azores for U-boats. But the aircraft based on Terceira proved very useful in protecting British-escorted north–south convoys against submarine and air attack; and the Santa Maria field was — and still is — immensely valuable for transatlantic air transport between the United States and Africa.

CHAPTER IV

New Training and Technical Developments

1. *The "Antisubmarine University"* [1]

THE Operational Training Command Atlantic Fleet ("Cotclant"), commanded by Rear Admiral Donald B. Beary,[2] was as important as the Tenth Fleet. In time of peace, training could best be conducted on board ships already in commission; but the Fleet was now too busy fighting to perform this function. Various *ad hoc* training schools had been set up when and as needed, but by 1943 it was time that all should be assembled in one family.

On 14 March 1943 Admiral Ingersoll commissioned Cotclant with the following functions: (1) to take over all existing training schools and training centers of the Atlantic Fleet, except those for submarines and landing craft; (2) to schedule and supervise (*a*) the precommissioning training of crews while being assembled for new construction and (*b*) training during the new ships' "shakedown";

---

[1] Monthly *Cotclant News Letter;* conversations with Admiral Ingersoll, Admiral Beary, and Capt. Denebrink in 1944.

[2] Donald Bradford Beary, b. Montana 1888; Naval Academy '10; M.S. Columbia Univ. '17. C.O. *Remlik* and *Lamson* in World War I and of three successive DDs 1921–23. Duty in fleet training div. C.N.O.; navigator *New Mexico* 1925, instructor in electrical engineering Naval Academy 1928, asst. chief of staff to Admiral M. M. Taylor, C. in C. Asiatic Fleet, 1931; duty in office of C.N.O. 1934, exec. *Colorado* 1937, C.O. *Richmond* 1939, C.O. *Mount Vernon* and Comtransdiv 19, 1941; Com N.O.B. Iceland July 1942; Cotclant 10 Feb. 1943–1 Oct. 1944. Organized and commanded Servron 6, one of the mobile service squadrons (see Vols. VII 106 and VIII 343–50) in the Okinawa campaign and until the end of the war with Japan, when he took charge of repatriating Japanese troops from China and the Pacific islands. Com. 12th Naval District and Western S.F. 1946. President Naval War College 1948; retired 1950.

and (3) to provide refresher training for crews of operating vessels.[3] The purpose of (2a) was to get away from the debilitating influence of receiving stations, where crews marked time waiting for their ships to be commissioned, and to place men under military control in a place where they could be trained with direct bearing on what they were about to do. The purpose of (2b) was to get away from the haphazard and uncoördinated shakedown training then in vogue; and (3), the "refresher," registered the conviction that training must continue in wartime or battle efficiency is lost.

Rear Admiral Beary was appointed to this new training command, located at Camp Allen near Norfolk, with Captain F. C. Denebrink his chief of staff. On 19 July 1943 the Antisubmarine Warfare Unit of the Atlantic Fleet [4] was brought under him insofar as its training functions were concerned. Captain P. R. Heineman, commander of that Unit, was designated Coördinator of Antisubmarine Warfare Training on 22 September. Admiral Beary directed him as follows: —

> The paramount tasks of your task group are to accomplish the most effective training and indoctrination of all Antisubmarine Specialists and Attack Teacher Instructors ordered to your command and to insure that the methods and procedures of antisubmarine instruction at all surface craft training centers, under Cotclant's cognizance, are adequate and in strict accord with the latest approved standards, to the end that all personnel and units will be fully ready for active operations against enemy submarines upon the completion of their training periods.

Thus, Admiral Beary and Captain Heineman became, as it were, Chancellor and Vice Chancellor of the United States Antisubmarine University. It was organized on the Oxford pattern, with separate colleges consisting of several sound schools and 15 antisubmarine training and refresher centers. These were located along the Atlantic Coast of the Americas from Argentia to Recife, and at

---

[3] Cinclant's Atlantic Fleet Letter 15 Mar. 1943. Cotclant had no jurisdiction over basic ("boot") or officer indoctrination training, which remained as before under the Bureau of Naval Personnel. See Vol. I 214–17 for the Sound Schools which now came under Cotclant.

[4] See Vol. I 218–19 for the early history of this Unit.

Bermuda and Casablanca. As Captain Heineman's "alumni" graduated into that rough-and-tumble world of the Atlantic they spread the antisubmarine gospel throughout the Navy.

To prevent diluting crews that had been trained in antisubmarine warfare, Admiral King on 9 May 1943 suspended the traditional Navy practice of shifting officers from one type of duty to another. He directed that "in view of the urgency of building up quickly a large and efficient antisubmarine element . . . personnel especially trained for and experienced in antisubmarine operations and activities" be retained in such duties "to the maximum possible extent."

The Subchaser Training Center in Miami [5] retained and expanded its function of training officers and men for all antisubmarine surface craft smaller than destroyers, but had no facilities to take care of "shakedown." As yet there was no profitable employment for new destroyers or destroyer escorts between the time they were commissioned and that of readiness for active duty. Often these ships wandered from port to port begging for instruction and facilities. This not only prolonged the shakedown to six or eight weeks, but afforded an imperfect and haphazard preparation for combat.

Accordingly, one of the first acts of Admiral Beary was to establish the DD–DE Shakedown Task Force at Bermuda. Captain James L. Holloway, jr., who had unusual capacity for imparting enthusiasm as well as for organization, was relieved of the command of Desron 10 to head up this new task force. He broke his pennant in *Hamul*, mother ship of the group, and arrived at Bermuda on 13 April 1943, accompanied by destroyer escort *Andres*, fourth of that class to be commissioned.

Newly commissioned ships were staffed with officers and men who had had thorough schooling ashore, but very few of them had ever before been to sea. Captain Holloway based his program on the assumption that his business was to train ships in operations, and to take care of logistics, repairs and mechanical readjustments,

[5] See Vol. I 231–33.

while commanding officers concentrated on training their crews. The oceanic location had a good psychological effect. Since all physical ties with the United States were broken, there was no question of leave or liberty after the day's work was over; and of course Bermuda is one of the most beautiful spots in the Atlantic.

At first only destroyer escorts were sent to Bermuda, together with a few gunboats; but the DE shakedown training was such a success that the "cans" would not be denied, and by the end of September 1943 it was decided to give all new destroyers the full program. A mother ship, *Altair*, was sent to Bermuda especially for them. Upon arrival each ship moored alongside *Hamul* or *Altair* and staff experts came on board to check her equipment and provide for essential repairs. While these were being effected, officers and men were given attack-teacher training on board *Hamul* or ashore. Once at sea, the new ships formed training units and worked with planes and "tame" submarines, fired on towed targets and practised with gunfire, communications and radar. They had night battle practice as well as daytime maneuvers, and opportunities to use every piece of their equipment.

By November 1943, when Captain Holloway was relieved by Captain Dashiell L. Madeira, 99 destroyer escorts and 20 destroyers had passed through this shakedown training, and 25 other ships were at Bermuda receiving it. Shortly after, a number of Canadian corvettes and DEs built for the Royal Navy were enrolled. Captain Holloway's "Bermuda College" actually reduced the shakedown period to four weeks for destroyer escorts and five weeks for destroyers, besides affording a quality of training vastly superior to earlier methods.

The Aircraft Antisubmarine Development Detachment at Quonset Point, Rhode Island, commissioned on 1 April 1943, formed another "college" of "Antisubmarine University." [6] Here for the first time naval pilots and crewmen, technicians, and men of science worked side by side in the same detail with the one purpose of im-

[6] Conversations at Quonset in 1943-44 with Capt. D. W. Loomis, Cdr. John W. Gannon, and Lt. (jg) David Worcester USNR, who had been President of Hamilton College before the war.

proving the air aspects of antisubmarine warfare. And within four months, acting on the Navy doctrine that aircraft and ships should operate as one team, Admiral Ingersoll directed that the functions of the Detachment would be expanded to include: —

1. Tests and experiments with laboratory-developed antisubmarine equipment to determine its practical value.
2. Development of the best operational use of accepted equipment.
3. Development of coördinated antisubmarine tactics and communications procedures between aircraft and surface vessels.[7]

Because of this expansion, the word "Aircraft" was removed from the Detachment's title, and it became known as "Asdevlant."

Captain Aurelius B. Vosseller commanded the Detachment. A successful naval aviator and a natural leader, "Abe" Vosseller [8] enlarged his staff with men who had had experience in both air and surface aspects of antisubmarine warfare. He arranged for his "students" to experiment on United States submarines from the New London base. He procured the services of several civilian scientists and equipment for a research laboratory, to work out mathematical and other scientific aspects of the insistent problem. Every known or suggested method or device for thinning out Admiral Doenitz's wolf-packs could be tested at Quonset under realistic conditions. Ideas were removed from the field of speculation and given practical application.

[7] Admiral Ingersoll letter of 28 July 1943.
[8] Aurelius B. Vosseller, b. Illinois 1903, Naval Academy '24. Served at sea 1924–30 on board *Mississippi* and *Reno* and as asst. gunnery officer on staff of Com. Destroyers Battle Force. N.A.S. Pensacola 1930–31, with subsequent service as naval aviator in *Saratoga* and *Lexington;* M.S. Cal. Inst. Tech., 1934. After serving on board *Arizona, Ranger,* and *Lexington,* he reported to Buaër and was instrumental in developing the high-altitude oxygen mask. Com Patwing 5 1940; Com Patron 55 during "pioneer days" in Iceland 1941–42; Comasdevlant 1943; C.O. *Bogue* Apr.–Nov. 1944; Aviation Officer on staff of Com Fifth Fleet 1944; aide to Under Secnav July 1945; Com Naval Air Test Center Patuxent 1946; C.O. *Coral Sea* 1948, Comcardiv 18 1951, staff of Supreme Allied Commander Europe 1952.

2. *Technical Developments*

At the same time that antisubmarine warfare was being reorganized, the Navy was developing new weapons and devices.

Rocket projectiles were tested by Comasdevlant throughout 1943, and the first rocket attack by American aircraft on a submarine was made by planes from escort carrier *Block Island* on 11 January 1944.[9] During 1943 many improvements were made in sonar, the supersonic echo-ranging equipment of escort vessels. Hedgehog (Mark–10 and –11), the ahead-throwing weapon, was already in operation,[10] and the streamlined, fast-sinking Mark–9 depth charge, with settings up to 600 feet, produced in the summer of 1943, established a new trend and outmoded the cylindrical "ashcan."[11] For planes, there were developed the 500-pound depth bomb and the homing torpedo known as "Fido," which answered to the German acoustic torpedo.

A device developed in 1943 to assist aircraft in locating submarines was the sonobuoy, an expendable float which carried a hydrophone for listening under water and a radio transmitter to relay submarine sounds to a plane. First deliveries were made in June 1943.

A very important new development was the ASV airborne microwave (10-centimeter) radar. Its story goes back to 1940 when British scientists brought to the United States the resonant cavity magnetron, a device with which radar waves of less than 50 centimeters could be generated. It has been described as "the most valu-

[9] Rockets had already been used by R.A.F. and Fleet Air Arm. A rocket-equipped Swordfish from H.M.S. *Archer* sank *U–752* 23 May 1943.
[10] See Vol. I 211–12.
[11] Lt. Cdr. Buford Rowland USNR and Lt. Wm. B. Boyd USNR *U.S.N. Bureau of Ordnance in World War II* (1953) pp. 141–43, describes the perfection of the Mark–9 "after almost two years frustration." *U.S. Fleet A/S Bulletin* July 1943 pp. 35–36 has a short history of depth charges, and same April 1944 pp. 40–42 has statistics of all in use at the beginning of the year, with allowances to each type of ship.

able cargo ever brought to our shores," "the most important item in reverse lend lease." [12] A laboratory sponsored by the United States and British governments was then established at Massachusetts Institute of Technology for research in the microwave field. Experimental radars were produced in 1941, including the prototype of the Navy's SG shipboard radar. By July 1942 Army Air Force antisubmarine planes were using 10-centimeter radar, and sets were delivered to the British in time to be used in the Bay of Biscay offensive. The advantages of this ASV over longer wave sets were greater accuracy and definition, less liability to jamming or disturbance, and a saving in weight and space. The Germans considered it to be the principal factor in the defeat of the U-boat.

Loran (Long Range Aid to Navigation), invented by Alfred Loomis, was a system of radio stations sending out pulse signals which, when picked up by a suitable receiver in an aircraft or ship, enabled the navigator to plot his position in about two minutes, with accuracy comparable to good celestial navigation. In 1942 stations were set up in Nova Scotia, Newfoundland, Labrador and Greenland; and, as the war progressed, Loran coverage was extended over more than half the earth's surface.

In the summer of 1940 Squadron Leader H. deV. Leigh RAF, a veteran pilot of World War I, conceived the idea of installing a 24-inch searchlight in the lower turret of a Wellington bomber, to be used instead of flares for night search and spotting U-boats. By mid-1942 the problem was solved and "Leigh-light Wellingtons," as they were called, began to make night antisubmarine patrols over the Bay of Biscay. The later American L–7 was an airborne searchlight with a 24-inch mirror mounted in the wing, rated at 60–80 million candlepower. Fifty of this type were delivered by December 1943; later it was superseded by the L–8, with an 18-inch mirror.

Recommendations of the Atlantic Convoy Conference to extend the high-frequency direction-finder net were promptly carried out,

[12] J. Phinney Baxter *Scientists Against Time* p. 142.

and a small HF/DF set was developed for shipboard installation. Both were of primary importance in locating submarines through spotting their radio transmissions to Berlin.

Improved training, new equipment and better administration greatly assisted the Navy to carry out a vigorous offensive against submarines in the latter half of 1943. But it must not be supposed that the enemy had exhausted his bag of tricks.

CHAPTER V

The German Underwater Fleet[1]

1943 – 1945

1. *Hitler, Raeder and Doenitz*

IT WAS fortunate for the Allies that Roosevelt and Churchill were "former naval persons," well versed in the value of sea power, whilst Adolf Hitler was completely *landsinnig*, land-minded. Although he cared little for naval warfare and understood less, the Fuehrer felt himself qualified by intuition to interfere in naval strategy. Like Kaiser Wilhelm of World War I, and also like Mussolini, the only aspect of sea power which he did appreciate was that of the "fleet in being," capable only of "sudden, furtive action" (as Mahan expressed it): the concept that the mere exist-ence of an inferior fleet, even if it stayed in port, acted as a threat and forced the enemy to waste his strength in watching and wait-ing. Yet Hitler's ignorance of naval strategy was so complete and his Napoleonic obsession with land conquest so thorough that he could follow no consistent naval policy. Although furious over the loss of battleship *Bismarck*, he was violently impatient over *Tirpitz* and other capital ships staying in port; yet he so cramped and re-stricted their movements that they accomplished nothing.

Grim, cool, tightlipped Grossadmiral Raeder was the most ca-

---

[1] In addition to books and documents mentioned in the Preface, sources here are the O.N.I. documents "Battle Instructions for German Navy, May 1939," and "Documents Relating to Resignation of Grand Admiral Raeder and Decommis-sioning of German High Seas Fleet," and these essays prepared after the war: Vizeadmiral Eberhard Weichold "German Surface Ships – Policy and Operations"; Konteradmiral Gerhard Wagner "Critique" of same; Vizeadmiral Kurt Assmann "Relations between Supreme Command German Armed Forces and Naval Staff"; Vizeadmiral Frederick Ruge "German Supreme Command in World War II."

pable flag officer of the German Navy since Admiral Tirpitz of World War I. Raeder was largely responsible for rebuilding the German Navy, materially and morally. Caught unprepared by the British declaration of war, after Hitler had repeatedly assured him that England would not fight, he did very well with what he had; and by the end of May 1941 (during which he lost *Bismarck*), his surface warships and converted commerce raiders had sunk 885,493 tons of enemy shipping, in addition to the 3,748,766 tons sunk by his submariners.[2] By the test of destructiveness the German offensive against commerce reached top point under Raeder in 1942, although a far greater number of U-boats was operating in 1943 and 1944.

Raeder hated to visit Hitler — used to say the very thought of it made him sick; but when asked for advice he consistently urged that more attention be paid to securing the Mediterranean and that a conflict with Russia be avoided. The Fuehrer did the exact opposite. Early in 1942, Hitler ordered the German surface fleet to hole-up in the Norwegian fjords — against the advice of Raeder, who wished to continue surface raids against Allied shipping on the high seas. The German battle fleet thereafter made a few sorties against North Russian convoys, but with slight success, owing in part to lack of fuel, in part to the want of efficient air coverage which Marshal Goering either could not or would not provide.[3]

Christmas Day of 1942 marked anything but good will from the Fuehrer to his Navy. An order of Goering's, sanctioned by Hitler, practically placed all German naval forces in the Mediterranean under the orders of one of the Reichsmarschall's civilian deputies at Rome. Raeder, not trusting himself to maintain a respectful silence during a Hitler tirade, gave Vizeadmiral Theodor Krancke, his liaison officer at Fuehrer headquarters, the difficult mission of remonstrating. At a conference on 30 December Hitler informed Krancke that the German Navy was but a "miserable imitation" of the British, its ships "lying idle in the fjords, utterly useless like so much

[2] S. W. Roskill *The War At Sea* I 615-16.
[3] See Volume I 179-86, 366.

junk." Krancke hopefully produced a signal he had just received to the effect that heavy cruiser *Admiral Hipper*, light battleship *Lützow* and six destroyers had just been sent out to break up a North Russia convoy. Ordered to wait and give the Fuehrer a blow-by-blow account of the expected battle, he passed a very bad New Year's Day at Hitler's "Wolf's Den." First came in the British broadcast on the battle announcing that *Hipper* had been damaged, a German destroyer sunk, and the rest driven away. This set off another Hitlerian tirade against the German Navy — its ships were "utterly useless, nothing but a breeding ground for revolution" (remembering the mutinies of 1917–18). And before long, word came from German naval headquarters that the British version of the battle was correct.

That was too much for the Fuehrer. He decided to decommission all his heavy ships, and summoned Raeder to receive the bad news in person. The Commander in Chief reported on 6 January 1943, listened to a lecture on naval policy and, after a last protest against laying up heavy ships, handed in his resignation.[4]

Karl Doenitz, now promoted Grossadmiral [5] and appointed Commander in Chief of the German Navy at the age of fifty-one, also remained Commander in Chief Submarines. His position, therefore, was somewhat analogous to that of Admiral King when he became Commander Tenth Fleet as well as Cominch and Chief of Naval Operations. But there was an essential difference. The submarine command consumed by far the greater part of Doenitz's time and energy, while for Admiral King antisubmarine warfare was but one of many world-wide responsibilities.

Doenitz was a man of limited intelligence and of very different metal from Raeder.[6] A professional naval officer with no political

[4] O.N.I. "Documents Relating to the Resignation of Raeder"; a "souped-up" version of these interviews is in C. B. Bekker *Swastika at Sea* (London 1953).

[5] The equivalent of U.S.N. Fleet Admiral and Admiral of the Fleet R.N.

[6] The estimate of Admirals Raeder and Doenitz in this Volume differs from that of Volume I, as it is based on better knowledge. At the same time I wish to modify the statement made on p. 10 of Volume I about Doenitz's alleged atrocity order. What happened is this. On 12 Sept. 1942, *U-156* sank British troop transport *Laconia* carrying 1800 Italian prisoners, 250 miles NE of Ascension I., and took four crowded lifeboats in tow after signaling other U-boats and French warships

ambitions, he had risen under the Nazi régime and apparently had complete faith in the Fuehrer principle and in Hitler, whom he cultivated assiduously in order to get what he wanted for the Navy. Doenitz possessed good qualities of leadership and a special gift for dealing with young officers. He managed to maintain high morale in his U-boat crews to the very end, in spite of heavy losses. But in the course of this volume we shall find him making many strategical blunders.

Perhaps his greatest blunder was his "integral tonnage" concept; although his former operations officer does not regard it as a blunder, but as strategy imposed by Allied success in antisubmarine warfare. According to this concept the main task of U-boats was to sink enemy tonnage without regard to route, place or cargo, in the hope of keeping ahead of replacement by new construction. That was all very well as long as Germany was winning, but he persisted in it to the end, in order to sink as much tonnage as possible with the least losses. Thus, for him a Liberty ship returning from Africa was as good a target as a heavy-laden Liberty ship proceeding to Great Britain, since they had the same tonnage; hence, whenever U-boat operations against shipping in the North Atlantic proved difficult and costly, he sent his submarines elsewhere for easier targets to build up the score. And his desire to keep tactical control of his boats was so strong that, even after he knew that their radio conversations with him were being monitored by Allied HF/DF, he went right on doing it. At the same time, he never knew accurately what his submarines were accomplishing. He had

---

at Dakar to pick them up. A B-24 based on Ascension, not appreciating the situation, attacked *U-156* while so engaged. Doenitz issued on 17 Sept. his "*Laconia* Order" to make "no attempt of any kind . . at rescuing members of ships sunk," except to take masters and chief engineers prisoner. Korvettenkapitän Karl Möhle of 5th U-boat flotilla, Kiel, put his own interpretation on this order (which both Doenitz and Godt repudiated at Nuremburg), and instructed his submariners to annihilate survivors; but few if any obeyed. It is true, however, that Hitler in a conversation with the Japanese Ambassador to Germany had previously expressed the intention of "killing as many of the crew [of a sunk M/V] as possible," and to "shoot up the lifeboats" in the hope of discouraging the American merchant marine. Int. Military Tribunal *Trial of Major War Criminals* V 218–55, XIII 268–95, 366–79, 437–62, 496–558; Ruge *Der Seekrieg* p. 228; B.d.U. War Diary Sept. 1942 pp. 169–70, 178, 180 of trans. Paszek in *Air Univ. Rev.*, 1964 pp. 26–37.

no evaluation committee, like those in the Admiralty and Tenth
Fleet for antisubmarine attacks, to study the U-boat commanders'
reports and figure out exactly how much tonnage they had sunk.
Their reports, almost always exaggerated, were checked from the
neutral press, from information derived from Allied survivors taken
prisoner, and other sources. The Germans had very unreliable intelligence in enemy countries, but plenty of agents in Spain and
Morocco to "count noses" in convoys passing Gibraltar.

One reason for the defeat of the German Navy was its lack of
an air arm. Doenitz and Marshal Goering disliked each other and the
Luftwaffe coöperated very ill with the U-boats. In 1941 Doenitz
managed to get one air squadron placed under his operational control, but Goering soon got it back, although Hitler ordered that it
continue to support the submarines. This squadron (KG-40), based
on French airfields, had a maximum strength of 30 bombers which
was insufficient for reconnaissance of convoys and support of
U-boats when entering and leaving port. Two other squadrons
(KG-26 and KG-30), based in northern Norway and Finland
were supposed to coöperate with the U-boats against North Russia convoys, but their efforts were constantly complained of by
the submarine commanders.

It is to his credit that Doenitz became a convert to Raeder's active surface fleet concept after Raeder had resigned. After four
weeks in office he persuaded Hitler to keep most of the modern
German warships in commission, and used them in a few unsuccessful raids on North Russia convoys. He never seriously considered calling off the U-boat offensive, even after the heavy losses
of U-boats in May 1943. The matter was brought up at a Fuehrer
Conference, where Hitler resolutely declared on 3 June 1943:
"There can be no talk of let-up in submarine warfare. The enemy
forces tied up by our submarine warfare are tremendous, even
though the actual losses inflicted by us are no longer great." [7]

Hitler and Doenitz were obsessed with this "tying up" or "pinning down" concept. Actually most of the British and American

[7] *Fuehrer Conferences* (1943) p. 75.

ships that were used in antisubmarine warfare would have been of slight use in the invasion of Europe. It would be more to the point to say that by submarine warfare Hitler "pinned down" men and matériel that might have been employed to repel invasion.

2. *German Submarine Construction*

The principal U-boat types which we shall encounter in this volume are as follows: —[8]

Type	Tons	Length, Feet	Beam, Feet	Speed in Knots Surface	Speed in Knots Submerged	Torpedo Capacity	Maximum Range at 12 knots in miles	Total Number Built
VII–C	500	220	20	17	7.6	14	6,500	660
IX–C	740	244	21	18.2	7.3	21–23	11,000	146
IX–D	1200	290	20	19.2	6.9	27	23,700	32
XIV	1600	220	30	14.4	6.2	9	9,300	10
								848

Grossadmiral Doenitz, in conjunction with Herr Speer, German Minister for War Production and a high Nazi, embarked on an ambitious submarine building program in order to meet the crisis of "Black May" 1943. U-boats were then being sunk faster than they could be built, and the loss of Allied shipping had fallen to the lowest point since 1941. Speer delegated to an automobile production expert named O. H. Merker — said never to have seen a ship, much less a submarine — full responsibility for increasing U-boat production from 25 per month to 40 or better. And Merker promptly adopted for U-boats the Henry Kaiser method of assembling prefabricated sections. By building these in widely dispersed factories, better protection was obtained against Allied air bomb-

[8] The tonnages in first column are those given in USSBS *German Submarine Industry* Report Exhibit "C," and which have been used throughout this history, and in most naval Allied documents. Displacement tonnages are higher: VII–C displaced 712 tons and IX–C 900 tons. Gröner *Die Schiffe der Deutschen Kriegsmarine* (1954), from which this table has been corrected, uses cubic-meter displacement. The total number of U-boats built during the war was 1158, including 250-tonners but excluding one- and two-man midgets.

ings, and the capacity of the shipyards to turn out finished boats was increased almost fourfold.

Doenitz also planned to replace the standard 500-ton and 740-ton boats by a new type with a submerged speed of 22.4 knots and greater endurance. German designers had been working on a closed-cycle propulsion boat, Type XXVI, generally called the "Walter," since 1940. Orders were placed for 180 Walters in June 1943, but Doenitz canceled them in November, since the propulsion machinery could not be produced rapidly enough, and only two experimental prototypes were completed. The Walter would certainly have been a menace if it had been successfully produced, as it was supposed to have almost unlimited endurance under water, and no breather device was necessary.

In place of the Walter, a naval architect named Cords designed, and Merker put into production, a 1500-ton streamlined U-boat known as Type XXI. It had diesel-electric engines and very powerful batteries of a new kind, but needed a snorkel or breather to operate. It could move submerged at 17.5 knots for small distances, and had a surface range of 19,000 miles at six knots. A full-sized mock-up of Type XXI was ready in December 1943. Doenitz ordered 290 to be built by the prefabricated section method by 1 March 1945. And for North Sea or Mediterranean service he ordered several hundred units of a new 300-tonner with the same propulsion, known as Type XXIII. In the meantime, 153 of the older types which were already on the stocks were completed by conventional methods, most of them before 1 July 1944.

U-2501, first of Type XXI, was launched on Hitler's 55th birthday, 20 April 1944. It proved so defective that several months' more work were required before it could go to sea for trials; and its fellows were equally full of "bugs" or *Kinderkrankheiten* (teething troubles), in German parlance. Nevertheless, no fewer than 119 units of Type XXI were completed before the end of the war; between 16 and 21 of these were then ready to operate, but only three actually departed on combat missions, and they did nothing. About 63 of Type XXIII were delivered before the end of the war and ten actually made combat patrols, enjoying some measure of success around the British Isles.[9]

This story of submarine production illustrates the folly of embarking on an unlimited war with limited means, as well as the wisdom of the basic Allied strategy of beating Germany first. Type XXI and the Walter would probably never have been the menace that Doenitz hoped for, but both had dangerous possibilities.

U-boat production was not much delayed by the Allied bombing offensive against Germany. The violent attacks on Hamburg from 24 July to 2 August 1943 reduced the waterfront of that port to rubble and knocked out the leading Blohm & Voss shipyard, so that an estimated six weeks' production time was lost; nevertheless 30 new U-boats, all but three of them Types XXI and XXIII, were completed in December 1944, and the total production for 1944 surpassed that of 1943 by 43 per cent.[10] Later bombing raids on the submarine building yards failed to suspend submarine production until April 1945, when the war was almost over. So cleverly had the prefabrication of U-boat sections been dispersed and placed underground, that air-bombing never became a considerable factor in the antisubmarine war.[11] Repeated attempts in 1942–43 by the R.A.F. and the VIII U.S. Army Air Force to break up the U-boat pens in French ports had failed to penetrate their heavy concrete roofs, and resulted only in a heavy loss of planes to antiaircraft fire.[12]

In May 1943, when Doenitz realized that his blitz against the

[9] Figures from Dr. Jürgen Rohwer.

[10] Annual production of U-boats: 196 in 1941, 244 in 1942, 270 in 1943, 387 in 1944 (153 by conventional methods, 132 "pre-fabs," 3 Walters and 99 midgets), 155 in 1945 (29 Type XXI, 21 Type XXIII, 2 Walters, 103 midgets). USSBS "German Submarine Industry" p. 26. The number commissioned each year, after the prolonged trials which followed delivery, differed materially from the above: e.g. 237 in 1944, 87 in 1945. (Figures from Dr. Rohwer.)

[11] USSBS "German Submarine Industry Report" p. 34.

[12] Craven and Cate II 250–51. The Admiralty had vainly urged the R.A.F. Bomber Command to bomb these pens when they were under construction in 1940–41, and when (according to Konteradmiral Godt) their completion might have been prevented. After repeated urgings by the Admiralty and the U.S. Navy the bombing was laid on in 1942; it was then too late.

North Atlantic convoys had fizzled out, he adopted certain *ad interim* tactics and procedures pending the full production of Type XXI and XXIII, which he confidently expected would turn the tide toward stalemate if not victory. These expedients, which we shall describe in detail as we reach their adoption, were, in brief, increased antiaircraft armament and "fight back" tactics against attacking aircraft, attempts to mine American and other distant harbors, nuisance operations by a few boats in areas that had been let alone for months, the "Zaunkönig" acoustic torpedo for sinking escorts, and the snorkel or breather. But Doenitz's strategy always remained that of the hit-and-run raid. The German underwater fleet was incapable of a sustained offensive against shipping in any one area, because Allied antisubmarine forces, measures and techniques had been developed to a point where a fresh challenge could always be met and repulsed after an initial blitz. This inescapable fact, coupled with Doenitz's desire to show results in terms of shipping sunk, no matter what or where, resulted in a succession of brief offensives in widely scattered areas. In 1943 the principal theaters for U-boats were the northern transatlantic convoy route, the Caribbean, the South Atlantic and the Indian Ocean. In 1944, with a larger U-boat fleet than ever before fighting a proportionally stronger antisubmarine fleet, Doenitz tried one more jab at the North Atlantic, followed by operations in the Indian Ocean and around the Cape Verde Islands. Every one failed; and the Allies were able to pull off the greatest invasion in modern history, that of France, and to sustain it by sea, with insignificant interference by U-boats. No more striking evidence of the collapse of Hitler's policy and Doenitz's strategy could be adduced.

Thus, through the period covered by this volume, the German Navy was fighting a series of defensive operations, comparable to the rear-guard actions of the Italian campaign and punctuated by "sudden, furtive action." As with the French commerce-raiding strategy of the Napoleonic wars, the U-boat campaign inflicted great loss of life and of tonnage; but never enough to disrupt Atlantic communications or to win the war. Even in their palmiest days of 1942, the Axis submarines never came within measurable distance of victory. In World War I, largely because of the Allies' tardiness in setting up merchant convoys, the U-boats almost won the decision before the United States entered the war. In World War II, the German submarine campaign may have postponed, but did not affect the outcome. Yet it might have accomplished far more, might even have ruptured the Allied lifelines and won the war for Hitler, but for the intensive, long-sustained and well-coordinated efforts of the British and American Navies, assisted by the R.A.F., for a time by the A.A.F., and, from first to last, by the devoted and skillful researches of men of science.

NOTE ON ITALIAN SUBMARINES

Although Italian submarines were considered by American naval officers to be superior to the German 500- and 740-tonners, they were not operated nearly so skillfully or aggressively. During the period covered by this volume up to the surrender of the Italian fleet in September 1943, Italian submarines with few exceptions operated only in the Mediterranean. Their futile efforts to break up the invasion of Sicily are described in our Volume IX. According to Admiralty statistics for the entire war, 32 Italian submarines entered the Atlantic from the Mediterranean and ten returned. Sixteen were sunk in the Atlantic; two were taken over by the Germans at Bordeaux (and one of these was sunk later); three were taken over by the Japanese and one surrendered to the British at Durban.

CHAPTER VI

Northern Transatlantic Convoys

April–May 1943

1. *The Ordeal of ONS–5* [1]

FIRST in importance to the Western Allies, in April 1943, were the ships crossing the North Atlantic; and so they would remain, except for a brief period when heavy troop movements to the Mediterranean were under way. This northern route was not only Great Britain's lifeline for food and supplies of every description; it was vital in the build-up of American armed forces in Britain for the invasion of France.

March of 1943 had been a fruitful month for U-boats in the North Atlantic, and a terror to the Allies. Of 687 ships in convoy, 49 of 296,000 gross tons had been sunk by submarines. In the entire Atlantic and Arctic Oceans, U-boats cost the Allies 567,000 tons. During the first 20 days of March the enemy came very near to disrupting communications in the North Atlantic, sinking 85 ships, including those not in convoy, at the cost of only six U-boats.[2] By 1 April, after ten days happily free of ship losses, Allied optimists thought that the crisis had passed, but they were wrong. Doenitz had called off his wolves only for rest and redeployment.

The Grossadmiral had always been bothered by the evasive routing of convoys by the Allies to escape known concentrations of U-boats. He now set up three submarine "fences" which he ex-

---

[1] Admiralty documents and reports of this convoy in the Div. of Naval History, Washington; information from Lt. Cdr. M. R. Tawes commanding U.S.S. *Sapelo;* conversations with Commo. P. W. Gretton RN in 1951 and 1955. All times are Zone plus 2.

[2] Vol I is incorrect in stating that only one U-boat was sunk at this period.

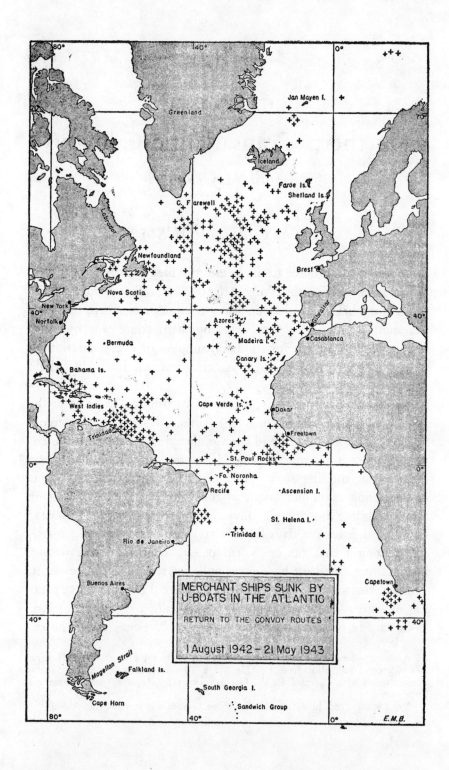

MERCHANT SHIPS SUNK BY
U-BOATS IN THE ATLANTIC

RETURN TO THE CONVOY ROUTES

1 August 1942 – 21 May 1943

E.M.B.

pected no northern transatlantic convoy could evade; some of them were in the "black pit" southeast of Greenland where no air support could reach the convoys. By 0700 April 28, Submarine Group "Star," 15 boats, had taken station along a north–south line between lats. 56° 30′ and 61° 30′ N, about 420 miles east of Cape Farewell, in the hope of catching convoys that were swinging north to avoid the usual danger point. At the same time Group "Specht" of 19 boats was set up on a WNW–ESE line about halfway between Cape Farewell and Flemish Cap, the small fishing bank off the Grand Bank of Newfoundland. Group "Amsel" of 13 boats, which had been chasing another convoy unsuccessfully, received orders the same day to move in along a line southeast of "Specht." As thus stationed, these 47 boats (later augmented to 51) straddled every North Atlantic convoy route known to the Germans. The stage was now set for one of the fiercest convoy battles of the war.

Convoy ONS–5, Commodore J. Brooks RNR, proved a star performer. It was a slow convoy of over 40 merchantmen, 5 of them American,[3] and all lightly ballasted for homeward passage to the United States and Canada. The British mid-ocean escort group, under Commander P. W. Gretton RN, comprised two destroyers, a frigate, four corvettes of the "flower" class, and two armed trawlers for rescue purposes. All except flagship H.M.S. *Duncan*, which had just finished refit, had worked together for four months — which was fortunate, since they were destined to encounter an unprecedented number of submarines.

Departing from the mouth of the Clyde on 22 April, ONS–5 encountered head winds as it plodded along in eleven columns. On the 26th it was joined by a small "feeder" convoy from Iceland, which brought the number of merchant ships up to 43, and brought the second destroyer, H.M.S. *Vidette*, to the escort. That night the

---

[3] S.S. *West Madaket, West Maximus, McKeesport, Argon;* U.S.S. *Sapelo.* The last-named, a naval tanker, had delivered a cargo of oil in the U.K. and was returning in ballast. The merchantmen in the convoy included two Greeks, one Panamanian, two Dutch, one Polish, one Norwegian and one Yugoslav. Two British tankers were included, but the escorts were able to fuel from only one, owing to heavy seas; the other did not have suitable gear for rough weather fueling.

convoy ran into a southwest gale. Inevitably there was straggling; and, as Gretton remarked, "the stragglers' lot, from a study of submarine dispositions, promised to be no happy one." On the 27th the weather cleared and three escorts were able to fuel, covered by Hudsons from Iceland. That day the convoy passed the meridian of western Iceland, without mishap.

On 28 April, shortly after sunrise, as ONS–5 was passing between the two northernmost patrol stations of Group "Star," it was sighted and reported by *U–650*. Promptly and silently all 15 boats closed in on the convoy. But as evening fell each U-boat skipper had to send his daily "bedtime story" to "Papa" Doenitz at Berlin, which enabled the HF/DF mounted in two British destroyers to plot the positions of these baleful "Stars."

Commander Gretton now directed a series of offensive sweeps away from the convoy, employing the so-called "scare" tactics which Royal Navy escort groups had adopted to force the U-boats down. His escorts, running down the bearings of HF/DF locations, forced one stalker after another to submerge. Either these tactics or a communications failure resulted in such garbled reports reaching Doenitz that he was unable to coach his wolves; and without their usual orders from Berlin they made straggling and badly co-ordinated attacks on the night of 28–29 April. Corvette *Sunflower* drove off *U–386;* hit-and-run sorties by *Duncan, Tay* and *Snowflake* frustrated several different threats; and as a result two boats of Group "Star" were so badly shaken by depth charges that they ceased to be effective, and at least seven stalkers were driven down. "The night had been a busy one," remarked Commander Gretton; "the convoy unscathed, and I felt that the U-boats must be discouraged by our night tactics and might try day attack."

He was right. Tenacious contact-keeping by *U–650* enabled *U–258* at dawn 29 April to make a successful submerged attack. Slipping through the screen, this boat torpedoed American S.S. *McKeesport* in the center column. The freighter's Naval Armed Guard, commanded by Ensign Irving H. Smith USNR, stood by their guns until ordered to abandon ship, but never sighted the target. All but one of the merchant and naval crew, 68 men, were rescued by trawler *Northern Gem.*

A full gale was now building up from the W and WSW, and for several days it blew continuously, punctuated by fierce gusts and blinding snow squalls. Fortunately ONS–5 was still within the range of Iceland-based Catalinas and Liberators, and at 0600 April 30 it came within the scope of shorter-range planes based on Ivigtut, Greenland. These air squadrons were now so hardened to Arctic conditions that they never flinched from supporting the convoy, blow and snow as it might. At dusk 29 April a Catalina from Iceland piloted by Lieutenant William A. Shevlin USNR flushed an outlying stalker of Group "Star," *U–258,* stove in its bow with a string of bombs, and forced it to break off pursuit and make for France. Late that night *U–192* approached the convoy through very heavy seas, only to be driven off by corvette *Snowflake.*

Only one escort, destroyer *Oribi,* which had left an unthreatened convoy to strengthen the screen of ONS–5, was able to fuel on 30 April. The merchant ships, now dispersed over some thirty square miles, slogged ahead at 2½ to 3 knots through pan ice and among small icebergs. By sundown 1 May, when the wind had risen to force 10, only 15 merchantmen and the flagship could be seen from U.S.S. *Sapelo.* "Two Liberators from Iceland were homed during the day watches and gave valuable aid in appalling weather." The U-boats were constantly harassed by Mitchell bombers based on Greenland and by Liberators from Iceland, even at night. *U–381* reported to Berlin on 1 May: "During the last night a boat reported continuous air patrol, probably based on Greenland. The same boat observed what was probably a new type of location gear. The Commander repeatedly noticed planes approaching at great height and carrying a light like a planet that went on and off." [4]

During the morning watch 2 May, as the gale abated, Commander Gretton, anticipating more attacks, depleted his fuel tanks

[4] B.d.U. War Diary 1 May 1943, p. 302 of trans.

to round up stragglers. All but ten merchantmen were back in the herd by 0900 when a snowstorm blew from the southwest. It ceased at 1145, but heavy fog set in an hour later. The ten laggards were now organized in two "straggler convoys" escorted by frigate *Tay* and corvette *Pink*.

Now came to the rescue the first fruit of a tactical innovation by "Cincwa," Admiral Sir Max Horton. This was the organizing of support groups, composed of destroyers, corvettes, frigates and sloops, so deployed that they could be thrown in at short notice to assist a harassed convoy.[5] It was the 3rd Support Group, Captain J. A. McCoy RN in destroyer *Offa*, that came out from St. John's and joined Gretton on the afternoon of 2 May when wind and sea were making up again from the WSW. Unfortunately most of McCoy's ships, like Gretton's, were so "short-legged" that aggressive patrolling depleted their fuel tanks quickly and it was too rough to fuel at sea. Destroyer *Impulsive* had to be detached on the 2nd to fuel at Iceland. *Duncan* had to peel off at noon 3 May to seek replenishment at St. John's, where she arrived with only 4 per cent of her fuel left; she would not have had that but for fine weather and a boost from the Labrador Current. Two more of Captain McCoy's ships had to return next day.

At the departure of *Duncan*, Lieutenant Commander R. E. Sherwood RN in *Tay* relieved Gretton as escort commander. Forenoon watch 4 May found the screen with only seven vessels, and German radio activity was observed to be mounting ominously, as 51 U-boats were carefully reorganized to trap Convoy ONS-5 between Cape Farewell and Flemish Cap. Thirty boats, redesignated Group "Fink," were stationed along lat. 55° N, barring every possible course, while the other 21 (Group "Amsel") were divided four ways, in groups of five or six each, two along lat. 51° N athwart the convoy, two on a north-south line east of Flemish Cap. The two latter groups were so located that they could either pile

[5] A partial list of captains and flagships of R.N. Support Groups is in Chalmers *Max Horton* p. 188; a fuller one will be printed in Roskill Vol. II. The composition of these groups varied a good deal.

in on ONS-5 or intercept other and more southerly routed convoys.

Throughout the daylight hours of 4 May, while the wind moderated and the sea abated, R.C.A.F. Cansos (as the Canadians called their Catalinas), kept the U-boats down; one Canso 600 miles from its Gander base caught *U-630* approaching a straggler, and neatly sent it to the bottom. *U-438* fought it out with another Canso on the surface, and escaped. Catalinas made too big a target for antiaircraft fire and were not equipped for night battle.

Convoy ONS-5 was now entering the most dangerous section of its passage. Alerted by a message from Doenitz, "Don't overrate the enemy; strike him dead," the 30 boats of Group "Fink" closed in ahead, astern and on each flank, to envelop the convoy in a deadly embrace. At this critical juncture the weather improved. By nightfall 4 May the ships were plowing through a calm, gently heaving sea about 300 miles south of Cape Farewell, silhouetted against northern lights. Conditions were ideal for attack. Working in pairs and threes, members of Group "Fink" picked off stragglers and hurled torpedoes into the crowded main body of the convoy. That night (4–5 May) they sank seven merchantmen, including American freighter *West Maximus*. The seven escorts did their best, and their best was amazingly good; it is a wonder that thirty submarines, under exceptionally favorable conditions for attack, did not make a higher score.

During the next two days this running fight continued along the route to "Westomp" (Western Ocean Meeting Point), where a Canadian escort group would take over. Daylight 5 May brought no relief to the harassed escorts. Day stations were complete by 0500 and two hours later trawler *Northern Spray*, with almost 150 survivors on board, was detached to proceed to St. John's. Heavy radio activity indicated plenty of U-boats around, and at 0900 members of Group "Fink" started popping up all around the convoy. Lieutenant Commander Sherwood met the challenge courageously. He sent *Oribi* to beat off the more distant boats by scare tactics, leaving only six warships in the close screen. Corvette *Pink*,

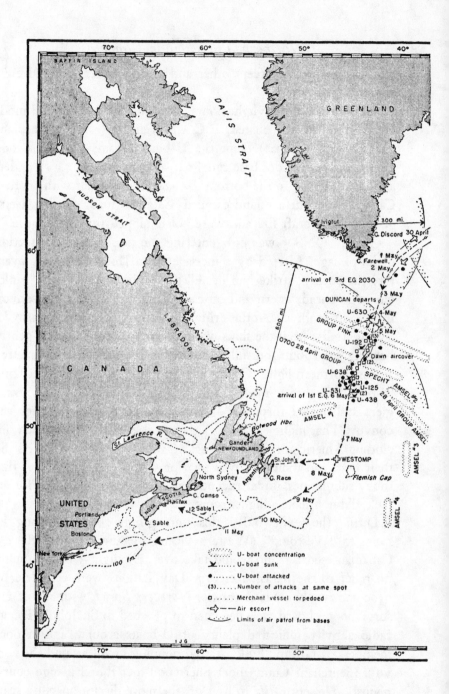

BAFFIN ISLAND

DAVIS STRAIT

GREENLAND

HUDSON STRAIT

Ivigtut

300 mi.

C. Discord 30 April

1 May

C. Farewell
2 May

arrival of 3rd E.G. 2030

3 May

DUNCAN departs

U-630   4 May

GROUP FINK   5 May
(5)
U-192

0700 28 April GROUP

Dawn aircover
(2)

(5)

U-638   SPECHT   AMSEL #2
(2)
arrival of 1st E.G. 6 May   U-531   U-125
(2)
U-438   28 April GROUP AMSEL

AMSEL   7 May

LABRADOR

CANADA

Botwood Hbr.

Gander
NEWFOUNDLAND   WESTOMP

St John's   Flemish Cap

St. Lawrence R.   Argentia

G. Race   8 May

North Sydney   9 May

NOVA   C. Canso
SCOTIA
UNITED   Halifax   10 May
Portland   2 Sable I.
STATES   C. Sable   11 May
Boston

New York

100 fm.

600 mi.

AMSEL #3

AMSEL #4

.... U-boat concentration
⌄....... U-boat sunk
●....... U-boat attacked
(3)...... Number of attacks at same spot
□...... Merchant vessel torpedoed
⟡— — Air escort
.... Limits of air patrol from bases

IJG

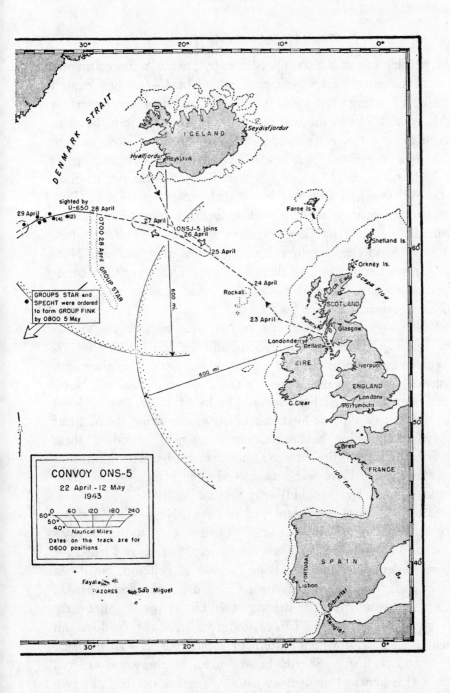

DENMARK STRAIT

ICELAND

Seydisfjordur

Hvalfjordur   Reykjavik

sighted by
U-650 28 April
29 April   0700 28 April
  (4) (2)   27 April   ONSJ-5 joins
                                         26 April
                                     25 April   Faroe Is.

                          GROUP STAR
                                                   Shetland Is.

                                                   Orkney Is.   60°

                                         24 April   Scapa Flow
GROUPS STAR and   Rockall   L. Ewe
SPECHT were ordered
to form GROUP FINK   23 April SCOTLAND
by 0800 5 May   NORTH
                                                      Glasgow
                                         Londonderry Belfast
                                                      EIRE   Liverpool
                          600 mi   ENGLAND
                                                               London
                                         C. Clear   Portsmouth

                                                      Brest
                                                                  50°
                                                      FRANCE

CONVOY ONS-5
22 April–12 May
1943
60° 0 60 120 180 240
50°
40°   Nautical Miles
Dates on the track are for
0600 positions
                                                      SPAIN
                                                               40°
                                         PORTUGAL
                                         Lisbon
  Fayal
  AZORES   São Miguel   Gibraltar
                                         Tangier

still herding one of the stragglers' convoys, made "a most firm and excellent contact" on what turned out to be *U-192*. She hunted this boat for three hours and 40 minutes, making seven hedgehog attacks; and, just as she was picking up speed to rejoin the merchant ships, a "powerful underwater explosion . . . low in note and like a deep growl," was heard. That was *U-192* breaking up.

In the meantime, *U-584* had broken the back of the twenty-five-year-old American freighter *West Madaket* with a torpedo. *Pink* rescued her entire complement of 61, including the Naval Armed Guard. Main convoy fared even worse than did the stragglers. During the afternoon, three British merchantmen and one Norwegian were sunk, three of them by *U-266*. Destroyer *Offa* counterattacked and damaged the culprit, which had to pull out to effect emergency repairs.

Following this distressing 5th of May, fog reduced the visibility, but submarines were still about, and the seven weary escorts prepared for another tough night. It was well that they did. Doenitz, realizing that the nearer the convoy approached Newfoundland the more efficient would be its air cover, now ordered his wolves to make one final, disruptive attack during the night of 5–6 May. Exhorting them to the "utmost energy," he ordered them to fight aircraft on the surface rather than spoil an attack on ships by submerging. Here was another early appearance of the "fight back" tactics which would shortly become doctrine.

Fifteen U-boats were deployed to trap ONS–5 when a dense fog bank, reducing visibility to a ship's length, came to the convoy's rescue. The submariners were completely baffled as Lieutenant Commander Sherwood, accepting the risk of collision, ran down every radar or sound-gear contact and dropped depth charges. Corvette *Loosestrife*, after driving down *U-267* with gunfire early in the first watch, located *U-638*, dodged a brace of torpedoes, and smothered it with a fatal pattern of depth charges — all in black night and thick fog. Shortly before midnight Sherwood ordered *Oribi* (Lieutenant Commander J. C. A. Ingram RN) to assist two other corvettes, which were slugging it out with another U-boat.

En route to the fight, Ingram sighted *U–125* coming out of the fog barely a cable length on his starboard bow; he changed course to ram, and hit the 740-tonner abaft the conning tower. The boat slewed around and disappeared in the foggy darkness. Ingram, after ascertaining that his forward bulkheads were intact, regained sound contact and, 25 minutes after the ramming, dropped a single depth charge which added to the U-boat's damage. Half an hour later, just as *U–125* was requesting Doenitz to direct another boat to stand by, it was sighted by *Snowflake* and sunk with gunfire.

"All ships worked hard, capably and with intelligence *and considerable humour*," recorded Commander Sherwood, "and the situation was always well in hand." [6]

These and subsequent counterattacks broke the back of the assault. In the small hours of 6 May, in a dense fog, *Vidette* sank *U–531* with a hedgehog attack, and *Sunflower* rammed but failed to sink *U–533*. Shortly before dawn the First Escort Group (sloop *Pelican*, flag [7]) arrived from St. John's and swept ahead and astern of the convoy. *Pelican* surprised *U–438* with a salvo of gunfire and sank it with depth charges. *Sennen* riddled the conning tower of *U–267*, which escaped by a deep dive.

It now became clear to Doenitz that the game was up; for ONS–5 would be sailing under an "air umbrella" as soon as the fog lifted. At 0915 May 6 he ordered all boats to break off and head eastward for replenishment. The long battle, the latter phase of which had lasted almost continuously for forty-four hours, was over. And in the evening of 7 May the convoy reached Westomp, sixteen days out from the Clyde.

But it was not yet out of danger; for forty-eight hours it steamed through a dense fog, merchant ships keeping station by whistle; and the group which peeled off for Halifax approached so near

[6] As a sample of the humor, Capt. McCoy of 3rd Escort Group signaled to *Oribi*, "Speaking without my book, I should say you have done bloody well during the past 24 hours." The "Yellow Book" credits *U–125* to *Vidette*, but I believe that *Snowflake* did it. It was, however, *Vidette* not *Oribi* that sank *U–531*.

[7] The others were gunboat *Sennen* (ex-U.S.C.G.C. *Champlain*) and frigates *Jed*, *Wear*, and *Spey*, Capt. C. N. Brewer RN. The same morning of the 6th, *Sunflower* and *Snowflake* were detached to escort 3 ships of the convoy to St. John's.

Sable Island that H.M.S. *Montgomery* had to take station as close to that famous ocean graveyard as she dared, to warn them off by radio. Early 9 May the fog lifted, and on the 10th Mr. Churchill signaled the convoy commodore, "The Prime Minister compliments the convoy on steady courage during the late attacks."

An amusing anticlimax to this hazardous crossing was the holding up of the main convoy off Ambrose Channel, New York, for want of the proper recognition signal, which had been changed while the convoy was at sea.

The events of the passage of ONS–5 added up to a great victory. The 51 U-boats that were deployed to destroy ONS–5 should have done so, and probably would have done so a year earlier. But only 13 merchantmen (three of them American) were lost out of 43, and five submarines had been sunk by an escort that never numbered more than nine ships and was usually weaker. (The sixth sub, *U–630*, was sunk by aircraft.) Rescue work, moreover, was so efficient, despite the heavy weather, that loss of life from the merchantmen was not very great.[8] Never again would an Allied convoy be attacked so vigorously or with so great a force. All honor to the ever vigilant and aggressive escorts, to the aircraft pilots who braved the worst of weather, and to the steadfast, well-disciplined merchantmen.

2. Debut of the Escort Carrier Group

Twelve convoys other than ONS–5 crossed the North Atlantic to and from Britain during the last days of April and the first three weeks of May. Only three of them suffered damage, losing five merchant ships in all; the rest got across intact. And the air and surface escorts of these twelve convoys accounted for no fewer than 13 U-boats, besides sending several others home for repairs. For lack of space we shall have to leave the detailed story of most

---

[8] Seven merchant mariners and one bluejacket from the three American ships sunk; 86 British and 5 Norwegians from the other ships.

of these convoys to the historians of the Royal and Canadian Navies which escorted them, and confine ourselves to those which had the support of escort carrier groups.

The pioneer United States escort carrier group in convoy support was built around *Bogue*, with a screen of four World War I destroyers: *Belknap, Lea, Greene* and *Osmond Ingram*. Captain Giles E. Short, task group commander, had put *Bogue* in commission at Tacoma, and his crew, a large number of whom were survivors of *Lexington* of Coral Sea fame, were more than eager for action. But their first three missions, in support of Convoys HX–228 and SC–123 in March, and of HX–235 in April, were uneventful. For a large part of the time the weather was too wild for flight operations. The pilots of *Bogue's* 9 Wildcats and 12 Avengers sighted only two submarines and sank neither one. After her third mission, concluded 25 April, the *Bogue* group was given two weeks' work at the British antisubmarine training centers in Liverpool and Northern Ireland, where a HF/DF set was installed.

In the meantime, slow convoy ONS–6 of 30 merchantmen had departed the British Isles 30 April. It was stalked off Iceland 6 May, by *U–418* whose efforts to home-in a waiting wolf-pack were frustrated by what a German skipper described as "unlimited numbers of aircraft" based on Iceland. During the night of 7–8 May, Convoy ONS–6 had to pick its way gingerly among a flock of icebergs. On the morning of the 9th, it was joined by an escort carrier group built around H.M.S. *Archer*. This flattop and her three destroyers took station astern and provided air cover which completely protected the convoy as it steamed southerly through waters recently churned by the savage attacks on ONS–5. The next slow convoy, ONS–7, lost S.S. *Aymeric* on 17 May to an attack by *U–640*, which was sunk an hour later by H. M. frigate *Swale* of the screen. *Aymeric* was the last merchant ship sunk from a northern transatlantic convoy until mid-September.

Convoy HX–237, departing New York 1 May, had the benefit of the 5th Support Group, escort carrier H.M.S. *Biter* (Captain

E. M. C. Abel-Smith RN) with a screen commanded by Captain E. H. Chavasse RN, from 7 May on. Doenitz managed to learn exactly where to find this convoy. *Biter's* Swordfish planes discouraged every U-boat that approached until 12 May, when a fresh group of seven boats, which had been operating off the Azores, sank two merchantmen and a tanker which were romping ahead of the convoy. Quick revenge was inflicted by the escort carrier group. On the second morning a Swordfish flushed *U–89* six miles ahead of the convoy and homed in Captain Chevasse's flagship, H.M.S. *Broadway*,[9] and frigate H.M.S. *Lagan*, for a clean kill. Later in the day HX–237 came within range of Coastal Command Liberators based at Aldergrove in Northern Ireland, one of which so badly damaged *U–456* that it had to signal to Doenitz for assistance. The transmission was intercepted by H.M.S. *Pathfinder*, which headed down the bearing and, assisted by a Swordfish, finished off *U–456* that afternoon.

Three more members of the wolf-pack were still shadowing HX–237, hoping to make a dawn attack on 13 May. A British Sunderland of Coastal Command found *U–753* just before daybreak, and before being driven off by antiaircraft fire homed-in two escorts, *Lagan* and H.M.C.S. *Drumheller*. Between them they sank that U-boat with shellfire and hedgehog. A succession of Coastal Liberators frustrated all efforts of the two remaining U-boats to attack by daylight. Konteradmiral Godt, Doenitz's operations officer, reporting on the ill success of this wolf-pack, observed that he was not surprised at the loss of three U-boats out of seven, since HX–237 was protected by an escort carrier. That was not only a tribute to the new Allied tactics but a warning that Doenitz had better make a fresh redeployment.

"Cincwa" detached the *Biter* group on 13 May to assist slow eastbound Convoy SC–129 which had just had a rough encounter with units of a 27-boat wolf-pack, Group "Elbe." Two merchantmen had been sunk, and one submarine, *U–186*, by H.M.S. *Hesperus*. This seems to have discouraged eleven other members of

9 Formerly U.S.S. *Hunt*, one of the four-pipers turned over to the R.N. in 1941.

the group that were supposed to be stalking the convoy, so that when *Biter* hove in sight on the 13th there were no plums left for her Swordfish to pluck. But on 14 May a Coastal Liberator, flying a noon-to-midnight patrol, spotted *U-266* ten miles ahead of the convoy and sank it with bombs. This was the boat that had sunk three merchantmen out of Convoy ONS-5.

The relative ease with which these heavily laden eastbound convoys eluded U-boat barriers of unprecedented strength sadly perplexed the Grossadmiral and his staff; and their depression deepened when news of the next eastbound convoy came through. This was SC-130 of 38 ships, under Commodore H. C. C. Forsythe RNR, happily escorted by Commander Gretton's group which had distinguished itself protecting ONS-5. Not only did SC-130 escape 32 boats of Groups "Donau" and "Oder" that were deployed to intercept it and reached port intact and undamaged; Gretton's screen, and vessels of Captain Brewer's 1st Support Group, which joined in mid-passage, sank two U-boats; and the convoy's air support, R.A.F. Liberators and Hudsons from Iceland, sank three more.[10]

All this between 16 and 20 May. Thus, if ONS-5 had the fiercest battle, SC-130 made the most successful transit of any convoy against which 30 or more U-boats were deployed.

Although Doenitz's blitz on the northern transatlantic convoys had boomeranged and he had little to show for the 43 U-boats lost in the Atlantic north of lat. 23° since 28 April,[11] on 19 May he grimly ordered 42 boats to form a new barrier between the Grand Bank and Greenland. This combined Group "Donau-Mosel" never took station; it was swept aside by two Allied convoys, like express trains brushing stranded bicycles and motor cars off a grade crossing.

The first of these express trains was fast westbound Convoy ON-184, 39 merchant ships with seven escorts and three rescue vessels, which debouched from the Western Approaches on 16 May

---

[10] *U-954*, sunk by a Liberator, carried down a son of Admiral Doenitz. A sixth boat, *U-646*, which was operating independently about 100 miles SE of Iceland, was sunk by an Iceland-based Hudson 17 May.

[11] Also one in the South Atlantic and two by collision.

and was joined off Iceland on the 19th by the *Bogue* escort carrier group.

In her earlier and unfruitful crossings, *Bogue* had added her screen to the convoy screen, and had taken station between the two center columns of merchant ships. This procedure, adopted because the flattops were vulnerable yet not expendable, involved constant danger of collision with the merchantmen whenever planes were launched and recovered, and drove the carrier's deck officers to exhaustion.[12] On this mission with ON–184, *Bogue* first took station astern of the convoy commodore's column, then pulled her own escorts out of the screen and operated as one group within visual signaling distance of the convoy.

Things began to happen on 21 May when the convoy was steaming S by W, 520 miles SE of Cape Farewell. At 2110, in the northern summer twilight of a perfect day, the air squadron commander, Lieutenant Commander William M. Drane, piloting an Avenger painted with the then standard "duck egg" camouflage (blue and gray), attacked *U–231* 60 miles ahead of the carrier and the convoy. He wrecked the boat's bridge and forced its skipper to head eastward to repair damage. U.S.S. *Osmond Ingram* and H.M.C.S. *St. Laurent* now ranged ahead of the convoy and kept down potential attackers all night. At 0635 May 22, a partly cloudy day, a second Avenger piloted by Lieutenant (jg) Roger C. Kuhn USNR sighted *U–468* broaching about 55 miles southeast of the carrier. Taking cloud cover, Kuhn dove for a bombing attack on the now fully surfaced submarine, but was kept at bay by antiaircraft fire. *U–468* then enjoyed an hour's respite from attack on the surface, which it improved to make temporary repairs, and escaped. Communications failures were responsible. Kuhn reported his position inaccurately and his plane was in a "null area" not covered by radar from the carrier, then over 60 miles distant. So neither the relief planes nor the surface escort sent out to help reached the spot in time.

One of the Avengers that was searching for Lieutenant Kuhn

[12] All carriers, especially those 18-knot escort carriers, had to head up into the wind to launch and recover planes. They dropped behind the convoy to do it. Times used here are Zone N (plus 1).

and *U-468* sighted *U-305* cruising 35 miles ahead of the convoy, and immediately throttled down for a strafing attack. This boat, commanded by Kapitänleutnant Rudolf Bahr, dove before the Avenger came near enough to shoot. At 0958 Ensign Stewart E. Doty USNR, piloting another Avenger, sighted *U-305* and succeeded in rupturing its pressure hull with one of four bombs; but Bahr dove, made temporary repairs undisturbed by *Osmond Ingram's* efforts to locate him, and resurfaced shortly after noon, just in time to be bombed by Lieutenant (jg) Robert L. Stearns's TBF. Bahr submerged a third time, evaded the sonar groping of two surface escorts, completed his emergency repairs, gave up his attempts to find HX-239, and pulled out eastward for Brest.

On the same eventful afternoon of 22 May, *Bogue's* HF/DF located *U-569*, then 20 miles on her port quarter, just as Avenger pilot Lieutenant (jg) William F. Chamberlain USNR sighted the boat. Chamberlain dropped four bombs close to the conning tower. *U-569* submerged but had to surface again at 1740. Chamberlain's relief, Lieutenant Howard S. Roberts USNR, was right there on top of the boat and gave it an accurate spread of depth charges, and *U-569* up-ended and plunged to a depth of 350 feet. Its skipper then blew all tanks and surfaced. The German crew, some waving tablecloths to discourage Roberts from strafing, jumped overboard while the engineer officer slipped below and opened the flood valves, thus foiling the intention of H.M.C.S. *St. Laurent* to board and capture the boat. The Canadians nevertheless pulled 24 survivors out of a very rough sea. *U-569* was the only kill credited to the *Bogue* group on this passage; but Convoy ON-184 got through unscathed, and the Avengers had proved their worth as antisubmarine planes. They carried four depth charges each, were flexible enough to deliver the low-angle glide approach now inculcated at Quonset, and had the speed to bomb before their target could dive and to retire quickly beyond antiaircraft range. An important factor this, since U-boats would soon consistently practice the new tactic of staying on the surface and fighting it out with aircraft.

While Convoy ON-184 was thus engaged, HX-239 ran afoul of other elements of the still inchoate "Donau-Mosel" barrier to the southeast. This fast east-bound convoy of 43 ships, with a combined escort led by Commander M. J. Evans in H.M.S. *Keppel*, passed Westomp 19 May in the midst of a heavy northwest gale. On the 21st it was joined by a British escort carrier group built around H.M.S. *Archer*. Shortly after noon on the 22nd, a Swordfish pilot sighted *U-468*, surfaced and with guns manned, about 20 miles on the convoy's port bow. Since attack by a slow Swordfish under such conditions would have been suicidal, the pilot circled out of range and homed-in two surface escorts; but *U-468* escaped.

In the meantime *U-218* had sighted the convoy about 700 miles north of Flores, as its skipper informed Doenitz at 1416. Kapitän-leutnant Karl Schroeter of *U-752*, the one boat now available for an attack on the convoy from the scattered and dispirited "Donau-Mosel" group, made the mistake of "talking" to Berlin shortly before dawn 23 May. H.M.S. *Keppel* intercepted the transmission and headed down its bearing, arriving within sight of *U-752* just as a Swordfish from *Archer* delivered a depth-bomb attack which failed to inflict damage. Schroeter, eager to score after two fruitless patrols, surfaced prematurely at 0850 and promptly became the target of a plane equipped with antisubmarine rockets, one of the first attacks of that kind.[13] Bursting rockets penetrated the boat's hull at several points; Schroeter took it down, resurfaced promptly as he was unable to cope with flooding, and then found himself so briskly engaged by three Swordfish and a Martlet that he abandoned and scuttled his boat. Thirteen survivors were rescued by a destroyer, and ten more were picked up some hours later by *U-91*, whose report to Berlin seems finally to have convinced Doenitz that his northern transatlantic blitz had dismally flickered out. It was hopeless to expect U-boat barriers to stop convoys protected by aggressive surface and air escorts and almost continuous land-based air cover.

On 23 May when *U-752* went down, Convoy HX-239 was only

[13] Saunders *R.A.F. 1939-1945* III 69.

a little more than halfway across the Atlantic, but completed the passage without another submarine contact, every ship present and accounted for.

Including those sunk in the Bay of Biscay offensive (which will be related in due course) and one each in the Mediterranean, the Caribbean, and the South Atlantic, the German Navy had lost 41 submarines in May. In the same month U-boats had sunk only 211,929 tons of Allied and neutral shipping. The "rate of exchange" of submarines lost in relation to Allied tonnage sunk, which had been over one to 100,000 at the heyday of U-boat success, had so fallen in May that one boat was lost for every 5169 tons sunk. And Doenitz knew almost the whole of this devastating score. In his war diary for 24 May he admitted the loss of 31 boats since the first of the month, 20 of them to air attack, including those by escort carriers. Losses "have therefore reached impossible heights." He attributed them "to the increased use of land-based aircraft and aircraft carriers, combined with the possibility of surprise through the enemy radar location by day and night." [14] That was, of course, the combination of ASV, the plane-mounted microwave radar, and the Leigh searchlight, which both Doenitz and Hitler constantly used as an excuse for the heavy losses; actually this combination so far had been effective only in the Bay of Biscay, and with Iceland-based Liberators.

On 24 May Doenitz recalled most of his U-boats from the North Atlantic, in preparation for strengthening their antiaircraft armament, and in the hope that the development of new and faster submarines, of an acoustic torpedo, and of a jamming device against microwave radar, would neutralize the hard-won Allied superiority. On the same day, 24 May, he broadcast a ringing appeal to all officers of submarines: —

"You alone can, at the moment, make an offensive attack against the enemy and beat him. The U-boat must, by continuous sinking of ships with war matériel and the necessary supplies for the British

[14] B.d.U. War Diary 24 May 1943, pp. 428–29 of trans.

Isles, force the enemy to continual losses which must slowly but steadily sap the strength of the strongest force. The German people have long felt that our boats constitute the keenest and most decisive weapon and that the outcome of the war depends on the success or failure of the Battle of the Atlantic. . . . The time will soon come in which you will be superior to the enemy with new and stronger weapons and will be able to triumph over your worst enemy — the aircraft and the destroyer."

In the meantime, the Grossadmiral planned a redeployment of U-boats to areas where escorts were not so aggressive nor air coverage so plentiful as in the North Atlantic. But he left a dozen or so there so that the Allies would not suspect what was up.

During the four weeks that preceded Doenitz's decisions, the Allies had demonstrated that both fast and slow convoys, if provided with air as well as surface escort and support, could cross the North Atlantic in either direction with slight if any loss, no matter how many U-boats were deployed against them; and that, during the passage, submarines could be killed by surface and air escorts before they ever came within sight of merchant-ship targets.

CHAPTER VII
Ushant to Finisterre
1943

1. Coastal Command and Army Air Force [1]

DURING the first four months of 1943 about 28 per cent of the U-boats that departed on war patrols reached the broad ocean via the North Sea and the coast of Norway. But the majority, the other 72 per cent, departed from five westward-facing French ports, Brest, Lorient, St. Nazaire, La Pallice (the port of La Rochelle) and Bordeaux; [2] all but the first on the Bay of Biscay. These were much the most important of the U-boat bases. Heavy bombproof concrete pens had been built to protect the boats, and in the nearby towns numerous bars, brothels and hotels were set aside for the recreation of German submariners. When a submarine came in from a patrol, one third of the crew was given nine

[1] Times in this chapter are in Zone N (plus 1). Hilary St. G. Saunders *Royal Air Force 1939–1945* III chap. ii; C. M. Sternhell & A. M. Thorndike *Antisubmarine Warfare in World War II* (Operations Evaluation Group Report No. 51, Washington 1946) chap. 6; Historical Division Asst. Chief of Air "Army Air Force Anti-Submarine Command (1945); B.d.U. War Diary for the period. This chapter profited by review and correction in 1953 at the hands of Capt. D. V. Peyton-Ward RN (Ret.).

[2] Submarines Entering and Departing Atlantic Ports under German Control, compiled from B.d.U. War Diary Jan.–Apr. 1943. See note 30 at end of chapter for May–Dec. 1943.

FRENCH PORTS				NORTH SEA PORTS		
	Entered	*Departed*			*Entered*	*Departed*
Brest	51	60		Kiel	4	74
Lorient	54	61		Bergen	4	12
St. Nazaire	56	62		Trondheim	—	1
La Pallice	28	30			8	87
Bordeaux	12	8				
	201	221				

days' liberty ashore, and lodged there; one third went by special train for nine days' leave in Germany; and the remaining third worked for nine days at repairs and upkeep. Every novena these rôles were reversed so that in the 28 days between patrols each submariner had an equal whack of leave, liberty and labor. The Allied bombing attacks on Brest, Lorient and St. Nazaire in 1942 accomplished nothing except destruction of the towns, and letting daylight through the roof of one pen at Brest.

All boats based on French ports, except some of those at Brest, had to transit the Bay of Biscay twice in every war patrol. Consequently it was logical to attempt to choke off this noxious stream of submarine traffic at source. The Bay, as Air Vice Marshal Slessor put it in a memorandum of 20 April 1943 to the Anti–U-boat Subcommittee, "is the trunk of the Atlantic U-boat menace, the roots being in the Biscay ports and the branches spreading far and wide. . . ." The tree should be felled by severing its trunk — the "little patch of water about 300 miles by 120 in the Bay of Biscay, through which five out of six U-boats operating in the Atlantic had to pass." [3]

Back in World War I when U.S. destroyers, initially coal burners, were based on Brest, the bluejackets used to sing: —

> In the English Channel and the Irish Sea
> Fritz is raisin' hell, he's runnin' free;
> But in the Bay of Biscay who wears the pants?
> It's the old coal-burners that are based on France!

It was different now. Fritz "wore the pants," and it was up to the Allied Navies and Air Forces to pull them down. And since the Bay was an area of British responsibility, the majority of forces were British. The United States Army Air Force participated to a limited extent during the most exciting phases of the "Bay Offensive," and United States naval aircraft entered toward the close. Surface ships of the Royal Navy got in a few good licks; but the offensive was predominantly an R.A.F. show.

[3] Saunders III 47. "Five out of six" needs correction to "three out of four."

Coastal Command aircraft had been patrolling the Bay of Biscay since 1940 with very meager results. And so had six boats of United States Navy Submarine Squadron 50 (Captain Norman S. Ives), based at Rosneath on the Clyde, which at the request of the Admiralty began to patrol the Galician shore of the Bay early in 1943.[4] The main mission of these boats of the 1525-ton *Gato* class was to break up the iron ore and other contraband traffic from Spanish ports to Bayonne and Bordeaux. They were also intended to intercept blockade runners returning from Japan, and perhaps sink U-boats. Their first problem was ship identification; American submariners were supposed to be able to distinguish blockade runners from hundreds of neutral freighters and fishermen plying the Biscayan coast, which they were not allowed to molest for fear of stirring up General Franco and Dr. Salazar. They had to operate within twenty minutes' flying time from Luftwaffe bases, but that was the least of their worries. The main frustrating factor was the bad quality of torpedoes with which they had been supplied.[5] For instance, two torpedoes fired by *Shad* at an ore carrier passed harmlessly under the target's keel; on 21 March 1943 *Shad* made a hit on a German "Narvik" class destroyer, but the torpedo failed to explode; and on the same day *Herring* fired two torpedoes at a U-boat off Ferrol but they "prematured." *Shad* made one good hit on blockade runner *Pietro Orseolo*, which managed nevertheless to get into Bordeaux after jettisoning several tons of crude rubber.

Admiral King, concluding that these submarines were "doing virtually nothing to further the war effort," on 23 March authorized Admiral Stark to negotiate with the Admiralty about their redeployment. That was done in early April. Admiral King did not insist on the boats' being sent back to American waters; he expressly told Admiral Stark to use them in whatever manner the Admiralty wished, and as long as they were useful. First Sea Lord decided to release them after they performed several missions north of Scotland, and in June 1943 the Subron 50 detachment was transferred

[4] Admiralty Historical Division "The Work of U.S. Subron 50 in European Waters," a study made in 1948.

[5] On this painful subject see Vol. IV 191–94, 200–202, 214, 221–22, 230–32.

to the Pacific Fleet. With better torpedoes, it did very well in the Pacific war.

Air Chief Marshal Philip Joubert of Coastal Command laid on the first real Bay of Biscay offensive in February 1943. About 36 Liberators of the 1st and 2nd Antisubmarine Air Squadrons, United States Army Air Force, commanded by Lieutenant Colonel Jack Roberts USA,[6] got into five out of six battles with U-boats around the Bay. One B-24 known as "Tidewater Tillie," piloted by 1st Lieutenant W. L. Sanford USA, sank *U-519* on 10 February about 660 miles west of Lorient. This was the only kill that month which could properly be credited to the Bay offensive; four other U-boats sunk by aircraft the same week were downed by the R.A.F. while supporting convoys. Consequently Admiral King was confirmed in his opinion that escort-of-convoy was the best method of employing air power against submarines. He was not disposed to divert more Liberators to the Bay offensive, particularly in the roughest part of the North Atlantic winter; on the contrary, he believed that the Moroccan Sea Frontier, now threatened by a redeployment of U-boats,[7] had an urgent need for Liberators. Accordingly, invoking the Air Forces' favorite principle of flexibility, Admiral King and General Marshall decided to transfer Colonel Roberts's two antisubmarine squadrons to Port Lyautey.[8] This movement, begun and completed in March 1943, greatly strengthened air reconnaissance and convoy coverage during the build-up of forces in North Africa.

Although in retrospect, and judged by results, this diversion of A.A.F. Liberators was justified, it was executed without sufficient warning to or consultation with the Royal Air Force.

[6] See Vol. I 244.

[7] Doenitz ordered a number of U-boats into the approaches to Gibraltar and Casablanca on 20-22 Feb. 1943 and in mid-March these sank 4 ships from Convoy UGS-6 east of the Azores (see Vol. I 357-8); they would probably have got more but for air support from Port Lyautey.

[8] See following chapter, section 3, for their activities off Morocco, reorganized as 480th A/S Group.

2. *The Bay Offensive, March–June*

Air Vice Marshal Slessor, undismayed by the slight results of the February air offensive in the Bay, made repeated efforts to obtain more American Liberators to help hack away at the U-boats' "tree trunk." But from March to mid-July, Coastal's British axemen were doing it all.

Plans for this Bay Offensive against U-boats departing or seeking French bases had been developed by Air Chief Marshal Joubert. Sir John Slessor at this point "had in his hand the weapon which his predecessors had forged. It was now for him to use it with vigor and address," [9] qualities with which he was exceptionally well furnished. He placed the operation under the tactical command of Air Vice Marshal Geoffrey R. Bromet RAF, commanding 19th Air Group R.A.F., but always kept his finger on the pulse. To him, this was "one of the decisive battles of the war."

One of the factors that had defeated the February offensive was the German radar search receiver called Metox, which enabled U-boat skippers to detect Allied planes using the best radar available at that time. But, on 20 March, Coastal uncorked ASV — the 10-centimeter-wave radar on which British and American scientists had long been working.[10] The combination of ASV, whose beams the Germans were unable to detect, with the 80,000,000-candle-power Leigh searchlight on a Wellington bomber, made it possible to attack U-boats at night from the air with great success. As soon as a surfaced U-boat was picked up on ASV, the plane made a radar approach undetected, turned on its blinding searchlight at a few hundred yards' distance, and attacked before the boat even knew that it had been sighted.

Slowly the campaign got under way. On 22 March 1943 a Wel-

---

[9] Saunders *Royal Air Force* III 35. Slessor was knighted 2 June 1943.

[10] See chap. iii, and Saunders II 109. U.S. Army Liberators had it first, and it was that model which British scientists adapted. But Bomber Command had priority, and not until it was realized what Metox was doing could Joubert obtain ASV for Coastal.

lington sank *U-665* at night about 280 miles WSW of Brest, in the Bay patrol area. On the same day, *U-338* evened the score by shooting down an Australian-manned Halifax and taking a prisoner. By early April the Germans began "fight back" tactics, although these had not yet become doctrine. Before long, all boats that sortied were equipped with powerful antiaircraft batteries, usually a 37-mm antiaircraft cannon mounted on an enclosed platform like a small bandstand abaft the conning tower, and a quad of 20-mm machine guns within the conning tower itself.[11] "There were some long faces in Whitehall at this development," wrote Slessor; and well there might be, because a submarine thus equipped could outgun any Allied aircraft, even a Liberator.

During April 1943, 42 U-boats entered and 75 departed French ports; 48 sightings were made by Allied planes and 27 attacks, but only one kill. Yet the loss of that one, *U-376*, together with news of other night attacks in which the plane's approach was undetected, so wrought on Doenitz that he ordered boats in transit to submerge all night, surface in daylight to recharge batteries, and, if surprised, to fight back. This proved to be a serious tactical blunder.

At this juncture there developed a struggle between Admiralty and R.A.F. for suitable aircraft. The operational scientists working under the Admiralty reported that 260 LR or VLR bombers would be required to cover the Bay effectively, but Coastal then had only 70. The Admiralty therefore requested the transfer of 190 Lancasters from Bomber Command R.A.F. to Coastal. Slessor, however, refused to endorse this request. He declared that the scientists' estimate was excessive, and backed up Air Chief Marshal Portal's assertion that no heavy bombers could be spared from the strategic bombing of Germany. As a substitute, Slessor requested that six squadrons (72 units) of Liberators of the United States

[11] The first quadruple-mounted 20-mm were placed on two boats (one of them *U-758*) in April and May 1943. The schedule called for 24 more to be so equipped by 25 July, and another 24 by 15 Sept. On 8 June, Doenitz issued orders that all boats be given at least four 20-mm before putting to sea, and on 1 Dec. he started the 37-mm Bofors equipment. B.d.U. War Diary 16 June p. 498, 1 Dec. p. 346.

Army Antisubmarine Command be transferred from the United States to the United Kingdom, for use over the Bay. The Anti-U-boat Committee of the Admiralty endorsed this request and on 21 April passed it along to the Joint Chiefs of Staff in Washington.[12]

Admiral King, faced with meeting the terrific concentration of U-boats against northern transatlantic convoys, and needing Liberators for reconnaissance in the Pacific, where a great forward movement was just beginning, was in no mood to weaken air strength in Newfoundland or Iceland, the only bases from which such planes could be transferred. To Slessor's plea that there were plenty of suitable aircraft in the then peaceful Eastern and Gulf Sea Frontiers that could be spared, he retorted (in a letter to Admiral Stark 3 May) that for the British "their own locality is the key to what concerns them — vitally, to be sure, but there are also other localities in which vital considerations exist, or may arise at any moment." In any case, the British notion that the Pacific and Eastern Sea Frontier were swarming with Liberators was a complete delusion.[13]

Air Marshal Slessor's urgency arose in part from his desire to take full advantage of U-boat targets presented in daylight, as required by Doenitz's new tactics. Air Vice Marshal Bromet's 19th Air Group was temporarily strengthened by shifting planes from other Coastal Command units operating over the English Channel and the Northern Transit Area north of Scotland, and these planes were strengthened by the addition of more and heavier forward-firing guns. During the first week of May the British Sunderlands and Halifaxes sank four U-boats in the Bay, and two more collided with fatal results. Another kill was made on the 15th, but no more

---

[12] Saunders *Royal Air Force* III 41–2. Admiral Stark to King, 4 Apr. 1943, states that Mr. Churchill backed up the R.A.F., and was "adamant against weakening by one iota the bombing of Germany."

[13] See table in Chapter III for actual numbers of Liberators in the U.S. sea frontiers and elsewhere. There were none in the Eastern Sea Frontier on 31 May or 1 June. By 1 July 1943, 209 Liberators had been delivered to the Navy; by the 20th, the Pacific Fleet had 72; most of the PB4Ys at that date were still undergoing tests or being used in training.

until the 31st, when two were disposed of by air attack. And *U–441*, specially equipped as a flak boat with machine guns, a 37-mm cannon, and rockets, and ordered to cruise about and knock down aircraft, was badly damaged by a Sunderland (which it shot down) on 24 May and forced to return to port. Altogether, the Bay offensive score for May was good: 98 sightings were made on 120 U-boats in transit, 64 were attacked, 7 sunk and 7 damaged; all at a cost of 6 aircraft.[14]

June opened hopefully with the sinking of *U–418* on the 1st, but only six more U-boats were sighted in or near the Bay before the 10th. Doenitz was trying new tactics. On 1 June he ordered all boats to make the transit in groups, surfaced (outward in fives, inward in deuces and treys) with the hope that their combined flak would drive off aircraft. This was not popular with the U-boat skippers, but it worked for a time; the first two pairs made Brest safely on 7 and 11 June.

On the 12th, when five boats in company were spotted by three unarmed British aircraft 90 miles north of Cape Ortegal, the new game was detected. The three planes hung around for an hour and a half, hoping to attract armed help, then departed; and at 2218 the five boats submerged for a night's run to clear the Bay. That they did, but next evening they were spotted some 250 miles west of Finisterre by a far-ranging Sunderland. Gallantly attacking through a fountain of flak thrown up by all five boats, the British pilot straddled *U–564* with a stick of bombs that ruptured its pressure hull, flew limping homeward and splashed 80 miles short of Scilly. While three units continued seaward, *U–185* escorted damaged *U–564* back into the Bay. On 14 June this pair was sighted 150 miles NW of Finisterre by the pilot of a training-command Whitley which had been lent to Marshal Bromet, and the Whitley sank *U–564*. *U–185* picked up 19 survivors and reached base, escorted by a German destroyer sent out from Royan.

On the same day, two transiting groups north of Cape Ortegal,

[14] Sternhell & Thorndike *Antisubmarine Warfare* p. 144 has tables of transits, sightings, and flying hours of patrolling planes for every month of the Bay offensive through July 1943.

one of five and the other of two U-boats, became targets of a prolonged air attack. None were sunk, and Coastal lost at least one
plane; but two boats were forced to return to Lorient for repairs.
As a result of these conflicts, Doenitz issued a new general order
that very night, to the effect that "groups of U-boats will proceed
through Biscay mainly submerged and will surface only to charge
batteries." [15]

A firm believer in joint air-surface operations, Slessor had hoped
for assistance from the Royal Navy; but until the back of the
North Atlantic blitz was broken in May, the Navy could spare no
escort vessels from convoy duty. "It was a happy day in the middle of June," wrote the Coastal chief, when the support group commanded by Captain Frederick J. Walker RN, consisting of sloops
Starling, Wren, Woodpecker, Kite and *Wild Goose,* was assigned
to the Bay offensive.

A group of three U-boats attempting to enter the Bay on 24
June encountered Walker's birds, 170 miles NW of Finisterre.
Starling blasted to the surface a 1600-ton minelayer, *U–119,*
rammed and sent it to the bottom with all hands. *Kite* then snuffed
up *U–449,* which fell victim to a series of creeping attacks by the
entire surface group.

These were the only kills of "passengers" in and out of the Bay
in June, and three more Coastal aircraft were lost on patrol. Nine
of the eleven-boat "Monsun" group, destined for the Indian Ocean,
whose fortunes we shall follow in a later chapter, made the transit
safely in late June and early July.[16]

3. *"Madcats" and B–24s in the Big Slaughter,*
20 July–2 August

Sir John Slessor, still in need of more aircraft to push his offensive, flew to Washington in June. Admiral King, impressed by

[15] B.d.U. War Diary 14 June.
[16] Wolfgang Frank *The Sea Wolves* p. 183.

the recent score, agreed to give him six squadrons of Liberators, and to transfer two at once, from Iceland and Newfoundland. Before the end of June, Army B–24s commanded by Colonel Howard Moore USA began to arrive at Dunkeswell in Devon; by 7 July two full squadrons (24 planes), the 4th and 19th, were there, and on the 13th they flew their first Biscay mission.

The offensive was now at high water; U-boats were entering and leaving in small groups and the hunting was excellent. Coastal Command planes had sunk five more boats since the first of July. On the morning of the 20th, a newly-arrived B–24, piloted by 1st Lieutenant C. F. Gallmeier USA, bombed *U–558* off the mouth of the Bay, and the lieutenant had the satisfaction of seeing the U-boat's crew abandon ship just as he had to return to base on three engines. A British Halifax and a second Liberator then bore out of the haze, straddled the boat, and hastened the sinking. That same day a third Liberator, piloted by 1st Lieutenant H. E. Dyment USA, was shot down by a pair of U-boats not far from the spot where *U–558* had gone down, and all hands were lost.

Transiting groups were now generally encountered on the surface. An Allied plane which made contact — usually by eyesight in the daytime or by microwave radar at night — homed in other planes, and also Walker's support group if available, to deliver a surprise attack. Doenitz thought that by operating in groups his boats would obtain mutual antiaircraft support; but that did not work out. When surprised, as they usually were, it was every U-boat for itself; each turned in a tight circle firing furiously, and if the planes were persistent some skipper would sooner or later lose his nerve and straighten out preparatory to diving. That was the signal for the planes to begin a bombing run.

In July the United States Navy got into the Biscay show.[17] At Slessor's request, and as earnest of the forthcoming relief of Army

---

[17] "The Story of the Madcats: a History of Patrol Bombing Squadron 63," April–June 1943, Division of Naval History.

Liberators in Britain by the Navy, Admiral King sent over Patron 63, Catalina flying boats, in the last week of July. This squadron, under Lieutenant Commander Edwin O. Wagner, was equipped with the Navy's new magnetic airborne detector (MAD), and hence adopted the nickname "Madcats." Based at Pembroke Dock in South Wales, Patron 63 began to patrol the Bay on 25 July. Two Catalinas flushed *U–262* and *U–760* about 150 miles NW of Finisterre on the 28th and engaged them at medium range while awaiting air reinforcement; but the boats escaped. The MAD proved to be of little or no use in the Bay, but one of the "Madcats" played an important if minor part in one of the fiercest battles of this campaign.

Until late August U-boats in transit were given very little protection by the Luftwaffe, whose capabilities, with several bases near the coast of France, were very great. The reason, apparently, was the feud between Goering and Doenitz. The portly Reichsmarschall did not care to build up the Grossadmiral's prestige at his own expense. The very thin fighter-and-bomber patrol that he put on over the Bay of Biscay accounted for only one victim, a "Madcat." This was a Catalina nicknamed "Aunt Minnie" piloted by Lieutenant William P. Tanner USNR, who as pilot of a PBY patrolling off Pearl Harbor had sighted a Japanese midget submarine on the morning of 7 December 1941.[18] Unfortunate "Minnie" was attacked by 8 to 12 Ju–88s on 1 August. She splashed one on the first pass, then came under a fatal crossfire, burst into flames from wing to wing, and had to be ditched. Tanner with his co-pilot and waist-gunner climbed on board a life raft and were rescued, after 24 hours, by H.M.S. *Bideford*.

Although the Germans claimed that the Madcats had been chased away, they stuck to it until the end of 1943; and by that time had carried out more Bay patrols than any other squadron in Air Vice Marshal Bromet's 19th Group.

The six days 28 July–2 August witnessed what Coastal called the "big Bay slaughter," in which nine U-boats were sunk. It began

[18] See Vol. III 96.

with *U–404* on 28 July, slain by an Anglo-American Liberator team. *U–614* on the 29th was sunk by a Leigh-light Wellington. And on the 30th two submarine tankers and a 740-tonner were disposed of by superb teamwork among a British Halifax and a Sunderland, three United States Army Liberators, a United States Navy Catalina, and Captain Walker's sloops.

An American Liberator spotted this trio on the calm, clear morning of 30 July about 150 miles NW of Cape Ortegal. Outward bound from Bordeaux, *U–461*, *U–462*, and *U–504* were steaming merrily along in company; the first two were 1600-ton "milch cows" en route to the Cape Verdes to fuel boats bound for the Indian Ocean. As the Liberator had just enough fuel to get home, the pilot called in a Sunderland and a Catalina before he had to depart. The PBY, too, went off to search for Walker's sloops, leaving the Sunderland alone for over an hour to stalk the boats. While thus engaged, the Sunderland homed-in an American Liberator and a Halifax. When these arrived on the scene about 1048, the U-boats began to circle and fire. The Halifax made a high-level bombing attack which overshot the target; then it too had to leave for want of fuel.

The Germans were now congratulating themselves on having driven off all assailants when, at 1100, there arrived a second Halifax whose pilot boldly wove his way through flak bursts to drop a homing torpedo which ruptured the pressure tank of *U–462*. The American Liberator already on the scene had its bomb-release gear shot away by German gunfire, but its pilot, 1st Lieutenant Anthony L. Leal USA, turned back to strafe. The Halifax followed with a high-level bombing run, and by 1105 the pack began to scatter. Now a Royal Australian Air Force Sunderland slipped in at mast level and straddled *U–461*. The big milch cow sank, leaving some 30 survivors afloat; and a Halifax finished off *U–462* at 1116. Two down!

In the meantime, Captain Walker appeared on the scene, his flagship *Kite* flying the long-disused signal "General Chase." His sloops, after firing on the two tankers as they were about to go

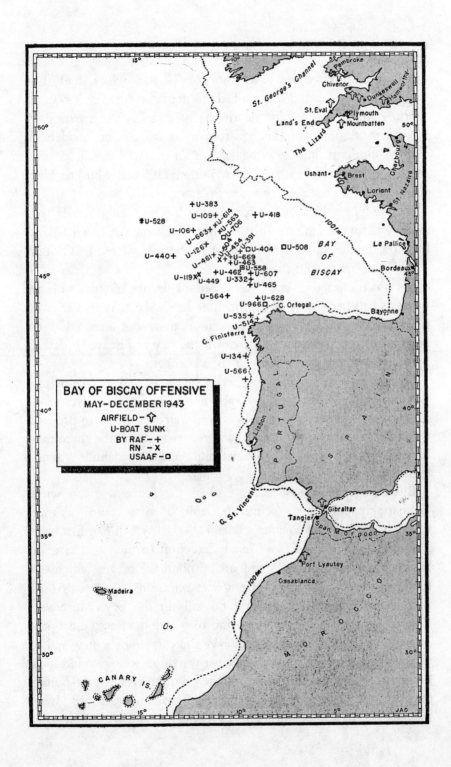

BAY OF BISCAY OFFENSIVE
MAY–DECEMBER 1943
AIRFIELD – 🛪
U-BOAT SUNK
BY RAF – +
RN – X
USAAF – ◻

down, concentrated on searching for *U–504*, which had submerged. Walker found it at 50-fathom depth at 1132, and went to work. A series of creeping depth-charge attacks over a period of two hours disposed of this 740-tonner. A search for "evidence" yielded clothing, human remains, "and some well-cured bacon," after which survivors from the two other U-boats, who had been waiting in their life rafts, were recovered.

To complete the score of nine in the big Bay slaughter, *U–454* and *U–383* were sunk by British Sunderlands on 1 August; *U–106* by three Sunderlands, and *U–706* by a Liberator piloted by Captain J. L. Hamilton usa on the 2nd.

"It was too good to last," wrote Slessor; in one month's time 16 U-boats had been sunk in transit, nine in six days. War diaries of surviving German submarines indicate that by 1 August a U-boat could seldom come up for air in or off the Bay of Biscay, by day or by night, without being jumped by a bomber.

Late on the evening of 2 August, as heavy air and surface patrols were sweeping northwest of Cape Ortegal in search of fresh victims, Doenitz ordered four U-boats on their way home to proceed through Spanish coastal waters without regard for the three-mile limit. It looked as though Bromet and Walker had built a fence across the Bay.

But the gap at the southern end of the fence was too wide. U-boat skippers quickly found that this "Piening route," as they called it, from Adolf Piening's boat (*U–155*) which had first used it in July, freed them from radar detection because of the close backdrop of the Pyrenees and other mountain ranges which extend almost to Finisterre. During the remaining 29 days, Allied patrols made few sightings and no kills in the Bay. Moreover, Doenitz had at last induced Goering to give him effective coöperation, partly in the form of Focke-Wulfs carrying the new radio-controlled glide-bombs for use against warships, which would soon be used off Salerno. In their first use on 27 August, glide-bombs sank H.M. sloop *Egret* and damaged Canadian destroyer *Athabaskan* SW of Cape Finisterre. Consequently the Admiralty ordered all ships to retire westward 200 miles, out of German air range, and air-surface coöperation suffered.

The Germans were still seriously disturbed because they were unable to ascertain the cause of so many successful surprise attacks on U-boats at night, and out of fog and clouds. In August Doenitz thought he had the answer: that his Metox radar receiver was sending out impulses which guided the planes to their quarry. Metox was promptly scrapped and replaced by a new type; but the Grossadmiral's diagnosis was wrong. It was the ASV microwave radar which led to so many sightings and attacks, as the Germans finally learned in December 1943; and not until March 1944, after studying a microwave set recovered from a crashed bomber, did they manage to install an efficient receiver in U-boats.[19]

4. *PB4Ys in the Bay Offensive, August–December*

Sir John Slessor regarded Coastal Command of the R.A.F. as the loser in the famous "horse trade" between United States Navy and Army Air Force, by virtue of which the Army retired from antisubmarine warfare and in Britain was replaced by United States Navy Liberators.[20] Perhaps the main reason for his objection to the deal was psychological. The United States Army Air Antisubmarine Command looked on Coastal as its guide, elder brother, and the model of what it wished to be and actually became after the war — part of an independent air force, coëqual with Army and Navy. The Air Arm of the United States Navy, on the contrary, regarded itself as a *corps d'élite* analogous to the Marines, and was not overly disposed to take orders or advice from the R.A.F. The Army Air Force accepted the somewhat primitive accommodations of St. Eval, glad to share privations with its brothers in arms;

[19] Frank *Sea Wolves* pp. 191, 196–97 has an interesting account of the stuffiness in German naval headquarters which so long postponed this important discovery. In fact, his whole book is a significant record of discoveries made too late, owing fundamentally to Hitler's distrust of scientists.

[20] See Chapter II, sec. 3 above.

but the Navy complained of the cold and the plumbing at Dunkeswell. Slessor, to be sure, puts his objection to the "horse trade" on a higher level – that "a large number of experienced Army antisubmarine crews were relieved by relatively inexperienced Naval crews." But the Navy crews who began to arrive in the United Kingdom on 17 August from Argentia had had plenty of practice in hunting submarines; they were inexperienced only in Coastal Command signals and procedures. Be that as it may, the United States Navy Liberators began to fly combat missions within two weeks of their arrival in England; they consistently flew more missions per plane per week than did those of the R.A.F. in Coastal, and they sank two U-boats during the November flare-up in the Bay, which was one more than all the rest of Coastal did in the same period or, for that matter, during the last four months of 1943.

A more legitimate grievance of Sir John Slessor, however, was based on the fact that he did not obtain in 1943 the full six squadrons (72 units) of Navy Liberators for which Admiral King had raised his hopes in June. The transfer took time; by the end of September only three squadrons had arrived, and at the end of the year there were still only three, one having been transferred to the Moroccan Sea Frontier shortly after it arrived, whither Patron 63, the "Madcats," had also flown.[21] But by the time the invasion of Normandy began, in June 1944, Coastal included no fewer than eight squadrons of United States Navy PB4Ys.

Captain William H. Hamilton, commanding Fleet Air Wing Seven, arrived in England 13 August and established his staff at Mount Wise, close to the Plymouth area combined headquarters of the British services. Bombron 103, Lieutenant Commander William G. von Bracht, consisting of 12 PB4Y-1s, arrived from Argentia at the St. Eval (Cornwall) base on the 17th, and began to patrol the Bay of Biscay on 30 August. As the Squadron's historian observes, "It was the beginning of a very rugged week." [22]

[21] Fairwing Seven War Diary. These were not full squadrons; they then comprised only 30 units. The 14 "Madcats" were also under this Fleet Air Wing.
[22] Patron 103 War History p. 4; Fairwing Seven War Diary 17 Aug. On 30 Sept.

A change had taken place in the tactical situation since the big slaughter had ended on 2 August, owing to Marshal Goering's decision to afford Doenitz more and better assistance. Besides bombers equipped with radio-controlled glide-bombs, flights of German fighter planes appeared, to frustrate the Sunderlands and Liberators. Their first victim, on 2 September, was a Navy Liberator piloted by Lieutenant K. W. Wickstrom USNR. Two days later a second Liberator was jumped by six Ju–88s and, after destroying one of them, went down in flames 75 miles NW of Finisterre. Thanks to brilliant handling by the pilot, Lieutenant (jg) J. H. Alexander USNR, all hands survived the ditching and were rescued by friendly Spanish fishermen and returned to England. On 18 September a third Navy Liberator, skippered by Lieutenant (jg) W. B. Krause USNR, came unscathed through a battle with eight Ju–88s. By the end of September this situation was somewhat relieved by a vigorous bombing, by the United States VIII Army Air Force, of German fighter bases in western France.

At the end of September the Navy had 44 combatant aircraft (30 Liberators and 14 Catalinas) under Coastal Command, and was relieving the Army Liberators, which now joined the VIII Army Air Force for the strategic bombing of Germany. But the second half of September and the entire month of October were relatively quiet in the Bay. One reason for the poor hunting was the fact that the Germans had now completed their submarine pens at Bergen in Norway, and Doenitz was ordering U-boats thither instead of to France.[23] Another was the use of the Piening route along shore.[24] United States Navy planes made only two sightings of U-boats and one attack in October. Air Marshal Bromet's entire 19th Group (to which the Navy Liberators belonged) made only 16 attacks in September and October, and one kill. Admiral King,

---

they moved to Dunkeswell. Capt. Hamilton was promoted Commodore in November.

[23] Only 13 U-boats entered the 5 French ports in Oct. 1943, and 23 departed.

[24] B.d.U. War Diary Aug. and 3 Sept. 1943. Returning boats were allowed to hug the coast at their discretion, and were allowed to surface only at night. Apparently the Piening route was used little if at all by departing boats.

on looking at these figures, naturally concluded that the Biscayan area had become inactive and, again applying the air force principle of flexibility, ordered Liberator Squadron 111 transferred to Port Lyautey on 3 November.[25]

Two days later, ironically enough, the Bay became the hottest area in the North Atlantic. Doenitz had decided to give up "Pie-ning" and resume direct transit. On 5 November a British Wellington flushed a boat 215 miles north of Finisterre but failed to sink it. Later the same day, the Navy Liberator of Lieutenant O. P. Johnstone USNR was jumped by six Ju–88s and barely escaped. On the 8th Lieutenant W. E. Grumble USNR reported his Liberator under air attack, and never returned.

A prolonged battle between four Liberators (three of them American) and *U–966* on 10 November 1943 was one of the highlights of this new offensive. A British Wellington with ASV raised *U–966* sixty miles off the Spanish coast at 0400. Shortly before 0800 a Liberator of VB–105, piloted by Lieutenant L. E. Harmon, obtained radar contact on the same boat at a range of nine miles and made two strafing attacks; heavy return gunfire from the submarine crippled his release gear and spoiled a bombing attack. An hour later, a British fighter plane strafed the submarine and made off. Harmon's Liberator returned for another exchange of gunfire at 0943 and riddled the boat's conning tower but at 1000 had to depart for want of fuel. A Liberator of VB–103, piloted by Lieutenant (jg) K. L. Wright USNR, receiving word from base that *U–966* had last been seen at lat. 44°39′ N, long. 9°08′ W, shaped a course for Ferrol and then backtracked — a maneuver which at 1040 resulted in a good radar contact at 12 miles. Wright delivered a low strafing attack and circled the U-boat until 1145, drop-

[25] After Air Vice Marshal B. E. Baker RAF had relieved Air Vice Marshal Bromet in October, the same command situation arose between him and Commo. Hamilton as had existed between the U.S. Navy and U.S. Army Air Forces operating under Navy command. On at least one occasion Baker tried to give orders to U.S.N. squadrons without consulting Hamilton, who insisted that the planes of Fairwing Seven should be sent out by no one except himself. Admiral Stark supported Hamilton in this controversy, and Slessor acquiesced. Stark to Vice Admiral F. J. Horne 22 Nov.; Hamilton to Stark 2 Dec.; Slessor to Stark 20 Dec. 1943.

ping five depth bombs. Although he straddled the submarine, which began to settle by the stern, it maintained speed and course and threw up so much flak that Wright was forced to orbit outside antiaircraft range until noon, when he too had to depart for want of fuel.

Scarcely had he broken off when a Liberator of VB–110 piloted by Lieutenant W. W. Parish USNR, sent out by Commodore Hamilton from Dunkeswell, picked up *U–966* by radar at 20 miles' distance and attacked down-sun. At 1235 Parish dropped six bombs which fell short to starboard, causing the U-boat to roll and skid to port; nevertheless it righted itself and resumed course toward Spain. Parish shadowed it as long as his fuel held out, until 1315. Half an hour earlier, an R.A.F. Liberator manned by a Czechoslovak crew had sighted the boat and started a bombing run, but was forced off in the face of intense antiaircraft fire. Returning to the attack, the Czechs battled *U–966* all the way to the cliffs, routing its crew topside and overboard with a rocket attack, just before it ran aground a short distance from Ortiguiera.[26]

Another PB4Y of VB–103, piloted by Lieutenant (jg) R. B. Brownell USNR, sank 740-ton *U–508* at 0116 November 12, about 95 miles north of Cape Peñas. But the Liberator itself was shot down, and not one man survived from boat or plane to tell the tale of what must have been a grim battle.

Increasingly foul weather, for which the Bay of Biscay is notorious, combined with aggressive German fighter plane activity, gave the transiting U-boats another month's grace. The sinking of *U–391* by a British Liberator on 13 December was the next kill, and the last of 1943. Shortly after, Commander Wagner's "Madcat" squadron, rendered ineffective by German fighter-plane activity, was transferred to Port Lyautey, where it rendered excellent service in barring the Strait of Gibraltar.

As winter days grew shorter, air reconnaissance disclosed that the German Navy was collecting a squadron of destroyers in the

26 *U.S. Fleet A/S Bulletin* Jan. 1944 p. 23; War Histories of VB–105 and VB–110; B.d.U. War Diary 11 Nov. 1943.

western ports of France, obviously for escort of blockade runners.
On 18 December Coastal Command aircraft torpedoed German
runner *Pietro Orseolo,* which had been hit by United States submarine *Shad* on 1 April in Concarneau Bay, but not sunk. *Osorno,* reported by an aviator from U.S.S. *Card* on 1 December,[27] got
through to the Gironde after a running fight between escorting destroyers and several Wellingtons, Halifaxes, and U.S. Navy Liberators. She ran aground but saved her cargo.

On 27 December 1943, a British Sunderland patrolling about 500
miles NNW of Cape Finisterre sighted 2700-ton blockade runner
Alsterufer, which had left Japan in October. Other aircraft were
homed-in, and the ship was set afire by a well-placed bomb and a
flight of rockets from a Czech-manned Liberator; she was last seen
exploding as her crew abandoned ship. Next morning, Lieutenant
S. D. Johnson USNR, pilot of a Navy Liberator on routine patrol,
sighted four German "Narvik" class destroyers and four 1300-ton
torpedo boats which had been dispatched from French ports to escort *Alsterufer,* and radioed their position to base. Word went out
to light cruisers H.M.S. *Glasgow* and *Enterprise,* then between the
destroyers and France, to get on their trail. The cruisers gave chase
and sighted the enemy shortly after noon. There followed a notable running battle — Halifaxes, Sunderlands, and United States
Navy PB4Ys, covered by Beaufighters and Mosquitoes, hurling
bombs at the fleeing destroyers and tangling with Ju–88s and
Focke-Wulfs. Lieutenant S. D. Johnson joined the fight, as did another unit of his squadron, piloted by Lieutenant L. E. Harmon,
who splashed a FW–200. When the German ships split into two
groups, the cruisers concentrated on the nearest four targets and
pursued them the entire afternoon, sinking *T–25, T–26,* and *Z–27*
by gunfire.[28] Commodore Hamilton and Air Vice Marshal Baker,

[27] See below, Chapter XI.
[28] Admiralty announcement London *Times* 30 Dec.; *Coastal Command Review*
Dec. 1943; War Diary German Naval Command Operations Div. 29 Dec.; VB–105
Action Report 11 Jan. 1944. Fairwing Seven, VB–103 and VB–110 War Histories;
Z–32 War Diary; Doenitz "War at Sea" sec. 124. One of the U.S.N. Liberators
crashed in England on its return, and the crew of another had to bail out over
Spain.

in the meantime, had dispatched 15 Liberators and 4 Halifaxes with fighter support to the scene of the fray. After driving off a dozen Ju–88s, they spotted destroyers Z–32 and Z–37. Under cover of darkness the two German vessels, though repeatedly strafed and straddled, managed to escape. Coastal planes had so long been practising on slow-moving submarines that they were baffled by nimble surface craft.

This battle with the destroyers concluded events of 1943 in the Bay of Biscay and its approaches. Between 1 May and 31 December, 32 U-boats had been destroyed while attempting the transit, or immediately after.[29] That was all to the good; but, in the same period of seven months, 258 U-boats entered and 247 departed the French ports, in addition to the 40 that entered and 145 that departed Kiel and Norwegian ports.[30] Thus the Bay offensive destroyed only 4½ per cent of the total movement of U-boats to and from their home ports. Moreover, in the same period of 215 days, the Germans lost a total of 183 U-boats in areas other than the Bay.

Advocates of land-based air power are fond of citing the Biscay Offensive as an argument for what the Air Forces might have done if they had been given enough planes to drench the Bay with air power and enough ships to follow up every air contact. But it seems hardly fair to blame these wants on the United States Navy

[29] The score, from the Yellow Book, is Royal Air Force, 21; Canadian Air Force, 1; Royal Navy, 5; U.S. Army Air Force, 2; U.S. Naval Air Arm, 2; and one by R.A.F. and U.S.A.F. combined. I have not counted two sunk by collision 3 May, or *U–528*, which ran afoul of a convoy on 11 May at lat. 46°55′ N, long. 14°44′ W and was sunk by H.M.S. *Fleetwood* and a Halifax.

[30] Compiled from the B.d.U. War Diary, the figures break down as follows:—

SUBMARINES ENTERING AND DEPARTING ATLANTIC PORTS
UNDER GERMAN CONTROL, MAY–DEC. 1943

French Ports	ENTERED	DEPARTED	North Sea Ports	ENTERED	DEPARTED
Brest	61	66	Kiel	0	100
Lorient	61	49	Bergen	30	27
St. Nazaire	77	78	Trondheim	7	17
La Pallice	31	33	Narvik	1	0
Bordeaux	28	21	Kristiansand	2	1
	258	247		40	145

in general, and Admiral King in particular, in view of Sir John Slessor's refusal to back up the British Admiralty in its request for 190 units from Bomber Command. Further, the relatively meager achievements of the Bay offensive are cited as a brilliant example of the "offensive" strategy of Sir Philip Joubert and General Arnold, in comparison with the "defensive" strategy of the Admiralty and the United States Navy. To obtain the decisive results that the air marshals and air generals confidently predicted, it would have been necessary to cripple the bomber offensive in Germany, and strip Atlantic convoys of their surface escorts and air support, exposing to submarine attack the troop, tanker and freighter convoys destined for the Sicilian and Italian campaigns, as well as those that were building up forces for OVERLORD.

Although the Bay offensive may have proved nothing in the eternal controversy of air vs. surface or "offensive" search-strike vs. "defensive" convoys, it helped materially in the final defeat of the U-boat. Two German admirals after the end of the war said that it was the most disconcerting offensive that they had experienced because they could not discover how or why their boats were being sunk.[31] It helped to raise the score of enemy submarines sunk in July to the record high of 45,[32] which was almost double the number of merchant ships (24) disposed of by enemy submarines that month. What a contrast to May of 1942, when the two Axis partners lost only four U-boats but sank 120 merchant ships! It was a costly offensive and deserved Sir John Slessor's tribute "to the gallantry of the crews who patrolled those grey waters day after day in all weathers, frequently under attack by enemy fighters, and who, hundreds of miles from land and with very little hope of rescue if they were shot down into the sea, went in to plant their depth charges practically at sea level against the formidable flak armament of the U-boats."

[31] Gladisch & Assmann "Report" 10 Feb. 1946 p. 161 of trans. Confirmed by Konteradm. Godt in 1955.

[32] Including 8 Italians. In May the total score of Axis subs lost is 45, but this includes 2 by collision and 3 by unknown causes, whilst all 45 in July were sunk in action.

Few sailors can think of the Bay of Biscay without humming a few lines of Andrew Cherry's old chanty, with a stanza of which it seems appropriate to close this chapter: —

> At length the wished-for morrow
>   Broke through the hazy sky;
> Absorbed in silent sorrow,
>   Each heaved a bitter sigh;
> The dismal wreck to view
>   Struck horror to the crew,
> As she lay, on that day,
>   In the Bay of Biscay, O!

CHAPTER VIII

The Central Atlantic and Azores[1]

May–August 1943

1. *CVEs, Supporting Convoys and on the Loose, May–June*

THERE WAS a disposition in some Allied quarters to regard the war against the U-boats won because of the Bay Offensive and the spirited defense of northern transatlantic convoys. That was far from the truth. On 24 May 1943 Doenitz signaled to all U-boat captains, "The situation in the North Atlantic now forces a temporary shift of operations to areas less endangered by aircraft." [2] As his actions proved, the "less endangered" regions were two areas of American responsibility, the Central Transatlantic Convoy Route and the South Atlantic; and the Indian Ocean. If the Navies had now failed the merchantmen, there would have been a tonnage slaughter comparable to that of 1942. As it was, the Central Atlantic convoy route became the scene of a major tactical triumph over the U-boats, that of the U.S. escort carrier groups.

On 26 May the Grossadmiral, having selected the horse latitudes as his best chance to fill his empty bag of merchant tonnage, ordered Group "Trutz" of 17 boats to form a north–south patrol line along the 43rd meridian between latitudes 32° and 39° N. Theoretically, he was providing a field day for the "defiant" U-boats. Their new patrol line straddled an Atlantic highway teeming with valu-

---

[1] See Vol. I 352–58 for the inauguration of the convoys, and Appendix IV below for task organizations of the CVE groups. There is a folder for each convoy in the Division of Naval History, as well as a host of Action Reports by C.O.s and aircraft pilots.

[2] Quoted in Saunders *Royal Air Force* III 46.

able targets. The United States Navy was then convoying hundreds of troop transports, fast tankers, and slow freighters crammed with military supplies, in preparation for the invasion of Sicily in July and of Italy in September.[3] Unfortunately for German hopes, the Navy was uncommonly well prepared to protect troop convoys with fast escorts and escort carriers, and as soon as Group "Trutz" was on station it became the victim of an antisubmarine offensive unique for the rapidity with which tactical innovations were introduced.

Commander in Chief Atlantic Fleet, Admiral Royal E. Ingersoll, had long been awaiting this opportunity. In January 1943 he had written to Admiral King that the central transatlantic route ran so far from Allied island bases other than Bermuda that air coverage by land-based planes could be furnished only near Bermuda and at each end. He intended to assign the new American escort carriers to this route as soon as available, but it seemed an interminable time before they were.[4] U.S.S. *Bogue*, as we have seen, had to lend a hand to defeat the North Atlantic blitz; and the next of her class to be completed, U.S.S. *Card* (Captain Isbell),[5] only finished her shakedown in early May.

"Buster" Isbell was a keen young naval air officer who had just made his fourth stripe before being given command of a new CVE group. *Card* and her destroyer screen (*Bristol, Ludlow, Woolsey*) made rendezvous off the Capes of the Chesapeake with Gibraltar-bound UGS–8A. This whale of a convoy, starting with 78 merchant ships, 12 LSTs and 9 escorts besides the escort carrier group, was beefed up to 129 merchant vessels and 19 escorts off Gibraltar. It then covered almost 70 square miles of ocean and, in tonnage,

[3] See Vol. II 271–74, and Vol. IX.

[4] Letter to Admiral King 25 Jan. 1943, Cominch files. Of the older CVEs *Santee* was on runner-interception duty in the South Atlantic and others of *Sangamon* class had been sent to the Pacific.

[5] Arnold J. Isbell, born Iowa 1899, Annapolis '20; naval aviator and specialist in aviation ordnance engineering; served in various naval aviation assignments; Sept. 1940, as C.O. of VP-54 was instrumental in survey and selection of U.S. bases in Newfoundland; C.O. N.A.S. Sitka 1942–1943; C.O. *Card* April 1943. Killed 19 March 1945 by air attack while serving temporarily in carrier *Franklin;* he had just been appointed C.O. of *Yorktown.*

had probably become the largest in history.[6] At this time, because of the vulnerability of escort carriers and their crews' lack of experience in operating them, they steamed inside the convoy, dropping astern for flight operations within visual signal distance. *Card's* planes furnished continuous daylight air cover all the way across, and on moonlight nights too; all good practice, but as yet there were no U-boats in those waters. After delivering UGS–8A safely to air coverage by Army Liberators out of Port Lyautey, Morocco, the *Card* group peeled off to support westbound Convoy GUS–8.

Transports returning from the Mediterranean carried thousands of German prisoners who had surrendered at the close of the Tunisia campaign. Because of a rumor spread through Rommel's Afrika Korps to the effect that U-boats were sinking practically every Allied ship in the Atlantic, a few stout fellows among the prisoners tried to jump ship when passing through the Straits and swim ashore, and a few had to be shot to discourage the rest.[7] Their surprise at crossing an ocean empty of U-boats was equaled only by their astonishment at beholding the skyline of New York, since Nazi propaganda had persuaded them that that proud city had already been reduced to rubble by German bombers.

Even before the safe arrival of Convoy GUS–8 in June, Admiral Ingersoll decided that close air support of central transatlantic convoys was a waste of effort; that it would be better to leave the commanders of escort carrier groups complete discretion to hunt down submarines where HF/DF fixes indicated, or to transfer their support to another convoy that needed close protection. The discretionary orders that he issued were a joy to the young carrier group commanders, making them feel as free off soundings as Paul Jones or Lord Nelson.

First to profit by this freedom of action was Captain Short of

[6] There were more ships than this in some of the West Indies and other convoys of the Seven Years' and earlier wars; the outbound Smyrna Fleet in 1693 comprised nearly 400 sail, but the average tonnage was only 150 to 300. The record of UGS–8A was broken in August 1944 when the Royal Canadian Navy escorted 167 ships safely across the North Atlantic.

[7] Capt. Roy Pfaff report on convoy GUS–8 and report on GUS–9 in Convoy and Routing Files.

Bogue, which, with flush-deck destroyers *Clemson*, *George E. Badger*, *Greene*, and *Osmond Ingram* as screen, departed Argentia 30 May with orders to conduct offensive operations in support of North African convoys, as long as logistic requirements permitted. As Captain Short analyzed the situation, his problem was a nice one: to exploit U-boat concentration . . . without moving so far away that he could not "render direct support to specific convoys." Upon reaching his initial patrol station 1 June, he decided to support westbound Convoy GUS–7A, then rounding the southern end of the "Trutz" patrol line which Doenitz had just set up. Favored as usual in these latitudes by excellent flying weather, *Bogue's* planes swept a path 120 miles broad, hoping to hit the German patrol line head on; and Doenitz was so accommodating as to shift Group "Trutz" to a new line, in order to intercept this very convoy.[8]

On the afternoon of 4 June, just as Captain Short was advised from Washington as to the new position of Group "Trutz," his Avengers sighted and attacked three U-boats in rapid succession but failed to sink any. *U–641* in particular showed such great skill in antiaircraft fire and in dodging bombs, that the squadron commander, Lieutenant Commander William M. Drane, who led the attack, was lucky to get back alive. On the same day Ensign Edward R. Hodgson USNR, pilot of a *Bogue* Avenger, saved a convoy of Africa-bound LCIs from attack by driving down nearby *U–603* with three bombs, one of which struck the submarine's jump-wire but bounced off and exploded harmlessly.

The 5th of June opened clear with a light haze, a calm sea and a soft south wind. A Wildcat piloted by Lieutenant Richard S. Rogers and an Avenger piloted by Lieutenant (jg) Alexander C. McAuslan USNR executed a well-coördinated attack on *U–217*, then some 63 miles from *Bogue*. McAuslan signaled to Rogers to attack first. The Wildcat, in three successive strafing runs, killed several gunners and started a fire in the conning tower, after which

[8] Between lats. 37°17′ and 30°36′ N, along long. 43° W. B.d.U. War Diary 1 June 1943. The Germans had accurate information, obtained from agents in Spain, of convoys that left the Mediterranean.

McAuslan dove out of the sun, releasing depth charges from an altitude of 100 feet. The U-boat plunged, and, while its stern was still high in the air, Rogers gave it a final strafing that helped it to the bottom.

This first victim of *Bogue* in her new field of activity happened to be the southernmost boat of Group "Trutz," and no more were located during the next two days. Captain Short then turned east to render close support to eastbound Convoy UGS–9, which had been diverted to escape the U-boat barrier. Konteradmiral Godt, who had been following both U-boat and convoy movements in Berlin as if playing a game of chess by telegraph, made a bad guess as to what UGS–9 would do, and it escaped without a contact. The U-boat chief then ordered Group "Trutz" to fuel from milch cow *U–488*, which was waiting for them somewhat to the north-eastward.

Captain Short, now satisfied that Convoy UGS–9 was safe, steamed back and forth, searching for more targets. At 1507 June 8, a clear and completely calm day with glassy sea, Radioman J. H. Finch of a *Bogue* Avenger, then at an altitude of 5500 feet, sighted *U–758* moving "at extremely high speed." The pilot, Lieutenant (jg) L. S. Balliett USNR, took the Avenger down in a steep dive, out of the sun. This boat happened to be the first of the German submarine fleet to be equipped with a quadruple mount of 20-mm antiaircraft guns.[9] It put up a terrific fire which caused Balliett's bombs to miss and, when a second Avenger piloted by Lieutenant (jg) W. S. Fowler USNR attacked, that plane was hit in sundry places and the radioman was wounded before it even reached the bomb-release point. Fowler bravely continued his run, dropped four depth charges from 100 feet close aboard *U–758*, pulled out with his cockpit full of smoke and the engine leaking oil.

The fight was not half over. Kapitänleutnant Helmut Manseck of *U–758*, merely shaken by Fowler's bombs, circled slowly on the surface as if unable to submerge, tempting one Wildcat pilot after another to try his luck. All were forced out of range except Lieu-

[9] B.d.U. War Diary 16 June 1943. *U–758* was heading for the Caribbean.

tenant (jg) Phil Perabo USNR who piled in, jammed the German 20-mm Oerlikons with strafing bullets, and mowed down most of the gunners. Manseck then decided it was time to dive; and as he did so, at 1528, an Avenger piloted by Lieutenant (jg) F. D. Fogde USNR delivered a load of bombs from an altitude of 70 feet, which should have been fatal. They did flood a compartment, forcing the boat to break surface ten minutes later. Two Wildcats then pounced on him but were driven off by heavy gunfire and retired, hoping for heavier support; but none was forthcoming. To the chagrin of his squadron commander, Captain Short refused to commit his last four serviceable Avengers, since he wished to reserve them for precautionary sweeps ahead of the next convoy.[10] And two of three screening destroyers which Short had dispatched to the scene of action had been withdrawn, owing to signals from the aviators that they needed no surface assistance. The third destroyer, *Clemson*, which arrived 40 minutes later, made one "scare" attack which merely pinned Manseck down until midnight. In the early hours of 9 June, he stole silently away. Heavy antiaircraft fire and smart cagey tactics saved *U–758*; and incidentally encouraged all its team-mates in the fatal belief that "fight back" doctrine was the answer to a German submariner's prayer.

On 9 June, *Bogue* began running down enemy radio bearings. Throughout that day and the next she scoured waters ahead and on both flanks of Convoy UGS–9. At dusk on the 10th, when the first Morocco-based Liberator arrived in support, Captain Short peeled off and headed west along lat. 30° N, in the hope of flushing more boats. Group "Trutz" was no longer looking for a fight, and not until 1147 June 12 [11] did one of *Bogue's* patrol teams make a fresh contact. A really solid contact it was: *U–118*, a 1600-ton milch cow cruising on the surface 20 miles astern of the carrier. It was a clear, cool day with a light northeast wind that barely ruffled the water, and a slight swell that flattened out toward noon.

The big fellow did not fight back with anything like the vigor

[10] Interview with Capt. Short and Lt. Cdr. Drane 22 June, transcribed 8 July 1943 in Air Information Office, Bureau of Aeronautics.

[11] Zone O (plus 2).

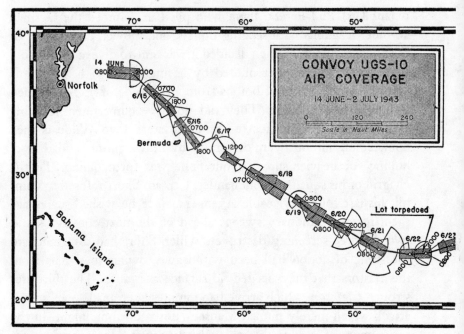

CONVOY UGS-10
AIR COVERAGE
14 JUNE – 2 JULY 1943

0   120   240
Scale in Naut. Miles

of *U–758*, but was hard to sink. Seven planes took part in the attack. Lieutenant (jg) Harry E. Fryatt USNR, who at 1205 dropped a depth bomb which exploded in the submarine's mine compartment, also dropped a life raft to swimming survivors, who waved their thanks, and *Osmond Ingram* rescued 17, including some of the wounded from *U–758*. This was probably the first kill of a milch cow in the favorite pasture of that breed near the Azores.

Captain Short swept through the now abandoned "Trutz" patrol line to cover the approach of Convoy UGS–9, but made no more contacts. And since *Bogue's* overworked catapult was damaged, and fuel was running low, Cinclant ordered the group to return home. Entering Hampton Roads 20 June, it was greeted by a signal from Admiral Ingersoll: "Well done. Results indicate hard work and thorough training." [12]

Considering the increased antiaircraft armament of some of the

[12] During most of this cruise the wind had varied from 8 knots down to dead calm, planes had to be recovered with a wind of 18 to 20 knots over the flight deck, and practically all launchings had to be made by the catapult, which had become dangerous to operate.

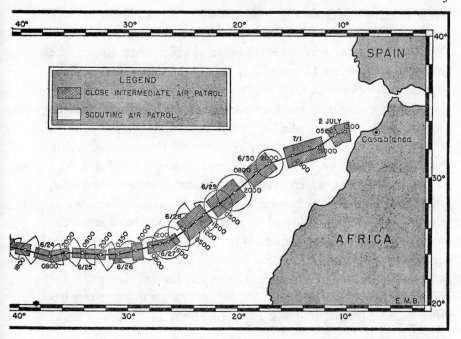

submarines encountered by *Bogue's* aviators, they had indeed done well. The escorting destroyers had not helped very much, simply because there were not enough to perform the double task of screening the carrier and assisting aircraft to make kills. Shortage of United States escorts was still a problem and would so continue through 1943, although in less degree after the destroyer escort divisions began to operate in August.[13]

Doenitz had lost only one submarine out of Group "Trutz," together with the big supply boat; but the group had not sunk a single Allied vessel. He now set up a new "Trutz" concentration, of 15 boats in three north–south lines 20 miles apart, with the center 850 miles east of Bermuda, in the hope of catching convoys in mid-Atlantic. As usual, HF/DF fixes on their transmissions to Berlin gave Tenth Fleet and Admiralty rough approximations of their positions.

Escort carrier *Santee* (Captain Harold F. Fick), now released

[13] According to Cinclant War Diary, Cortdiv 6, departing Hampton Roads 16 Aug. 1943, was the first to get into action.

from hunting raiders in the South Atlantic, furnished almost continuous air cover to 70-ship Convoy UGS–10, which departed New York 13 June. It was routed south to lat. 22° N in order to clear the new "Trutz" barrier. Ill disciplined, some of the ships failed to keep station, showed lights, had one bad collision, and broke radio silence with a transmission of such character as to indicate that an enemy agent was concealed on board one of the merchantmen. *U–572*, outward bound to harry convoys off the Guianas, would have passed Convoy UGS–10 wide and missed it but for one of these transmissions, which gave Oberleutnant Günther Kummetat, the U-boat's skipper, a beeline to a profitable target. Even so, he should not have been allowed to penetrate the screen of seven destroyers and two minesweepers, as he did, exploding two torpedoes on French naval tanker *Lot*. She sank in three minutes on 22 June with loss of 23 officers and men. Destroyers hunted Kummetat for five hours but he got away and made more havoc in other seas before being brought to book by a Liberator off Trinidad on 3 August.

Admiral Doenitz, exasperated by the failure of Group "Trutz" to intercept convoys, ordered these boats eastward on 21 June. *Card*, breaking off from Convoy GUS–8 that evening to scour the reported positions of these submarines naturally drew a blank. Group "Trutz" was now ordered to set up a new barrier south of Flores. After this, too, had been successfully evaded by two westbound convoys, the group was dissolved 29 June and divided into three small packs of four boats each, called "Geier," to operate west of Gibraltar and off the coast of Portugal.[14]

2. *The Azores Happy Hunting Ground, July–August*

Doenitz had not abandoned the Central Atlantic. Although no organized patrol line replaced the frustrated "Trutz," on 12 July there were sixteen U-boats, including several milch cows, in waters

[14] See section 3 of this chapter.

east and south of the Azores. Some were in transit to or from the South Atlantic, others were fueling; and only one, *U–183*, was patrolling between Santa Maria and the Formigas Rocks. These were the next targets for the escort carriers. Battles between them and the submarines provided some of the finest actions of the naval war.

The series of kills that we are about to record was made possible by a tactical transition: the evolution of the close-support escort carrier group into a roving convoy support group, and finally into an independent hunter-killer group. *Bogue* had shown the way; and after Captain Isbell departed Casablanca with *Card* on 9 June 1943 he received orders "that it was not necessary to keep a continuous umbrella over the convoy, and that we could operate independently against any reported concentration (of U-boats) within striking distance, as long as we could get back to the convoy before the concentration could reach it.[15] Thus, instead of hanging on the flanks of a convoy all the way across the ocean, a carrier group could go a-roving in search of game on orders from Cinclant or according to the group commander's judgment.

The earliest kills as a result of roving tactics were scored by the *Core* and *Santee* groups south of the Azores in mid-July 1943. *Core*, commanded by Captain Marshall R. Greer, an experienced naval aviator who had supervised her construction at Tacoma, stood out from the Capes of the Chesapeake 27 June on her first war cruise. Screened by destroyers *Bulmer*, *George E. Badger* and *Barker*, she remained within hailing distance of 61-ship Convoy UGS–11 until 11 July when it was about 700 miles south of São Miguel. Captain Greer then received a signal from Cinclant to join westbound Convoy GUS–9, hitherto covered by the *Santee* group.

On the afternoon of 13 July one of *Core's* Wildcat-Avenger patrol teams, having reached a point about 720 miles SSW of Fayal, sighted the 1600-ton tanker *U–487*. The German crew, amusing themselves by pulling on board a floating bale of cotton, were

[15] Capt. Isbell Interview Nov. 1943 in Division of Naval History.

completely surprised; but discipline was quickly established and the deck gunners shot down the Wildcat. Its pilot, Lieutenant (jg) Earl H. Steiger USNR, was never recovered. Lieutenant Commander Charles W. Brewer, *Core's* squadron commander, was already on the scene with three planes, one of which dropped four bombs. *U–487* went down; 33 survivors were recovered.

Three days later, 16 July, the *Core* group made a second kill. Lieutenant Robert P. Williams USNR on dawn patrol reported a U-boat 842 miles SW by W of Flores. This was *U–67* looking for a "drink" of diesel oil after an unproductive patrol between the Caribbean and the Chesapeake Capes. At 0511 Williams delivered a bombing attack that needed no follow-up except for rescue. Destroyer *McCormick*, reaching the scene at 0630, could find only three submariners afloat. On the morning of 17 July Captain Greer, believing that Convoy GUS–9 was safe for the rest of the homeward passage, headed southeast.

We may now return to *Santee* (Captain Fick) which, with destroyers *Bainbridge*, *Overton* and *MacLeish*, had been equally successful. When relieved from support of GUS–9 on 12 July, this group had been sent toward the Azores in the hope of intercepting U-boats which were operating through that area. An Avenger-Wildcat team, patrolling about 150 miles north of the carrier at 0803 July 14, sighted *U–160*. *Santee's* air squadron was now equipped with the homing torpedo "Fido," for which a new form of attack had been worked out. The Wildcat forced the sub to dive; the Avenger, piloted by Lieutenant (jg) John H. Ballantine USNR, dropped a Fido which quickly found its target. *U–160* went to the bottom with all hands.

Next victim was another 740-tonner, *U–509*, sighted on the surface at 0818 July 15 about 180 miles south of Santa Maria. Again the Wildcat forced the boat down and the Avenger dropped the fatal Fido. There were no survivors.

The dozen U-boats remaining south of the Azores had learned their lesson; warned by Spanish steamers that American escort carriers were abroad, they pulled out to the north; *Santee* had an un-productive week. But on 24 July at 0819 one of her patrol teams encountered *U–373*, 133 miles west of Madeira. This boat was sup-posed to mine the mouth of the Wadi Sebou, which leads up to Port Lyautey. If successful, this would have been very annoying to ships supplying that important Moroccan airfield. *U–373* was sufficiently damaged to head back for France and the Sebou continued to flow unvexed to the sea.

Captain Fick's *Santee* group now joined westbound Convoy GUS–10. Upon its reaching mid-ocean on 30 July, a Wildcat pilot sighted two submarines; *U–43* on a mining mission to Lagos on the Gold Coast, then doubling as milch cow and preparing to fuel *U–403*. The fighter plane's strafing runs forced both boats to sub-merge; but while the larger still had decks awash an Avenger, piloted by Lieutenant (jg) Robert F. Richmond USNR, dropped two depth bombs and a Fido near enough to do the trick. *U–43* was literally "hoist with his own petard." His mines exploded and the boat disintegrated.

Unfortunately for the future success of Fido, Doenitz was on to him; and in a signal of 5 August warned his submarine commanders of "new, more dangerous bombs" that their enemies were carrying. "Do not report too much bad news," he added, "so as not to depress the other boats; every radio message goes the rounds of the crew in every boat." [16]

Bogue, with her old screen (less *Greene*), but a new com-mander, Captain Joseph B. Dunn, supported eastbound Convoy UGS–12. She remained within hailing distance of the convoy for only 7 out of 21 days on this passage, spending the other fortnight running down distant HF/DF fixes. These efforts were unproduc-tive; but just as the group was rejoining the convoy 23 July, at a point 194 miles SW of São Miguel, destroyer *George E. Badger* (Lieutenant Thomas H. Byrd USNR) made a sound contact at 1100 yards. It was *U–613*, bound for Jacksonville with a load of mines.

[16] Addendum to B.d.U. War Diary 5 Aug. 1943 p. 107.

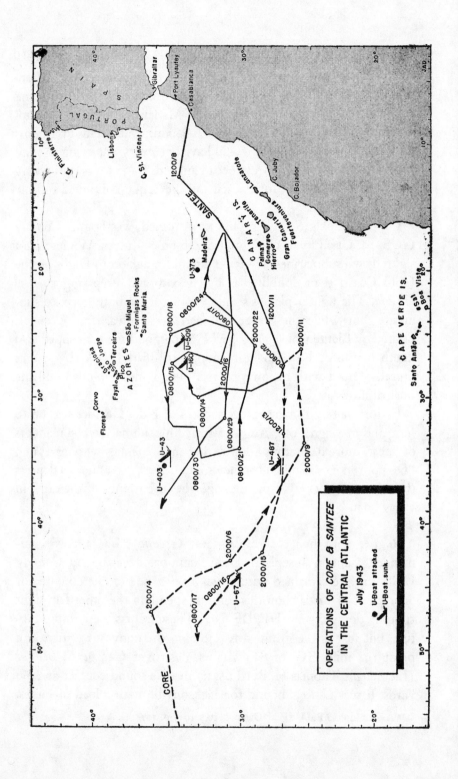

OPERATIONS OF *CORE & SANTEE*
IN THE CENTRAL ATLANTIC
July 1943

● U-Boat attacked
⚓ U-Boat sunk.

The day was clear and sunny, the sea smooth, the wind only force 3 At 0923 the destroyer dropped a pattern of eight depth charges Relocating the boat at a depth of 600 feet, Byrd dropped two more patterns, opened range, obtained another contact at 1012, used both rudder and engines skillfully to keep within the submarine's turning circle (normally much smaller than that of a destroyer), and delivered a third attack seven minutes later. Shortly were heard sounds that are music to a submarine hunter's ears — the horrible roarings, rumblings, cracklings, belchings and bubblings that mark the breaking-up of a U-boat.[17] Debris appeared on the surface: shattered woodwork, mattresses and clothing, dismembered and mutilated human bodies. Finally (appropriate conclusion), the sea spewed up a German translation of Poe's *Murders in the Rue Morgue.*

At noon 23 July, when the *Bogue* group was about 55 miles from Convoy UGS-12, the gunner of an Avenger piloted by Lieutenant (jg) Robert L. Stearns USNR sighted two U-boats cruising board-and-board only a few yards apart. These were 740-ton *U-527*, going home from the Gulf of Mexico and fueling from *U-648*, a 500-tonner acting as relief supply boat. The latter dove in time to escape attack, while *U-527* tried to slide under a nearby fog bank. Its skipper, Kapitänleutnant Herbert Uhlig, who had successfully dodged Catalinas in the Gulf of Mexico, miscalculated the speed of Avengers. Stearns quickly climbed to 600 feet, nosed down from dead astern of the boat, and dropped depth charges so accurately that most of the Germans on deck were blown overboard and the boat was sunk. Thirteen survivors, including Uhlig, were recovered by a destroyer.

Bogue broke off from the convoy 26 July on dispatch orders from Cinclant, cruised about Madeira without result, and headed for Casablanca just as the *Card* group got into the picture again.[18]

[17] These were well described by the classically educated skipper of a British corvette in the onomatopoeia which Aristophanes used for a froggy underwater chorus in *Frogs* 249: "pompholugopaphlasmasin." Roskill *The War at Sea* II, 337*n*.
[18] TG 21.14 Report of A/S Operations 27 July-15 Sept. 1943; interview with Capt. Isbell 15 Nov. 1943 in files of Air Technical Analysis Div. Deputy C.N.O. for Air; conversations with other officers of *Card*.

She had departed Hampton Roads 27 July, loosely attached to Convoy UGS–13. *Card's* planes had just been repainted a bluish white, which the squadron commander thought would be a better camouflage in those waters than the previous "duck egg" scheme, and she was provided with a new screen – destroyers *Barry*, *Goff* and *Borie*. These 22-year-old "flush-deckers" were fragile and short-legged; but, pending arrival of the much-desired destroyer escorts, they made a fair screen for escort carriers because of their speed and their veteran crews. *Borie's* officers, in particular, had "blood in the eye" because they had seen several merchant ships torpedoed but had not caught one U-boat. A naval constructor who had come on board at the time of their last upkeep had found members of the wardroom practising marksmanship by throwing bowie knives at the bulletin board and dishes at mess attendants. That would come in useful before long.

Card took on more fuel oil at Bermuda, joined Convoy UGS–13 August 1, topped off destroyers from the escort tanker, and next day peeled off to hunt. Captain Isbell's plan was to charge straight through the reported center of any submarine concentration, with patrols flying 100 miles ahead and on each flank. These tactics resulted in a five-day battle.

On 3 August at 1628, a *Card* patrol team encountered *U–66* at a point 457 miles WSW of Flores.[19] The veteran skipper of this boat, Kapitänleutnant Friedrich Markworth, was homeward bound after a patrol of almost 14 weeks, and had made two kills off the East Coast. Wildcat strafing fatally wounded his officer of the deck and the men topside rang the diving alarm, but the skipper came roaring up the hatch, belayed the dive and ordered guns manned. An Avenger piloted by Lieutenant (jg) Richard L. Cormier USNR now encouraged the boat to dive with two depth bombs, followed by a Fido which missed the scent. Markworth surfaced to fight back and was badly wounded; his next in command then took the boat down. He surfaced that night to radio Doenitz that he needed assistance and was ordered to rendezvous with *U–117*, the nearest refueler.

[19] Time Zone P (plus 3).

The two boats met shortly before midnight 6 August, when Ober-leutnant Frerks came on board to relieve Markworth.

At 0648 next morning, 7 August, Lieutenant (jg) A. H. Sal-lenger USNR, pilot of a *Card* Avenger, flying 83 miles west of the carrier, spotted the two submarines at a point 320 miles due west of Flores, steaming parallel to each other about 500 yards apart. It was a glaringly bright morning and Sallenger had no fighter cover, but he boldly dove down-sun, made a perfect straddle on *U–66* and delivered a few machine-gun blasts on the deck of the big milch cow. After radioing to Captain Isbell for support, Sallenger hovered out of range for about 25 minutes until three more planes appeared, when *U–66* started to submerge; he swooped down again to drop a Fido, through a hail of fire from *U–117*. This big boat had the new German antiaircraft armament, but Sallenger reported that its gun-fire was "rotten — all around us, but no hits."

U–66 got away again, but *U–117's* afterdeck was ruptured by one of the depth bombs intended for its consort. Unable to sub-merge, *U–117* was a "sitting duck" for two Avengers who dis-patched it with depth bombs about an hour after the original sighting.

Next morning, 8 August, Lieutenant Sallenger's Avenger and a Wildcat piloted by Ensign John F. Sprague USNR did not return on schedule. Captain Isbell turned *Card* toward the center of their patrol area, where destroyer *Barry* found Sallenger and his gunner sitting on a rubber raft. The aviators had run into another pair of submarines, *U–664* and *U–262*, which had just battled their way out of the Bay of Biscay and were full of prunes and vinegar. They made two shell hits on the Avenger, which Sallenger had to ditch, though not before straddling *U–664* with two bombs, *U–262* shot down the Wildcat, killing young Sprague and Sallenger's radioman. Both boats escaped.

The skipper of *U–664*, Kapitänleutnant Adolph Graef, an un-popular and unskillful martinet, was amusing himself by playing chess. His game was interrupted at about 2000 by a shout from the watch officer that a big tanker was just visible in the twilight. Graef tried three shots at the "tanker" and missed — fortunately for her, as the target was escort carrier *Card*, whose crew did not even sight the torpedo wakes.

At 1216 next day, 9 August, 65 miles from the carrier, Lieutenant (jg) G. G. Hogan USNR spotted *U–664* on the surface charging batteries. Captain Isbell and his squadron commander, Lieutenant Commander Carl E. Jones USNR, had profitably spent the previous night working out tactics to smother U-boats which insisted on fighting it out with aircraft. The patrol team now numbered three, a Wildcat and two Avengers, one armed with two instantaneous 500-pound bombs, the other with two depth bombs and one torpedo. The 500-pounders proved a great success. Hogan dropped one which exploded close on the U-boat's bow, spraying its deck with fragments and discouraging its already disgruntled crew. Lieutenant Norman D. Hodson USNR strafed ten seconds later. Within a minute, just as the submarine dove, Lieutenant (jg) R. H. Forney USNR dropped two depth bombs with 25-foot settings. Exploding beneath the unhappy boat, they blew it back to the surface. Graef managed to take his boat down about 50 feet, but it leaked so badly that after ten or fifteen minutes he decided to blow tanks and surface. There, met by more strafing and bombing, he gave the word to abandon, and at 1420 the boat up-ended and sank. The planes dropped rafts and lifejackets. *Borie*, sent to rescue survivors, recovered 44 men and might have done even better if another U-boat had not launched five torpedoes at her while she was so engaged. Next time she would not be so eager to save enemy lives.

Card, after taking survivors on board, headed north of the Azores, where HF/DF had ascertained that Doenitz was now routing his outward-bound boats. On the afternoon of 11 August, a Wildcat-Avenger team [20] sighted *U–525*, a 740-ton supply submarine, 376 miles WNW of Corvo, drove it down by strafing, then depth-charged and finished it off with a Fido. There were no survivors.

[20] Pilots Ens. Jack Stewart USNR and Lt. (jg) C. G. Hewitt USNR.

Captain Isbell's group entered Casablanca 16 August to await a homeward-bound convoy, while the *Core* group patrolled south of the Azores. But before relating their next missions, we shall describe the very mixed-up cruise of a newcomer to the flattop fleet, U.S.S. *Croatan* (Captain John B. Lyon).

Croatan, with a screen of old flush-deck destroyers, *Paul Jones*, *Parrott* and *Belknap*, departed Hampton Roads 6 August 1943 as roving support to Convoy UGS–14. On the 12th she was diverted to hunt a submarine which had been engaged by weather-reporting Coast Guard cutter *Menemsha* at a point near the great-circle track from Bermuda to Flores.[21] *Menemsha* lay 155 miles distant when Captain Lyon got the word; his planes searched as thoroughly as they could in very squally weather, but found "neither hide nor hair" of the U-boat. The group rejoined UGS–14 on 15 August, as it approached the Azores, and *Croatan's* screen was refueled from the escort oiler.

Captain Lyon stayed with the convoy until the night of 19 August, when he received orders from Admiral Ingersoll to hunt northeast of the Azores. No organized pack was operating there but several boats happened to be passing, including Japanese transport submarine *I–151*, which was looking for *U–161* in order to pick up a pilot for the Bay of Biscay passage. *Croatan's* fliers did not have the good fortune to encounter that interesting couple; but on the afternoon of 21 August a patrol team sighted *U–134* on its way home after shooting down Navy blimp *K–74* off Key West on 18 July.[22] Neither plane succeeded in damaging *U–134* after a fight lasting 55 minutes. But three days later, off Cape Finisterre, British Coastal Command bombers would finish the colorful career of this U-boat.

"Old Crow," as the bluejackets were beginning to call their three-month-old *Croatan*, had more than her share of bad luck. On the afternoon of 21 August two Wildcats crashed on recovery and that night a main fuel pump broke down, reducing her speed to 10

[21] *Menemsha* sighted the submarine 600 yards on her starboard bow near midnight 11 Aug., took it under gunfire; but the boat, *U–760*, slipped away in a fog.
[22] See Chapter XI, sec. 3.

knots. While she was crawling at this rate under bright moonlight, the surface search radar conked out, making her an easy torpedo target; but a protecting angel had seen to it that no U-boats were about. Next day the catapult broke down, the wind blew only 4 knots, and it was impossible to launch planes.[23] So Captain Lyon made for Casablanca.

Temporary repairs effected, *Croatan* left port 30 August, made air contact with the *Card* group on 2 September, supported west-bound Convoy GUS–13 for three days, then reversed course for a sweep south of the Azores. At about 92 miles SSW of Santa Maria she almost scored. Lieutenant (jg) Joseph W. Steere USNR, on noon patrol 9 September, sighted *U–214* on the surface 25 miles from the carrier. He ducked into a cloud, determined by his radar that the boat was heading southwest, emerged, called for fighter support, but attacked before it arrived since the boat showed signs of submerging. The German gunners loosed a terrific salvo which made several hits and caused the Avenger's four depth charges to miss. Steere saved his plane and the lives of his crew, although his engine had been damaged and the hydraulic system knocked out by exploding shells. No fewer than five Avengers and four Wild-cats searched for *U–214* until sundown, but in vain; the boat continued unharmed to the Panama Canal approaches where it laid mines off Colon breakwater and got home safely.[24] "This action," reported Captain Lyon to Admiral King, "emphasizes the fact that if a submarine is not disabled by the first attack there is small chance of reinforcements effecting a kill." With a screen of only three vessels he could not do much in the way of surface hunting.

The *Croatan* group entered Hampton Roads 22 September with only experience to show for its first war cruise of 43 days, during which the carrier had logged 15,300 miles.

We shall now return to the *Core* group which had relieved *Card* in the happy hunting ground off the Azores. Captain Greer's avia-

[23] The Avengers, reported Capt. Lyon, needed a 30-knot wind over the deck for normal launching with full fuel and bomb load, and 24 knots for recovering. These figures had already been reduced on the other CVEs by practice.
[24] See Chapter XI, sec. 3.

tors, patrolling well ahead of Convoy UGS-15 on the morning of 23 August, sighted *U-84* searching for a milch cow about 750 miles southwest of Fayal. That U-boat escaped, though not for long. The next one encountered, *U-185*, also looking for a drink after a cruise off Brazil, was not so fortunate. Spotted at 0639 [25] August 24 by Lieutenant (jg) M. G. O'Neill USNR, as the early morning sun was reflected by its light gray conning tower, *U-185* became the object of a well-planned attack by Squadron Commander Brewer, in which Lieutenant Robert P. Williams USNR, O'Neill and several other pilots took part. As *U-185* began to go down and its crew darted topside, a strange drama was enacted below, which a survivor related. Kapitänleutnant Höltring, rescued by *U-185* after his boat (*U-604*) had been sunk off the coast of Brazil,[26] was lying in his bunk with pistol close at hand, and in the forward torpedo room were two badly wounded members of his former crew. As water flooded the battery compartment, releasing chlorine gas, Höltring burst in on the torpedo room, pistol in hand. The two wounded men begged him to shoot them. He obliged, then blew his own brains out. Attacking planes withheld fire from the wretched submariners clustering about the conning tower, and 35 were rescued.

At about noon the same day, 24 August, another *Core* Avenger piloted by Lieutenant (jg) William A. Felter USNR sighted *U-84* (unsuccessfully attacked on the 23rd) emerging from a rain squall ten miles from the spot where *U-185* had gone down. This boat was returning from an unproductive patrol off Cuba. Not yet indoctrinated with the "fight back" technique, the skipper took his boat down as Felter banked for the bombing run; but a Fido got him.

Core, already ordered home for repairs to her turbines, which vibrated dangerously at any speed above 12 knots, now relinquished the Azorean hunting ground to *Card*. Captain Isbell's group had departed Casablanca, with no convoy responsibilities, on the scent of a submarine concentration north and east of the Azores. On 27

---

[25] Zone O (plus 2) time.
[26] See Chapter XII, sec. 3.

August *U–508* was sighted by Lieutenant Hogan's Avenger, armed (according to a new attack plan) with one 500-pound bomb and one homing torpedo. The boat maneuvered so briskly as to avoid damage by the 500-pounder, and dove so deep that Fido could not connect. Half an hour later, at 1102, Lieutenant Ralph W. Long USNR sighted 740-ton *U–847*. That boat, the center of a fueling group since 19 August, had already supplied five others with fuel and provisions.[27] Two Wildcats attacked and forced the boat down; Lieutenant Long dropped a homing torpedo just ahead of the swirl, and *U–847* was finished.[28]

This was the sixteenth submarine, and the eighth milch cow, that Admiral Ingersoll's escort carrier groups had accounted for in 98 days. During the same period, the U-boats had managed to sink only one merchantman (tanker *Lot*) in the Central Atlantic, and had shot down only three planes.

The vital importance of this destruction of supply and tanker submarines is proved by German records. By the end of May 1943, "U-tankers of Types XIV and X had refueled and replenished nearly 400 U-boats in the waters south and north of the Azores, losing only one of their number in the process. But by 12 June only one out of the four tankers in the area was left, and some of the larger boats had to be sent out as auxiliary tankers. . . . Tanker losses persisted and by August only three of the twelve 'milch cows' remained." [29] Doenitz's War Diary for 5 August states that the loss of three milch cows which were to have supplied U-boats returning from the Caribbean and South Atlantic had forced him to order them home prematurely. "There are no more reserve tankers available," he recorded; "only the most essential supply operations can be carried out, and then only on an outward passage." [30] U-boat operations in the Central Atlantic had to be abandoned much earlier than had been expected, owing to the lack of milch cows.

*   *   *

[27] B.d.U. War Diary 18 and 29 Aug. 1943.
[28] The explosions were heard on board *U–508*.
[29] Frank *Sea Wolves* p. 181.
[30] B.d.U. War Diary pp. 100, 144 of translation for 2nd half of 1943.

Thus, the operations that we have been describing in this and in the previous chapter had a deleterious effect on all future U-boat activities in the Central and South Atlantic, in the Caribbean, and in the Indian Ocean. Admiral Ingersoll's acumen in sending the escort carrier groups against fueling concentrations deserves the highest praise.

3. *Finisterre to Cape Juby, July–August* [31]

The two United States Army Liberator squadrons under Lieutenant Colonel Roberts, which shifted their base of operations from the United Kingdom to Morocco in March 1943, found plenty to do. Navy Catalinas of Captain T. A. Turner's Fleet Air Wing 15, based on Port Lyautey and Agadir, and R.A.F. planes based on Gibraltar,[32] had kept approaches to the Strait clear of U-boats for several months; but it was correctly anticipated that Doenitz would have another try in that direction as soon as he was forced to haul out of the North Atlantic. The arrival of the B–24s made it possible for Rear Admiral Frank J. Lowry,[33] Commander Moroccan Sea Frontier, to fly air patrols over a thousand miles out, to the eastern Azores, Cape Finisterre and Madeira. As early as 22 March, Lieutenant Sanford's "Tidewater Tillie," which had scored in the Bay Offensive, sank *U–524* about 160 miles northwest of Porto Santo.

B–24 pilots wished to continue the sort of operations to which they had been accustomed in the Bay of Biscay; but "search-strike" tactics were deemed unsuitable by a naval officer whose primary duty was to protect convoys. Nevertheless, "by informal agreement with understanding Naval commands . . . the group was given increasingly substantial freedom in planning its missions." [34]

[31] John R. Pellam "Analysis of A/S Warfare in Moroccan Sea Frontier, 1942–43," a study made for Asworg in 1943; "A.A.F. Anti-Submarine Command"; Henry Grattan "Three Historical Essays." The Liberators in the Moroccan Sea Frontier were organized as 480th Group A.A.F.
[32] At Gibraltar in July there were 12 Wellingtons, 32 Hudsons and 12 Catalinas.
[33] Brief biography in Vol. IX 325*n*. Relieved 26 Sept. 1943 by Commo. B. V. McCandlish.
[34] Craven & Cate II 398.

A difficulty in that area, however, was the division of authority between R.A.F. at Gibraltar and Commander Moroccan Sea Frontier at Port Lyautey. The one controlled north–south convoys between Britain, Gibraltar and West Africa; the other, convoys between America and the Mediterranean. It was something like having two traffic policemen at the same crossroads; and a wonder it is that there were no serious collisions. Both American and British air commanders in the Mediterranean theater agreed in early April 1943 that, with the invasion of Sicily coming up, operational control of all Allied aircraft in the Moroccan Sea Frontier should be transferred to the Royal Air Force commander at Gibraltar, who was responsible to Air Chief Marshall Tedder, top Allied air commander in the Mediterranean. But this proposal was vetoed by Admiral Hewitt, who felt that the logistic supply line to General Eisenhower's army in Africa must remain under American control and responsibility. Admiral King concurred.[35]

After a barren three months of convoy coverage and distant patrolling, the Army Liberators began to find targets. Doenitz had just broken up Group "Trutz," into three groups "Geier" of three or four boats each. These were ordered to cover waters southwest of Cape Finisterre through which convoys between Great Britain and the Mediterranean and Africa had to pass. The first "Geier" to be sunk, though not the first to be attacked, was *U–951*, a victim of 1st Lieutenant W. S. McDonnel's B–24 on 7 July, patrolling about 300 miles WSW of Lisbon. The second, *U–232*, was attacked next day by 1st Lieutenant James H. Darden's Liberator, about 200 miles northwest of the Tagus estuary. His microwave radar gave him a contact at seven miles; using cloud cover he roared down suddenly and began to be hammered by heavy flak at a range of 300 yards. The bombardier, 2nd Lieutenant C. J. Froccaro USA, dropped four 650-lb. bombs from an altitude of only 50 feet. The German deck crew huddled in the conning tower

[35] Grattan "Three Essays" III 44–45; conversations with Rear Admiral Low, 1951, and Capt. Vest (who attended a conference on the subject), 1954; Admiral Hewitt, 1957. The R.A.F. command at Gibraltar.

until plumes of spray had subsided, then sprang to their guns and jammed the bomb doors of the Liberator as it returned for a second attack. Froccaro, although wounded, managed to force the doors open before the third run, during which the two remaining bombs were dropped so accurately that the submarine actually broke in two, the after part rising twelve feet out of the water and rolling over. No survivors were visible.

The "Geier" groups had been so harried by land-based bombers, without encountering a single merchant ship, that Doenitz on the evening of 8 July gave them permission to return to France at their skippers' discretion. It was high time. On the 9th *U–642* and *U–953* were attacked by United States Army Liberators and badly shaken up, and *U–435* was sunk by a British Wellington out of Gibraltar. The eight remaining "Geiers" managed to transit the Bay of Biscay safely. But a 740-ton boat which had just sortied from Lorient, *U–506*, was caught on 12 July 320 miles west of Finisterre and sunk by a far-ranging Army Liberator out of Port Lyautey, piloted by 2nd Lieutenant Ernst Salm USA.

The only convoy to be attacked off Moroccan Sea Frontier in July was OS–51, United Kingdom to Freetown, when threading the narrow passage between Fuerteventura Island of the Canaries and Cape Juby, Africa. A lone wolf, *U–135*, was there lying in wait. On 15 July it torpedoed a freighter. H.M.S. *Rochester*, *Mignonette* and *Balsam* of the screen forced the boat to the surface after dropping 90 depth charges, and were exchanging gunfire with it when an Agadir-based Catalina piloted by Lieutenant (jg) Robert J. Finnie USNR appeared, routed the submariners from their guns with .30-caliber machine-gun bursts, and dropped four depth bombs. Covered by the strafing flying boat, *Balsam* then moved in and rammed *U–135*. There were 42 survivors.[36]

Coastal Command and Moroccan Sea Frontier between them had so effectively protected the north–south convoys off the Portuguese

[36] Lt. Finnie "A/S Action by Aircraft" 15 July 1943; in the Yellow Book he is not credited with his part.

coast, as well as those between America and Gibraltar or Casa-blanca, that Doenitz was at his wits' end. The U-boat command war diary for 11 July contains this significant entry: —

The ocean over which the U.S.–Gibraltar convoys operate permits them to make radical evading movements without unduly prolonging their passage. Consequently there seems no purpose in sending another group to intercept U.S.–Gibraltar convoys, as long as the boats are unable to detect radar transmissions from enemy aircraft. . . . Presence of escort aircraft carriers with the convoys make operating conditions so difficult for the U-boats that they are not likely to meet with success.

Shortly after, the Germans began to patrol Moroccan Sea Frontier with 4-engined FW–200s, their counterpart to the B–24. On 17 August one of Colonel Roberts's Liberators had a battle with two FW–200s, one of which was shot down and the other damaged; but the B–24 crew had to ditch; most of them were rescued. Two other B–24s were lost during the month, but so were four more of the big German bombers.

In the Atlantic as a whole,[37] August was a banner month for anti-submarine warfare. For the second time since the war began, more submarines than merchant ships were sunk; 26 of the former, as against only four of the latter. It really looked as if we had them "on the ropes," but Doenitz was not yet ready to throw in the sponge.

[37] Including Arctic, Baltic and Mediterranean.

CHAPTER IX

North Atlantic Crossings

September–November 1943

1. *Troop and Tanker Convoys to Britain* [1]

BY MID–MAY 1943 Operation BOLERO, the build-up of American armed forces to Britain for an Allied invasion of the Continent, was being handled by the Cunarders *Queen Mary* and *Queen Elizabeth; Mauretania, Aquitania*, French line *Pasteur* and Canadian *Empress of Scotland* also participated. The "Queens," of 81,235 and 83,675 tons respectively, had been in that service since August 1942, when their troop-carrying capacity was increased from 6000 to 15,000 men each. They maintained a steady speed of 28½ knots, which meant that no escort vessel could keep up with them; nor were any necessary.[2] Every so often the Germans claimed to have sunk one; but so far as can be ascertained no U-boats ever got a crack at them.

By September 1943 the Queens and their consorts could no longer cope with the increased stream of American troops. On the 5th, four days before the Salerno landings, the first of a new series of all-American troop convoys departed New York for the United Kingdom.

These convoys, designated UT, traveled at 14 or 15 knots, which in itself was almost enough to escape submarine attack. For even better protection they were given a strong escort of American destroyers, fast minesweepers or destroyer escorts, with a battleship

[1] Reports by convoy commodores and escort commanders in Convoy & Routing files; first draft narrative "History of Convoy and Routing" in Naval Administration series, pp. 102–3.
[2] Roskill *The War at Sea* II.

added on the chance that a German raider might get loose. So fast and well protected were the troop convoys that their crossings were almost completely uneventful; but, as indispensable feeders for the coming campaign of France, they merit a place in history.

UT–2, second of these troop convoys, consisted of 20 transports and troopships. It was escorted by 9 destroyers, 4 fast mine-sweepers, a destroyer escort and battleship *Nevada*, veteran of World War I and of Pearl Harbor, in which Rear Admiral Carleton F. Bryant, the escort commander, flew his two-star flag.[3] Departing New York 5 September 1943, it swung north to latitude 55°, and made a ten-day passage to the North Channel between Ireland and Scotland. Not one submarine contact was made, although Doenitz was then moving Group "Leuthen" into position for his September blitz; and a similar evasion was made by the same ships returning in late September as Convoy TU–2.

UT–3, the next eastbound, with the venerable 32-year-old battleship *Arkansas* as Rear Admiral Cooke's flagship, successfully skirted the battleground of Liberators vs. U-boats, southwest of Iceland, in October. Its immunity from attack was the result of skillful routing by Tenth Fleet close to the northern Azores, and by the Admiralty east of the chop line.

Rear Admiral Cooke [4] shared the conduct of these troop convoys with Rear Admiral Bryant; Convoy TU–5, under his command, was the only one of this series to be threatened. On 23 December 1943 it was sighted about 300 miles west of Rockall Bank by *U–471*, which took *Nevada* to be a cruiser, selected a target from the main body of the convoy, fired a torpedo which missed so wide

[3] See Vol. III 108–10 for picture and account of *Nevada* at Pearl Harbor, and Vol. II 176 for an earlier successful handling of a convoy in a tight spot by Admiral Bryant. Born in New York City 1892, Naval Academy '14, served in *Wyoming* in World War I, M.S. Lehigh Univ. 1921, specializing in ordnance, and performed several duties in that field; gunnery officer *Saratoga* 1927–30; C.O. *Oahu* and *Stewart* on Asiatic Station 1933–34; C.O. *Charleston* 1937–39 and *Arkansas* 1941–43; commanded a gunfire support group in OVERLORD and DRAGOON 1944; retired as Vice Admiral 1946.

[4] Henry D. Cooke, b. Washington 1879, Naval Academy '03, a destroyer commander prior to World War I in which he was C.O. of destroyers in convoy duty. After various commands between wars he retired in 1939 but returned to active duty to command troop convoys.

that nobody saw it, and was unable to catch up with the convoy to try another shot. The same day, when engaged in a hopeless stern chase, *U–471* was badly damaged by a Coastal Command Liberator, but survived.

Second only in importance to the troop convoys were the oil convoys, most of which were sent to Great Britain after the Italian armistice. The CU (Curaçao–United Kingdom) convoys had been sailing throughout 1943.[5] In mid-October Convoy & Routing Tenth Fleet made a change; all tankers from the Dutch West Indies followed the then safe East Coast route to New York, where they were formed into convoys with a screen of new destroyer escorts. These convoys were routed along the 40th parallel to a point about 380 miles west of Flores, thence to Liverpool. When Convoy UC–6 — 24 ships and 6 destroyer escorts — which departed England 18 November, made a submarine contact a few days later, the escort commander disappointed his skippers by refusing to let them peel off in search of the U-boat; he kept them in a close screen around his empty tankers, and soon left the submarine well astern. That was doctrine in tanker convoys.

2. *The Zaunkönig Blitz on Convoy ON–202* [6]

In a speech to the House of Commons on 21 September 1943, Winston Churchill announced, with unusual gusto even for him, that "for the four months which ended on 18th September, no merchant vessel was sunk by enemy action in the North Atlantic." Ship losses in August, he continued, were "the lowest we have ever had since the United States entered the war. . . . During the first fortnight in this September, no Allied ships were sunk by U-boat action in any part of the world. This is altogether unprecedented in

[5] See Vol. I 353–54.
[6] "History of Convoy and Routing" in Naval Administrative Series; Wemyss *Walker's Group in Western Approaches; Fuehrer Conferences* for 1943; Doenitz "The War at Sea"; B.d.U. War Diary. Times in this section and the next are Zone O (plus 2).

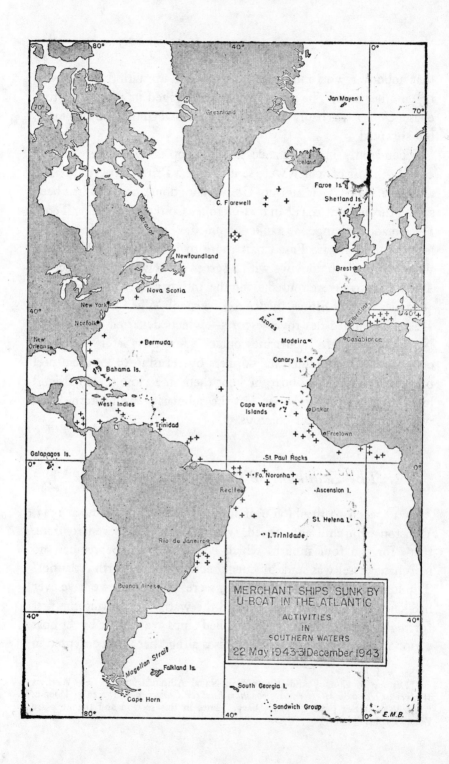

MERCHANT SHIPS SUNK BY
U-BOAT IN THE ATLANTIC
ACTIVITIES
IN
SOUTHERN WATERS
22 May 1943-31 December 1943

the whole history of the U-boat struggle, either in this war or in the last." Respecting new construction of merchant vessels, he stated that more than six million merchant tonnage had been built in excess of "losses of all kinds, including marine risks, since the beginning of the year; . . . and should the present favourable conditions hold, we shall soon have replaced all the losses suffered by the United Nations since the beginning of the war."

The situation was equally bright in civilian supplies: —

"The House will also realise that we have taken full advantage of the lull in the U-boat attack to bring the largest possible convoys, and that we have replenished the reserves in these Islands of all essential commodities, especially oil fuel, which is almost at its highest level since the outbreak of the war, and we have substantial margins between us and what is called the 'danger level,' on which we have never trenched even at the worst time."

And to whom is credit due for all this? "It is the result of the most astonishing and praiseworthy efforts of industry and organization on both sides of the Atlantic. It is also the result of hard, faithful, unwearying service given by the multitudes of escort vessels of all kinds; and most of all, so far as last year is concerned, it is the result of the startling intervention of the long-range aircraft of the British Empire and the United States, and especially of our Coastal Command. Besides this the large numbers of auxiliary aircraft carriers which are now coming into service are able to give a measure of air protection to the convoys, and to conduct an aggressive warfare against U-boats, in those ocean spaces which are beyond the reach even of the very-long-range aircraft . . . of the two countries." [7]

This oration was greeted by "loud and prolonged cheering" in the House. Broadcast around the world, it evoked a cheer in many a United States ship engaged in convoy duty and brought joy to thousands of people in the families of soldiers and sailors then afloat on the great deep.

[7] Charles Eade ed. *Onward to Victory, War Speeches by Churchill 1943* (London 1944) pp. 193-5. Also in Eade's U.S. edition called *War Speeches* (1953) III 7.

If we define the North Atlantic as extending only to lat. 40° N, Mr. Churchill's statements are almost literally correct.[8] But there had been at least 26 British and 19 American ships and 10 of other countries sunk in the Central and South Atlantic and Mediterranean during the previous four months, and the Allied merchant marines had suffered exceptionally heavy losses in the Indian Ocean in July. The Prime Minister was careful to state that a new North Atlantic blitz by U-boats "fitted with what is thought to be the best and latest apparatus" had already begun, but that he could give "no guarantee of a continuance of these favourable conditions."

The apparatus to which Mr. Churchill referred was the acoustic torpedo, officially called *T–5* and code named *Zaunkönig* ("Wren").[9] This weapon, in production by August 1943, was so designed as to be attracted by the pitch of an escort's propellers (that of a merchant vessel's was generally different) so that, even if aimed inaccurately, it would explode under the ship's stern. Each boat was provided with two — later with four — Wrens, in addition to its regular complement of ordinary torpedoes. Skippers were instructed to blast their way through the screen of a convoy with Zaunkönig and then sink the merchant vessels.

Another new piece of apparatus was a radar decoy called "Aphrodite," a balloon trailing plates covered with tinfoil which could be launched from a submarine to bewilder Allied radar operators.

Group "Leuthen" of 21 U-boats, most of them provided with

[8] Exceptions: On 31 May S.S. *Catford* was sunk by mine in English Channel; and on 9 Sept. S.S. *Larchbank* was sunk by submarine in Indian Ocean. But note this summary of Northern transatlantic convoys 18 May–18 Sept. 1943: —

DESIGNATION		CONVOYS	SHIPS	ESCORTS	
HX–238	to –256	18	1,190	160	
SC–130	to –142	13	698	112	
ON–182	to –201	19	1,181	170	*no losses*
ONS–8	to –17	10	452	110	
UT–1	and –2	2	25	20	
	Total	62	3,546	572	

[9] The Admiralty called it "Gnat," abbreviation of German Naval Acoustic Torpedo. The great majority of torpedoes used by U-boats against merchant shipping were of the 30-knot electric type, range slightly over 5000 yards and showing no wake. Most of the boats also carried a few of the older, air-driven type for long-range shots.

both pieces of apparatus as well as the full antiaircraft armament, had sortied, 18 of them from French ports, by 9 September. They were directed by Doenitz to form a north-south patrol line 17 miles apart, starting at a point about 500 miles east of Cape Farewell, in order to straddle the great circle route between Halifax and the United Kingdom. It was rightly assumed that the trade convoys, after almost four months' immunity from attack, would follow that shortest route. Doenitz ordered Group "Leuthen" to keep radio silence during transit, in order to throw HF/DF off the scent, and sent them to sea with a ringing radio message which ended: —

"The Fuehrer is watching every phase of your struggle. Attack, follow up, sink!"

Unfortunately for Group "Leuthen," the sleuth-hounds of the Admiralty knew it had left port and guessed its intention. But the guess was not good enough for two westbound convoys to be routed clear.

Convoy ON–202 of 41 ships departed Western Approaches 16 September. The escort commander, Commander P. W. Burnett RN in Canadian destroyer *Gatineau*, had one other destroyer, frigate *Lagan*, and three corvettes in his screen. ON–202 was rerouted northwesterly on the evening of 18 September, in the hope that this would clear Group "Leuthen." Next morning, however, a Canadian Liberator which was flying to Newfoundland flushed *U–341* at lat. 58°40′ N, long. 25°30′ W, some 165 miles north of the convoy. Its bombing attack sent that submarine to the bottom; but the news of this exploit was received with mixed feelings at the Admiralty, since it indicated that Group "Leuthen" was stationed much farther north than had been suspected.

The slow convoy, ONS–18, which had sailed first, did clear Group "Leuthen"; but ON–202, less fortunate, ran right into the middle of it. Shortly after one bell in the midwatch 20 September, H.M.S. *Lagan* was hit in the stern by an acoustic torpedo launched from *U–270*, which was then driven off by *Gatineau*. *Lagan's* flooding was checked and she made home safely, but the convoy had to plunge into the "Leuthen" line with a reduced screen.

At 0209 September 20, H.M.S. *Polyanthus* illuminated and depth-charged *U–238* (Oberleutnant Horst Hepp). It escaped, stalked the convoy on the surface, and moved in undetected for a dawn attack. Lining up four freighters in his sights, Hepp gave them the contents of his bow tubes. The two Liberty ships that he hit were empty of cargo; he could not have selected two American freighters whose loss would inflict less damage yet create more mischief.

The first, named *Theodore Dwight Weld* after a prominent abolitionist, was a good ship with an average crew. Abreast of her steamed *Frederick Douglass*, named after a celebrated freedman of the Civil War era. This vessel had a Negro master, several Negro officers, and a crew that was about half Negro and half white. Consequently, she was considered an experiment in race relations, and the conduct of officers and crew under stress became the subject of unreasonable detraction and equally extravagant laudation. *Douglass* was also experimenting with a very cumbersome and ineffective anti-torpedo device rigged on large paravanes; she had experienced more or less engine trouble on the passage, and her first engineer, a white man who claimed to have been sunk thrice on the North Russia run, boasted that if again torpedoed he would be the first to abandon ship.

At 0540 September 20, as day broke bright and cold on a fairly rough sea with WNW wind making up to force 4–5, *Theodore Dwight Weld* took a torpedo from *U–238* in her engine room. The boilers exploded, cutting the ship in two parts, one of which sank within two and a half minutes of the ringing of the alarm bell. There was no time to launch lifeboats, and all the crew and Naval Armed Guard who survived either jumped overboard or were thrown into the water, which quickly became covered with a viscous film of fuel oil.

Within a few seconds of this hit, *Frederick Douglass* was struck by a torpedo which exploded in the sand ballast of her after cargo hold. The entire "black gang" (partly white in color) abandoned the engine room without closing the watertight door to the driveshaft tunnel, which had been holed; consequently the engine room flooded. The Negro master, Adrian Richardson, on the bridge when the torpedo exploded, went below to investigate damage. During his absence the chief engineer and the second officer, both white, ordered Abandon Ship. They were joined by most of the crew, who had pilfered the master's liquor, collecting a lot of gear; and by a Negro girl stowaway who had been concealed by the colored boatswain and the white "Chips." The Naval Armed Guard, all white, stood to their posts, as did the first officer (white) and a few of the crew. When the master came on deck, three out of four lifeboats were already in the water. He stood by his ship until about 1010, when he abandoned on orders from the escort commander. He then caused the fourth lifeboat to be lowered and took off the Armed Guard and the rest of his crew. *Douglass* could have been salvaged if the engine room bulkhead had been closed, for she floated until after dark, when another U-boat sank her.

In the meantime the convoy's rescue vessel, the British S.S. *Rathlin*, was doing her best to pick up the floating survivors of *Weld*, unaided by the lifeboats which had prematurely abandoned *Douglass*. At 0600 she lowered a boat which in 25 minutes picked up a dozen men with great difficulty, owing to the heavy layer of fuel oil which choked the boat's circulating system and eventually forced it to return to the ship. *Rathlin* in the meantime had scooped up several floating survivors with life nets swung out on booms, and continued to rescue men in that fashion until 2045, when the launch was lowered again and took off one lone seaman who had clung to the floating bow of *Weld*. The men in the *Douglass* lifeboats also were taken on board, but the gear that they tried to bring with them was indignantly hurled overboard by members of *Rathlin's* crew. All hands of *Douglass* — 70 including the stowaway — were rescued but only 38 of *Weld's* crew (one of whom died shortly after), and 15 of her Naval Armed Guard.

These unfortunate events, duplicated dozens of times in the history of World War II convoys, would have called for no particular comment but for the racial composition of *Douglass's* crew, and the feeling of some of *Weld's* survivors that the *Douglass* lifeboats might have made an effort to rescue them. In this writer's opinion, the personnel of the torpedoed vessels reacted as individuals; some well and courageously and others in a despicable and cowardly manner; Captain Richardson behaved according to the best traditions of the sea.[10]

While *Gatineau* and *Polyanthus* swept the scene of the sinking for a submarine contact, Hepp took *U–238* deep, and escaped. But on the same day (20 September) an Iceland-based Coastal Command Liberator sighted and bombed *U–338* six miles abeam of the convoy, and it never surfaced again.

Convoy ON–202 was now in a precarious situation. In obedience to orders from Cincwa, it altered course around noon to join ONS–18 before dark and combine the two screens. Owing to communications difficulties, the two convoys had some difficulty finding each other and "gyrated majestically round the ocean . . . watched appreciatively by a growing swarm of U-boats." They were still groping for each other when *U–386*, which had been stalking ONS–18 for an hour in a heavy sea, moved in. The boat was so badly damaged by an encounter with the screen that it had to haul out for home.

At 1600 September 20 the two convoys finally joined, with another welcome accession of six British and Canadian destroyers and corvettes under Commander M. J. Evans RN, who now became O.T.C. The combined convoy of 66 ships now had 15 escorts, which under other circumstances would have been ample protection; but six U-boats armed with Wrens were stalking it. At 1756, H.M.C.S. *St. Croix* took an acoustic torpedo near her port propeller. The U-boat dove, surfaced an hour later, and sank the de-

[10] Testimony taken at investigation 6 Oct. 1943, in Casualty Review section, U.S.C.G. Hq. New York; Summary of Statements of Survivors in Armed Guard files; Commandant 3rd Naval Dist. to C.N.O. 15 Oct.; U.S. Naval Observer Halifax to V.C.N.O. 4 Oct., and Summary of Statements of Survivors of S.S. *Weld* 30 Oct., in Statistical Analysis Office O.N.I.; Report of Interview with Master of S.S. *Rathlin* in Merchant Navy Interview Section, Admiralty; Letter of Cadet-Midshipman F. H. Cain of *Weld* to District Cadet-Midshipman Supervisor N.Y. 5 Oct. 1943; letters of several surviving officers of the ships' Naval Armed Guards to writer, January 1955.

stroyer with another Zaunkönig. A third exploded 30 feet on the port quarter of *Itchen* as she was searching for survivors. H.M.S. *Polyanthus* now made a fatal encounter with *U-641*, whose seasoned crew had given U.S.S. *Bogue's* planes an impressive demonstration of "fight back" tactics off the Azores. At 2030 *U-641* hit the corvette with a Zaunkönig which disintegrated her completely. Only one man of her crew was rescued, and he was lost from *Itchen* next day. *Narcissus* succeeded in driving off the rest of the stalkers, but five U-boats were still trying to get at the big convoy from ahead.

During the midwatch 21 September the convoy ran into a heavy fog bank which protected it during the next two watches, while Group "Leuthen" became confused by contradictory reports. When the fog lifted around noon, it was discovered that the two menaced convoys were in an excellent though unplanned disposition — "organized by a Higher Authority," commented Commander Evans — for resisting attack. Smoke screens and aggressive patrolling frustrated nine separate attacks by stalking boats during the afternoon and first dog watches. Doenitz from Berlin now commanded his wolves to deliver *der Hauptschlag* (the big blow) under cover of fog and darkness.

French corvette *Roselys* found the first attacker about 1900 September 21. On HF/DF bearings furnished by the outer screen, and using their own radar, escorts moved boldly through the fog-mull and nailed down every U-boat that approached the convoy. Near midnight H.M.C.S. *Chambly* scored a 4-inch hit on the conning tower of *U-584* just as it was submerging, and dodged a Wren. In the midwatch 22 September British trawler *Northern Foam* (655 tons) bracketed *U-952* with star shell and scored a few hits; she almost managed to ram this boat, and depth-charged it so vigorously that its skipper was forced to blow tanks and retreat on the surface. An hour later, Commander Evans in *Keppel* moved 13 miles astern to personally direct an attack on a shadower. Sighting the boat at first light, around 0425, Evans opened with gunfire and rammed, crashing over the submarine's afterdeck and im-

mediately thereafter throwing ten depth charges which finished
U–229.

Der Hauptschlag had gone wild, but Doenitz was not yet
through with Convoys ON–202 and ONS–18. Ordering his boats
to hang on until the following night, when *der Wettergott* might
favor, he sat back to await the result. The fog lifted around noon
22 September; Commander Evans observed that it was "very nice
to come into the open air and find it filled with Liberators" —
R.C.A.F. B–24s based on Newfoundland. The two convoys had
drifted about four miles apart in the fog. Now the slow one
took station astern of the fast, and the order was given for a radical change of course after dark. *U–270* had its pressure hull ruptured that afternoon by a Liberator's bombs and was forced to
retire. A second Liberator, coming up to assist, barely failed to
sink *U–377* twelve miles astern of the slow convoy at 1502 [11]
and, having expended its bombs, was driven off by the gunfire of
U–402. Toward dusk the crafty Germans began jamming voice
telephone circuits with bogus messages to the aviators to "return
to base forthwith," and, although the source of these orders was
suspected, decreasing visibility frustrated any further attempts at
air attack.

So a third night (22–23 September) began with only the screen
to protect the combined convoy, now spread out over seven
miles. But the HF/DF in the outer screen of five ships enabled
Commander Evans to direct a series of sharp attacks on stalkers.
Plucky *Itchen* started the night's proceedings at 1900 by detecting
and nailing down the first U-boat that tried to penetrate the screen.
During the next ten hours Doenitz directed at least 15 attacks
from ahead, astern and on each flank. A radical change of convoy
course, 60 degrees to starboard at around 2000, threw off the
boats that were boring in on the port hand, but ran afoul of those
that were cruising ahead; and these managed to deliver a well-
coördinated attack during the first watch. *U–666,* sighting *Itchen*
and H.M.C.S. *Morden,* which were dealing with one of its fellows

[11] We now enter Zone P (plus 3) time.

just ahead of the oncoming convoy, at 2155 executed a one-two attack with acoustic torpedoes, one of which exploded in *Itchen's* magazine. Sheets of blue and red flame and dense smoke arose from her hull. American S.S. *James Smith*, rapidly closing the scene at the head of the third convoy column, got into the fight; her Naval Armed Guard fired one round at the submarine's conning tower, briefly sighted in the light of a flare. The master, Bernhard G. F. Kuckens, gallantly stopped engines when he heard shouts from survivors, and dropped life rings and rafts. The loss of *Itchen* was particularly tragic, as she was carrying survivors from *St. Croix* and *Polyanthus*. From the crews of these three ships only three men survived.

Four more boats moved in to attack during the long midwatch. All were driven away by the indefatigable screen, which almost lost another of its units, *Chambly*. An acoustic torpedo exploded a hundred yards astern of her. Next, *U–238*, which had sunk *Douglass* and *Weld* two nights before, put in another appearance, evaded three vessels of the screen and loosed torpedoes at four merchantmen, three of which were hit and sunk. *U–238* plunged back through the screen and escaped. Other U-boats in the vicinity failed to profit by the uproar and confusion; not until shortly before dawn did *U–952* deliver another attack. With two torpedoes it finished the career of American S.S. *Steel Voyager* and hit S.S. *James Gordon Bennett* with a dud.

As the convoy was now approaching Newfoundland, too near for the comfort of German submarines, Doenitz decided to call the fight off. At dawn 23 September he ordered Group "Leuthen" to move eastward, which it did after a few Parthian shots. During the night of 23–24 September there were two attacks, both driven off by the screen.

By the morning of 24 September the battered convoys had plenty of air support and were free of stalkers. On the 25th, they again ran into a fog-mull, but ON–202 made New York, and ONS–18 arrived at Halifax, with no further incident.

Both sides were well pleased with this convoy battle. Commander in Chief Western Approaches praised "the fine offensive spirit" of the escorts which had "resulted in comparatively slight losses to the convoy and prevented the enemy from ever seizing the initiative." That was a little short of the truth. Grossadmiral Doenitz, not satisfied with his actual score of six merchant ships and three escort vessels sunk, claimed 12 destroyers actually and 3 probably sunk, together with 9 merchant vessels, and probably two more! [12] Zaunkönig, he said, "had won its laurels"; its threat indeed was serious. Fortunately, "the National Defense Research Council was hard at work on countermeasures to the acoustic torpedo long before its introduction by the Germans." [13] and assisted by Asworg produced the FXR or "Foxer" gear. Ready at the end of September, it was promptly installed on all transatlantic escort vessels.

Doenitz apparently realized that his brief success against these convoys was only a flare-up, since he later recorded that this battle made it "finally clear that surface warfare for U-boats had come to an end. It was now a matter of filling in time till the new type should be ready for action." [14]

3. *The Blitz Fizzles Out, October–November*

Time-filling activities cost Admiral Doenitz a few more U-boats. In early October he sent a group which he named "Rossbach" — after one of Frederick the Great's famous comeback battles — to look for Convoy ON–204 in waters dangerously close to Iceland. On 4 October a United States Navy Ventura, piloted by Commander Charles L. Westhofen, sighted *U–336*, the potential convoy contact-keeper, about 230 miles southwest of Reykjavik. The boat dove as the plane burst out of the clouds. Westhofen used the gambit tactics of retiring over the horizon, then returning in ex-

[12] B.d.U. War Diary 24 Sept. 1943. This excessive claim is still made in Wolfgang Frank *Sea Wolves* p. 190.
[13] Baxter *Scientists Against Time* p. 34.
[14] Doenitz "The War at Sea" sec. vi p. 24.

pectation that the boat would have surfaced. Sure enough, it had. Diving through heavy flak Westhofen strewed three depth charges close on the boat's starboard side. As the high plumes of water subsided, Germans were seen boiling out of the conning tower. Westhofen then had his turret gunner, D. R. Seifert, rake the motionless boat from stem to stern. After exhausting their ammunition the Ventura crew had the satisfaction of seeing *U–336* upend and go down. Westhofen's efforts to call a ship to pick up survivors were thwarted by the enemy's having shot up his radio.[15]

Less than an hour later, and 65 miles westward, a British Liberator of the 120th Squadron sank *U–279;* and next morning a rocket-equipped Hudson of British Squadron 269 got *U–389,* only 160 miles southwest of Iceland. Doenitz now diverted the rest of Group "Rossbach" southward to await an eastbound convoy.

In accordance with this plan, *U–731* on the morning of 7 October sighted a destroyer of Convoy SC–143, nine days out of Halifax. At dusk Doenitz ordered Group "Rossbach" into this convoy's estimated path, with the order "Blast destroyers, scuttle ships and reward yourselves for your long wait."

The Admiralty, anticipating a rough night ahead for the 39 merchantmen of Convoy SC–143 and its eight-unit escort, had ordered a support group, H.M.S. *Musketeer, Oribi, Orwell,* and Polish destroyer *Orkan,* to join and strengthen the screen. The Pole, provided with HF/DF, got a bearing on a stalker thirty miles astern of the convoy and that afternoon, 7 October, stood out with *Musketeer* to attack. At 1900 an acoustic torpedo from *U–758* exploded harmlessly in *Orkan's* wake. She and *Musketeer,* aided by other ships of the screen, managed to keep the stalkers at bay all night; but when hastening to rejoin the convoy, just after eight bells had ushered in the morning watch 8 October, *Orkan* received a torpedo fired by *U–378.* It exploded in the after magazine, and she sank within five minutes. Commander Stanislaw Hryniewiecki,

---

[15] Admiral Low called this action "worthy of emulation by all aircraft engaged in antisubmarine activities." Tenth Fleet Incident No. 4670.

senior officer of all Polish destroyers and a distinguished veteran of World War I, went down with his ship, only 44 members of the crew were saved. The U-boat escaped.[16]

Iceland-based aircraft prevented the development of any attack on the convoy that day, and three more units of Group "Rossbach" fell victims to Iceland-based planes: *U–419* to a Liberator of British Squadron 86; *U–643* to a second of the same squadron, assisted by one of Squadron 120; *U–610* to a Canadian Sunderland.

During the morning watch of 9 October *U–645*, the lone "Rossbach" that was still stalking Convoy SC–143, sank American S.S. *Yorkmar;* 54 survivors were rescued by the screen. The score for Group "Rossbach" was one merchantman and a destroyer in exchange for six U-boats.

Doenitz never seemed to know when he had had enough. On 13 October he ordered a fresh pack of 13 boats, called Group "Schlieffen," to a new patrol line starting about 500 miles southeast of Cape Farewell. Two days later *U–844*, the contact-keeper of this group, was located by H.M.S. *Duncan* (Commander Gretton) and *Vanquisher* when trailing Convoy ON–206. They pinned it down until dawn 16 October when it was sunk by Liberators of Coastal Command. Gretton's veterans kept off the rest of this group "Schlieffen," and on the 17th one of its number, *U–540*, was sent to the bottom by Iceland-based British Liberators. The convoy lost nothing but sleep.

Westbound ONS–20 of 52 merchant ships, escorted by a group of British destroyer escorts [17] and a couple of armed trawlers, first met "Schlieffen" on the morning of 16 October, 400 miles south of Iceland — where it was sighted by *U–964*. This boat shadowed the convoy until the afternoon, when a Liberator of R.A.F. Squadron 86 pounced on it and sank it with four depth bombs. A hundred miles northwestward, *U–470* met a similar fate at the hands of another Liberator. Both boats used fight-back tactics to no avail.

[16] B.d.U. War Diary credits *U–758* with the sinking of *Orkan* on the 7th, and we have no log of *U–378;* but it is certain, from a comparison of the logs of other U-boats in the vicinity, and in view of the time, that *U–378* did it.

[17] H.M.S. *Bentinck* flag. The R.N. called their DEs "Captain" Class Frigates.

After dark 16 October the rest of Group "Schlieffen" moved in on Convoy ONS–20 when a part of its screen was making an offensive sweep. *U–426* sank a merchantman and was then kept down by the screen. The following afternoon, 17 October, H.M.S. *Byard* of the screen spotted *U–841* trailing the convoy nine miles astern. A depth-charge attack blew the boat to the surface, where it immediately came under the frigate's fire. As German submariners swarmed out of the conning tower the skipper, furious at being caught, returned fire with his pistol, while an Austrian member of the crew, more realistic, waved a white handkerchief. Upon sighting this improvised flag of truce, the frigate moved in and rescued 27 men.

Convoy ONS–20 had now come within the orbit of Commander Gretton's roving support, which had recently peeled off from ON–206. On the same day, 17 October, that the British DEs were blooded, the veteran corvette H.M.S. *Sunflower* sank *U–631*. Henceforth, that convoy was allowed to proceed in peace. Admiral Sir Max Horton of the Western Approaches congratulated Commander H. R. Paramor RN, who commanded the screen, on the successful first passage of a DE escort group.

Thus, the renewal of U-boat activity against the North Atlantic convoys had resulted in more U-boat losses — no fewer than 15 between latitudes 54° and 62°, together with three sunk by *Card's* aviators around the Azores, and some in other parts of the Atlantic. These losses might have been acceptable if the damage to the Allies had been commensurate; but the Germans had only sunk four escorts and eight merchantmen during the thirty-day period 20 September to 19 October. Doenitz had formerly defended his losses to the Fuehrer on the ground that the U-boats were sinking merchant tonnage faster than the Allies could replace it. But the ships constructed monthly were now equivalent to ten-fold the monthly losses; new construction by the end of October had more than replaced the total losses of all Allied merchant shipping since the beginning of the war.

Ineluctable facts brought about a change of strategy and tactics at U-boat headquarters. On 18 October 1943 Doenitz ordered the remains of Group "Schlieffen" to dive immediately upon sighting hostile aircraft.[18] Thus he virtually admitted that his much vaunted "fight back" policy had been a costly tactical error. But he still thought that the acoustic torpedo was a huge success, and continued in that opinion at least as late as 1 July 1944, when the official war diary made up a bloated score of one cruiser and 128 destroyers and other escorts sunk by the Wren.

Doenitz was marking time awaiting the appearance of snorkel-equipped U-boats. As a naval commander he had been overpowered by his enemies' antisubmarine forces, overwhelmed by their superior seamanship and tactics, "out-improved" by their new devices.

It was consistent with the Fuehrer's love of Wagner that Doenitz named his next concentration Group "Siegfried" and sent it into waters where there seemed to be some chance of making a few sinkings worth boasting about.[19] The "Siegfried" boats moved cautiously westward, submerged by day and keeping radio silence by night, toward patrol stations along the 39th meridian, east of Flemish Cap. Their presence there became known at Tenth Fleet headquarters on 28 October, in ample time to permit evasive convoy routings. For three weeks Group "Siegfried" and its successors sought in vain, and often in the fog, for targets. Largely because of the new tactics — staying submerged in daylight and rising to periscope depth once an hour for a look-see — no targets were sighted. Although these U-boats seldom exposed themselves, four were sunk, and they failed to reduce Allied sea power by even as much as one merchant vessel. The German submarine staff complained that it had been thwarted by evasive convoy routings and by the absence of air reconnaissance on their side. Without it, noted their war diarist on 17 October, the submarines' assignment was hopeless.

[18] This message is recorded in *U-426* War Diary for 18 Oct. 1943: — *"Bei Auftreten von Luft unter Wasser bleiben. Opera-abbrechen."* Also recorded in Operations Division German Naval Staff War Diary 19 Oct. 1943.

[19] Information from *U-426* War Diary; that of B.d.U. is wanting for this period. "Siegfried" was split in two groups 30 Oct., and they were re-formed as five "Tirpitz" groups of 4 boats each on 5 November.

The first unit of Group "Siegfried" to be sunk was *U–420*, victim of a Royal Canadian Air Force Liberator on 26 October. For the next two, British escort carriers, helped by Captain Walker's group, were responsible.

On 19 October 1943 Captain Walker, with his tried team of sloops, sailed out of Lough Foyle before a southeast gale in H.M.S. *Starling,* and rendezvoused with escort carrier H.M.S. *Tracker* in the North Channel. His general mission was to cover convoys between Iceland and the Azores, one remaining "hole" in the North Atlantic still deprived of air coverage. At 1700 October 20 the group joined westbound Convoy ON–207, in the midst of which *Tracker* took her station. This was what the British called a "bait convoy," routed directly through a U-boat group for the express purpose of trapping the enemy.[20] Commander Gretton's distant support group, steaming more or less parallel to the convoy and a hundred miles northward, attacked and sank *U–274* on 23 October, greatly to the delight of his officers and men, since the hunting was apt to be poor for anyone else when Walker was about. Two days later, having detected no U-boat concentrations, Gretton, Walker and the *Tracker* groups broke off from ON–207, and on the 26th joined eastbound Convoy HX–262, 483 miles north of Graciosa. There followed three uneventful days, on the last of which the escorts refueled. Captain Walker left HX–262 on 29 October and turned west to look for a reported concentration of U-boats. The weather, already rough, became so foul on 1 November that flight operations had to be canceled and the entire group hove-to; *Tracker* rolled so badly — up to 52 degrees — that all but three of her Swordfish were badly damaged. A fifth sloop, H.M.S. *Kite,* joined that afternoon, and it was she who found the first submarine during the pitch-black midwatch 6 November.

This was *U–226*, a member of one of the "Tirpitz" groups into which "Siegfried" had been resolved. Walker clung to the contact all night and directed a creeping attack at sunrise, laying down

[20] Wemyss *Walker's Groups* pp. 98–104; information from Commo. Gretton, 1955.

26 depth charges which finished the career of *U–226*, about 200 miles southeast of Flemish Cap. This kill was made without benefit of aircraft, as was the next. Owing doubtless to the new German tactics of remaining submerged during daytime, neither *Tracker's* aircraft nor a Liberator from Newfoundland could locate *U–842*; but, by proceeding to its position indicated by an HF/DF bearing, Walker's sloops at 1300 November 6 successfully depth-charged *U–842* in the deep where it was lurking. After debris appeared on the surface Captain Walker gave an order which unfortunately has disappeared from the bone-dry United States Navy, "Splice the Main Brace!"

Two days later H.M.S. *Tracker* narrowly escaped an untimely end. *U–648* sighted her by moonlight, pitching wildly in a heavy sea, about 630 miles E by S of Cape Race, and fired three torpedoes which missed; an acoustic torpedo fired at an escort detonated prematurely. That night (8 November) the wind built up to 80 knots — hurricane strength — and the group again had to heave-to. Fortunately the U-boat, too, was hampered by the storm — and never regained contact with its intended victim. On 12 November the *Tracker* and Walker groups, thoroughly exhausted, took refuge at Argentia.

Doenitz, on 7 November, split Group "Tirpitz" into nine groups of three boats each which were deployed along the North Atlantic convoy route. They were unable to locate a single convoy, although twice moved to action stations, and were bothered by the excessive battery consumption resulting from running submerged all day. On 15 November, the Grossadmiral decided to take another whack at the Mediterranean convoys; and by the 20th all but four boats had retired from the North Atlantic routes.

This concludes the story of submarine attacks on North Atlantic convoys for 1943.[21]

[21] One exception: on 30 Dec. 1943 *U–545* sighted an unescorted group of stragglers from westbound Convoy ON–217, about 200 miles south of Iceland, and torpedoed S.S. *Empire Housman*, which was again torpedoed by *U–744* on 2 Jan. 1944, and sank when under tow three days later.

CHAPTER X

The Central Atlantic Grind[1]

October–December 1943

1. Central Atlantic Convoys

ECCE ET NAVES – There go the Ships. Always we come back to the convoys. Although the name is three centuries old, there had been nothing like these in all maritime history, and possibly never will be again: seventy to a hundred freighters and tankers of divers Allied and neutral flags — American, British, Panamanian, Brazilian, Dutch, Russian, French, Norwegian and Greek; after 1943, Italian — manned by merchant mariners of every race and nation under the sun, from Finns with parchment-like faces to brown Lascars and black Africans; of all ages and conditions, from boys too young for the Navy to bearded and toothless old salts.

All American and British merchant vessels at this period, and many, too, under foreign flags, have guns and Naval Armed Guards.[2] Besides the master on the bridge of an American vessel in a UGS–GUS convoy is the commodore, and in another is the vice-commodore, who will take over if the flagship is sunk. On this route, both are retired officers of the United States Navy recalled to active duty, having the authority to crack the whip over smokers,

[1] Some of the fights in this chapter took place as far north as lat. 50°, but as the CVE groups were operating in wide support of Central Atlantic convoys, I have thought best to relate them here.

[2] A surplus of Armed Guard crews developed in September, and 3 months later the training program was reduced. By 1 May 1943 2066 U.S. ships and 229 under other flags, mainly Panamanian, had received guns and U.S. Naval Armed Guards. By the end of the year the figures were 3045 and 245; by 1 May 1945 they were 3460 and 251 – all cumulative. For earlier figures see Vol. I Appendix III.

stragglers and rompers; [3] for no ego can be tolerated in these fleets of heavy-laden freighters, "fraught with the ministers and instruments of cruel war."

Before the war most master mariners jeered at the idea of a convoy keeping uniform speed — it "couldn't be done" with a fleet made up of perhaps thirty different types of hulls and engines; but it was done in World War I without radar and again in World War II with radar, greatest boon of scientist to sailorman since the chronometer. Even so, to an old-timer it seems a fresh miracle every morning when the rising sun lights the same ships, in the same order as those dark shapes which faded in the deepening twilight the night before. And any vessel, even a Hog Islander or an average Norwegian tramp with more rust than red-lead topside, is transfigured to a fair argosy when flooded by the first rosy light from the sun rising out of Africa.

Outside the compact main body of the convoy, in which the 10 to 15 columns are 800 to 1000 yards apart, and each ship's bow not less than 500 yards ahead of the next one's bow, plies the screen. The majority of its units are United States destroyers or DEs, with a few fast minesweepers and perhaps a couple of Fighting French corvettes to escort provision ships to North Africa when the convoy breaks up. Nine to eleven is the proper number now. The advanced screen may steam as much as ten miles ahead of the convoy, in order to detect surfaced U-boats; the close screen, according to weather, number of ships, or other circumstances, may be 5000 to 8000 yards outside the merchant ships, in a circular disposition. [4] Each is continually questing for underwater enemies with the monotonous "ping" of her sonar, and for surfaced or flying enemies with the rotating grids of her radar sets. At the rear of the center column steams an escort tanker which breaks

---

[3] A straggler is a ship separated from a convoy through engine trouble or other cause, and at least 10 miles away; a romper is one that has moved more than 10 miles ahead of the convoy.

[4] The ideal disposition, seldom realized, was to station the escorts near enough to each other so that a U-boat could not get through the sonar screen, yet far enough out so that a torpedo launched from seaward of the screen could not reach the convoy.

off when the screen needs oil, and fuels two ships at a time along-side at fair speed while two others of the screen mount radar and sonar guard. The escort commander, a destroyer division or squadron commander, has the direction of the entire disposition even though he be junior by twenty years to the convoy commodore. It is he who receives orders and messages from Cinclant or Tenth Fleet from the twice-daily Fox schedule [5] and transmits them by blinker in daylight or short-range voice radio by night to whomsoever in the convoy they may concern; for merchant ships must keep radio silence. And often against the skyline can be seen the welcome silhouette of an escort carrier, with planes coming and going like bees around a hive.

Suppose we follow the fortunes of a routine UGS (United States-Gibraltar slow) convoy before taking up again the exploits of the escort carrier hunter-killer groups on this route. Convoy UGS–21 sails from Norfolk 15 October 1943. The New York section has been waiting a couple of days in Lynnhaven Bay for the Chesapeake section to be made up. At 1400 the day before sailing, the convoy conference is held in a great room at N.O.B. Norfolk. Escort commander, convoy commodore and vice-commodore, port director, the president of the Virginia Pilots' Association, and every master or first officer of a merchant vessel must be there. The first three are in naval khaki (or blues if the day is nippy); a few masters wear the new merchant marine uniform, but most are in civilian suits and flannel shirts without ties. A varied-looking lot they are, of all ages from 21 to 70, and of several nations; some recent graduates of King's Point, crisp and taut; others stooped, bewhiskered, and weather-beaten; but almost every man lean and serious, with the eyes of a sailor used to long-distance gazing.

Here are the writer's notes taken at one of these conferences: —

(*The mimeographed convoy instructions are first distributed.*)

PORT DIRECTOR: Are ye all ready for sea?

A MASTER: I have to sign on some crew at Newport News.

[5] See Vol. I 103–5.

Two Masters: We haven't cleared ship yet.

A Fourth Master: I have three men yet to come aboard.

Port Director: Well, hurry up and get yer business done.

Convoy Commodore: The signal for departure will be given at 0500 tomorrow morning by one prolonged blast of my whistle. Each ship must hoist the convoy signal number. When ye enter the Med., no more zigzagging, no balloons, show all yer lights, and any submarines you encounter are friendly. (*Sensation among the masters!*)[6] Get yer mates familiar with the contents of the convoy instructions. Give 'em authority to turn on signal light at night, after passing Europa Point, whence you will all proceed independently to your destinations. Columns 1 through 4 will consist of the vessels joining us from New York. Watch yer green officers; see that they keep closed up 500 yards to the ship ahead.

Escort Commander: When an escort comes alongside steer the steady convoy course. If you see lights in another ship, signal him by whistle, one blast for forward, three for amidships, two for aft. Three of our escort vessels have surgeons on board who can be transferred to you by boatswain's chair if you have any serious cases on board.

Convoy Commodore: Use blue stern light and dim running lights in visibility so poor that you cannot make out other ships.

Pilots' Association President: I will have 37 pilots available to take you through the swept channel. The first 35 ships to sortie should have anchor cables hove short, engines in stand-by, and ladder lowered on the port side.

Convoy Commodore: Good sailing!

Port Director: Beer in the rear — Good luck — Scram!

(*One of the masters, an Oriental by his looks, asks me, "Does that mean the blue stern light?" Fortunately not; it means free beer in the rear of the room!*)

The conference disperses after a few handshakes and backslappings. Motor lifeboats take the members on board, and precisely at 0500 next morning anchors are weighed and the convoy stands out of the Capes, through the swept channel in a single column 25 miles long, forming up outside while a blimp maneuvers overhead and land-based planes slice across the sky.

Over our particular Convoy, UGS–21, Captain James D. Ma-

---

[6] This happened in Nov. 1944 after the Germans had been driven out of the Mediterranean.

loney USN (Ret.) is convoy commodore in S.S. *Atenas*. There are 69 merchant ships, 51 American, including a dozen tankers carrying oil and gasoline for the armies, fleets and air forces in Africa and Italy. Some merchant vessels are destined for Casablanca, others for various Mediterranean ports, and a substantial number will pass through the Suez Canal. Their ocean escort, under Commander W. J. Marshall in *Baldwin*, comprises six U.S. destroyers, three minesweepers, one subchaser, and oiler *Chepachet*. A support group — consisting of escort carrier *Block Island* (Captain Logan C. Ramsey), destroyers *Parrott*, *Paul Jones*, and *Badger* is loosely attached.

Admiral Ingersoll shortly relieves the *Block Island* group of close support duty in order to hunt U-boats reported to be about 500 miles north of the Azores. Two of the destroyers make an unsuccessful attack, but the carrier's planes sink *U–220* on 28 October.

The ocean passage is uneventful. There is some straggling and poor station-keeping on the part of merchantmen unable to maintain the convoy speed of 9½ knots in rough weather. Ancient coal-burners cannot help smoking on occasion and there is one minor collision. On 17 October a minesweeper peels off to escort a merchant ship into Bermuda for repairs, and French destroyer *Simoun* and sweeper *Annamite* join to take care of the Casablanca section, which breaks off on 30 October. Next day several ships from Casablanca under French local escort join the convoy. The Rock is sighted that afternoon and cheery news arrives that a couple of U-boats have been sunk near the Strait.[7] Off Gibraltar, seven merchant ships break off, and Commander Marshall turns over the rest of the convoy to a British escort consisting of anti-aircraft cruiser *Palomares*, two destroyers and four "Flower" class corvettes. A local escort picks up the Oran section — fifteen merchant ships including those destined for Sicily and Italy —

[7] Actually one, *U–732*, by H.M.S. *Imperialist* and *Douglas*; but three other ships of the Royal Navy, with R.A.F. assistance, got *U–340* next day.

on 1 November; nine eastbound vessels join from Oran. Convoy UGS–21 is finally dispersed at Port Said. Ships bound for the Indian Ocean steam independently through the Canal and the Red Sea to Aden, where they form up with others from the United Kingdom into small convoys which the Royal Navy escorts to final destinations in Colombo, Bandar-Shapur, Abadan, and Khorramshahr.

Westbound we may follow Convoy GUS–18, fifty-five merchant ships, most of them from Italy and the Middle and Far East. Formed at Port Said, it calls at Oran and at Gibraltar, where, on 17 October 1943, the British escort commander turns it over to Commander John Connor in *Stevenson*, whose escort group comprises eight destroyers and U.S.C.G.C. *Spencer*. Captain G. L. Woodruff USN (ret.) is convoy commodore in S.S. *Thomas Pinckney*. Three ships join off Gibraltar and four are detached; off Casablanca, nine more merchant vessels, sweeper *Staff* and escort oiler *Kennebec* join. The convoy now forms up in 13 columns, the center ones with five ships each, tapering off to two-ship columns on the wings, a circular formation that facilitates patrol by the screen. Steaming against the autumn westerlies, the speed of advance is set at 8 knots, and stations are well kept. Captain Woodruff, however, thinks that the escort commander indulges in too much signaling, and after the voyage dryly recommends that he be provided with another 12-inch signal light "for use exclusively in communication with escort commander." Destroyer *Turner*, one of the advanced screen 7½ miles ahead of the convoy center, runs down a radar contact in the evening of 23 October and sights a U-boat close aboard; she attacks with gunfire and depth charges and has the satisfaction of seeing the submarine assume an angle of 70 degrees and plunge. All she gets from the hard-boiled Tenth Fleet assessors is "insufficient evidence of damage," which turns out to be correct — that submarine escaped.

During the first two days of November, Convoy GUS–18 is scattered by foul weather over an area roughly 40 miles square, but re-forms successfully as soon as the storm abates. It enjoys continuous air coverage from departure to 25 October, and again from the 31st until the Norfolk and New York sections part company off the Capes on 4 November. An escort carrier group built around U.S.S. *Card* has furnished a part of this air support; but *Card* and her destroyers have had a good deal else to do during this passage, as we shall now relate.

2. CARD *and* CORE *Score Four,*[8] *3–20 October*

Well-blooded escort carrier *Card*, still commanded by Captain Isbell, had lost her original Composite Squadron One but had taken over *Bogue's* VC-9, together with her screen of 1917-vintage flushdeckers *Borie, Barry* and *Goff*. While *Card* was undergoing two weeks' overhaul at Norfolk in September, her escorts were fitted with the new FXR ("Foxer") gear, a contraption of parallel rods which clacked together when towed, making an unholy racket designed to attract and detonate the new German acoustic torpedo. That it did, and very successfully, as *Card's* next cruise proved; unfortunately the noise drowned out the delicate sound gear on the towing ship at 10 knots or more, nullifying her principal means of sparring with a submerged U-boat. As no scientist came up with a remedy, some destroyer skippers took to stationing a bluejacket on the fantail with a sharp axe, ready to cut away Foxer when sound contact was established.

On his next eastward passage, in wide support of Convoy UGS–19, Captain Isbell at 0901 October 4 [9] received a radio signal from one of his Avenger pilots: he had sighted a veritable jackpot — four submarines fueling within a radius of 500 yards! The biggest, *U–460*, had just topped off *U–264* and was getting lines across to *U–422* while *U–455* stood by for its turn. *Card*, 83

---

[8] "U.S.S. *Card* History" dated June 1945; *Card* Operations Log and War Diary for Oct. Capt. Isbell "Three Months' Experience as CTG 21.14," an interview of 15 Nov. 1943 in files of Technical Analysis Div. C.N.O. for Air.
[9] Times for this action are Zone O (plus 1).

miles distant, launched three more planes. Lieutenant R. L. Stearns
USNR, who sent the message, attacked at once. Weaving his way
among antiaircraft bursts from all four boats, he planted a 500-
pound bomb between *U-264* and the milch cow. Doenitz had
ordered every member of his thinning group of 1600-tonners to
submerge immediately if attacked; but the commander of *U-460*,
instead of so doing, argued with the skipper of *U-264* over who
should dive first. As a result, only *U-455* had submerged when
Stearns's air reinforcements appeared. A Wildcat and an Avenger
buzzed the surface trio like a pair of hornets, silencing the antiaircraft fire of two of the boats after taking numerous hits. The skipper of the 1600-tonner now belatedly tried to submerge, but Stearns
dropped a 500-pound bomb just ahead of the swirl, and the big
boat disintegrated, spewing forth gruesome human debris.

Captain Isbell at 1038 launched five Avengers and three Wildcats, which joined the three already in action; four of them found
U-264, which fought back so skillfully as to force an attacking
Avenger to drop its bombs prematurely. It looked as if three out
of the four had escaped; but later in the same day damaged *U-422*
had to broach five miles from the scene of battle and was promptly
jumped by a waiting fighter-bomber team piloted by Lieutenants (jg) S. B. Holt USNR and S. E. Doty USNR. A 500-pound bomb
released by Holt finished this boat — the sixth kill by the *Card*
group.

Foul weather now set in. On 7 October, *Card* lost an Avenger,
snapped off the flight deck in a sudden lurch, with the pilot and
a crew member.[10] Captain Isbell turned south in search of better
flying conditions, fueled, and moved north at flank speed as wind
and sea abated. On Columbus Day, 12 October, his airmen flushed
the nucleus of another fueling concentration, supply boat *U-488*.[11]
Twice attacked, it was damaged and ordered home. On 13 Octo-

---

[10] In the same gale H.M.S. *Fencer* lost a Swordfish near the Azores; Capt. Isbell
also searched for this pilot, but in vain.

[11] At a point about 600 miles N of Flores. This boat had been ordered to fuel,
under cover of night, 3 or 4 units of Group "Rossbach" which had recently been
decimated by Iceland-based Liberators.

ber *U-402*, hopefully nosing along toward its milch cow, was forced to dive by an Avenger piloted by Ensign B. C. Sheela USNR, and sunk by a 500-pound bomb dropped by squadron commander Howard M. Avery's Wildcat. *U-378*, unsuccessfully attacked near the same spot on the same day, survived long enough to increase the score of U.S.S. *Core* within a week.

The weather had now made up again, with WSW wind up to force 10, and a very rough sea. The vicissitudes of escort carrier planes in rough weather are illustrated by the recovery of an Avenger piloted by Lieutenant (jg) H. E. Fryatt USNR after this last attack. A shot from the submarine had jammed his right wheel, *Card* was pitching and rolling horribly, and darkness had fallen. Captain Isbell ordered the flight deck to be dimly lighted and Fryatt to be waved in for an emergency landing. Approaching with one wheel and a prayer, Fryatt missed the arresting cable, crashed through the midship barrier, caromed off the island, and was finally stopped by another TBF which was knocked overboard by the collision. The pilot coolly swam clear of his sinking plane, flashed a light, and was rescued by U.S.S. *Barry*.

That was the last incident on *Card's* outward passage. She put in at Casablanca 18 October, and on the same day the *Core* group made its first appearance north of the Azores. *Core*, now commanded by Captain James R. Dudley, had departed Hampton Roads 5 October with old flush-deck destroyers *Greene*, *Belknap*, and *Goldsborough* as screen, in support of Convoy UGS-20. On the afternoon of 19 October one of her patrol pairs encountered *U-378*, the boat that had sunk Polish destroyer *Orkan* and had since eluded *Card's* pilots. The leader of *Core's* squadron VC-13, Lieutenant Commander Charles W. Brewer, who was piloting the Wildcat, strafed so vigorously as to blow German gunners off the "bandstand" and explode ammunition in the conning tower. And at 1352 his Avenger partner, Lieutenant R. W. Hayman USNR, planted two sticks of bombs that finished *U-378*.

If *Core* had been equipped for night flying she might have hit a jackpot that very night, for *U-488* was fueling three U-boats not far away. Next morning (21 October) one of her Avengers on dawn patrol spotted *U–271* about 35 miles SW of the carrier and knocked out one of its antiaircraft batteries, but the boat submerged before air reinforcements arrived from Terceira, and eluded a subsequent sound search by *Belknap*. Captain Dudley, concluding that Isbell had left him slim pickings in that area, turned southeasterly and entered Casablanca 27 October.

3. Borie's *Last Battle,*[12] 1–2 November

Captain Isbell's group provided cover for Convoy GUS–18 until it was well clear of the Azores, doubled back around Santa Maria, then turned NW to break up a submarine fueling concentration some 500 miles north of Flores. The fringe of this concentration had just been cracked, and 1600-ton *U–220* sunk by the *Block Island* escort carrier group.[18] On the afternoon of 30 October Lieutenant Fryatt, one of *Card's* "hottest" Avenger pilots, flushed a U–boat at lat. 48° 43′ N, long. 32° 19′ W. In accordance with Grossadmiral Doenitz's latest instructions, canceling his previous "fight back" tactics, the submarine dove before Fryatt could drop a 500-pounder, and escaped. But another fueling pair that Lieutenant (jg) W. S. Fowler USNR spotted next day failed to obey the new doctrine. One of them, *U–91*, got away; but Fowler and Lieutenant (jg) L. S. Balliett USNR (who had been promptly vectored to the scene) each planted a 500-pound bomb which sent *U–584* into a 2000-fathom deep about 656 miles north of Flores.

Captain Isbell had no intention of allowing *U–91*, which he mistakenly assumed to be a milch cow, to escape. It was too late in the day for flight operations, and his carrier needed her three-destroyer screen as protection against submarines known to be

[12] *Borie* Action Report 1 Nov. 1943; Capt. Isbell Interview, and Lt. Hutchins's personal narrative, 15 Nov., in Division of Naval History.

[13] *U–220* had just completed a mining operation off St. John's, Newfoundland, that cost the Allies two small merchantmen. It was looking for a supply boat in the vicinity when sunk by an Avenger from *Block Island* at lat. 48°53′ N, long. 33°30′ W, on 28 Oct. 1943.

nearby; but he decided nevertheless to send destroyer *Borie* to search for *U–91.*

U.S.S. *Borie* was that old flush-decker commanded by Lieutenant Charles H. Hutchins USNR whose officers had astounded a naval constructor at New York with their proficiency at throwing knives and dishes about the wardroom. Although the junior C.O. of the screen, Lieutenant Hutchins's energy and initiative had impressed Captain Isbell, who chose him for this mission as the skipper most likely to get results. And he certainly got them, in the shape of an old-fashioned slug-fest recalling the fight of U.S.S. *Constitution* with H.M.S. *Java* in 1812.

Borie reached the scene of the recent sinkings after dark 31 October, and before long obtained a radar contact on a surfaced boat. Lieutenant Hutchins made three attacks in heavy seas, saw the submarine go down, heard an underwater explosion, and signaled *Card* "Scratch one pig boat!" That particular enemy, *U–256,* managed to limp back to Brest; but Hutchins continued searching nearby. At 0145 November 1,[14] he made another radar contact at 800 yards. The target dove when the range closed to 2800 yards, sound contact was made at 2200 yards, and *Borie* attacked when about a quarter of a mile distant. Every depth charge then in her racks was expended because something had gone wrong with the release mechanism; but this proved to be a lucky break. The submarine, 500-ton *U–405,* responded to this shower of deadly confetti by coming to the surface where her whitish, 220-foot hull, silhouetted by a flickering float light, looked as big as a battleship.

Then followed a gunfire-torpedo duel. Hutchins trained his 24-inch searchlight on the target and opened fire with main battery and machine guns, starting at 1400 yards, and also trying to ram. German sailors swarmed out of the conning tower, some wearing only skivvies, many with long hair and brightly colored bandannas, which offended our bluejackets' sense of propriety and made them the more eager for a kill. A few submariners reached their guns and slammed shells into *Borie's* forward engine room and bridge,

[14] Zone O (plus 2).

but many were cut down by the destroyer's 20-mm machine-gun fire; and *U–405*'s largest gun was literally blasted over the side by a well-directed 4-inch shell.

After the antagonists had steered parallel courses for several minutes, *Borie* firing continuously, she closed the boat's starboard quarter and turned left to ram. Just before the crash, *U–405* also turned hard left. *Borie* struck it on an angle about 30 feet abaft the stem and rode up and over the forecastle. The two ships remained locked in mortal combat, one under the other, at an angle of 25 to 30 degrees, for ten minutes. Two of *Borie's* main battery guns and three 20-mm machine guns kept a continuous fire on the sub's conning tower and deck, which were still above water. Negro mess attendants who manned a 20-mm battery fired through the metal weather screen; bluejackets not otherwise occupied fired tommy guns, pistols, shotguns, rifles or whatever they could lay hands on, at the Germans. In a fairly heavy sea — waves twenty feet from trough to crest — the two vessels pounded and rolled against each other, adding the noise of grinding steel to the roar of gunfire, the clatter of machine guns and human shouts and screams.

Lieutenant Hutchins's exec., Lieutenant Philip B. Brown USNR, had told his men exactly what to do if they came to close grips with a submarine, and they did it. Brown himself bounded out of the now useless combat information center to the bridge, whence he sprayed the U-boat's decks with a tommy gun. A sheath knife hurled by Fireman First Class D. F. Southwick buried itself in the belly of a German running to man a gun; another "Kraut" was knocked overboard by an empty 4-inch shell case thrown by Chief Boatswain's Mate Walter C. Kruz.

Although some 30 submariners were killed in this close fighting, as against none of the destroyer's crew, the Germans below decks were far safer than *Borie's* "black gang," which was making a gallant fight to keep up steam. The destroyer's plates, light enough at her birth in 1920, had by now been chipped and rusted almost paper-thin, and the whole port side became crushed and holed

as it ground against the U-boat's hard pressure hull. All hands
stuck to their stations, and, under the lead of Engineer Officer Lieutenant Morrison R. Brown USNR, managed to keep up full power
even when salt water was lapping the boilers. Firemen working in water chest-high were pounded by heavy gratings as
Borie lurched from port to starboard. Brown remained at the
throttle with the water level shoulder-high. Motor Machinist's Mate
Irving R. Saum dove into the oily water of the after engine room
to close a drain fitting which made it possible to place all suction
pumps on that room. Thus *Borie* kept on fighting.

After ten minutes of this mêlée the submarine managed to back
out from under and opened the range to 400 yards; then went into
a tight turn. *Borie*, which had a larger turning circle, ran around
the submarine, trying to get into a position to ram, and firing
furiously. Four-inch hits on the starboard diesel exhaust probably
penetrated the after torpedo room of *U–405*, and certainly did it
no good. *Borie* fired a torpedo which missed. Lieutenant Hutchins, observing that the submarine's after "stinger" tubes were pointing right at him, doused his searchlight, hoping that the enemy
would straighten out and try to escape, which he did. Now, ordering depth charges set shallow, Hutchins bent on 27 knots, turned
on the searchlight and closed to ram. He was on collision course
with the U-boat, on his starboard bow, when it swung hard left and
endeavored to ram *Borie* on her starboard quarter. Hutchins, with
great presence of mind, ordered hard left rudder and, with port
engine backing full and starboard engine stopped, slewed his fantail with its depth-charge projectors right across the path of the
submarine. Three charges fired a couple of seconds later made a
perfect straddle around the conning tower, lifting *U–405* bodily
and stopping it dead when its stem was only six feet from *Borie's*
stern. The submarine backed its engines and attempted to pull out.
Borie swung rapidly to port and pursued, firing with all her guns
and, as the range opened, launching a torpedo which missed. One
4-inch shell blew Korvettenkapitän Hopman and his bridge crew
overboard; another shell made a "very, very effective hit" on the

U-boat's exhaust tube, and the boat glided to a halt. Submariners were now coming on deck with hands raised and firing white Very flares in lieu of a white flag; but, as some were running toward their guns, *Borie* continued to fire until cries of *"Kamerad!"* were heard. At 0257 November 1, 72 minutes after the first contact, *U–405* plunged stem first and exploded under water. A yell of triumph went up from the deck of battered *Borie*.

Hutchins intended to pick up survivors, but the Germans, in life rafts only 60 feet away, set off colored flares which were answered from a distance, obviously by another submarine. *Borie* had to ring up flank speed to dodge a torpedo from the direction of the distant answering flare, and in so doing ran down a number of Germans. She zigzagged clear of the area on one engine.

So many of *Borie's* thin plates had been stove by the pounding that she was in a dangerous condition. One engine was out, generators died and the sea was rising. Hutchins fired all torpedoes and most of his ammunition, and jettisoned everything possible, from anchors to guns and torpedo tubes, in order to keep afloat and make the planned rendezvous with *Card*. The remaining condenser was not working properly, and both feed and fuel tanks were badly contaminated with salt water. Salt locked the blades on the remaining turbine, and at 0900 *Borie* went dead in the water. When fuel for the radio's auxiliary generator was on the point of exhaustion, it was spliced with lighter fluid, kerosene, and rubbing alcohol, so that a message could be put through to the escort carrier at 1100: "Commenced Sinking."

Captain Isbell, consumed with anxiety over *Borie* — his planes could not find her in the low visibility — got an HF/DF bearing on Hutchins's far-from-cheery message and immediately launched two Avengers. One of these sighted the destroyer at 1129, only 14 miles from the carrier, dead in the water, wallowing heavily and down by the stern. Next he sent *Goff* with hose and handy-billies to pump fresh water for *Borie's* boilers, but it was now so rough, with swells up to 40 feet, that she could not get alongside. Late in the afternoon the task group commander communicated by TBS with

Goff, one of whose leather-lunged chief petty officers shouted to *Borie* by megaphone that Lieutenant Hutchins had better consider abandoning ship, since it would be dark in an hour's time and the weather would be worse before it got better. Shortly before sunset 1 November, Hutchins reluctantly gave the word.[15] Captain Isbell sent *Barry*, his one remaining escort, to assist in the difficult process, leaving his carrier stripped of her entire screen. The abandonment, which began at 1644 November 1, was seamanlike and orderly; but the waves were running so high that it was almost impossible for boats and rafts to close the rescue ships. Some men were killed by a plunging propeller guard; three officers and 24 men left their rafts to swim through very cold water to the rescue ships, and were drowned.

Throughout the first watch and into the midwatch of 2 November, *Goff* and *Barry* searched for survivors in heavy seas and under pouring rain until a total of 7 officers and 120 men were rescued. All through those hours of heroism and misery, *Card* circled nearby at 10 knots — what a target for a roving submarine! And one was after her, too. In pitch darkness, as eight bells marked the beginning of the morning watch, her radar registered a contact at 4000 yards. Isbell closed the two destroyers and signaled: "Submarine on our tail . . . pick it off!" *Barry* and *Goff* tried to make contact; the submarine's distance from *Card* narrowed to 2800 yards before its blip disappeared from radar screens — probably frightened away.

The feeling of relief was only momentary since, according to information received from Cominch and the Admiralty, there were still 50 submarines (an exaggeration) within 300 miles of *Card*. Captain Isbell decided that, in order to save his carrier, he must abandon further efforts at rescue. He sent *Barry* to torpedo the derelict hulk of *Borie*. Three torpedoes missed, but four depth bombs from an Avenger sent the gallant old ship to the bottom at 0954 November 2.

This memorable battle took place in one of the loneliest stretches

---

[15] He knew that *Borie* could not make New York under her own power, and it was not feasible to await a tug in those sub-infested waters.

of the Atlantic about halfway between Cape Race, Newfoundland, and Cape Clear, Ireland.

Since *Card* was in no situation to prolong her cruise, Captain Isbell now turned his group toward Hampton Roads. The pilots were exhausted, but with undaunted spirit and splendid stamina they continued daily flight operations, catapulting Avengers at 40-second intervals when the carrier was pitching so violently that catapult shots had to await a comparatively smooth spot. The cruise ended at Norfolk 9 November. But the final blow to German supply submarine activity in the Atlantic was yet to be delivered.

4. Bogue *Gets Four More, November–December*

Captain Joseph B. Dunn's task group, composed of escort carrier *Bogue* and the aged destroyers *George E. Badger, Osmond Ingram, Clemson* and *DuPont*,[16] was next chosen by Cinclant to continue the Azorean offensive. Departing Hampton Roads in mid-November 1943 as close support to UGS–24, it broke off to hunt east of Bermuda but made no promising contact until 385 miles east of Terceira. That was on the 29th. A perfectly coördinated attack by four aircraft, some carrying 500-pound bombs, abruptly ended the career of *U–86*. Next day *U–238*, commanded by Oberleutnant Horst Hepp, regarded as one of the most skillful and aggressive German submariners, beat off an attack by three of *Bogue's* planes, but suffered so many casualties that Doenitz ordered it home.[17]

Captain Dunn's group spent four days at Casablanca, and on 9 December sortied with orders from Cinclant to support Convoy GUS–23 until it had cleared a concentration indicated by HF/DF to be shaping up at lat. 27° N, long. 30° W, the center of a 650-mile circle that cuts Santa Maria, Madeira, and Tenerife. Admiral

[16] These were flush-deckers of 1919–20 vintage; the first three had been converted to seaplane tenders before the war and were still classified as AVDs, but would soon be reconverted to destroyers, and were operating as such. Their main battery was 3-inch .50 caliber.
[17] B.d.U. War Diary 30 Nov. 1943.

Ingersoll was leaving unswept no part of the ocean for which he was responsible. The object of his present interest and of *Bogue's* hunting was a 1600-ton milch cow, *U–219*, about to fuel *U–172*, outward bound to the Indian Ocean.

At 0723 December 12, Lieutenant (jg) E. C. Gaylord sighted *U–172* less than 40 miles south of the carrier.[18] Damaged by a 500-pound bomb, the boat submerged. Within 40 minutes three more aircraft arrived and laid a sonobuoy pattern. Next on the scene, at 1014, were *G. E. Badger* and *DuPont*, which between them delivered 20 hedgehog and depth-charge attacks; but the 740-ton boat managed to keep below this barrage by diving to the vast depth, so its skipper claimed, of 700 feet.

The surface hunt continued all day and far into the night. Finally at around 2100 *G. E. Badger's* radar indicated that the boat had surfaced and was slowly steaming north, four and a half miles away. The ancient destroyer's youthful skipper, Lieutenant E. M. Higgins USNR, began a creeping attack. Pinging with sonar was hushed and the ship slowed down while Combat Information Center [19] plotted the enemy's course and speed by radar. The destroyer stole quietly up on the U-boat in the path of a bright moon just past full. At 6400 yards' range the enemy stopped dead, suggesting that he had sighted his hunter and was about to submerge. Star shell was then fired. The U-boat, however, resumed its course, and *G. E. Badger* closed at 17 knots, the maximum speed at which it was possible to man the forward gun in the moderately rough sea. Gunfire opened at 4000 yards and after three rounds had been fired, the U-boat retaliated with an acoustic torpedo which missed by a wide margin, and promptly dove — at 2218. Sound contact was reëstablished. At 2224 the thirteenth depth-charge attack was delivered by the destroyer, and at 2315 the fourteenth and last. These attacks broke all gauges in the submarine and put one diesel engine

[18] Times, for this fight, are Zone O (plus 2).

[19] C.I.C.s, where all information received by voice telephone, radio gear and radar is collected, where the course of the enemy is plotted and whence information is sent to bridge and gunnery officer, were installed in almost all U.S. fighting ships by the second half of 1943. In destroyers they occupy the commodore's old cabin in the superstructure.

and all radio and electrical circuits permanently out of commission. *DuPont* in the meantime had joined, and both destroyers continued searching until about o600 December 13 when Captain Dunn ordered them back to his screen.

An hour later, one of the carrier's planes sighted a moving oil slick about seven miles SW of the midnight conflict. *Clemson* and *Osmond Ingram*, followed by *G. E. Badger*, reached the scene shortly, and at o907 the first-named rocked the boat with nine depth charges. Lieutenant Higgins in *G. E. Badger*, with only three "ashcans" left after the night action, coached the other two destroyers on four more runs, giving out ranges and bearings over voice radio as he maneuvered at low speed within 2500 yards of the boat, while two Avengers hovered overhead dropping sonobuoys and giving useful advice. Three minutes after the last attack by *Clemson*, at 1016, *U–172* broached. It was damaged and leaking badly, but the crew, though stifling for want of oxygen, came up fighting. The aggressive C.O. of *Osmond Ingram*, Lieutenant Commander R. F. Miller USNR, wanted to ram, but Captain Dunn refused permission, remembering what had happened to *Borie*. *Osmond Ingram* then closed to 500 yards and exchanged gunfire, suffering the loss of one killed and six wounded. The other two destroyers also opened fire at about 1400 yards with their 3-inch guns. The submarine's conning tower burst into flames, the deck crew jumped overboard, and *U–172* sank at 1021 December 13, exploding underwater. The skipper and 45 of his crew were rescued by the destroyers.

This fight was a hunt to exhaustion, illustrating a proper coördination among planes and ships, correct choice of weapons and individual proficiency. That was Tenth Fleet doctrine.

U–219, the milch cow in that vicinity, escaped, and finished the war as Japanese *I–505*. The *Bogue* group drew blanks for a week as it worked north and by west. On the afternoon of 20 December, at a point 610 miles southwest of Fayal and 170 miles distant from *Bogue*, Lieutenant (jg) W. A. La Fleur USNR sighted *U–850*, one of three boats near the Central Atlantic convoy lanes. This new

740-tonner was completely surprised, but the Avenger's bomb release jammed. Pulling just out of range, La Fleur circled, waiting reinforcement; and the U-boat commander, electing to fight it out on the surface, was so busy trying to shoot down the Avenger that he failed to notice four relief planes as they approached and bore in for a coördinated attack. A couple of 500-pound bombs which hit abaft the conning tower up-ended his stern; and, as the great fountain of spray raised by the explosions subsided, the bow lifted almost 90 degrees and *U–850* went down stern first. Destroyers which reached the scene some hours later recovered "dismembered bodies, pieces of clothing" and other debris; but no survivors.

5. CARD *Scores Again, but Loses* LEARY
17–25 December [20]

As *Bogue* and company steamed westward to keep Christmas at Bermuda, the *Card* group was approaching the scene of her own, and *Bogue's*, former exploits. Following the sinking of *Borie*, Captain Isbell had been given a screen of flush-deckers dating from 1919 — destroyers *Leary, Schenck, Decatur* and *Babbitt;* but the last-named developed engine trouble and had to return to New York for repairs. The outward passage was uneventful. After two days at Casablanca they departed 17 December, initially in support of Convoy GUS–24. On orders from Washington soon after, the *Card* group was detached to track down a submarine concentration reported to be around lat. 45° N, long. 22° W.

In expectation of foul weather, the crews of *Card* and consorts had eaten Christmas dinner in Casablanca before sailing; and were very glad they had, for winter weather in the Western Ocean does

[20] CTG 21.14 (Capt. A. J. Isbell) "Report of A/S Operations 24 Nov. 1943–2 Jan. 1944"; *Leary* senior survivor, Lt. R. B. Watson USNR, Action Report 30 Dec. 1943; oral information from Lt. Watson and interview with Chief Quartermaster N. N. Rollings, in Div. of Naval History; *Card* "Summary of Air Operations" 23 Dec., and mimeographed "War History" 13 June 1945; B.d.U. and *U–415* War Diaries, 18–24 Dec. 1943.

not agree with aged destroyers, escort carriers or planes. At daybreak 23 December, around lat. 47° N, long. 19° W (about 695 miles west of St. Nazaire), the sea was so rough that planes could not even be taxied to the catapult. One Wildcat which managed to take off at 1025 sighted a merchantman steaming north and flying the red ensign. She failed to answer his challenge correctly, and the pilot reported to Captain Isbell that he suspected the ship's colors to be false. Nevertheless the group commander decided not to send destroyers to investigate, since his destroyers were low on fuel, and U-boats were already about. After consulting Gibraltar by radio, Captain Isbell realized that this ship was the German blockade runner *Osorno*. She was bound from Kobe to Bordeaux with a load of rubber. Doenitz had sent Group "Borkum" of 13 U-boats to patrol lat. 45° 25′ N between the 21st and 24th meridians, in order to help her get home safely; and these were the boats that *Card* had been sent north to find. The Luftwaffe, too, was looking for *Osorno*, and one of the German pilots the previous afternoon had sighted *Card*.

The seas were so heavy that just before dusk 23 December, after the one search plane had been safely recovered, a Wildcat on the flight deck, with its pilot, was tossed over the side by a violent lurch, and both were lost. All three destroyers were already more than half water-ballasted, and one (*Decatur*) had to be steered by hand after a heavy sea flooded her steering-engine room. Captain Isbell had already decided to make best speed to the Azores in order to refuel in sheltered waters. But the northwest wind was blowing a full gale, roughing up the sea to such an extent that the carrier, all the previous night, was forced to head between 135° and 110° instead of 197°, the rhumb for Pico Channel; and by the time it was possible to lay the correct course, at 0850 December 23, the U-boat group "Borkum" lay 85 miles dead ahead, barring his route. Washington so informed him; but Captain Isbell decided to go on rather than evade. In consequence of the Luftwaffe's sighting report on the 22nd, Doenitz had diverted Group "Borkum" from shepherding the blockade runner to attacking *Card*, of whose movements he was well apprised through a second aircraft sighting that afternoon. All moved north so as to intercept the carrier group on the night of 23–24 December.

At 2120 December 23, *Card* began to fish up enemy transmissions on her HF/DF. A quarter-hour later she began to get surface radar contacts, and at about 2200 *U–305* sighted her and signaled the pack to close. At 2230 *Card's* radar spotted a target at 13,000 yards; and before long so many were popping up that it was impossible to investigate every one.[21] *Card* had only three escorts, her planes were not equipped for night flying, and Captain Isbell dared not open with gunfire lest the flashes reveal his position. So he ordered *Schenck* to attack and took evasive action, escorted by *Leary* and by *Decatur*, the latter steering by hand.

Events followed in rapid succession. *Card's* "evasive" course took her into the range of *U–415*, which she sighted as "large black object trailing" 3700 yards astern. She was unaware that the "object" had already fired three torpedoes at her. Having heard that *Schenck* was already tangling with *U–305*, Captain Isbell detached *Leary* to assist her, and turned *Card* to course 220°, making best speed away in hope of avoiding torpedoes until he had light enough to launch planes. He signaled *Leary* over TBS at 0111 December 24: "Keep subs down during night. Rendezvous at 0600, forty miles SW of *Schenck's* last contact. Good Luck." One or more submarines pressed *Card* vigorously and continuously until daylight; at 0630, when she commenced catapulting planes, one was 7000 yards on her port quarter. But for Isbell's keen tactical sense and a liberal supply of luck, *Card* might have received a "fish" that wild night.

In the meantime, two destroyers were engaged in a grim battle with two members of Group "Borkum." *Schenck* (Lieutenant Commander E. W. Logsdon) scored several hits on a contact that

21 "At one time our own C.I.C. . . . became so confused that it was necessary to turn on the SK radar in order to observe our own ships' ABKs so that we might differentiate between our destroyers, the two subs on our port beam and the subs on our starboard quarter." Capt. Isbell's "Addendum" to TG 21.14 Report. The SK is surface search radar, and the ABK is an interrogator-responsor equipment of the I.F.F. system, which can be observed only on the radar screen.

she made before midnight, and then joined *Leary* in a systematic search. At about 0130 December 24 they made three radar contacts five to seven miles north. As *Leary* moved out to run down the more distant, *Schenck* made a fourth contact, lost it at 2500 yards, sighted the U-boat diving, evaded a torpedo, closed to 800 yards, and at 0145 dropped a nine-charge pattern. This probably damaged *U-645* since that boat surfaced about half an hour later. *Schenck's* radar picked it up at 4000 yards. Again the boat dove; *Schenck* found it again at 1900 yards by sonar, and dropped a shallow nine-charge pattern at 0227, when the range had closed to 200 yards. Two minutes later an explosion was heard. German records prove that this marked the end of *U-645*.

Schenck could not stay around to gather evidence since *Leary* (Commander James E. Kyes), five miles distant, had just reported that she had been torpedoed. After leaving *Schenck* she had experienced a series of minor mishaps which added up to her destruction. At 0158, upon making radar contact at 6500 yards, she tried to illuminate the target (*U-275*) by star shell and succeeded only in lighting up herself. As the U-boat submerged to periscope depth, one of the destroyer's guns, by a misunderstanding, went right on firing star shell. The noise created by gunfire blasts and by the Foxer gear prevented sound contacts being regained soon enough to permit swinging ship to start a proper depth-charge attack. At 0208, when sound contact was finally made at 750 yards, the "squawk box" between sound room and bridge failed to function, and almost two minutes elapsed before Commander Kyes got the word and, too late, ordered Hard Right Rudder.

U-275, whose commander, Oberleutnant Bork, had enjoyed a periscope view of *Leary* for almost ten minutes, already had two torpedoes in the water, well aimed under the bright illumination unwittingly provided by his victim. At 0210, when the last star shell was fading and just as *Leary* commenced her turn, two Zaunkönig torpedoes hit her in quick succession, one in the after engine room and one in the after hold. All power was lost; the ship listed 25 degrees and settled so rapidly by the stern that a forehanded

group of seamen barely had time to set the depth charges on safe.
The entire after part of the ship became a tangle of jagged and
twisted steel, mixed with arms and legs and other human debris.
Radio Technician Francis R. Hauer started the auxiliary generator
and called *Schenck*, which had neither seen the flash nor heard the
explosion.

Three or four minutes after the second torpedo struck, the exec.,
Lieutenant R. B. Watson USNR, concluded a quick inspection.[22] He
reported to the captain that *Leary* was settling fast. Kyes ordered
Abandon Ship. Boatswain's Mate Walter Eshelman calmly directed
men to jettison all floatable gear, and abandonment was orderly, as
if it were a drill. Watson then reported that everyone except himself and the skipper had left, and obtained permission to make one
more look-around to see if any wounded man had been forgotten.
A moment later another unit of Group "Borkum," *U-382*, moved
in close and launched a third torpedo which at 0241 exploded with
a burst of orange flame in the forward engine space. *Leary* began
to go down fast. Commander Kyes, last to go over the side, gave
his lifejacket to a colored mess attendant in the water who had
none, and was never seen again.

This supreme act of devotion was the finest incident in the story
of a devoted crew. Over 60 men were killed by the explosions,
about 100 abandoned ship, but only 59 survived the four hours of
darkness in cold water. The sea was not rough, but a brisk rain-
squall whipped up whitecaps, and the men had only two life rafts
and some cork-buoyed nets to keep them up. Lieutenant Watson
ordered them to keep quiet lest they attract attention from the
U-boat; and for four hours he personally kept a mess attendant
afloat.[23] Water Tender F. M. Norris "instilled hope and confidence
in those who were near the point of exhaustion."

The three officers and 56 men of *Leary* who were saved owed

---

[22] In the course of this inspection, Lt. Watson found the deck covered with a
thick, "gooey" substance, and was astonished to see two seamen seated on a torpedo
tube, calmly eating Boston cream pie. The cook had just baked a batch, and the
explosion had spattered most of the cream over the deck.
[23] This lad died of exposure after rescue. "That hurt me more than anything
else," said Lt. Watson; "he was such a game, plucky little fellow."

their lives to the fine seamanship and good judgment of Lieutenant
Commander Logsdon, skipper of *Schenck*. While passing the wreck
at 15 knots in search of the submarine, he lowered his gig to recover survivors and continued the hunt while his boat crew pulled
benumbed sailors from the water. "*Leary* survivors will never forget his courage and skill in maneuvering his ship into position, both
to effect transfers from the gig and to rescue scattered groups
direct from the water." By 1000 December 24, the last had been
taken on board.

Two old "cans," terriers of the fleet, had fought a good fight with
their traditional verve, skill and courage. Even the pilots remarked,
"Who said this was an airman's war?"

Fortunately *U–275* and the rest of Group "Borkum" hightailed
out of that area, ignoring the big target near at hand, because
Doenitz had ordered them to concentrate on the next Gibraltar-
bound convoy. *Card* at that time lay fifteen miles from *Schenck*,
zigzagging at full speed, with only *Decatur* as screen. The sea now
moderated so that the carrier could fuel both destroyers on Christmas Day and take over the survivors from *Schenck*, without seeking shelter in the Azores. It was a sad Christmas at sea after the loss
of so many shipmates — two thirds of *Leary's* complement. On 2
January 1944 the group reached Hampton Roads without further
incident.

Against the loss of two destroyers and several planes, these escort
carrier groups had made a brilliant record during the second half
of 1943. *Card* was still tops with 11 to her credit; *Bogue* had moved
into second place with 8; *Core* had 5, *Santee* 3; H.M.S. *Tracker*
and *Biter* were tied with 2 each; *Block Island* had one. Aviators of
Composite Squadron 9, flying from two different carriers, had sunk
eight of these. Even under the handicap of winter weather, carrier
groups had proved to be the most efficacious means yet devised of
sinking submarines in the far reaches of the ocean beyond land-
based air protection. They had projected aircraft thousands of miles
from land in an effective partnership with destroyers. They had

given a demonstration of the warfare of the future, for all who had the sense to heed.

Captain Isbell concluded his account of their missions, "CVE task groups can cruise through enemy sub concentrations at night with reasonable safety." Grossadmiral Doenitz had already admitted as much. Addressing a conference of flag officers at Weimar on 17 December, he declared that, thanks to superior Anglo-American high-frequency electronic research, the Allied air-sea forces had thwarted the latest U-boat offensive. There were, as we have seen, many other causes, some more potent than the microwave radar; but Doenitz always used that as a sort of whipping boy. But he had no thought of relaxing the struggle, pending production of new submarine types, in view of the currently expected invasion of *Festung Europa*. The Battle of the Atlantic must go on to victory or a bitter end — and a bitter end it was.

CHAPTER XI

East Coast and Caribbean

April–December 1943

1. *Eastern Sea Frontier "Nuisances," [1] April–July*

BETWEEN 15 July 1942 and 22 April 1943 not one merchantman was sunk by enemy action in the waters between Cape
Sable and the Straits of Florida, for the simple reason that no U-
boats were there. Hundreds of merchant vessels, mostly in convoy,
steamed along the coast with no other hazards but the eternal ones
of the sea; converted yachts in ship lane or coastal picket patrol
enjoyed a series of pleasure cruises, even though the weather was
cold and the water rough; airplanes flew routine patrol and investi-
gated contacts which always turned out to be friendly; amateur
strategists imagined that the U-boats had been permanently driven
from North American waters.

Eastern Sea Frontier had peculiar problems, owing to its close
integration with the populous cities of the Eastern seaboard, and
consequent political and social pressure. The commander, Vice
Admiral Adolphus Andrews,[2] was better fitted by training and
temperament to cope with these factors than with the let-down in
morale and keenness among his substantial frontier forces during
nine months' routine activity. Within the Navy it was anticipated
that Doenitz would strike again along the East Coast as soon as
other waters became unprofitable; but the pressure for escorts and

[1] Eastern Sea Frontier War Diary; B.d.U. War Diary; the War Histories and
Action Reports of the plane squadrons involved are the general sources for this
section. Times, unless otherwise stated, are Zone Q (plus 4) Eastern Daylight Saving Time.
[2] See Vol. I 208n for brief biography of Admiral Andrews. He retired 11 Nov.
1943 and died 1948. See also Vol. I 207–8 for organization of Eastern Sea Frontier.

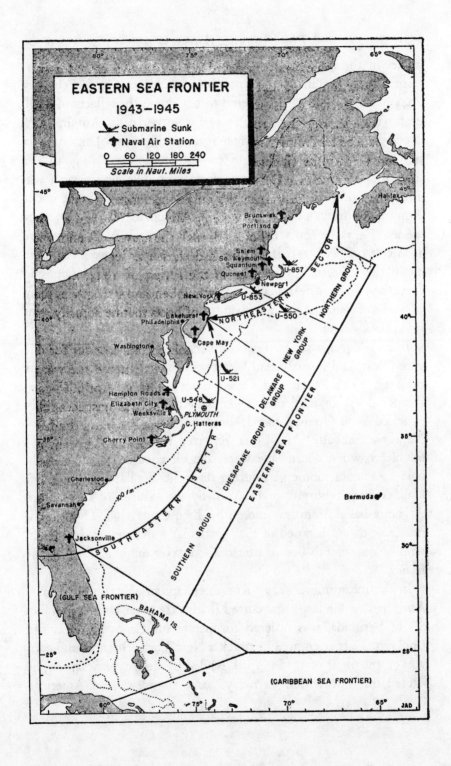

EASTERN SEA FRONTIER
1943–1945

Submarine Sunk
Naval Air Station

0   60   120   180   240
Scale in Naut. Miles

Halifax

Brunswick
Portland

Salem
So. Weymouth
Squantum
Quonset
Newport   U-857

New York
Lakehurst   U-853
Philadelphia   U-550

Cape May   NORTHEASTERN SECTOR

Washington   NORTHERN GROUP

                              NEW YORK GROUP

                       U-521

Hampton Roads   U-548
Elizabeth City
Weeksville   PLYMOUTH   DELAWARE GROUP
C. Hatteras

Cherry Point   CHESAPEAKE GROUP

                               EASTERN SEA FRONTIER

Charleston   SOUTHEASTERN SECTOR

Savannah   Bermuda

                       100 fm   SOUTHERN GROUP

Jacksonville

(GULF SEA FRONTIER)

BAHAMA IS.

(CARIBBEAN SEA FRONTIER)

JAD

planes in the immediately menaced trade convoys caused a substantial reduction in frontier antisubmarine forces. On 26 February 1943 naval districts were ordered to cut down their fleets of small craft (those shorter than 100 feet) by 40 per cent. Admiral Andrews reduced his frontier surface forces, which on 1 January 1943 numbered 210 units (including 11 destroyers) by 1 May to 172 units including neither DEs nor destroyers. His air strength was also reduced. On 1 July 1943 the only long-range aircraft under Admiral Andrews's command were 55 Mitchells (B–25s), 15 Fortresses (B–17s), 10 ancient Bolos (B–18s); the only VLR ones were 17 Venturas (PV–1s). If Doenitz had chosen to loose a real blitz along the Eastern Sea Frontier in the spring of 1943, opposing forces would have been inadequate in numbers and strength, as they proved to be against the mere handful of boats that he actually sent into those waters.

In mid-March 1943 two 740-tonners sailed from Lorient for the East Coast, and in early April four more boats entered the waters between Nova Scotia and Cape Hatteras. On 12 April, *U–161*, skippered by Kapitänleutnant "Ajax" Achilles, was unsuccessfully attacked by a Quonset-based Kingfisher about 75 miles south of Nantucket Shoals. "Ajax" then reported to Doenitz that convoys in this crowded ocean lane were so well covered that he would have to remain submerged during daylight. Similar conditions off Halifax were reported on 17 April by the skipper of *U–174*. An Argentia-based Ventura, piloted by Lieutenant (jg) Thomas Kinaszczuk USNR, disposed of that particular nuisance ten days later, with a neat depth-bomb attack about 150 miles ESE of Sable Island.

In the meantime *U–129* (Korvettenkapitän Witt) which on 2 April had sunk a large unescorted British freighter about 450 miles SE of Bermuda, was ordered to operate off Capes Hatteras and Lookout. Witt attempted to attack a New York–Guantanamo convoy on the night of 21–22 April. Baffled by destroyer *Swanson*, he hauled off, but within two days sank an unescorted American freighter carrying gasoline and ammunition, about 375 miles SE of Hatteras.[3] The entire crew of 95 was rescued by Swedish S.S. *Venezia*. Witt then moved inshore and on 4 May picked up tanker *Panam*, a convoy straggler, as she was rounding Cape Lookout, finished her with two torpedoes and shook off a swarm of ships and aircraft that were dispatched to hunt him down.[4] *U-129* then returned to France; as did *U-161* after sinking Canadian barkentine *Angelus* halfway between Bermuda and Cape Sable.

The above-mentioned boats were promptly relieved by a fresh trio — *U-66* and *U-521* which departed Lorient at the end of April 1943, and *U-190* which was sighted 250 miles east of Cape Henry 28 May — and attacked the same day by an Army Liberator piloted by 1st Lieutenant J. M. Vivian usa. It barely escaped destruction, causing the skipper to adopt such cautious tactics that he returned home with an empty bag after a cruise of two months. *U-521* was sighted by a Norfolk-based plane about 225 miles off Hatteras on 31 May. The boat evaded attack and began to work toward the Capes of the Delaware, mostly submerged; its sound operators must have been asleep when a Guantanamo-bound convoy approached. One of that convoy's escorts was *PC-565*, a 173-foot patrol craft commanded by Lieutenant Walter T. Flynn usnr. Like other young reserve officers, Flynn had been laughed at for errors due to overeagerness and lack of experience, and he had taken these things to heart.

Shortly after noon on a beautiful June day (the 2nd), about 85 miles southeast of Five-Fathom Bank Lightship, *PC-565* made

[3] *Santa Catalina*, at 0556 April 24.

[4] On 4 May, U.S. Army transport *Oneida* foundered in heavy seas off Cape Charles with a loss of 31 seamen. This was attributed at the time to submarine attack, as survivors reported hearing two muffled explosions astern; but it is certain from German records that no U-boat was responsible. As for the alleged ramming of a U-boat by motor tanker *British Prestige* 350 miles east of Jacksonville on 1 May, she reported striking only a "submerged object"; but when, later in the year, Dr. Goebbels broadcast a story of the near-miraculous survival of a U-boat that had been rammed in American coastal waters, the Admiralty assessment committee connected the two events and gave credit to *British Prestige*. Actually, no U-boat was near at the time. The German story was a souped-up version of the escape by *U-333* on 18 Nov. 1943 from a ramming attack NE of the Azores.

sound contact on *U–521*. Although the convoy was pounding along a mile astern, the patrol craft managed to steal up on the U-boat undetected. The skipper, Kapitänleutnant Klaus Bargsten, was in his bunk reading a German translation of the Lynds' *Middletown*, and doubtless gloating over the decay of American democracy, when five depth charges from *PC–565* exploded close aboard. *U–521* was so severely damaged that the skipper ordered all tanks blown, and, as soon as it broached, came up on the bridge. There, seeing the patrol craft blazing away with her guns and bearing down to ram, and also *Brisk* boring in, he yelled below to all hands to abandon ship. The commanding officer rushed topside in a state of panic, but before anyone else could follow him water poured down the conning tower hatch and *U–521* went to the bottom, expedited by more depth charges from *PC–565*. Bargsten was the only survivor.

It was particularly gratifying that one of the PC fleet, which had carried the burden of coastal convoying so long, gallantly and uncomfortably, should have sunk a submarine; and Bargsten was an "ace," having been awarded the Knight's Cross for allegedly sinking 39,000 tons of shipping on a previous 79-day cruise. The loss of his boat seemed to worry him less than the fact that his conqueror and rescuer had been a landlubber lawyer only two years before.

Another boat of this "nuisance" trio, *U–66*, had good luck. Under the command of Kapitänleutnant Markworth, this boat moved into the Gulf Stream off Savannah at the end of May, escaped detection for over a week, and on 9 June took a crack at a couple of northbound tankers, but missed. Next day *Esso Gettysburg*, a heavy-laden tanker escorted only by a blimp which was then dodging a thunder squall, steamed right into the view of *U–66*. Two torpedoes exploded in her engine room and after holds and lighted a violent fire that quickly enveloped her stern. Ensign John S. Arnold usnr, commanding the Naval Armed Guard, was sprayed with burning oil. After extinguishing the flames by rolling on the deck he led a party of his bluejackets forward and managed to get off one round from his bow gun. As the blimp made off without reëstablishing contact ⁵ the sinking of *Esso Gettysburg* was not reported for over 24 hours, when an Army B–25 escorting transport *George Washington* sighted 15 pitiful survivors and homed-in the ship to pick them up.⁶

This sinking, sadly reminiscent of the 1942 massacre, touched off a vigorous but barren hunt for the culprit by surface and air forces of the Eastern Sea Frontier. *U–66* simply lay low until the excitement subsided and allowed several convoys to pass unmolested. Shortly after midnight 1 July, Markworth selected another tanker victim about 40 miles north of the spot where the *Esso* had gone down. This was *Bloody Marsh*, steaming north unescorted, her blimp having departed two hours earlier because of thunderstorms, to which the "lighter-than-air" ships are very sensitive. The tanker was making 16 to 18 knots at 0008 July 2 when *U–66* shot a torpedo into her after engine room. She at once began to settle, and within three minutes her boilers burst. While the crew were abandoning ship the Naval Armed Guard sighted *U–66* and tried unsuccessfully to bring their two guns to bear. Markworth, ignoring their shots, approached the tanker's port beam, running down a lifeboat en route, and gave her a second torpedo which broke her in two; all but three of the crew were rescued by a subchaser. Although this sinking took place only 90 miles southeast of Charleston and a signal from *Bloody Marsh* had been received, and although Markworth surfaced to report to Berlin, eight ships, led by a destroyer and a dozen blimps, Catalinas, and Mitchells, nevertheless combed the sea in vain for *U–66*.

On his way home, Markworth made two hits on water-ballasted tanker *Cherry Valley* in Mona Passage but failed to sink her, and was discouraged from further efforts by the Naval Armed Guard led by Lieutenant (jg) A. C. Matthews USNR. *U–66* then turned toward a mid-ocean fueling point near the Azores, where it ran into trouble at the hands of U.S.S. *Card*.

⁵ It had radar and radio trouble and failed to receive an order from shore to continue mission.
⁶ Standard Oil Co. *Ships of the Esso Fleet* (1946) pp. 454–59. Ens. Arnold survived, though badly burned.

2. *Mining Offensive, June–October*

A new pot of trouble had already been brewed by Doenitz — a mining offensive. His plans for the summer of 1943 included mining missions to St. John's, Halifax, New York, Norfolk, Charleston and Jacksonville. *U-119*, first to depart, mined the approaches to Halifax and thereby sank one small freighter on 1 June; but it was sunk itself, returning, in the Bay of Biscay. Six out of nine mine-laden U-boats that left France in July 1943 were destroyed or damaged around the Azores, as we have seen; the other three ran the gantlet of the escort carrier groups.

U-566 and *U-230* claimed to have sown 20 mines off the Lower Middle Ground inside the Virginia Capes on the nights of 30 and 31 July. Yet no trace of them was ever found, which created the suspicion that they were jettisoned in water so deep that they were never activated.[7]

Nevertheless, Kapitänleutnant Hans Hornkohl of *U-566* took no empty bag home to Doenitz. Unwittingly he triggered off an air-surface hunt which showed up Eastern Sea Frontier at its weakest. A Norfolk-based Martin Mariner first sighted the boat on the evening of 2 August about 250 miles east of Cape Henry, and made a brief but unsuccessful attack. The helter-skelter hunt by planes and small craft that followed was regarded with such contempt by Hornkohl that instead of hauling offshore he closed Cape Charles to lie in wait for convoys. He had just sighted one at 1427 August 5 when gunboat *Plymouth* (ex-yacht *Alva*) of the escort picked him up on her sound gear. Within a minute, just as she was straightening out for a depth-charge attack, she was hit by a torpedo abaft the bridge, burst into flames, and went down rapidly. Her skipper, Lieutenant O. M. Mitchell USNR, though badly wounded by the explosion, directed an orderly abandonment and survived; Ensign

---

[7] B.d.U. and *U-230* and *U-566* War Diaries for July 1943; the E.S.F. and Fifth Naval District Local Defense Force War Diaries show that their presence was suspected. See Appendix III for list of mine fields laid by U-boats.

Rubin Keltch USNR lost his life helping the "black gang" to get out of the engine room.[8]

Next to make contact with *U-566* was a formidable search mission of eleven bombers accompanied by a blimp. At 0720 August 7 a Ventura pilot sighted the boat surfaced about 250 miles east of Cape Charles, and attacked. Hornkohl fought back vigorously with his antiaircraft battery, holing the plane so that it splashed before reaching base and the pilot was drowned. Owing to a slip-up in communications (which were usually bad in the Eastern Sea Frontier), headquarters knew nothing of this action. A second Ventura attacked and dropped bombs accurately, but all were duds; and the plane was shot down in flames with the loss of all hands. Five minutes later a Mariner out of Quonset appeared. *U-566* dove in time to evade, but was blown to the surface by bombs. Twice more the Mariner attacked and again the U-boat dove; bombs then forced the boat to the surface, where its gunners, undisturbed by two other planes and two blimps patrolling nearby, kept him at a respectful distance.

All efforts of shore authorities to send relief aircraft failed until after dark 7 August, when a second Mariner arrived, sighted *U-566* surfacing by moonlight midway in the first watch, and endeavored with voice radio to raise destroyer *Laub* (Commander J. F. Gallaher), which had been diverted to the spot from a homebound Mediterranean convoy. TBS failed to function. The Mariner then released flares but they refused to flare; and after searching for about 45 minutes it had to leave for want of fuel — just as *Laub* identified a surface target on its radar scope. That aircraft was then relieved by a third PBM from Elizabeth City, which picked up a promising target and dropped flares which this time did function — only to illuminate U.S.S. *Laub*.

In the small hours of 8 August, a Catalina out of Halifax sighted the elusive boat 225 miles SE of Nantucket Shoals Lightship, and

---

[8] About half the crew of 183 officers and men were rescued by U.S.C.G.C. *Calypso*, with the help of a fleet tugboat of the Royal Navy that happened to be in the vicinity.

three new destroyer escorts out of Norfolk made sound contact on it at the same time, fired star shell and forced Hornkohl to make a quick dive. He used the German radar decoy called "Aphrodite" to mislead the DEs, and made good his escape.[9]

A comparison of this hunt with the events that we have already described, around the ocean convoys and in the Bay of Biscay, is startling, to say the least. And, as in the Battle of Savo Island, so many mistakes were made by so many people — blunders in procedure and communications, "failures of bomb release gear, of bombs to explode, of guns to operate, and of radios to function" [10] — that one cannot blame any particular person or command. Obviously the long immunity to attack enjoyed by this sea frontier had impaired its efficiency. And almost everyone who took part was a novice, since it was the policy of the Atlantic Fleet to use sea frontier forces to train new recruits and recently commissioned officers. The Navy had been expanding so rapidly that some part of it had to take on this function, and the normally inactive sea frontier forces were the natural choice. The poor performance of Navy planes is explained by the fact that they had just relieved those of the Army Air Force Antisubmarine Command, in accordance with the recent "horse trade." [11]

Nor was the Eastern Sea Frontier the only stretch of coastal waters where sailors and aviators became slack. About 100 miles off Freeport, West Africa, in April 1943, Convoy TS–37, provided with a screen of only one British corvette and three trawlers, was badly battered, owing to delays in communications. U–515 sank 7 merchant vessels out of 18 before help arrived. And in May, three

---

[9] E.S.F. War Diary Aug. 1943, including Appendix "A," a scorching letter from Capt. W. G. Tomlinson, Com Fleet Air Wing Five, to the squadron commanders 4 Aug., and Appendix "B," a candid analysis of the hunt by Capt. Stephen B. Robinson of E.S.F. staff; U–566 War Diary. Information from Capt. Gallaher, former C.O. of *Laub*.

[10] Capt. Robinson's Appendix, sec. 15.

[11] See chap. ii sec. 3 above. The one organizational defect that this hunt revealed, the split of sea frontier air command into three or more semi-independent units, was shortly afterward remedied. In Sept. 1943 Admiral King concentrated all antisubmarine squadrons on the East Coast, including the blimps, in one fleet air wing responsible directly to Commander Eastern Sea Frontier.

other U-boats operating off West Africa sank four more merchant-men. Mr. Churchill described these losses as "deplorable," and the Admiralty "had again to point out how we were always liable to suffer from a sudden reappearance of U-boats in an area which had for a long time been free from them." [12]

A third minelaying boat which departed Lorient in July and got through was 740-ton *U–107*, charged with mining Charleston Harbor. It approached the Carolina coast slowly and circumspectly, moved inshore on the night of 26–27 August, laid 12 mines (so the skipper claimed) southwest of the harbor entrance, and promptly hauled off in hope of bagging some heavy traffic outside. On the morning of the 28th it sighted freighter *Albert Gallatin* off Savannah, escorted by blimp *K–34*, and fired three torpedoes which hit but failed to detonate. The blimp radioed ashore promptly and held *U–107* down while the freighter escaped and assistance winged its way to the spot. An Army B–25 sighted the boat at 1515 as it was heading north at high speed, and attacked through light overcast, dropping four depth bombs which missed. Within an hour of receiving the B–25's sighting report, Eastern Sea Frontier headquarters ordered eleven ships to make an intensive search, and *K–34* stayed out to home them in. At dawn 29 August destroyer *Biddle*, Charleston-bound from Guantanamo, set up a search line with two destroyer escorts and nine small craft. They stuck to it all day and the next, with only three fruitless sound contacts.

At 2014 August 31, Tenth Fleet headquarters reported a high-frequency direction-finder fix at 233 miles east of Cape Lookout. Whatever this may have indicated, it was not *U–107*, then hundreds of miles away; but Eastern Sea Frontier naturally assumed that it was, and directed to the spot a search which continued for several days.

U–107 returned safely home, ignorant of the hullabaloo it had raised, but smugly conscious of having done a good minelaying job.

Ironically enough, that is exactly what it had not done. Although

[12] Roskill *The War at Sea* II.

guided by lighted gas buoys up Charleston Harbor, *U–107* had laid
the mines so far outside the main channel that ships entered and
departed innocent until 20 September when British motor minesweeper *J–967*, while making a routine sweep, exploded one with
no damage to itself.[13] Sixth Naval District then put on a sweep
which disposed of the remainder.

U–220, which was sent across in September to plant mines, on
9–10 October laid about 66 off St. John's, Newfoundland, which
sank two small freighters on the 19th. *U–220* got away but encountered the *Block Island* escort carrier group when making for
the Azores, and on 28 October was sunk by her Avengers.

Apparently Doenitz never suspected how much of a nuisance
these operations had been. He had, to be sure, lost five boats [14] of
the thirteen that he had dispatched to those waters over a period of
five months, for which their bag of four merchant ships was a poor
exchange; and their mining operations were almost worthless. But
his main objective, the pinning down of surface and air forces, was
achieved. Admiral Andrews felt obliged to build up his frontier
forces again; on 3 September 1943 he had under his command 16
squadrons of planes, 4 squadrons of blimps, 2 frigates, 15 gunboats
and 225 other vessels, including about a hundred 85-foot Coast
Guard cutters.

3. *Caribbean Blitz, July–August* [15]

In April 1943, for the first time since early 1942, the Caribbean
Sea and the Gulf of Mexico enjoyed complete immunity from
enemy submarine operations. Since both Mexico and the Spanish
Main were important sources of petroleum products for Allied
war operations, and of other strategic materials such as bauxite,

[13] E.S.F. and Sixth Naval Dist. War Diaries. This mine lay 6½ miles 128° from
buoy 2 AC.

[14] *U–174, U–117, U–521, U–220, U–613.*

[15] Gulf and Caribbean Sea Frontier War Diaries; N.O.B. Trinidad War Diary;
N.O.B. Trinidad Combat Information and Statistical Section "Statistical Report of
the A/S Flying Effort in the Trinidad Sector April 1–30, 1943," June 8.

their adjacent waters had not been neglected by the enemy.[16] Between 1 March and 6 April 1943, six U-boats patrolling the Gulf and Caribbean sank eleven ships with a tonnage approaching 60,000. When these boats were withdrawn to the North Atlantic in mid-April, the American forces in Gulf and Caribbean settled down to routine air patrol and escort-of-convoy.

Rear Admiral Munroe,[17] Commander Gulf Sea Frontier with headquarters at Miami, was responsible for the protection of both coasts of Florida, the Gulf of Mexico, the Yucatan Channel, and most of Cuba. His sea frontier forces comprised only one 173-foot PC, thirty 100-foot SCs, 31 Coast Guard cutters (mainly 85-footers), and 25 small craft.

Caribbean Sea Frontier, commanded by Vice Admiral John H. Hoover[18] with headquarters at San Juan de Puerto Rico, was less centralized than any of the others; by the nature of things, sector commanders at Guantanamo, Curaçao and Trinidad were allowed a wide measure of autonomy. The surface forces at their disposal in April 1943 comprised 9 destroyers based at Guantanamo and Trinidad, 3 gunboats, 9 Coast Guard cutters, 24 SCs and about 40 smaller craft. The air forces (Fleet Air Wing Eleven) included 31 PBM and 35 PBY flying boats divided among Trinidad, San Juan, Guantanamo, Great Exuma (Bahamas), Coco Solo (Panama) and Corpus Christi, Texas; together with the better part of Blimp Squadron 30, whose bases were dispersed from Richmond in Florida to Zandery in British Guiana. Port of Spain and the Gulf of

16 See Vol. I 144–54, 346–52.
17 William R. Munroe, b. Texas 1886, Naval Academy '08; C.O. of several submarines in succession, 1913–19; navigator of *Mississippi* 1920–21; U.S. Naval Mission to Brazil 1922–25; C.O. *Paul Hamilton* 1925–27; Naval aide to Presidents Coolidge and Hoover; commander of a submarine division 1930; service in O.N.I., and as aide to Asst. Secnav 1932–39; C.O. *Mississippi* 1939; Com Batdiv 3 1941; Com 7th Naval Dist. and Gulf S.F. Apr. 1943; relieved Admiral Ingram as C. in C. Fourth Fleet Nov. 1944. Com Carib. S.F. 1945; retired 1947.
18 John Howard Hoover, b. Ohio 1887, Naval Academy '07. Served in various ships 1908–16; C.O. destroyer *Cushing* 1918. Qualified as naval aviator and submariner 1924–29; served as subron commander; exec. *Lexington* 1929–31; Com N.A.S. San Diego 1931–34 and N.A.S. Norfolk 1937; C.O. *Lexington* 1938; Com Carib. S. F. 1941; Com Aircraft Central Pacific 1943–44; Commander Marianas 1945; General Board 1946; retired 1948.

Paria, now the crossroads between North and South Atlantic, had never before known such a press of shipping. A convoy of eight to ten merchant vessels and several unescorted merchantmen arrived or departed almost every day. In addition, small bauxite freighters were constantly shuttling that precious ore from the Guianas to Trinidad; 77 on an average cleared monthly from Port of Spain between March and September 1943, and not one was molested by the enemy. The Navy blimps based on Edinburgh Field, Trinidad, were useful escorts for the bauxite route, and for covering other convoys while forming up in the Gulf of Paria. There is nothing like a blimp to make a convoy feel easy at that critical moment.

Before really laying it on in the Caribbean, Doenitz tried a few nuisance raids. *U-176* (Kapitänleutnant Reiner Dierksen) came through Crooked Island Passage in early May 1943 to operate in the Old Bahama Channel. Dierksen first revealed his presence on the 13th by attacking a small Cuban convoy east of Nuevitas, sinking a small tanker and S.S. *Nickeliner*, which had just been converted for carrying ammonia water. The Cuban escort commander forgot to report this attack for several hours, so it was not until well into the night that subchasers and Kingfishers began to comb the waters off Cayo Frances, while destroyer escort *Brennan*, four PCs and a blimp undertook to work over the western exits of the Old Bahama Channel. In one of these, Nicolas Channel, on 15 May a King-fisher spotted *U-176* submerging just as a Cuban convoy hove in sight. The pilot dropped depth bombs and a smoke pot which attracted the attention of the Cuban naval escort. Subchaser *CS-13*, commanded by Alférez de Fragata Mario Ramírez Delgado, peeled off, closed the smoke, made good sound contact and delivered two perfect depth-charge attacks that disposed of *U-176*. As the only successful attack on a U-boat in the Western Atlantic by any surface craft smaller than a 173-foot PC, this kill by an 83-foot subchaser is properly regarded with great pride by the small but efficient Cuban Navy.[19]

[19] Letter of Comodoro José Aguila Ruiz, Chief of the Cuban Naval General Staff, 19 Feb. 1947; and his report "La Marina de Guerra Cubana en la Segunda Guerra

Even more of a nuisance to American authorities than *U–176* was the situation at Martinique. Amiral Georges Robert, with a fleet carrier, two cruisers and a few auxiliaries, was still holding out for Marshal Pétain at Fort de France. Numerous U.S. Navy planes were uselessly employed in watching lest he attempt to escape and join the Axis; a small but noisy group of patriotic French at Cayenne, French Guiana, were demanding transportation from Admiral Hoover to capture Robert's Vichyite fleet. The French sailors were restive and mutinous; the colored population of Martinique was hungry and rebellious; and on 13 July, the local garrison revolted. Next day a high commissioner appointed by General Giraud arrived at Martinique in the French destroyer *Le Terrible* and took over the island with ceremonies appropriate to Bastille Day. Thenceforth the French Antilles collaborated with the Western Allies.[20]

This settlement of the long-standing Martinique question came not a moment too soon, because Doenitz had just unleashed his Caribbean blitz. Only ten boats participated; most of them were sunk, and their bag of shipping was small, but they tested the skill and determination of sailors and naval aviators to the utmost.

U–759 slipped through the Mona Passage and accomplished nothing for six weeks. On 5 July it cut a freighter out of a small convoy within sight of Navassa Island and avoided attack by the subchaser escort. Next afternoon it encountered a convoy of eight ships with six escorts ten miles off Morant Point, Jamaica, sank a Dutch merchantman, and evaded depth-charging by destroyer *Tattnall*. A Kingfisher out of Guantanamo sighted the boat off Cape Maysi on 8 July, dropped depth bombs, and summoned surface aid; but the boat shook everything off after a close pursuit of seven hours and resumed patrolling off Jamaica. *U–759* was not heard of

Mundial"; Gulf Sea Frontier War Diary; Chief U.S. Naval Mission to Cuba letter to Rear Admiral Munroe 17 May. *CS–13* was one of twelve 83-foot U.S.C.G. cutters transferred to the Cuban Navy under Lend Lease.

[20] Vol. I 30–3; W. L. Langer *Our Vichy Gamble* (1947) pp. 216–7; Cdr. C. A. Smith USNR "Martinique in World War II," U.S. Naval Inst. *Proceedings* LXXXI (Feb. 1955) 169–74.

again until 26 July, when a Mariner piloted by Lieutenant R. W. Rawson, sweeping ahead of a convoy south of Navassa, sighted the boat before dawn, illuminated it with a flare, and loosed a string of depth bombs that crumpled the pressure hull and sent it to the bottom with all hands.

In the meantime six other submarines had moved in; *U–159* slipped past "Spanish Hat" and through the Anegada Passage on 12 July. Heading for the Canal entrance on the 15th, it was surprised by a big gray Mariner, swooping down out of an overcast with guns blazing. The pilot, Lieutenant R. C. Mayo USNR, flew so low that he could even look down the U-boat's hatch while his bombs were falling. Banking for a second run to get a photograph, he saw *U–159* disappear. There were no survivors.

U–84 and *U–732* threaded the Windward Passage 10–11 July, unseen by blimps and planes guarding that entrance to the Caribbean between Cuba and Hispaniola. The first-named worked westward to the Yucatan Channel and around the west end of Cuba to the Florida cays. This boat, a veteran of the 1942 blitz, found conditions very different. In those days submariners could relax topside enjoying the scenery and acquiring a sun tan, submerge to periscope depth upon sighting smoke on the horizon, knock off a freighter or two and easily evade the frantic efforts of ill-trained small craft. Now one could surface only at night and even then had to keep a sharp lookout for planes. *U–84's* skipper must have been too cautious to look for targets or too frightened to attack them, as he emerged from the Straits of Florida in late July without logging a single one. On 24 August, as we have already noted, he fell victim to U.S.S. *Core.*

U–732, least cautious of the Caribbean raiders, was commanded by Oberleutnant C. P. Carlsen, a veteran of the attack on Convoy ONS–5. Jumped by two Kingfishers on 12 July near Navassa Island, he submerged in time, headed south, then returned to the Windward Passage looking for targets. On the night of 28 July, off Cape Maysi, he encountered three naval repair ships escorted by three destroyer escorts, one of which (by a curious coincidence

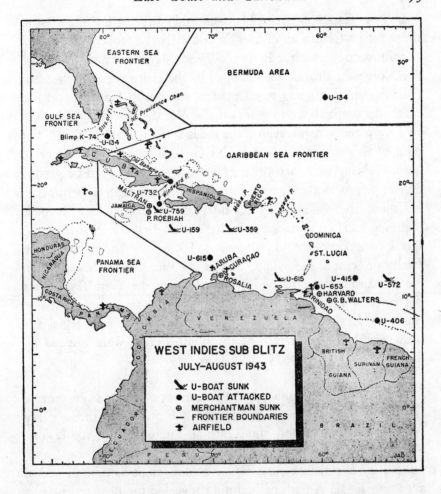

named *Carlson*) drove him off with a "scare" attack. *U–732* then headed toward the Old Bahama Channel and at midnight 1 August met southbound Convoy NG–376, twenty-seven ships and five escorts, about 30 miles west of Great Inagua, and was driven down by gunboat *Brisk*. Stalking all night, Carlsen delivered an attack at dawn 2 August and claimed to have torpedoed two merchantmen; but the convoy, unaware of his presence, plodded on and reached Guantanamo intact. *U–732* turned north through Crooked Island Passage and returned home with only a phantom-filled bag.

U–134 (Kapitänleutnant Hans-Günther Brosin) had the most to show for its Caribbean cruise. En route from France it had an inconclusive fight with a Bermuda-based Mariner. Passing through the Northeast Providence Channel in the Bahamas, it bucked the Gulf Stream, intending to take patrol station off Havana; and had reached a point about 30 miles off the Florida cays about midnight 18 July when it registered on the radar screen of blimp *K–74*. The pilot of this airship, Lieutenant N. G. Grills USNR, had been told before leaving base that a tanker and a freighter would be passing that night; so, with the thought of protecting them uppermost in his mind, he violated lighter-than-air doctrine which forbade bombing runs on surfaced submarines, and bravely bore in at top speed of 47 knots. *U–134* spouted flak at the enormous target, fatally punctured the balloon and kindled fires in the fuselage; but the airship's impetus carried it directly over the boat. Then, by a sad turn of fate, the long disused bomb-release gear refused to function. As the blimp settled in the water *U–134* submerged and made off. Nine out of ten of the blimp's crew were rescued by destroyer *Dahlgren* off North Elbow Cay.[21]

Admiral Munroe now diverted convoys, ordered unescorted freighters to keep clear of the Straits of Florida, and threw every available ship, plane and blimp into an intensive hunt for *U–134*. Shortly before midnight 19 July, a Ventura out of Boca Chica, piloted by Lieutenant John C. Lawrence, came within an ace of avenging *K–74*. A flash of lightning revealed the boat on the surface; the plane plummeted down and planted a string of three bombs which exploded under Brosin's bow. He submerged, effected temporary repairs and crossed the Atlantic, but was sunk by British bombers off the Bay of Biscay.

---

[21] Lt. Grills "A/S Action by Aircraft" 21 July 1943; Gulf Sea Frontier War Diary; Com Fleet Airship Wing Two to Cominch 27 July; *U–134* War Diary; conversations in 1952 with former members of the Blimpron staff. Plans to court-martial Lt. Grills were shelved when he pointed out that two weeks earlier the wing commander had urged his pilots to use more aggressive tactics against U-boats in order to dispel the talk that blimps were good only for reconnaissance.

Three boats ordered to the Caribbean never entered. *U-653* in mid-July began to patrol off the Guianas, where so many of the crew came down with tropical fever that the skipper pulled out, having accomplished nothing. *U-415* and *U-572* operated south of Barbados in hope of catching a tanker convoy. The former, spotted 60 miles off the mouth of the Orinoco, became the target of an intensive air search out of Trinidad, in the course of which a Mariner made a series of attacks just before midnight 24 July. The pilot had to break off after expending his last flare, since Navy planes in the Caribbean as yet had no searchlights. *U-415* reached home safely with nothing to show for its cruise.

Not so *U-572*. After sinking two local schooners with a combined burthen of 290 tons, it became party to a duel in which both contestants were annihilated. A Mariner of VP-205, piloted by Lieutenant (jg) Clifford C. Cox, radioed to Trinidad at 0025 August 3, "Sighted submarine, making attack." Evidently he attacked successfully, as his target, *U-572*, was never heard from again; [22] but neither was the Mariner. As a careful search recovered neither survivors nor wreckage, the story of that night encounter will never be known.

We have now accounted for every boat engaged in the Caribbean blitz except *U-615*, which had entered by the Anegada Passage 13 July. Its skipper, Kapitänleutnant Ralph Kapitzky, had orders to break up the heavy tanker traffic between Lake Maracaibo and Aruba-Curaçao, which had been interrupted for a time by three U-boats early in 1942.[23] He prowled about the Dutch islands for a fortnight without scoring, but on 27 July sank a small lake tanker off Willemstad, Curaçao. The funeral pyre of this vessel made a fine spectacle and Kapitzky reported it by air to Berlin, which was his eventual undoing. The HF/DF trackers at San Juan picked up the transmission and sparked off an operation

[22] Twenty minutes earlier, as we learn from German records, it had transmitted to Berlin from near the position indicated by Cox in his signal.

[23] See Vol. I 144-45 and Stanton Hope *Tanker Fleet* (London 1948) pp. 54-58.

which provides perhaps the best example in the entire war of a fiercely aggressive, fearfully costly, but finally successful air anti-submarine hunt.[24]

First to attack was an Army B–18 out of Aruba on the night of 29 July 1943. The pilot, 2nd Lieutenant T. L. Merrill USA, made one good bombing attack but lost contact when his flares flickered out – again, no searchlight. On 1 August a B–24 out of Curaçao dropped one bomb on the submarine; next day *PC–1196* made a depth-charge attack of no avail. *U–615's* crew were working hard to make repairs, and the boat had made only 200 miles easting by the night of 5 August when it was caught surfaced near Blanquilla by a Trinidad-based Mariner commanded by Lieutenant (jg) J. M. Erskine USNR. This plane made three runs but failed to inflict further damage. The following afternoon another Mariner of the same squadron (VP–205), piloted by Lieutenant A. R. Matuski USNR, attacked once, caused heavy flooding, radioed to Port of Spain, "Sub damaged with bow out of water making only two knots, no casualties to plane or personnel," banked for a second attack and then radioed, "Damaged – damaged – fire." Those were Matuski's last words; *U–615* shot him down and all hands were lost.

In the meantime more aircraft were hastening to the spot or warming up at Trinidad. That very afternoon (6 August) a Mariner piloted by Lieutenant L. D. Crockett USNR located the crippled submarine a few miles from the latest contact, delivered a bombing attack against heavy antiaircraft fire, and received an incendiary bullet in the starboard wing, which immediately burst into flames. While the flight engineer smothered the blaze with CO_2 and his shirt, Lieutenant Crockett bore in and at 1631 dropped a string of bombs that detonated close on the submarine's port quarter. Nevertheless *U–615* managed to withstand five subsequent strafing attacks. At 1635, a Ventura piloted by Lieutenant (jg) T. M. Holmes USNR appeared on the scene, slipped through the U-boat's flak without a scratch, and straddled it. *U–615* submerged, surfaced within a minute, the submariners springing to their guns as Crockett, Holmes and, at 1815, a Mariner piloted by Lieutenant

[24] Times for this operation are in Zone Q (plus 4).

(jg) J. W. Dresbach USNR, prepared to make a coördinated attack. The U-boat's gunfire killed Dresbach and caused a premature release of his bombs; but the co-pilot, Lieutenant (jg) O. R. Christian USNR, pulled out of the dive and banked for a high-level bombing attack. By this time, the U-boat's deck was littered with dead and wounded. At 1834 August 6 arrived another PBM (fifth of that type to take part), making three aircraft on the spot; its pilot, Lieutenant Commander R. S. Null, made two attacks which resulted only in killing more Germans. Night was now falling and the planes were running out of gas; an Army B–18 from Zandery reached the scene and attacked at 2118, the boat lighted by flares from a sixth PBM. So ended this memorable 6th of August.

U–615 was still afloat at 0010 August 7 when a seventh PBM made radar contact and lighted flares but, uncertain whether the boat was friend or foe, dropped no bombs. Destroyer *Walker*, dispatched from Port of Spain the night before, sighted the submarine at 0552. Kapitzky, seeing the destroyer approaching, knew that his time was up, ordered all hands into life rafts, and grimly took his boat down for the last time.[25] *Walker* rescued 43 submariners.

Thus the midsummer blitz in the Caribbean ended on a note of triumph for the air forces guarding that sea, and Vice Admiral Hoover was able to turn over his command to Vice Admiral A. B. Cook on 12 August 1943 with a sense of achievement.[26] He gave full credit to Captain Adrian O. Rule, Commander Fleet Air Wing Eleven, although that wing had lost three PBMs together with eight damaged in recent antisubmarine operations.

[25] N.O.B. Trinidad "Statistical Report," gives the best account of this hunt. Also, blimp *K–68* arrived on the scene 6 Aug. on hearing that Crockett's plane was on fire, and remained so long in the hope of rendering assistance that it had to make a forced landing. Crockett stayed on the scene 4½ hours directing the whole show. The Yellow Book is wrong on date and position, which was 35 miles N of Blanquilla.

[26] Arthur B. Cook, b. Indiana 1881, Naval Academy '05. Served in *Georgia* during the worldwide cruise of the Fleet, in *South Carolina* 1910 and *Louisiana* 1913. Staff duty with Rear Adm. H. T. Mayo 1913–16; flag lieut. to Cinclant in World War I; C.O. *Long* 1919–21; C.O. *Case* 1923–24; exec. of *Idaho;* qualified as naval aviator 1928 and became C.O. *Langley.* Asst. chief Buaer 1931, C.O. *Lexington* 1934, chief of Buaer 1936; Com Aircraft Atlantic Fleet 1940–42; chief of air operational training 1942; Com Carib. S.F. Aug. 1943–May 1944; retired 1944.

The German submarine command's war diary for 23 August 1943 contains these remarks on conditions in the Caribbean: —

"Entire Caribbean area . . . strong to very strong air patrol, changing to continuous air activity on U-boat being observed. Convoy traffic as formerly. . . . Isolated traffic protected by air and surface escort. . . . Day and night [radar] location everywhere, especially strong radar in Trinidad area. Slight chances of success. . . . Strength of crews taxed to utmost by heat and moist atmosphere. On the other hand enemy conditions for defense are favorable. This is apparent from the losses."

For the enemy, his Caribbean blitz was a disaster. Ten U-boats in six weeks had sunk only 16,231 tons of shipping, a bag that would have been considered small for one boat in 1942. Five boats were sunk in the Caribbean itself, and two more never got home.[27] Doenitz called this offensive off before realizing how unsuccessful it was, because the sinking of his milch cows near the Azores rendered it imperative for the assault boats to get home.

4. *Panama Run-around, October–December* [28]

After withdrawing the battered remnants of his West Indies raiding group in early August, Grossadmiral Doenitz left the Car-

[27] This table of participants and the passage by which they entered (or where they operated), with date that they entered the Caribbean and record of sinking, was compiled from German and other records by Lt. Lundeberg.

DATE OF ENTRY	U-BOAT	PASSAGE	DATE SUNK	BY WHOM
29 June	*U-759*	Mona	26 July	VP-32
10 July	*U-84*	Windward	24 Aug.	*Core* Group
11 July	*U-732*	Windward		
12 July	*U-159*	Anegada	15 July	VP-32
13 July	*U-615*	Anegada	7 Aug.	VP-204, -205, -130, A.A.F. Bomron 10
14 July	*U-415*	(E. of Trinidad)		
14 July	*U-653*	(E. of Trinidad)		
15 July	*U-134*	NE Providence	24 Aug.	R.A.F. Bomron 179
21 July	*U-572*	(E. of Martinique)	3 Aug.	VP-205
23 July	*U-359*	Dominica	28 July	VP-32

[28] Times in this section are Zone R (plus 5). Panama Sea Frontier and Fairwing Three War Diaries; *U-214* War Diary; and A/S Action Reports by Navy pilots. Details obtained by the writer at Sea Frontier headquarters 1946.

ibbean undisturbed until October,[29] when he instituted a series of nuisance mining raids, having little hope of torpedoing ships in such heavily patrolled waters.

U-214, which we have already observed in action around the Azores, entered by the Dominica Passage in late September, steered straight across the Caribbean to Escudo de Veragua off the coast of Panama and approached the Canal entrance without being detected. Navigating by coastal lights, this boat impudently planted 15 mines within four miles [30] of Colon breakwater on 8 October. No damage was inflicted by the mines, ten of which were swept up by deep-running Oropesa gear within a month.

During its retirement *U-214* was the occasion, though not the cause, of a tragic accident to a United States submarine. *Dorado* (Lieutenant Commander Earle C. Schneider) departed New London 6 October, bound for the Canal and the Pacific. A Mariner pilot based on Guantanamo, who had not been correctly briefed about a submarine safety area set off to facilitate the passage of just such vessels as *Dorado*, had been warned to look out for the minelayer. When covering a Guantanamo-Trinidad convoy on the night of 12 October, he challenged a surfaced submarine, observed no recognition signal, and made a bombing attack which he believed to be unsuccessful. But it seems very probable that he sank the boat, and that it was *Dorado*. Two hours later, the same pilot sighted a boat which can be identified as *U-214* by its own war diary, and was driven away by gunfire.[31]

U-218, carrying another clutch of mines to be planted in Port of Spain, was then approaching the Antilles. It beat off an attack by a Mariner off Grenada, stole through the Bocas, laid its eggs in the Gulf of Paria on the night of 26 October and silently departed.

[29] One exception is *U-518* which passed through the Providence Channel and the Straits of Florida in late Sept., missing numerous chances because of the skipper's fear of air attack, and was ordered home 12 Oct.

[30] Information from Capt. E. D. McEathron, historian of U.S.N. minecraft, compiled from reports by Com Minesweepers Cristobal Section. The plant was 3½ miles off the breakwater entrance to the Colon side of the Canal. *Catbird*, *Curlew* and 7 YMSs did the sweeping.

[31] "Record of Proceedings of Court of Inquiry . . . to inquire into disappearance of U.S.S. *Dorado* — 13 Oct. 1943;" *U-214* War Diary.

This field troubled only the local minesweepers who swept the Gulf for months and found nothing.

Since the minelayers had produced no tangible results Doenitz decided in early November to try a three-boat attack on Caribbean shipping. *U-516* (Kapitänleutnant Hans Tillessen) made the most sensational raid on the Isthmus of Panama since the days of Drake; and, although he carried off no silver ingots or pieces of eight, he made a bigger bag of merchantmen than had all ten boats of the summer blitz.

Rear Admiral H. C. Train,[32] Commander of the Panama Sea Frontier which straddles the Isthmus, was responsible to Lieutenant General George H. Brett USA, Commanding General Canal Zone, for the Navy's share in Canal defense. From their point of view, any German submarine approaching through the Caribbean was a minor threat compared with that of a Japanese air, surface, or submarine attack on the Pacific side. Once the war was over, it became obvious that the Japanese were incapable of anything of the kind after the Battle of Midway, but in 1943 that was by no means clear; and from Chinese sources, which provided some of our most phony intelligence right through the war, the Navy received repeated and specific warnings that such an attempt would be made. This preoccupation with the imaginary Japanese menace explains why, on two occasions during the war when U-boats entered the bight between Cape Gracias á Dios and Punta Manzanilla, Panama Sea Frontier was unprepared to cope with them.[33] Nobody cared to run the risk of a second Pearl Harbor.

[32] Harold C. Train, b. Kansas City, 1887, Naval Academy '09, service in Nicaragua 1912; exec. of a Naval transport World War I; gunnery and engineer officer *New Hampshire* 1919–21; C.O. *Borie* and *Parrott* of Asiatic Fleet, 1924–46; General Board and Naval Limitation Conference; Naval aide to President Hoover on South American tour; various staff duties to 1935; exec. of *Mississippi* 1935. C.O. *Vestal* 1936; Director of officer personnel 1938; C.O. *Arizona* 1940; staff officer on board *California* in Pearl Harbor attack; assistant chief of staff to Admiral Nimitz in early 1942; Director of Naval Intelligence June 1942 to Sept. 1943, when became Com 15th Naval District, Panama S.F., and SE Pacific Force; on committee of J.C.S. 1944–45; retired 1946.
[33] For the June 1942 affair see Vol. I 151–4. As the War Diary of Fleet Air Wing Three for 29 Oct. and 11 Nov. 1943 reveals, there had been a full air alert against Japanese attack twice in two months.

In the Pacific the Bougainville campaign was now on, Tarawa was coming up, and every day tankers, LSTs, supply ships and combatant ships were passing through the Canal to reinforce the Pacific Fleet, while troop transports were returning empty from San Diego. Plenty of targets for an enterprising U-boat!

Unfortunately, at the very moment when *U–516* paid its unexpected call on the Caribbean side, all frontier defense forces were engaged in a tactical exercise on the Pacific side, taking advantage of two escort carriers that were about to pass through the Canal. Captain Dan Gallery in escort carrier *Guadalcanal*, in company with *Mission Bay* and a "tame" submarine, were trying to sneak up undetected within striking distance of Balboa; most of the available ships and aircraft were engaged in trying to locate and "sink" them.[34] Rear Admiral Train's meager surface forces comprised eleven PCs, 19 SCs, three small Coast Guard cutters, and a squadron of motor torpedo boats. His more ample air forces, two squadrons of Mariners and one of Catalinas, together with about 40 short-range planes, were only in part based at Naval Air Station, Coco Solo; most were at outlying stations of the frontier.[35] The VI A.A.F. Bomber Command, based at Albrook Field on the Isthmus, had four squadrons of Flying Fortresses and Liberators. A ring of sonobuoys moored around the Caribbean entrance to the Canal should have warned patrol planes of any submarine making a close approach.

And such an approach is what Tillessen made. *U–516* entered the Caribbean by the Dominica Passage on 5 November, and three days later, north of Curaçao, fired on a sailing vessel. The skipper of that craft, an unknown hero, managed to slip into a rain squall and outwit the U-boat. Around 1000 of the same day a Ventura sighted *U–516* north of Curaçao, bombed it unsuccessfully and retired, damaged by three shell hits.

[34] Admiral Gallery has an amusing account of this "exercise," and how he foxed his "enemy," in *Clear the Decks* pp. 84–89.

[35] All but 4 of the PBMs, together with 2 PBYs and 3 OS2Us, were divided among Jamaica, Salinas (Ecuador), Barranquilla (Colombia), Corinto (Nicaragua), and the Galapagos Islands.

The Navy operations officer at Panama, assuming that the U-boat would take the shortest route to the Canal, set a trap to catch it on 9 November. He sent three subchasers to perform continuous patrol over a 60-mile square athwart its estimated course, while three Kingfishers based at Barranquilla patrolled a slightly larger box by day. Tillessen evaded the trap by hugging the Spanish Main. He rounded Cabo de la Vela, and on the moonlit night of 12 November, about 60 miles northwest of Cartagena, sank S.S. *Pompoon,* a small Panamanian freighter with a United States Naval Armed Guard. No S O S got off because she sank in less than a minute, but she was reported overdue next day and an air search was put on. Yet three Armed Guard bluejackets and a sailor from *Pompoon* floated on a life raft for 23 days, sighting numerous unobservant ships and planes, before being rescued.

On 16 November the patrolling SCs, having reached the limit of their fuel endurance, put into Barranquilla and were relieved by three others. All Frontier forces and commercial pilots were alerted to keep a sharp lookout for the U-boat and for survivors. In the meantime, on 17 November, *U-516* shelled and sank the small Colombian schooner *Ruby* about 125 miles north of Cristobal. A Honduran fruiter picked up seven survivors on the 19th and landed them at Cristobal next day. But the U-boat was not sighted by a single patrol craft or plane, since they were mostly employed in escort-of-convoy, and Tillessen was shy of convoys. He lay low for three days watching the ships ply to and fro, waiting for a plump and easy target. On the night of 22 November he sighted unescorted American tanker *Elizabeth Kellogg* outward bound from Cristobal, loaded with 46,000 barrels of fuel oil; and at 0600 November 23 torpedoed her very near the spot where *Ruby* had gone down. The tanker burst into flames and the master ordered her abandoned, but she floated for 36 hours.[86] Next, at 0020 November 24, *U-516* torpedoed unescorted Liberty ship *Melville*

---

[86] A tug and small craft were sent out 25 Nov. for salvage, but by the time they got there she had sunk; 38 out of a crew of 48 were rescued.

Stone, 75 miles off the Canal entrance. She went down in ten minutes, losing 16 men, including the master, out of 89 passengers and crew. The other 73 were rescued by patrol craft sent to the scene of sinking.

At dawn 24 November, a few hours after sinking *Stone,* Tillessen saw smoke on the horizon and went to periscope depth. The smoke came from tanker *Point Breeze,* escorted only by a Kingfisher. This was the first aircraft that the German had seen for ten days. Its presence apparently spoiled the skipper's aim, and *Point Breeze* sailed on.

A search group consisting of 9 PCs, SCs and other small craft was dispatched to the scene of these events the same day (24 November), together with a number of Navy and Army planes. The surface search group became fouled up in its own communications and accomplished no good; but a B–24 flushed *U–516* about 100 miles north of Cape Tiburon that afternoon, just as it was surfacing. Tillessen dove promptly. The Liberator dropped two sticks of bombs on his swirl but failed to sink him; three PBMs and a PBY relieved the B–24 and searched all night, unsuccessfully.

Lieutenant General Brett, in Rear Admiral Train's absence,[37] on 25 November ordered almost every available plane, including twelve Avengers from escort carrier *Mission Bay,* to search the area during daylight; but only four radar-equipped planes were available for night patrol, and their pilots were not well trained in night flying. Tillessen pulled out northward, then returned to the scene of his former exploits and reported to Berlin on 1 December from a point only 150 miles north of Colon. All unescorted sailings of merchant vessels were stopped, and some of the convoys, of which several were arriving and departing Cristobal daily, were routed along the Mosquito Coast. One not so routed was attacked by *U–516* on 5 December about 40 miles northwest of Colon, but the boat was detected and driven off by the escort before doing any damage. This attack was not reported to the sea frontier, with the

[37] Rear Admiral Train had departed 19 Nov. on a diplomatic mission to Peru.

result that Tillessen's calculated impudence continued for two more days. On the night of 7 December his fuel account dictated an immediate start for home, and regretfully he departed.

The adventures of *U–516* were not yet finished. On 8 December, while Admiral Train, returning from his visit to Lima, was conferring with General Brett and Colombian officials at Bogotá, Tillessen torpedoed and sank his fifth victim, the 1175-ton coffee freighter *Colombia*, off Porvenir Island, Gulf of San Blas. Next day officials in Bogotá announced they were establishing an antisubmarine patrol along the Colombian coast, as the United States authorities had long wished them to do. *U–516* now headed eastward into a prolonged running fight.

The element of luck in antisubmarine warfare is brought out in the next effort to get *U–516*, an effort which drew a blank despite good organization and aggressiveness. This was a Christmastide submarine hunt, organized jointly by Rear Admiral Theodore E. Chandler,[38] commanding the Aruba-Curaçao sector, and Rear Admiral Arthur G. Robinson,[39] commanding the Trinidad sector Caribbean Sea Frontier. And a great hunt it was, even though the fox escaped. Tillessen on his eastward course outside the Dutch islands

[38] Theodore E. Chandler, b. Annapolis 1894 (son of Rear Adm. L. H. Chandler), Naval Academy '15. Served in *Conner* during World War I and as exec. of *Chandler* (named after his grandfather W. E. Chandler, Secnav under President Arthur) 1919; M.S. Univ. of Michigan 1922; duty in Buord; served in *West Virginia* and *Colorado* 1923-26, gunnery officer *Trenton* 1928; C.O. *Pope* in Yangtze Patrol 1929; various duties in Washington 1930-32, when became gunnery officer on staff of Rear Adm. Kalbfus in *Detroit;* C.O. *Buchanan* 1934; naval attaché at European embassies 1935-38; exec. *Nashville* 1938; C.O. *Omaha* 1941-43 (for his capture of a German runner see Vol. I 84); Commander All Forces Aruba-Curaçao Apr. 1943-July 1944; commanded a gunfire support group in Operation DRAGOON and a batdiv (flag in *Tennessee*) in Battle of Surigao Strait. Transferring his flag to cruiser *Louisville* he was badly wounded in a Japanese air attack 6 Jan. 1945 and died next day.

[39] Arthur G. Robinson, who became commandant Trinidad Sector April 1943, was b. Brooklyn 1892, Naval Academy '13, served in *Montana* World War I; C.O. *Robinson* 1920-21; on Asiatic Station as exec. *Preble* and *Palos* and C.O. *Monocacy* 1924-27; helped fit out *Salt Lake City* and served as her navigator 1929-32; instructor Naval Academy to 1935; Yangtze Patrol to 1937; duty in Buord; C.O. *Marblehead* (see Vol. III 299-303); Com Aruba-Curaçao Area from June 1942. Com U.S. Naval Ports and Bases Germany 1945; President of Military Commission for trial of Japanese war criminals 1946-49; retired 1951.

missed two tankers on 14 December; but on the 16th, in two attacks five hours apart, sank unescorted American tanker *McDowell* about 30 miles north of Aruba. Too late, except to pick up survivors, a PC, two small minesweepers, and a Ventura were sent to the spot from Willemstad. In the small hours of the 17th *SC–1299*, escorting a small San Juan–Aruba convoy, sighted *U–516* about 65 miles from the previous sinking, failed to deliver an attack, and was narrowly missed by an acoustic torpedo. This aroused Admiral Chandler to order a heavy aërial hold-down. Before dawn a Mariner covering a convoy out of San Juan followed up a radar contact a few miles east of the last sighting, and flushed *U–516*, but Tillessen beat off its first attack and submerged before a second could be delivered.

The PC and the YMSs that had picked up *McDowell* survivors were now diverted to the new position, and at 1300 U.S.C.G.C. *Duane* and three PCs came roaring out of the Bocas to assist; a fourth PC followed that night. Unescorted ships and convoys crossing the area were diverted; preparations were made for day air patrol, and for round-the-clock surface patrol of all likely exits from the Caribbean. Near the last sighting a swirl was noted, a marker dropped, and a pattern of sonobuoys placed, one on each corner of a four-mile square centered at the contact position; and at 1130 two Mariners began flying a twenty-mile box square around this point. Small craft arrived at 1620 and searched well into next day, while a PBM from San Juan covered an adjoining area to the northward. But Tillessen eluded them all by releasing "Aphrodite" radar decoy balloons, which kept them chasing the wrong scent.

At nightfall on the 18th, Admiral Robinson organized a rectangular search by three Mariners equipped with radar and the new L–7 searchlights. A PBM piloted by Lieutenant Robert E. Pearce made radar contact at 2113 before the moon rose, ran it down, and at 1500 yards' range illuminated *U–516*. Tillessen opened up at once with everything he had. Pearce returned the fire from twin .50s in the nose, and the two streams of tracers crossed, making red

patterns against the velvet tropic night. Bullets were seen rico-
cheting off the U-boat, but the plane never took a hit. It crossed
the target from starboard quarter to port bow at a speed of 144
knots, dropping four depth charges, all of which exploded; then
climbed to 1300 feet and released a flare which revealed the U-boat
dead in the water. Nevertheless, *U–516* managed to submerge while
Pearce was banking for another strafing run. The plane dropped a
float light where the U-boat had disappeared, and four sonobuoys
at the corners of a four-mile square around it; yet Tillessen resumed his dash for blue water.

Another PBM arrived to take over sonobuoy listening, while
Pearce flew a 20-mile box around the attack position, about
90 miles north of El Roque. A third PBM arrived to assist at 0345
December 19. *U–516* surfaced at first light and (according to its
war diary) made 19 knots. At noon a Ventura piloted by Lieutenant P. J. Townsend USNR sighted the boat's foaming wake 20 miles
away and delivered a depth-charge attack as it dove. Air bubbled to
the surface for 45 minutes; but the German's pressure hull was not
ruptured, his crew checked flooding and made emergency repairs,
and after a 5-hour breakdown he resurfaced on the morning of the
20th and resumed homeward course. No surface craft of the killer
group happened to be near enough at the time of Townsend's attack to be homed in; and, although they eventually turned up and
searched the area all night 19–20 December, with the aid of Venturas and searchlight-equipped Mariners, no contact was made. On
the 20th surface craft and PBMs patrolled a 70-mile parallelogram
northeast of the last attack and then departed to guard the sea pas-
sages between Antigua and St. Vincent. Similar patrols and sweeps
continued until Christmas Day, but to no purpose. Late Christmas
Eve, Tillessen's lookouts glimpsed the lights of St. Eustatius through
a rain squall. After celebrating Christmas Day submerged near
"Statia," *U–516* reached the open sea by the seldom-used passage
between Saint-Barthélemy and Barbuda, one which the sea frontier
commanders thought not worth patrolling. The boat reached home
safely and returned next year.

"December was a very quiet month in this sector," concluded, probably with tongue in cheek, the Trinidad naval chronicler who reported this hunt.[40]

[40] Although their exploits were eclipsed by those of *U–516*, brief mention must be made of two 740-tonners that were operating at the same time. *U–193* worked through the Florida Strait into the Gulf of Mexico, torpedoed and sank American tanker *Touchet* on 3 Dec. about 185 miles west of Dry Tortugas. Lt. (jg) Absalom F. Bray USNR and 9 Naval Armed Guards, who stuck to their guns as *Touchet* went down, were lost. *U–193* continued to Tampico, and returned safely through Yucatan Channel and Windward Passage, evading two attacks by PBMs. *U–530* came in north of Martinique 21 Nov., patrolled the Gulf of Darien, missed a tanker off San Blas Point, and torpedoed but failed to sink tanker *Chapultepec* on 26 Dec. off Colon. It was rammed by its next intended victim, tanker *Esso Buffalo*, on 29 Dec., but escaped.

CHAPTER XII

South Atlantic[1]

May 1943–January 1944

1. *Fourth Fleet*

OFF BRAZIL and the South Atlantic, Vice Admiral Ingram's Fourth Fleet waged relentless war against raiders, runners and submarines, with the loyal coöperation of the Brazilian government and armed forces. Jonas Ingram had been more noted for brawn than brains in his Academy days; but he had learned much since World War I, while retaining at the age of fifty-seven a lusty physique, and displaying a certain magnificence that recalled the era of Dom Pedro to our Brazilian allies. He and President Vargas were thick as thieves, and everything that he wanted the Brazilian armed forces to do was done. His chief of staff, Captain Clinton E. Braine, accepted eagerly the suggestions put out by Comasdevlant and by the Asworg scientist, Dr. Jacinto Steinhardt. The small, closely knit Fourth Fleet, less diluted by replacements than almost any other part of the Navy, ranked high in morale and aggressiveness.

The ships under Admiral Ingram's command on 1 May 1943 consisted of five light cruisers of the twenty-year-old *Omaha* class, eight destroyers, five gunboats, 16 patrol craft and a number of

---

[1] Times in this chapter are either Zone O (plus 2) or P (plus 3). Fourth Fleet War Diary; Fleet Air Wing Sixteen War Diary; Lt. D. V. Phillips (Combat Intelligence Officer Fourth Fleet) Memo to Admiral Ingram on A/S Operations Fourth Fleet in July 1943, Aug. 15; the ms. volume on South Atlantic Force in Navy Administrative History; Com Crudiv 2 (Rear Admiral O. M. Read) War Diary; Blimpron 41 War Diary and War History; Army Air Forces A/S Command Monthly Intelligence Reports for the period. For the history of this command and area from Sept. 1941 through Apr. 1943, see Vol. I chap. xv.

tenders, minesweepers and other auxiliaries. The Admiral flew his flag in cruiser *Memphis* at sea; otherwise in a sort of converted houseboat moored in Recife's harbor, with the curious name *Big Pebble*. The Força Naval do Nordeste of the Brazilian Navy, commanded by Contra-almirante Alfredo Soares Dutra, was under Ingram's operational control. It comprised two light cruisers built in 1909, four (later increased to six) modern minelayers of the *Carioca* class which doubled as corvettes, and a number of patrol craft and subchasers.

During May 1943, United States naval air strength in the South Atlantic was augmented by two squadrons (VB–127 and VB–129) of Venturas, based at Fortaleza and at Ipitanga near Bahia; and Squadron VP–83 exchanged its amphibian Catalinas for Liberators. Fleet Air Wing 16, Captain Rossmore D. Lyon, still had only 36 LR or VLR planes based at Natal, and a number of Brazilian aircraft, to cover the stretch of coastal waters from the border of French Guiana (Fourth Fleet's "chop" line with Caribbean Sea Frontier) down to Rio de Janeiro, together with the ocean more than halfway to Africa. The Royal Air Force West Africa command, based at Port Etienne, Dakar, Bathurst, Freetown, Harper, Takoradi, Lagos, Douala, Libreville, Pointe Noire and Banana, provided coverage for about 600 miles off the African coast from latitude 30° N to the mouth of the Congo.[2]

Admiral Ingram expected Grossadmiral Doenitz to move U-boats into his bailiwick as soon as the North Atlantic blitz was defeated; nor was he disappointed. As a prelude to a Brazilian blitz, the Grossadmiral in May 1943 sent two 740-tonners to operate south of Cape San Roque.

First to make itself known was *U–154*, which attacked a convoy straggler about 120 miles SE of Recife on 8 May; but the one torpedo that hit was a dud, and a Brazilian B–25, which appeared within three hours, forced *U–154* to break off pursuit. *U–128* ar-

[2] That portion of the Atlantic for which the Fourth Fleet was responsible lay "south of 10° N and west of the following lines: from lat. 20° N, long. 40° W, SE to Ascension Island including that island and its territorial waters, thence SW to lat. 40° S, long. 26° W." Fourth Fleet Operation Plan 1-43, May 20, 1943.

rived off Bahia 14 May, patrolling so close inshore that its crew could see the city lights. This submarine was a South Atlantic specialist; under another commander in 1942 it had sunk five unescorted ships off the Guianas and had since patrolled for 121 days between the Cape Verde Islands and Brazil.

Admiral Ingram, informed of the position of *U–128* by HF/DF fixes on its transmissions to Berlin, set up an intensive search beginning 9 May; but, as Captain Lyon's planes were equipped with low-frequency radar, the boats detected their presence and submerged. *U–128* was first sighted on the 16th. Ingram promptly ordered destroyers *Moffett* and *Jouett* to break off from escorting a convoy and proceed to the scene of action, while planes of the two navies conducted a hold-down patrol as planned by the Asworg scientists attached to Fourth Fleet staff. About two hours after sunrise 17 May, two Mariners almost simultaneously sighted the boat about 20 miles off shore and each delivered a depth-bomb attack as it submerged. The first blew it to the surface; the second, followed by intensive strafing, damaged *U–128* so severely that when the skipper sighted the two destroyers bearing down, he gave orders to abandon ship. *Moffett* and *Jouett* then sank the boat with gunfire and rescued 51 submariners, of whom 4 died on board and were buried at sea. So ended a well-coördinated hunt, which set up Fourth Fleet no end. But it soon received severe shocks.

2. *Nuisances and Precursors, May–June*

Disquieting reports of submarines were coming from Ascension Island, 1200 miles east of Recife. The Ascension airfield, which United States Army Engineers had constructed in 1942,[3] although intended primarily for staging American aircraft to South Africa, now supported five Army B–25s for antisubmarine patrol; but their radius was only 250 miles. Outside that range, *U–182* sank a Greek freighter on 1 May, and *U–195* sank a Liberty ship on the 6th.

Five days later *U–195* encountered 6800-ton S.S. *Cape Neddick*,

[3] See Vol. I 379–80.

Harry Stark master, whose merchant marine crew and Naval Armed Guard under Ensign M. A. Gurda USNR put up a stout fight. This ship was bound from New York to Suez, laden with locomotives, Sherman tanks and aviation gasoline. Tenth Fleet, unable to furnish her with an escort, had sent her by the widely evasive route of Panama Canal, West Coast of South America and Cape Horn. She had reached a point 500 miles SE by S of St. Helena at 0113 May 12 when a torpedo from *U–195* exploded in the forward part of the ship. A sheet of flame rose masthead high, followed by a deluge of water; but Captain Stark spotted the submarine and resolutely steered for it at top speed, intending to ram, while Armed Guard and merchant crew fired with the forward guns. *U–195* was so startled by this spirited reply that it dove and temporarily retired. The high speed of the attempted ram so flooded *Cape Neddick* forward that she had to be stopped, in danger of foundering; but the crew worked valiantly to shore bulkheads, and had her under way and zigzagging when *U–195* fired a second torpedo at 0245. It missed, and a few bursts from a forward 3-inch gun effectually discouraged the submarine. *Cape Neddick* made a safe passage to Suez.

U–197 sank a Dutch tanker on 20 May, within 150 miles of Ascension, took a crack with its flak at a passing ferry plane, submerged after a depth-bomb attack by an Army Mitchell of the Island garrison, and got away. On 2 June *U–180*, returning from Madagascar where it had transferred the Indian traitor Subhas Chandra Bose to a Japanese submarine, sank a Greek freighter about 270 miles from Ascension.

Trouble reached the coast of Brazil when *U–154*, having replenished from *U–515*, an auxiliary which Doenitz had stationed off the St. Paul Rocks, started back to its patrol station. On the night of 27 May it encountered a northbound Bahia-Trinidad convoy (BT-14) about 170 miles NE of Cape San Roque. The twelve ships had what seemed to be an adequate escort, consisting of flush-deck destroyer *Borie*,[4] three gunboats and *PC–592*. Shortly before midnight

---

[4] The sinking of this destroyer in November has already been related in Chapter X.

the U-boat penetrated the screen and fired six torpedoes at ships of the starboard column, clearly silhouetted in moonlight. A tanker and two freighters were hit, but brisk work by the escorts kept *U-154* from making a second attack; the freighters managed to continue with the convoy, and gunboat *Saucy* towed the tanker to Fortaleza. The U-boat reported that it had sunk five ships, got a *"Gut gemacht!"* from Doenitz, and retired northward.

These events underlined the need for more and longer-range antisubmarine planes at Ascension and along the Brazilian coast. Admiral Ingersoll saw to it that Fourth Fleet got them. By 1 July 1943, Fairwing Sixteen, air arm of Fourth Fleet, was composed of the following squadrons under Captain Lyon: —

VP-94	14 PBY-5A (Catalina), at Natal	Lt. Cdr. J. B. Tibbets
VB-127	12 PV-1 (Ventura), at Natal	Lt. Cdr. W. E. Gentner
VB-107 [5]	12 PB4Y-1 (Liberator), at Natal	Lt. Cdr. B. J. Prueher
VB-129	12 PV-1, at Recife	Lt. Cdr. J. E. Jones
VP-74	12 PBM-3 (Mariner), at Bahia	Lt. Cdr. J. C. Toth

By the end of the year these had been doubled by the addition of five more squadrons: —

VB-130	12 PV-1, at Fortaleza	Cdr. G. C. Price USNR
VB-145	12 PV-1, at Natal	Lt. Cdr. J. E. Owers
VB-203	14 PBM-3, at Bahia	Lt. Cdr. M. D. Burns
VP-211	12 PBM-3, at Rio de Janeiro	Lt. Cdr. C. F. Fischer USNR
VB-143	12 PV-1, at Recife	Lt. Cdr. C. D. Hoover

Contrary to the practice in other sea frontiers, Fourth Fleet put on few routine air patrols; the great majority of flights were either to cover convoys or in search of definite targets. On the other hand, Admiral Ingram maintained an almost continuous surface patrol of the South Atlantic under Rear Admiral O. M. Read,[6] who flew his flag in light cruiser *Omaha.* The main object of

[5] Formerly VP-83.

[6] Oliver Middleton Read, b. South Carolina 1889, Naval Academy '11; officer or C.O. of several submarines in World War I; Bu Engineering 1919-22 and 1926-28; C.O. *James K. Paulding* 1923-25; C.O. *Paul Jones* and *Canopus* 1932; Com Subdivs 5 and 10 1933-34; senior class Naval War College. In War Plans Div. C.N.O. at start of war; C.O. *Helena* 1942; Com Crudiv 2 under Fourth Fleet Oct. 1942 – March 1944; Com Destroyers Atlantic Fleet 1944-45; Com Batdiv 5 1945. Retired 1951.

this patrol, which started in 1942, was to intercept blockade runners and armed raiders; and two runners had already been sunk before April 1943. Patrol Force,[7] based on Recife, covered the waters between the St. Paul Rocks and Ascension, sometimes ranging north of the Line or south to Tristan da Cunha. Occasionally it broke off to escort ships to Ascension, or a coastwise convoy. Except for one "good will" visit to Montevideo, this was proving a very boring duty, since no target was encountered for eight months.

On 21 June 1943 Swedish S.S. *Venezia* was torpedoed and sunk about 300 miles southeast of Rio de Janeiro. The assailant, *U–513*, commanded by Kapitänleutnant Fritz Guggenberger who had sunk H.M.S. *Ark Royal* in 1941, was precursor of ten or a dozen boats which Doenitz had committed to the South Atlantic. *Venezia* went down so quickly that her radio operator was unable to send out an S O S, and her loss was unknown until her survivors drifted ashore. Admiral Ingram on 25 June declared a submarine alert between Bahia and the Brazilian capital and shifted aircraft south to patrol off Cape Frio. The new Naval Operating Base at Rio de Janeiro,[8] commanded by Captain Harold Dodd, was ready to handle convoys; and thenceforth all convoys to and from Trinidad began or ended at Rio instead of Bahia.

Commander Fourth Fleet was not pleased to hear of U-boats off Rio. Although his air arm had been increased, his surface fleet was off balance because cruiser *Milwaukee* and three destroyers had been sent to the United States for overhaul. Besides escorting the Trinidad-Rio convoys and local feeder convoys to other ports, he

---

[7] TF 41, Surface Patrol Force, Rear Admiral Oliver M. Read, was organized in 5 task groups, of which 3 were constantly at sea.

Omaha	Capt. C. D. Leffler	*Cincinnati*	Capt. D. F. Worth
Jouett	Cdr. J. C. Parham	*Davis*	Cdr. W. A. Dunn
Milwaukee	Capt. C. F. Fielding	*Marblehead*	Capt. E. W. Morris
Moffett	Lt. Cdr. G. H. Richards	*Winslow*	Lt. Cdr. W. T. Samuels
	Memphis	Capt. R. W. Hungerford	
	Somers	Cdr. W. C. Hughes	

[8] See Vol. I 389.

had to protect a large volume of shipping between Rio and southern Brazil and River Plate ports, as well as ships independently routed to South Africa. Since the Naval Air Arm at that time had no bases south of Bahia, and the Rio field was too small for B–24s and B–34s, a detachment of amphibian Catalinas was sent south to operate from its tender, U.S.S. *Barnegat*, in Rio's harbor.

While Admiral Ingram was making these dispositions, *U–513* moved south. It torpedoed American tanker *Eagle* a few miles off Cape Frio at 0350 June 25. That morning a Brazilian plane — an old German Focke-Wulf — while looking for *U–513* flushed its 1200-ton partner *U–199* off Cape Frio, but both boats escaped, eluding air and surface search as they continued south in search of easy targets. Late in the night of 27 June, *U–199* encountered an unescorted Liberty ship, *Charles Willson Peale*, G. S. Thompson master, about 50 miles south of Rio. Her merchant crew and Naval Armed Guard led by Lieutenant (jg) Roscoe E. Johnson USNR took advantage of a missed torpedo to fight back so energetically with gunfire, and the master handled her so skillfully, that she eluded the submarine and made Rio safely. But *U–513* sank a small Brazilian coffee freighter on the night of 30 June, and Liberty ship *Elihu B. Washburne* on 3 July.

The same day *U–199* was spotted by a pair of Brazilian planes and held down until evening, when a Mariner commanded by Lieutenant (jg) Harold C. Carey attacked. The plane was shot to pieces by the U-boat's flak, and all hands were lost. But "Jonas kept 'em sailing." Convoys arriving at Rio from the north were broken up into so-called "Coffee Coast Convoys" to and from Santos and other ports, escorted by destroyer *Winslow*, Brazilian cruiser *Baia* and *Carioca*-class corvettes, and by Brazilian and United States patrol craft and aircraft. These mixed escort groups worked very well in spite of the language barrier, and got their convoys through without the loss of a single ship.

3. *July Blitz off Brazil* [9]

Along the Brazilian coast between Guiana and the Amazon, and eastward to São Luiz, there occurred in July the biggest concentration of submarines that Fourth Fleet had yet encountered. The "July blitz," as Admiral Ingram called it, had been timed by Doenitz to strike north of the Bulge immediately after *U-513* and *U-199* had forced the U.S.–Brazilian forces to stretch southward like a rubber band.

First shot was fired 28 June when *U-172* sank an unescorted British freighter 550 miles east of Cape San Roque. On 4 July, *U-590* sank an escorted Brazilian freighter laden with badly needed aircraft engines and spare parts. A southbound convoy (TJ-1) of 20 ships escorted by *Somers*, four PCs and a Brazilian subchaser, lost a tanker and two freighters to *U-510* off Cayenne 8–9 July. As the decimated convoy plodded on, a Catalina of VP-94 sighted *U-590* and attacked in the face of strong antiaircraft fire. The Germans consistently practiced "fight back" tactics in this area — and flying boats make good targets; but Admiral Ingram's orders were "Attack first, then worry about gunfire," and Lieutenant (jg) Frank F. Hare USNR, the pilot, obeyed. An explosive shell entered his cockpit, killed him and wounded his radioman and knocked out almost every instrument. Co-pilot Lieutenant (jg) J. P. Phelps USNR took over the controls, and after attempting another run with the damaged plane, flew 350 miles to Belem and landed safely. *U-590* did not long survive; Lieutenant (jg) S. E. Auslander USNR of the same squadron caught it off Maraca Island two hours later and sank it with six bombs.

U-185, third unit of the German blitz, had encountered a northbound convoy of 20 ships escorted by three gunboats and a PC in the midwatch 7 July, about 90 miles north of Cape San Roque. It

[9] Lt. Phillips "Anti-Submarine Operations Fourth Fleet July 1943"; Summary of Statements by Survivors prepared by U.S. Naval Observer, Natal, 26 Aug.; Com Fairwing Sixteen to Cominch 6 Oct.; Report on Interrogation of Survivors from *U-604* and *U-185* Nov. 4.

penetrated the screen and torpedoed an American freighter and a tanker.

In the meantime Convoy TF–2 of 18 ships was pounding along ten days behind TJ–1. On 19 July, it was picked up by *U–662* north of the Amazon estuary. While stalking the convoy, this boat was jumped by an Army Liberator based on Surinam, but escaped. On the 20th an Army B–18 attacked *U–662* about 200 miles east of Cayenne. The boat held this ancient Bolo at bay for twenty minutes, then submerged and resumed its pursuit of the convoy, which next day received air cover by Navy Catalinas of VP–94 based at Amapá, northernmost airstrip in Brazil. One of them, piloted by Lieutenant "Stan" Auslander, had an hour's running fight with *U–662* that afternoon; but it fell to a second PBY, piloted by Lieutenant (jg) R. H. Howland USNR, to sink the boat on the 21st, within a hundred miles of the spot where *U–590* had gone down. The German skipper and three men were picked up by *PC–494* a week later.

Off Natal on the following day, 22 July, Lieutenant Commander Renfro Turner, exec. of VB–107, when on a training flight in a Liberator near Rocas Reef, sighted and attacked *U–598*. Other planes out of Natal maintained a hold-down for the rest of that day and night, and delivered three strafing attacks shortly after daybreak 23 July, which rendered the boat incapable of submerging. A Liberator piloted by Lieutenant (jg) Goree E. Waugh USNR, first of a pair that were homed-in, attacked the target from so slight an altitude that the explosion of its own bombs caused the big plane to splash; all hands, four officers and eight men, were lost. Within a minute, Lieutenant William R. Ford USNR of the second Liberator avenged his friends by sinking *U–598*. Two survivors were picked up by Navy tug *Seneca*.

U–510 and *U–653* hung around the mouths of the Amazon for two or three weeks, ignoring the many targets that passed, and started home 4 August, along with ten other boats in southern and Caribbean waters. "Tropical fever" was their skippers' excuse for lack of aggressiveness.

Rear Admiral Francis S. Low USN

Vice Admiral Patrick N. L. Bellinger USN

A "short-hull" destroyer escort, U.S.S. *Decker*

A "long-hull" destroyer escort, U.S.S. *Greenwood*

Destroyer Escorts

U.S.S. *Wake Island*

U.S.S. *Croatan*

Carriers

Carrier-based Avenger

Vega Ventura

Types of Antisubmarine Aircraft

Navy Catalina (PBY-5A) landing at Argentia

Navy Liberator (PB4Y) taking off for Bay of Biscay

Types of Antisubmarine Aircraft

U-569

U-118

U-boats under Attack by U.S.S. Bogue *Group*

U–117 (left) and *U–66*, by *Card*

U–185, by *Core*

U-boats under Attack by U.S.S. Card *and* Core *Groups*

Captain Joseph B. Dunn USN

Captain Arnold J. Isbell USN

Commanders of Escort Carrier Groups

Captain Marshall R. Greer USN

Captain Giles E. Short USN

Commanders of Escort Carrier Groups

A Transatlantic Convoy

U.S.S. *Leary*

"There Go the Ships"

U.S.S. *Borie*, damaged while successfully fighting two submarines,
being sunk after abandonment

Lieutenant Hutchins of *Borie* receives a citation from Admiral Ingersoll

Borie's *Last Battle*

U.S.S. *PC–565*

Lieutenant Flynn observes scene of battle

A Fighting Patrol Craft and Her Skipper

Admiral John H. Hoover USN
Commander Caribbean Sea Frontier

Vice Admiral Jonas H. Ingram USN
Commander in Chief Fourth Fleet

U–848 *under Attack by Liberators from Ascension Island*

U.S.S. *Niblack*

U.S.C.G.C. *Campbell* with a GUS convoy

Two Mediterranean Escort Ships

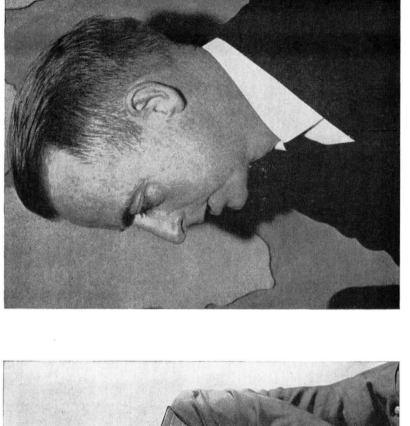

Captain Charles C. Hartman USN

Captain Adelbert F. Converse USN

Two Escort Commanders in the Mediterranean

U.S.S. *Buckley*

U.S.S. *Barr* after being hit by an acoustic torpedo

U-boat Fighters

Boarding party securing *U-505*

Captain Gallery on deck of "Can Do!"
Prize in background

"Captain Dan" and His Prize

Commodore William H. Hamilton USN

Crew of Liberator to which *U-249* surrendered welcomed ashore.
Squadron Commander Campbell is shaking hands with the skipper,
Lieutenant Schaum

Fleet Air Wing Seven

U–1229, with snorkel raised, under attack by aircraft of VC–42

U.S.S. *Bogue*

U.S.S. Bogue *and One of Her Victims*

U.S.S. *Frederick C. Davis*

The last of her

"Fightin' Freddy"

"Long May It Wave . . ."

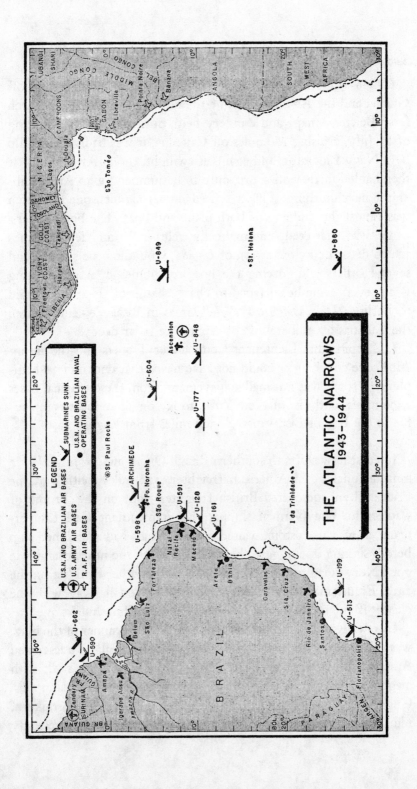

LEGEND

U.S.N. AND BRAZILIAN AIR BASES

U.S.ARMY AIR BASES

R.A.F. AIR BASES

SUBMARINES SUNK

U.S.N. AND BRAZILIAN NAVAL
OPERATING BASES

THE ATLANTIC NARROWS
1943-1944

U–466 (Oberleutnant Ernst Thäter), next to enter waters off Guiana and the Amazon, became the object of intensive air search from Belem, Amapá and Zandery field, Surinam. On the morning of 23 July, cruising 160 miles off Cayenne, it was badly shaken up by a Navy Liberator, and again, at twilight, by an Army B–18. It then hauled farther off shore, only to be jumped by an Army Liberator next morning. Thäter scored numerous hits, one of which was almost the undoing of both plane and boat. The bombardier's panel was shattered, automatically releasing four depth bombs which detonated close astern of *U–466*, wounding the skipper and several others and forcing the boat to submerge. After sighting B–24s every time he surfaced to charge batteries, Thäter reported to Berlin: *"Luft wie Biscaya"* — "Air as in Biscay" — and cleared the Guianas by a liberal use of Aphrodite radar decoys.

It is a pity that Lieutenant Commander Tibbets and the Army Air Force commander could not have heard that unconscious compliment; for it was no small achievement, from these tropical bases 2400 miles southeast of New York, to lay on air support comparable to the Bay of Biscay patrol, 300 miles from English bases.

Interest now shifts to southern Brazil. On 12 and 15 July *U–172* sank an unescorted American freighter, 225 miles south of Cape Frio; and an unescorted British freighter right on the Tropic of Capricorn. The German skipper, Kapitänleutnant Carl Emmermann, as was his custom, waited until all hands had abandoned ship before sinking it, and gave them the course to the nearest land. He got a Norwegian freighter on the 16th and another Britisher on the 24th. Emmermann sent that merchant crew on its way with the cheery if enigmatic slogan: "Have a drink to Churchill for me!"

U–513 (Kapitänleutnant Guggenberger), forerunner of the blitz, was still at large. On the afternoon of 16 July it sank an unescorted American freighter bound from Buenos Aires to New York with magnesium and tungsten ore, about 120 miles off Florianópolis. Guggenberger, who claimed to have spent seven years in Brooklyn, remarked to a survivor that he hadn't seen many papers recently and asked him how the Dodgers were doing. Sizing up the South Atlantic situation from a submariner's eye, he then sounded off to Berlin, expressing his contempt for Brazilian air patrols and suggesting that more U-boats be sent for easy pickings. His transmission served to home-in a Mariner which had just moved south to Florianopólis. The pilot, Lieutenant (jg) R. S. Whitcomb, caught *U-513* about 90 miles northeast of that city. Guggenberger, as he later admitted, thought that this was just another "old crate" to be shot down; but the Mariner, weaving expertly through his flak, made two direct hits that sent his boat down bow-first, propellers thrashing the air. The date was 19 July. Twenty survivors were observed afloat and *Barnegat* rescued seven, including gabby Guggenberger, five hours later.

His fellow nuisance, 1200-ton *U-199*, sank a British merchantman on 24 July, and started north to refuel from the milch cow near the St. Paul Rocks. En route it had the misfortune to run into a heavy air patrol laid on to cover the sortie of a convoy from Rio. Sighted in the early morning of 31 July only 60 miles off the Sugar Loaf, *U-199* was attacked by a Mariner piloted by Lieutenant (jg) William F. Smith with six Mark-47 depth bombs and so crippled that it dared not submerge. After expending all bombs, the Mariner exchanged gunfire with the submarine while signaling for help, which was furnished by the Brazilian Air Force. A Hudson attacked, missed, wheeled about and strafed most of the gunners overboard, enabling a Catalina piloted by Cadet Alberto M. Torres to make a lethal straddle which sent the German to the bottom. Twelve survivors were later picked up by *Barnegat*. This disposed of the last U-boat operating south of Cape Frio.

Fourth Fleet had recently acquired two squadrons of new Vega Venturas (PV-1) which were deployed at Fortaleza, Natal, Recife and Bahia. Their first kill occurred close to Recife on 30 July 1943, when a Ventura of VB-127, piloted by Lieutenant (jg) Walter C. Young USNR, sweeping 25 miles ahead of a convoy and flying at 4000 feet, sighted *U-591* distant 12 miles. It took the aircraft just three minutes to arrive over the submarine, which was taken completely by surprise. Straddled by six bombs, it sank in four minutes. Twenty-eight survivors including the skipper were later picked up by *Saucy.*

About noon of 30 July a Ventura from the other newly arrived squadron, VB–129, piloted by Lieutenant Commander Thomas D. Davies, took off from Bahia for an antisubmarine sweep ahead of Convoy TJ–2. At 1410 July 30 it sighted *U–604* about 100 miles off Maceió. The German skipper, Kapitänleutnant Horst Höltring, expected to patrol Brazilian waters for three or four weeks. He brought the Ventura abeam and opened fire. Davies straddled him with four Mark–47 bombs spaced 75 feet apart. *U–604* submerged, went ahead slowly, then broached at a steep angle, screws fanning the air, and went down. Davies returned to base and reported a sure kill. Nevertheless the boat managed to regain the surface. Höltring, having lost his executive officer, estimated that he could never coax his boat back to a French port, and reported his plight to Doenitz, who promised aid and arranged a rendezvous for 3 August between him and *U–172* and *U–185.*

As the three boats exchanged ideas by radio via Berlin,[10] Admiral Ingram suspected that a rendezvous was impending and saw to it that aircraft were dispatched to break it up. On 3 August at 0825 Lieutenant Commander B. J. Prueher, commanding Liberator Squadron VB–107 and flying his "Spirit of 83," sighted *U–604* and attacked with Mark–47 bombs after it had been submerged a few seconds. He was relieved by another Liberator, and Admiral Ingram had already dispatched destroyers *Moffett* and *Jouett* to the spot for a coördinated air-surface hunt. Prueher returned to the scene after refueling and rearming at Natal. At dusk a radar contact and a trail of oil directed him to *U–185,* Kapitänleutnant August Maus. In the gathering darkness he was first apprised of its location by a stream of tracer fire coming his way. He dropped four bombs and delivered a second attack through heavy antiaircraft fire, which hit one of his propellers and engines and perforated

[10] *U–185* had sunk a straggler from Convoy TJ–2 off Maceió around midnight 1 Aug. Survivors reported that the boat had exchanged blinker signals with another, which gave Fourth Fleet staff its lead.

the starboard wing. The U-boat, not seriously damaged, disappeared in the darkness and submerged.

Lieutenant Commander G. H. Richards of *Moffett*, after searching all day 3 August, at 1933 made a sound contact — not on *U-185*, but on badly wounded *U-604*. During the next two hours he made two depth-charge attacks and one with gunfire, but *U-604* survived. At 0340 August 4, a Liberator picked it up on radar and coached in *Moffett*, dropping flares as the destroyer closed the target. *U-604* surfaced about 95 miles north of Ilha da Trinidade at 0426, near enough to *Moffett* to be attacked with gunfire, and Lieutenant Commander Richards, deceived by an Aphrodite released by Höltring before he took the boat down, thought he had damaged it so that it could not submerge. *U-604* surfaced well out of *Moffett's* way and by radio arranged a new rendezvous with *U-185* and *U-172* for the following week.

The first-named, since its last attack (made by Lieutenant Commander Prueher on 3 August), had sunk a British freighter. Around noon 6 August, *U-185*, when sighted by *Moffett*, submerged, and escaped a depth-charging. But the chase had just begun. *Moffett* had to call at Ascension for replenishment 7 August, but planes scoured the ocean daily and kept in touch with the boats. On 11 August, Prueher started the long flight from Natal for the position where they were last reported. Two and a half hours later he reported to base, but was never heard from again; the rest of his story is derived from enemy sources.[11]

Prueher's "Spirit of 83" flew right into the rendezvous which had been effected between *U-604*, *U-185*, and undamaged *U-172* (Kapitänleutnant Carl Emmermann), about 500 miles NW of Ascension. Upon meeting *U-185*, the crew of damaged *U-604* began to transfer oil and provisions with the intention of abandoning ship. The transfer was almost complete when *U-172* arrived on orders from Doenitz to take over part of *U-604's* crew. This happy meeting of the three submarines was rudely interrupted when Prue-

11 Fourth Fleet Combat Intelligence Memo "*U-604* and Other Subs"; *U-172* War Diary.

her's far-ranging Liberator roared down from the overcast, strafing and bombing. *U–172* immediately submerged, but the other two opened fire, *U–185* circling its foundering fellow in order to protect it. Prueher made two runs but his bombs missed; and, as he was banking at about 1200 feet altitude to make a third run, *U–185* shot him down. "Spirit of 83" splashed with all hands. This was a sad loss to Fairwing Sixteen. "Bert" Prueher was an accomplished naval aviator, a born leader, and an inspiration to his squadron.

Preparations to scuttle *U–604* continued. *U–185* took over the rest of its crew, demolition charges were exploded, and *U–604* went down.

U–185 and *U–172* met again about noon on 14 or 15 August. Twenty-three lucky members of *U–604's* crew were transferred to *U–172*, after which it and *U–185* headed for home. As we have already told, when relating the exploits of escort carriers *Bogue* and *Core*, the Germans did not enjoy a peaceful return to the pleasures of Lorient.

An important additional factor in the defeat of this July blitz was the Germans' loss, in May, of milch cows *U–463* and *U–467*, and the premature return of *U–462*, owing to escort carrier operations around the Azores. Another trio of 1600-tonners was hurriedly dispatched from Biscayan ports in order to fuel the Brazilian and Caribbean blitzers, but all three — *U–459*, *U–461*, *U–462* — were sunk by Coastal Command bombers when crossing the Bay, as we have already related. And on 4 August, even before he knew that a fifth milch cow, *U–489*, had been sunk off Iceland, Doenitz notified all boats in the South Atlantic and West Indies that they would have to cut short their patrols in time to reach home without replenishment.

That is the main reason why no ships were sunk on the western side of the South Atlantic during the six weeks following 6 August, the date of *U–185's* last score. U-boat operations off Brazil had accounted for 18 merchantmen since 1 May; but had cost the German underwater fleet eight experienced submarines. The July blitz was analyzed by Konteradmiral Godt, Doenitz's operations officer:

Coast of Brazil from Natal to Rio — Six boats deployed, five lost; 10 merchant ships, totaling 59,000 tons, sunk.

As is apparent from the losses, the Brazilian Coast has shown itself to be a difficult and dangerous operations area. With one exception, an attack by surface forces (depth-charge attack on *U-604*), the defence took the form of fast daylight bombing attacks off the coast or heavy land- and sea-based aircraft up to 400 sea miles off the coast. Apart from *U-604*, which had to be abandoned and sunk as a result of damage sustained in air and depth-charge attacks, the boats remaining were most certainly lost in aircraft attacks.[12]

Once more, control of the air enhanced command of the sea.

4. *Air and Patrol Battles around Ascension, September–December*

Fourth Fleet air arm was powerfully reinforced by "lighter-than-air" in the fall and winter of 1943–44. Fleet Airship Wings Four and Five were commissioned, with bases at Maceió and Trinidad; and in September the blimps began to arrive. First to reach Brazil was *K–84*, which tied up at Fortaleza on the 27th. Igarápe Assu, Bahia, Ipitanga, São Luiz and Amapá also were used as lighter-than-air bases, and by 1 January 1944 blimps were operating south of Rio.[18]

The United States Navy had based blimps in France during World War I, but these were the first advanced operations conducted by lighter-than-air in World War II. The big aircraft enjoyed only one hangar, the old German dirigible base at Santa Cruz

[12] B.d.U. War Diary p. 143 of translation.
[18] The bases for Fleet Airship Wing Four were set up as follows: —

Squadron ZP-41		Squadron ZP-42	
São Luiz (HQ)	3 Dec. 1943	Maceió (HQ)	14 Dec. 1943
Amapá	26 Nov. 1943	Recife	1 Oct. 1943
Igarápe Assu	14 Oct. 1943	Ipitanga	26 Nov. 1943
Fortaleza	26 Mar. 1944	Vitoria	27 Mar. 1944
		Caravellas	Feb. 1944
		Santa Cruz	9 Mar. 1944

They Were Dependable, Airship Operation in World War II, 7 Dec. 1941 to Sept. 1945, prepared by Naval Airship Training and Experimental Command, Naval Air Station, Lakehurst, N.J. (1946); other data from Aviation Bases Office (Western Hemisphere).

near Rio, and possessed very little equipment; as their commander, Captain W. E. Zimmerman, remarked, they had to get used to "tying up to a coconut tree." They worked intimately with planes, each type being used in the manner for which it was best fitted. Blimps were particularly useful for night convoy coverage and patrol, and for rescue of pilots of planes which crashed in the jungle.[14]

In October 1943 the runway was completed at Fernando Noronha Island, 290 miles off the coast of Brazil, and three Venturas were sent to operate thence. Admiral Ingram now had enough aircraft to set up continuous air patrol between Natal and Ascension, to catch southbound U-boats. One of these, *U-161*, commanded by the well-known "Ajax" Achilles, sank a freighter on 20 September, turned north, and lay off the mouth of Rio São Francisco near Maceió, awaiting a chance to make a surprise attack. On the 26th it sank an unescorted Brazilian freighter. A PBM piloted by Lieutenant (jg) Harry B. Patterson USNR, which sighted *U-161* on the 27th, east of Bahia, worked over it to such good purpose that it was never heard from again.

Aware that another boat, which turned out to be *U-170*, had slipped through his air patrol and was moving south, Admiral Ingram decided to send Liberators to Ascension in order to extend the lethal range of the air garrison on that lonely island. These planes of VB-107, which arrived by mid-October under the command of Lieutenant Commander Renfro Turner, made a perfect score against U-boats during their first month's operation — two contacts and two kills.[15]

---

[14] An outstanding rescue was made 11 Feb. 1944 when two B-25s made belly landings in a dense jungle clearing near Amapá. *K-106*, Lt. Robert A. Powers USNR, dropped his boatswain who organized a "landing party" to cut away shrubs, and *K-106* managed to land and take on a load of passengers. *K-114*, Ens. William T. Raleigh USNR, came next, landing in the midst of a line squall; *K-106* made a third trip before dusk and rescued the remaining crewmen. (Blimpron 41 War History.)

[15] Com Fourth Fleet War Diary and Action Report to Cominch 14 Feb. 1943, Encl. A; "Narrative of Anti-Blockade Runner Operations So. Atlantic 1 Dec 1943 — 8 Jan. 1944"; Fairwing 16 War Diary; VPB-203 War History; O.N.I. Interrogation of Survivors from German Blockade Runners."

The first battle, on the morning of 5 November 1943 about 290 miles southwest of Ascension Island, was between *U-848* and four PB4Ys supported by two Army B-25s. Lieutenants C. A. Baldwin and W. R. Ford (both USNR) were searching some 200 miles apart for a submarine plotted SW of the island when Baldwin's bow lookout reported a ship, glimpsed between tradewind clouds. The pilot took one look and bellowed to his crew, "Heck, that ain't no ship, it's a Nazi submarine!" All hands scrambled to battle stations while their skipper made a diving turn through the clouds, swooped in on the German's port beam at only 75 feet, and made a perfect straddle. Lieutenant Ford's Liberator bore in half an hour later and inflicted further damage, but the boat's guns were still firing. Summoned from Ascension, a Liberator piloted by Lieutenant W. E. Hill USNR was greeted by heavy bursts of flak, one of which knocked out an engine so that this plane had to return to base. By midafternoon *U-848* was showing alarming signs of recuperation when two Army Mitchells appeared and dropped 500-pound demolition bombs from 4000 feet altitude. Naturally, they missed. Lieutenant Ford in the meantime had returned to Ascension, where Lieutenant Samuel K. Taylor USNR relieved him at the controls and flew to the scene of action. He reached it at 1555 and, in coordination with Baldwin's Liberator, blew up *U-848*. Twenty survivors were counted, three life rafts were dropped, and a freighter was signaled to pick them up; but only one survivor, delirious from hunger and thirst, was rescued a month later by *Marblehead*. "During the entire action the planes encountered heavy antiaircraft fire but, although hit, all returned safely to the base." [16]

Turner's Ascension-based Liberators were determined to give the Admiral something better than turkey for Thanksgiving. For one week they had been making daily long-range sweeps to regain a submarine contact made by *Memphis* on 17 November near the St. Paul Rocks. This was *U-849*, sister to *U-848*, outward bound for the Indian Ocean. Early Thanksgiving morning, 25 November,

[16] *All Wing No. 16* Nov. 6, 1943, a mimeographed weekly by Fairwing Sixteen issued in Recife for local use; *U.S. Fleet A/S Bulletin* Dec. 1943 pp. 19-23 has diagrams and illustrations.

came the payoff. Two Liberators took off from "Wideawake Field," Ascension, on a long search eastward. At about 1030 the one piloted by Lieutenant (jg) Marion Dawkins USNR, already 590 miles and four hours E by N of the base, sighted *U-849* from 5200 feet altitude at a range of ten miles. Lieutenant Dawkins cleverly maneuvered to make use of cloud cover and achieved complete surprise, catching the submariners as they were having lunch. Breaking through at 2000 feet, range one mile, Dawkins straddled *U-849* with six depth bombs dropped from a height of only 25 feet. One bomb bounced and damaged the Liberator's fin and rudder, but the pilot managed to keep his plane from splashing as he circled to observe results. The U-boat settled slowly by the stern, its crew scrambled overboard, and a few seconds later it blew up with a tremendous explosion which made a 200-foot fountain of spray. After dropping a life raft to survivors, and taking photographs, the seriously damaged PB4Y made Ascension successfully.[17]

Admiral Ingram observed at his conference that morning in Recife, "Today is Thanksgiving. I don't see any snow or football games, but we have a hell of a lot to be thankful for. In this global war there are lots of worse places to be than here." Brazil too had much to be thankful for, but she still had a long way to go before becoming a great naval power. Her activities were modestly summed up by a remark of her Navy Chief of Staff, Vice Admiral A. Viera de Mello: "We came from nearly nothing to just a little bit."

Turner's Ascension detachment wanted a lot more. In early December when a string of blockade runners, homeward bound from the Far East, was approaching the Atlantic Narrows, Admiral Ingram strengthened his South Atlantic patrol between Natal and Ascension; and his opposite number, Vice Admiral Frank H. Pegram RN of the Freetown Command, did the same between West Africa and Ascension. Captain Lyon set up the aërial section of the fence with one squadron of Mariners based at Natal and almost a

dozen Liberators and Mitchells, based at Ascension; [18] and Rear
Admiral Oliver M. Read's five surface task groups, eager for action
after long months of patrolling with no results, got into the act.

The first runner to come along, 7000-ton German *Osorno*, was
carrying tin, wolfram and rubber from Singapore and Japan. On
8 December she was sighted and challenged midway between Ascension and Fernando Noronha by a Liberator which maintained
contact for 40 minutes and then headed west in search of Task
Group 41.4. Captain Morris of *Marblehead*, confused by simultane-
ous reports of another suspicious-looking vessel (which turned out
to be friendly), failed to follow the Liberator's lead for three hours,
during which *Osorno* changed course and escaped. *U-510*, acting
as a red herring on *Osorno's* scent, led *Winslow* and two other
destroyers on an antisubmarine hunt. *Alsterufer*, next runner to
be sighted by aircraft, passed the barrier safely, only to be sunk by
Coastal Command off the Bay of Biscay.

Grossadmiral Doenitz, eager to get the runners through, now
ordered them to run the gantlet west of Ascension at two-day intervals. *Weserland* was spotted by a Liberator piloted by Lieutenant Robert T. Johnson USNR. Flak from the runner ruptured his
fuel tank; he had to ditch 70 miles short of Ascension and was lost
with all hands. *Somers* (Commander Hughes) sent *Weserland* to
the bottom with point-blank five-inch gunfire about halfway between Ascension and Caravellas, at 0826 January 3, 1944.

Admiral Read now seized the initiative and wound up the operation promptly. *Omaha*, accompanied by *Jouett*, sighted blockade
runner *Rio Grande* on 4 January 1944 in midpassage, about 650
miles off Cape San Roque. The German skipper sent out a bogus
call sign, that of an American merchantman; but Captain Leffler
of *Omaha* saw through it, closed to one-mile range, and found that
the crew were already preparing to scuttle. The two warships then

[18] Aërial Patrol Forces, Capt. R. D. Lyon (Fourth Fleet War Diary): —

Patron 203 (Lt. Cdr. M. D. Burns)	7 PBM, Natal
Bombron 107 (Lt. Cdr. R. Turner)	6 PB4Y, Ascension
1st Compron A.A.F. (Col. A. J. Ronin USA)	5 B-25, Ascension

moved beyond the runner's range and sank her with gunfire. Most of the crew were rescued.

On 5 January another of the Natal-based Mariners sighted a highly dubious customer some 640 miles east of Recife. Picking up the vessel at the extremity of his assigned sweep, Lieutenant Stanley V. Brown immediately challenged the 7320-tonner, which flashed the name *Floridian*. Brown, having no such ship on his location plot, was suspicious and transmitted such an accurate description of the vessel that Fourth Fleet headquarters identified her as blockade runner *Burgenland*. Orders were immediately issued for a bombing attack; but before another Mariner could locate the vessel, Admiral Read's group had again gone into action. *Omaha* altered course to intercept and, working up flank speed, picked up the runner that afternoon on her radar, 50 miles south of the scene of *Rio Grande's* destruction. Visual contact was made eight minutes later; and at 1722, shortly after the armed merchantman had transmitted a last message to Berlin, *Omaha* blinked a challenge; when the German failed to respond properly, she looped two shots across his bow and, at 1733, opened fire in earnest. *Burgenland* was already shaken by scuttling charges and disappeared amid a plume of steam. All but one of her 150 passengers and crew were rescued.

Admiral Read's task group now headed east in the hope of finding more game. Interrogation of German survivors, almost 400 of whom were rescued by American and Brazilian vessels from various ships, indicated that the blockade-running season was over. On 10 January 1944, after seagoing tugs had salvaged nearly 2000 bales of crude rubber — enough, it was estimated, to re-tire 5000 Luftwaffe bombers — Fourth Fleet forces turned their attention once more to submarines.

Thus, after an uncertain beginning, Fourth Fleet had barred the Atlantic Narrows to blockade runners and virtually ended the flow of raw materials from the Far East.

CHAPTER XIII

In Arctic Waters[1]

May–December 1943

1. High Jinks in High Latitudes

DURING the first half of the Battle of the Atlantic the most dangerous and uncomfortable Allied convoy route was that of the PQ–QP convoys between Scotland or Iceland, and the North Russia ports of Murmansk and Archangel. Although more heavily escorted than any in the war, 27 of these convoys lost 74 ships to the German Navy and Luftwaffe in 1942, and five more convoys lost five ships during the first three months of 1943.[2] In mid-March, as Arctic days were growing longer, the Admiralty decided that it needed all available escort vessels for the hard-pressed northern transatlantic route, and suspended the North Russia convoys.

At that time a task force of the United States Navy under Rear Admiral Hustvedt,[3] in heavy cruiser *Tuscaloosa*, was operating with the British Home Fleet based at Scapa Flow. During May,

---

[1] Admiralty documents; B.d.U. and F.d.U. Norway War Diaries.

[2] See Vol. I chap. vii and pp. 358–75. Also, 5 ships were sunk by "friendly" mines, 5 unescorted ships were sunk by enemy action, and one wrecked. Revised statistics on this chapter were furnished by Cdr. L. Pitcairn-Jones RN at the Admiralty.

[3] Olaf M. Hustvedt, b. Chicago 1886, Naval Academy '09, M. S. George Washington Univ. 1914. Served in *New York* during World War I; two periods of service in Buord 1918–27 as chief of experimental section. C.O. *Burns* 1922–24; divisional gunnery officer in Battle Fleet 1928; duty in Naval Gun Factory 1930; exec. of *Louisville* 1933; duty with C.N.O. 1935; C.O. *Detroit* 1938; Admiral Richardson's operations officer in *Pennsylvania* 1939; fitted out *North Carolina* and became her C.O. 1941; chief of staff to Admiral Ingersoll Oct. 1941; Com Battleships Atlantic Fleet May 1943; Batdiv commander in Pacific Fleet 1943–4; retired 1946.

June and July 1943, this force included the new battleship *Alabama* (Captain Fred D. Kirtland), and battleship *South Dakota* (Captain Lynde D. McCormick) which had just been repaired at Brooklyn after the battering she had received in the great Battle of Guadalcanal.[4] The object of sending them to Scotland was to tempt *Tirpitz* to come out and fight; but the German super-battleship, despite provocative cruises along the Norwegian coast by the two Americans and by major Home Fleet units, was ordered by Hitler to decline the challenge. Early in August *Alabama* and *South Dakota* with their destroyer screen departed for the Pacific.

German forces, all set for a profitable summer's hunting under the midnight sun, were left with nothing to do. Kapitän-zur-See Rudolph Peters, the submarine commander in northern waters, with 21 U-boats based between Narvik and Hammerfest, observed plaintively in his war diary on 19 April 1943, "There are still no' indications of the running of the next PQ convoy, which has been due for a long time." Owing partly to Hitler's "intuitions" (which British counter-intelligence took care to confirm), the Germans were alerted against an Allied landing on the coast of Norway in June, and Peters was ordered to set up a defensive screen of U-boats. When the Allied landings in Sicily on 10 July ended that false alarm, Peters's U-boats were again unemployed.

On 20 June 1943 a German weather-reporting party on Spitsbergen was chased out by an Anglo-Norwegian landing party. A U-boat sent by Peters to pick up the Germans reported that the Allies had set up a meteorological station of their own at Eisfjord, around lat. 78° N. That minor event gave the idle German surface fleet in northern waters something to do.

This fleet, commanded by Vizeadmiral Oskar Kummetz, was formidable on paper. Giant *Tirpitz*, fast battleship *Scharnhorst*, heavy cruiser *Lützow*, and 14 destroyers lay at the head of Altenfjord, waiting, waiting, and waiting. All summer long they continued to do nothing; a "fleet in being" but not in action. In September, when the impending surrender of the Italian Navy sug-

[4] See Vol. V 270–85.

gested that the British Home Fleet would soon be reinforced by heavy ships from the Mediterranean, Doenitz decided to justify the existence of this surface navy and give it a little exercise by wiping out the Allied installations at Spitsbergen. Accordingly, on the 7th, *Tirpitz*, *Scharnhorst*, and ten destroyers bombarded the village, landed troops who gutted the installations, re-embarked the troops and retired. One destroyer could easily have done the job.

Doenitz dared not set up a German base there, knowing that it would be at the mercy of Allied sea power; so the Norwegian garrison, which had escaped to the mountains, promptly returned and began to rebuild. On 19 October, Norwegian troops and matériel were brought in by a small task group consisting of U.S.S. *Tuscaloosa* (Captain J. B. Walker) and *Fitch*, and three British destroyers.[5] Spitsbergen remained in Allied hands for the rest of the war. But Operation ZITRONELLA, as the overstuffed German raid on Spitsbergen was called, assumed the proportions of a major victory in German propaganda.[6]

The British answer to ZITRONELLA was to send six midget submarines a thousand miles across the North Sea to attack the German Fleet. Three were lost in passage and the other three were sunk, but not before their gallant crews had seriously damaged *Tirpitz* with mines dropped under her bottom. She never sailed again, except to another northern anchorage where she was badly battered on 3 April 1944, by aircraft from a number of Royal Navy carriers.[7]

In October 1943 the Allies struck another blow: Operation LEADER, an air strike against German shipping in northern waters, led by C. in C. Home Fleet, Admiral Sir Bruce Fraser, in battleship *Duke of York*. Under his command were H.M.S. *Anson*, three cruisers, six destroyers, and Rear Admiral Hustvedt's task force, now comprising carrier *Ranger*, cruiser *Tuscaloosa* and a destroyer

[5] *Tuscaloosa* War Diary Oct. 1943. She claimed a "farthest north" for any United States warship in the war, having reached lat. 78°18'30" N. She also picked up Norwegian survivors from outlying points and islands, and transferred them to Iceland and Greenock.
[6] Doenitz "The War at Sea" sec. 133; *O.N.I. Weekly* 15 Sept. 1943.
[7] See Chapter XVI below, p. 308.

division. Their objective was the port of Bodö south of the Lofo-
ten Islands, a rendezvous for German and Quisling sea traffic. It lay
within a few minutes' flight of Luftwaffe bases, but so many planes,
including all torpedo bombers, had been withdrawn from Arctic
fields during the summer to reinforce dwindling Axis air power
in the Mediterranean that the risk of air attack had become
negligible.

Admiral Fraser's task force reached its launching position off
Vestfjord before dawn 4 October, completely undetected. At
0618 [8] Captain Gordon Rowe of U.S.S. *Ranger* launched his first
attack of 20 Dauntless dive-bombers escorted by 8 Wildcats, led
by Lieutenant Commander G. O. Klinsmann. The planes skimmed
low over the North Sea until they picked up Myken Light 18 miles
south of the target, then gained altitude and swung north. While
one division of SBDs peeled off to work over 8000-ton freighter
La Plata, the rest continued up the coast, ignoring numerous small
coasters and fishermen which Norwegian observers on board the
planes identified as friendly, and at 0730 pitched on a small German convoy. The American pilots, over half of them on first combat mission, were disconcerted by abundant flak; yet they succeeded in damaging severely a 10,000-ton tanker and a 4300-ton
transport with troops on board, before pressing on to their principal target, the shipping in Bodö roadstead. There they sank two out
of four small German merchantmen but lost two planes to shore-
and ship-based antiaircraft fire.

The Germans were so completely surprised, and their communications were so bad, that there was no air interception, even
of the second *Ranger* attack group (10 Avengers and 6 Wildcats
led by Commander J. A. Ruddy), launched 50 minutes after the
first. Ruddy's planes destroyed a 5000-ton German freighter with
the American name *Topeka* and a small coastal steamer, and
dropped another bomb or two on *La Plata* which caused that vessel
to be beached. They bombed and gutted yet another troop-laden
transport and, after losing three of their number to antiaircraft

[8] Zone N (plus 1) time.

fire, returned to *Ranger* before 0900. That afternoon (4 October) three German planes finally managed to locate the carrier, whose combat air patrol instantly shot down two of them.

Admiral "Pat" Bellinger, air commander of the Atlantic Fleet, was well pleased with Operation LEADER. Six steamers amounting to 23,000 tons had been destroyed, four others badly damaged, and about 200 troops killed; this from German records. And the raid created a feeling of insecurity in the once arrogant occupation forces in Norway. Possibly the most valuable result, for the far future, was the demonstration (in Admiral Hustvedt's words) that ships and air squadrons of the United States and Royal Navies could work in the same task force with "effectiveness, mutual understanding, and complete coöperation." [9]

2. *North Russia Run Reopened, November–December*

Kapitän-zur-See Peters had by this time been deprived of 9 U-boats out of 21 to help the September submarine offensive in the North Atlantic. Repair and upkeep facilities in the Norwegian fjords were so inadequate that in early October, when the North Russia convoys were revived, his normal operational strength was only half a dozen boats.

While the transpacific route, still unmolested by Japan,[10] continued to carry almost half the American supplies to Russia, and the Persian Gulf route was available, the northern one was much the shortest. And Russian cries of "More, more, more!" were so insistent, that Mr. Churchill ordered the Admiralty to resume sailings to Murmansk. Now that winter was beginning to throw its blanket of darkness over the Arctic Ocean and Barents Sea, it seemed a

[9] Comairlant (Vice Adm. P. N. L. Bellinger) to Cominch 13 Nov. 1943; Comnaveu (Admiral Stark) Letter to Cominch 30 Nov. 1943 enclosing Rear Admiral Hustvedt Report on Operation LEADER 18 Oct.; German Operations Div. Naval Staff War Diary 4–6 Oct.
[10] See Vol. I 158–9 and table near end of chap. xvi below.

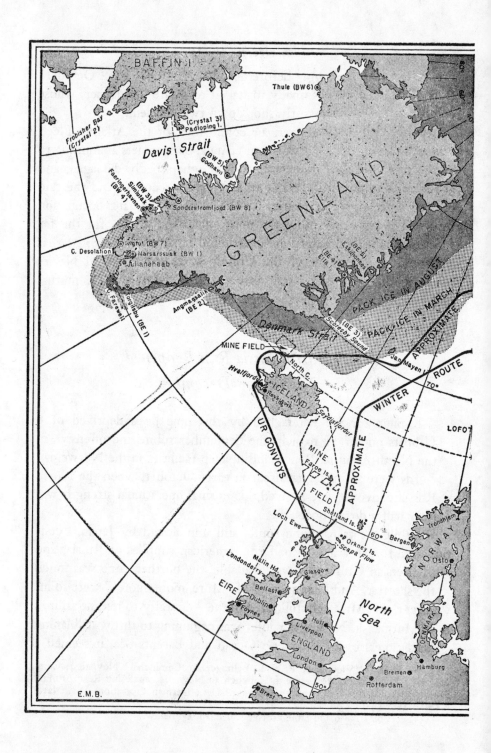

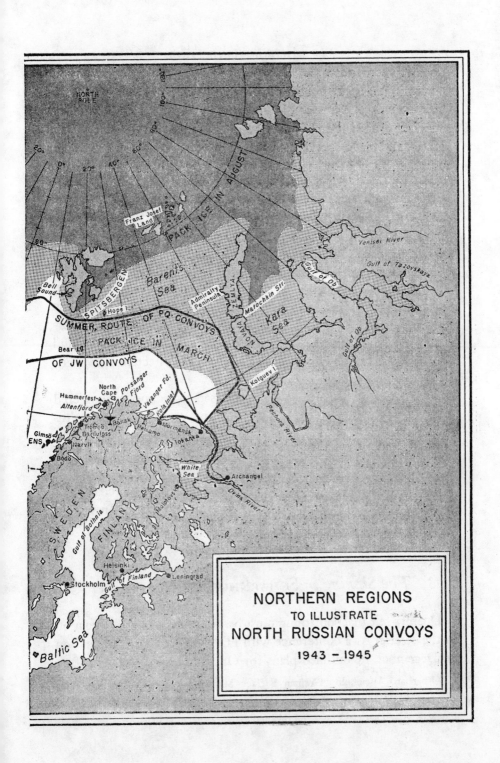

NORTHERN REGIONS
TO ILLUSTRATE
NORTH RUSSIAN CONVOYS
1943 – 1945

good time to start. On 1 November 1943 the first southbound convoy, RA–54A, consisting of 13 merchant vessels which had been waiting all summer for an escort to return, sailed from Archangel. It evaded four U-boats which were patrolling south of Bear Island, and made Scotland on the 14th. Next day JW–54A the first northbound convoy, 18 ships escorted by 8 destroyers and corvettes, departed Loch Ewe. Seven American minesweepers which had been transferred to Russia, in partial recompense for the slice of the Italian fleet that Stalin claimed, joined off Iceland. German U-boat headquarters at Narvik learned about this convoy on 22 November; but neither U-boat nor aircraft sighted it steaming toward Murmansk in total darkness 23 hours out of every 24. Admiral Kummetz blamed Peters for letting this convoy off so easily; the Kapitän-zur-See retorted that the Admiral had interfered with his patrol dispositions; but they found a common ground of agreement in blaming the Luftwaffe for ineffective reconnaissance.

U–307 of Peters's patrol (now increased to six boats) blundered into the second southbound convoy, but was immediately illuminated, depth-charged, and driven off; and the second northbound convoy got through like the first without making a single enemy contact of any kind. It was the same story to the end of 1943. During the first three weeks of December, 52 merchant vessels crammed with British and American goods for Russia got through without sighting a plane or a torpedo wake.

3. *The Sinking of* SCHARNHORST, *26 December* [11]

Doenitz felt that something must be done about this sad situation in the Arctic. At a conference with Hitler at the "Wolf's Den" on 20 December, he outlined plans for Operation OSTFRONT, a surface

[11] Eberhard Weichold "German Surface Ships, Policy and Operations" (an O.N.I. mimeographed publication) pp. 133–43, with messages. Fritz-Otto Busch *Tragödie am Nordkap* (Hannover 1952) and Admiralty sources; B.d.U. and F.d.U. Norway War Diaries; Times for this action are Zone A (minus 1).

raid on the next North Russia convoy by 11-inch-gunned *Scharnhorst*, the only available capital ship in the German Navy.[12]

He chose a time when there were plenty of targets, even more than he knew. He was aware that a northbound convoy was about to sail from Loch Ewe; but he did not know that a southbound one was to depart Murmansk a few days later; or that Admiral Fraser in battleship *Duke of York*, with cruiser *Jamaica* and four destroyers, would cover the one, while Vice Admiral R. L. Burnett in cruiser *Belfast*, with *Norfolk*, *Sheffield* and more destroyers, protected the other. The Admiralty had anticipated Doenitz's intentions. Admirals Fraser and Burnett planned a series of complex movements to intercept the German raiders before they could pounce on the two convoys when passing Bear Island on opposite courses.

Admiral Kummetz was skeptical about using *Scharnhorst* in the dark of the year when British radar superiority might be decisive; but Doenitz, eager to convince Hitler that capital ships were still useful, ordered her out. Querulous Kapitän Peters, though given eight more U-boats and supplied with acoustic torpedoes, damned the Luftwaffe; but it was a pilot of the Luftwaffe who spotted JW–55B, the northbound convoy, before it passed the Faroes, and delivered the first attack.

That 19-ship merchant convoy (Commodore Maitland Boucher RNR)[13] included nine American Liberty ships and was escorted by eight fleet destroyers and five smaller craft under Captain J. A. McCoy RN. During the forenoon of 23 December, in the Arctic twilight, five bombers attacked in succession; two were splashed and the rest driven off by gunfire. Such attacks, in 1942, would have heralded a full-scale blitz next day; and the convoy, knowing that Admiral Fraser's support force was still far behind, felt apprehensive. But nothing happened on the day before Christmas. Both sides continued to spar, probe and fight without benefit of assistance from the air.

[12] *Lützow* was in a German dockyard, *Hipper* had been paid off, and *Scheer* and *Nürnberg* were in the Baltic.
[13] A retired rear admiral RN.

In the meantime RA–55A, the 22-ship southbound convoy, escorted by eight fleet destroyers and six smaller craft, had neither been spotted nor suspected by the Germans. Admiral Fraser, cognizant that JW–55B was being shadowed by the Luftwaffe, correctly estimated that it would be the German target. Consequently, early on Christmas morning he ordered RA–55A to pass through the safe though icy channel north of Bear Island and to detach four destroyers from its screen to assist JW–55B. The southbound convoy, which included eleven American freighters, had to dodge plenty of ice to pass north of Bear Island, but broke through without mishap and entered Loch Ewe on New Year's Day.

Acting on information from the Luftwaffe, *U–601*, one of the eight boats sent out by Peters to patrol south of Bear Island, encountered Convoy JW–55B at 0900 Christmas morning. A gale working up from the SSE made the Arctic noon as dark as midnight, but *U–601* hung on grimly for five hours, when it was forced down by a "scare" barrage from the escorts; not, however, before the skipper had homed-in *U–716*. That boat was soon detected and, after launching an acoustic torpedo which failed to hit, was driven down, while the heavily-laden merchantmen, with half-frozen Naval Armed Guards on the alert, pitched and rolled in the heavy sea.[14] The convoy commodore, although a tank was adrift topside his flagship, refused to change course; it was better to take the wind on the starboard bow, as it then was. That decision, in the commodore's own words, "may really have been the intervention of Providence"; for it took his convoy out of the area of approaching combat and into thick weather where no plane could locate it.

The German Battle Group was keeping a not very merry Christmas in Altenfjord. Weather prospects were so bad that the task force commander, Konteradmiral Erich Bey,[15] wished to call the operation off, but Doenitz was adamant. Toward evening, Bey received the word to start. With a *"Heil und Sieg!"* from Doenitz

[14] Ens. John M. Broderick USNR commanding Naval Armed Guard S.S. *Will Rogers* Report to V.C.N.O. 29 Dec. 1943.
[15] Bey had temporarily relieved Kummetz, who was on leave. He was a destroyer man, and this task force was his first big command.

ringing in his ears, he broke his black-cross flag in *Scharnhorst* and at 2200 December 25 steamed out of Altenfjord escorted by five "Narvik" class destroyers.

By 0400 December 26 the northbound convoy, JW–55B, Captain McCoy commanding the screen of 14 destroyers, two sloops and a minesweeper, had reached a point about 50 miles south of Bear Island. *Scharnhorst* was speeding north, practically on a collision course with the convoy; Admiral Burnett's cruisers were about 150 miles east of it, steering SW by W at 18 knots, a course calculated to intercept the German battleship. Admiral Fraser in *Duke of York*, still 350 miles to the southwest, was feeling anxious lest *Scharnhorst* attack the convoy during the short period of partial daylight and retire before he could intercept her. He bent on 24 knots, the most that his destroyers could take in the strong wind and heavy sea. And he broke radio silence to request Captain Mc-Coy and Admiral Burnett to report their positions. Having received them, Admiral Fraser at 0628 ordered the convoy to alter course to northeast and Admiral Burnett to close it for close support. Burnett at 0712 altered the course of his cruisers to due West, and at 0815 to 300°, in order to approach the convoy from the south, as well as in the hope of getting the weather gauge on *Scharnhorst*. That was still an advantage, though not so important as in days of sail.

At 0840 the radar screen in *Belfast*, Admiral Burnett's flagship, picked up the enemy at 35,000 yards, bearing 295°, about WNW. *Scharnhorst* was then about 30 miles from the convoy. She was unescorted, Konteradmiral Bey having detached his destroyer screen to locate the merchant ships and coach him in. The five "Narviks" steamed to within ten miles of the convoy at 1300 without discovering it, and an hour later were ordered by Bey to break off and make for the Norwegian coast. They never again saw *Scharnhorst* or the convoy.

After his 0840 radar contact Admiral Burnett bent on 18 knots and had just formed a line of bearing when, at 0921, lookouts in cruiser *Sheffield* sighted through the dim twilight the tall, silver-gray German battleship, 13,000 yards distant, bearing south-west. After illuminating the target with star shell, *Norfolk* opened with her main battery and scored two 8-inch hits on the enemy's superstructure. The two 6-inch cruisers did not fire in this phase, nor did *Scharnhorst*. She opened range as if to give her 11-inch guns the advantage, but at 0955 was observed altering course to the northeast. Burnett almost instantly decided that Bey intended to work around him to the north and get at the convoy; and, as his cruisers in that weather (wind force 7 to 8, sea very rough) could not make more than 24 knots, while *Scharnhorst* was reported to be capable of 31½ knots, it behooved him to get between her and the convoy. He therefore altered course to 305° at 1000 and to 325° at 1014, with the result that his track diverged from that of the enemy and he lost radar contact at 1020. Four destroyers, H.M.S. *Musketeer, Matchless, Opportune* and *Virago*, which had been detached from the convoy, were now disposed as screen ahead of Burnett's three cruisers. Shortly before 1100 he picked up the convoy on his radar and commenced zigzagging about 10 miles ahead of it.

Almost at that moment Admiral Fraser in *Duke of York*, still about 125 miles away but coming fast, advised Admiral Burnett by radio that he would have little chance of regaining touch with *Scharnhorst* unless destroyers were detached to find and shadow her. In view of the weather and the enemy's superior speed Burnett did not think it proper to divide his force, feeling confident that *Scharnhorst* was seeking the convoy and so would have to reveal herself. Excellent judgment! In order to hasten the inevitable clash, cruisers and convoy alike altered course to NE and at 1204 Burnett's patience was rewarded by a radar contact on *Scharnhorst*. Bearing 75°, distant 14 miles; she was heading straight for the convoy. The British admiral promptly deployed his four destroyers on the starboard bow of his cruisers and shaped a course to intercept. At 1221, when *Sheffield's* lookouts sighted the white bow wave of the battleship (it was too dark to see the hull), he opened gunfire and ordered the destroyers to make a torpedo attack. At the same time the convoy altered course to SE, in order to keep the cruisers between it and the enemy.

Seamen in the American Liberty ships, sighting flashes over the horizon and hearing the rumble of distant gunfire, guessed that the "Limeys" were having it out with the "Krauts."

They certainly were. For twenty minutes there was a brisk exchange of gunfire between *Scharnhorst* and Burnett's cruisers at ranges from 9000 to 16,000 yards. *Norfolk* received two hits, one of which put a turret out of action; *Sheffield* was straddled. The cruisers made five or six hits on the battleship, but the destroyers were unable to get within torpedo range. *Scharnhorst* increased her speed, altered course from W around to SE, and soon was out of range. Bey, who had orders to break off action if capital ships appeared, was now interested only in getting home. Since neither he nor any of his officers survived, it is not known whether he had received reports from planes which had been shadowing *Duke of York*. Probably not, since the course 155°, on which he steadied, led into her lethal embrace.

Burnett shadowed *Scharnhorst* outside visible range (about 7½ miles), as the faint Arctic twilight faded into black night. *Sheffield* with shaft trouble had to drop astern, but *Norfolk* and *Belfast* kept radar contact on the German and sent frequent reports to Admiral Fraser, who shaped the correct course to intercept. At 1617 his radar found the enemy at 45,000 yards, bearing 20°; *Duke of York* was then steering almost due east, and the German about south-southeast. The range closed rapidly. At about 1645 *Duke of York* sent up a brilliant parachute flare which revealed *Scharnhorst*. Bey was completely surprised; his guns were still trained fore-and-aft when *Duke of York's* first 14-inch salvo, fired at 12,000 yards, straddled him and made one hit.

Scharnhorst reversed course, then steered easterly, hoping to escape this new enemy; she pulled away at such speed that for about an hour it looked as though she might escape. The cruisers fired a few salvos but were soon outdistanced. *Scharnhorst* would turn briefly southward, fire a broadside at her pursuers, then turn east

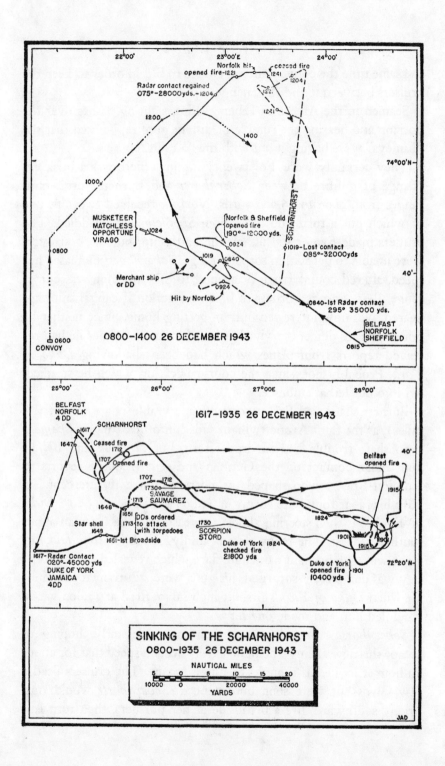

22°00' 23°00'E 24°00'

Norfolk hit
opened fire-1221 ceased fire
1241 1204

Radar contact regained
075°-28000 yds.-1204

1232

1200 1241

1400 74°00'N—

1000

MUSKETEER
MATCHLESS
OPPORTUNE 1024
VIRAGO

Norfolk & Sheffield
opened fire
190°-12000 yds.

0924

1019-Lost contact
085°-32000yds.

0800 1019 0840

Merchant ship 40'
or DD

0924

Hit by Norfolk 0840-1st Radar contact
295° 35000 yds.

BELFAST
NORFOLK
SHEFFIELD

0800-1400 26 DECEMBER 1943 0815

SCHARNHORST

0600
CONVOY

25°00' 26°00' 27°00E 28°00'

BELFAST
NORFOLK
4 DD 1617-1935 26 DECEMBER 1943

SCHARNHORST

1617 40'

1647 Ceased fire
1712 BELFAST
1707 Opened fire opened fire

1707 1712 1915o

1730
1648 SAVAGE
SAUMAREZ

1713 1824

1651 DDs ordered
Star shell 1713 to attack
with torpedoes
1649 1901o 1900

1651-1st Broadside 1730
SCORPION 1915
STORD

1617-Radar Contact Duke of York 1824 72°20'N—
020°-45000 yds checked fire
DUKE OF YORK 21800 yds
JAMAICA
4DD Duke of York
opened fire
10400 yds 1901

SINKING OF THE SCHARNHORST
0800-1935 26 DECEMBER 1943

NAUTICAL MILES
5 0 5 10 15 20

10000 0 20000 40000
YARDS

JAD

again at flank speed, making things as difficult as possible for the British gunners. *Duke of York* made three hits, and the cruisers about three more. None of the British ships were seriously damaged, but a mast of the *Duke* was penetrated by 11-inch shells and she was frequently straddled.

For two hours this stern chase continued in complete darkness, lighted only by the flashes of gunfire and the yellow-green glow of burning cordite on *Scharnhorst* when she was hit. By 1820 her main battery had been silenced; but she continued to fire wildly with her secondary armament at the destroyers, which were closing to fire torpedoes. At 1900 Konteradmiral Bey sent out the grim radio message "We fight to the last shell," and received appreciative acknowledgments from Hitler and Doenitz. *Duke of York* ceased firing at 1928 after her 77th salvo, in order to enable *Belfast*, *Jamaica* and the destroyers to deliver torpedo attacks. Together they fired 55 torpedoes; probably the last three, launched from *Jamaica* at 1937 from 3750 yards, finished the battleship. She went dead in the water. Now all that could be seen of her was a dull glow through a dense cloud of smoke, which even star shell and searchlight failed to penetrate. After a heavy explosion at about 1945, *Scharnhorst* sank. When *Belfast* reached the spot, there was nothing to be seen but wreckage and a few swimmers.

For over an hour cruisers and destroyers combed the icy, heaving waters for survivors, using searchlights to spot them for boat crews. Thirty-six men, but not a single officer, were recovered alive. About 1940 men perished.

George VI sent a "Well done, *Duke of York*, and all of you! I am proud of you." From Winston Churchill came: "Heartiest congratulations . . . on your brilliant action. All comes to him who knows how to wait." [16] And Commodore Boucher of the convoy did not forget the merchant mariners' part. United States Naval Armed Guards and the crews of the Liberty ships were gratified to receive his signal:—

[16] New York *Times* 27, 29 Dec. 1943 p. 1.

"I congratulate all captains, deck and engineer officers and men, on a fine feat of hard steaming, skill and endurance, in what has been, under God's hand, a successful and historic voyage. Good luck, and may we sail together again!" [17]

4. *General Conclusions for 1943*

What a year of successes and setbacks, surprises and satisfactions! Although the submarine menace ended only with the war, and a last, desperate attack on coastal shipping took place even in 1945, the Allied navies and air forces had obtained definite mastery over the U-boat before the end of 1943. In March and April the submarines had wrought great havoc along the North Atlantic convoy routes, in July they had put on a blitz in the South Atlantic, and in September they had boiled up into the high latitudes with new tactics and weapons. Yet the "rate of exchange," which at the beginning of the war was over ten merchant vessels sunk to every submarine lost, had become over two submarines sunk per merchant vessel in the last three months of 1943.[18] And the tonnage of new merchant ship construction was now soaring above that of tonnage lost.

Not only the "tonnage war" but every objective of submarine warfare had failed. Germany had counted on U-boats to cut off or at least interrupt the vast flow of supplies from America to Europe and from the Western Allies to Russia, to break up the American invasions of Africa and Italy, and to prevent the build-up of an American expeditionary force in Great Britain. In no respect had she succeeded. Even the consolation of "pinning down" forces was delusion. The several hundred planes, escorts and patrol ships employed in antisubmarine warfare were not needed for the great invasion. It is at least arguable that Hitler could have postponed defeat a few months if he had scrapped his U-boat fleet and em-

---

[17] Ens. Broderick's Report (see note 14).
[18] It was now 46 to 24; or, if we include the Mediterranean, 46 to 30.

ployed the men and matériel released from submarine construction in the defense of the Reich.

The U-boats themselves became distinctly less aggressive after the "Black May" of 1943 and at the same time Allied antisubmarines had wrought great havoc along the North Atlantic convoy marine warfare greatly improved. Tenth Fleet, Cotclant and Asdevlant made for efficiency in administration and uniformity in training; as soon as a new device was approved, it could be adopted with confidence that escorts and antisubmarine aircraft would be properly instructed in its use. The growing fleet of escort carriers and destroyer escorts had at last given the Navy adequate escorts both for convoys and for support and hunter-killer groups, with superior gunfire and antisubmarine equipment and better-trained crews. The pathetic expedients of 1942, such as fishermen observers, auxiliary sailing yachts and Q-ships, now faded out; and a tight, well-knit, adequately trained military organization of fighting ships and naval aircraft, operating as a unit and served by adequate intelligence, was gradually approaching that military perfection which is never quite attained in practice.

In 1943 aircraft found their definite place as equal members of the antisubmarine team. It was the combination of ships and planes that did the trick, whether in an organic escort carrier group or in the combination of land-based plane cover with escort-of-convoy. The limitations of the airplane had been revealed, as well as its powers. Doenitz's tactics of arming U-boats with antiaircraft guns and fighting it out with planes on the surface did destroy an appreciable number of planes; but in the end this method played into the hands of the Allied air forces by furnishing them with more surface targets. Many types of planes had been tried; the Ventura, Liberator, and Mariner had proved to be the best for antisubmarine work from land bases, and the Avenger from carrier decks. Experience proved that an airplane's offensive capabilities were fully realized at night only when it was equipped with microwave radar and searchlight.

Even more than 1942, 1943 was the year of the convoy. The

Interlocking Convoy System, now extended to Rio, became everywhere more effective by more and better escorts, improved convoy discipline and increased air coverage. During the last month of 1943, the average number of Allied merchant vessels daily at sea in the Atlantic Ocean was close to one thousand, of which 82.5 per cent were in convoy.[19] Besides merchant convoys, a procession of troop convoys escorted by the United States Navy, and of fast unescorted Atlantic liners under three or four different flags, was conveying American soldiers from the New World to the Old, without losing a man to enemy action.

The German high command made some significant admissions and omissions about the Battle of the Atlantic in end-of-the-year broadcasts. Goebbels, in his organ *Das Reich* of 6 December 1943, remarked: "Not for the last time has the theater of oceanic war passed through a transformation in which the U-boat offensive arm has been surprised by the progress of the enemy's defense." [20] Grossadmiral Doenitz, convinced that the British and Americans would attempt to force an entry into *Festung Europa*, lamented his lack of a sufficient number of submarines to attack and destroy every Allied convoy. In a speech at a conference of flag officers at Weimar on 17 December 1943, he admitted the Allies by their skill in "radio location" had wrested the advantage of surprise from the U-boats. Science, not superior strategy or tactics, he insisted, had done this; and, he added bitterly, he might have worsted the enemy in that realm if German scientists had not stupidly been absorbed into the armed forces instead of being kept at work in their laboratories. These men were now being released from military service in order "to catch up in the field of high-frequency research to equal the achievements of the enemy." As we shall see, they did catch up some of the slack in 1945.

By the summer of 1944, he predicted, U-boat production would be up to 66 a month, since prefabrication and mass production now made it possible to build a submarine for the German Navy in 6 or

[19] *U.S. Fleet A/S Bulletin* Jan. 1944 p. 5. These figures are incomplete and do not include the Arctic.
[20] Communicated to me through the kindness of Dorothy Thompson.

7 months instead of 22, as formerly. The 100,000 naval personnel procured in 1943 were not enough; he must have more. And commanding officers of U-boats now averaged 21 years of age. But, he concluded, U-boats were now the Fatherland's first line of defense, and as such called for feats of sacrifice never contemplated in the heyday of their success.[21]

The German home front broadcast of 30 December admitted: "This year the British and Americans managed after three years of preparation to gain a success against the U-boat. In the second half of the year, as far as U-boat exploits were concerned, sinkings have considerably fallen off." The commentator declared that total sinkings of Allied merchantmen were only 20 per cent less than in 1942; a gross misstatement, since the true figure was 56 per cent less than in 1942, a cut of over half. Moreover, the number of German and Italian submarines lost in 1943 was 263, compared with 108 in 1942. During the summer months the Allies were sinking them faster than the Germans could build new ones.

The most extraordinary admission came from the Fuehrer himself, in his Order of the Day to the German armed forces, 1 January 1944: "The obvious decline in U-boat successes has been due to only one invention of our enemy." [22]

The invention to which he alluded was ASV, the microwave search radar mounted in aircraft. But, while Hitler was right about the "obvious decline," he was wrong in attributing that unwelcome trend to a single invention. The United States and Allied Navies and merchant services thwarted the submarine by efforts all along the line, and in four dimensions: Doctrine; Research; Training; Production. They thwarted the U-boat by fighting it with whatever weapons they had, and by persisting through the dark winter of 1942–43 until the necessary means and know-how were acquired. The results were a triumph of intelligence as well as cour-

---

[21] This speech was printed in Germany, classified top secret, and circulated among officers of the fleet. Translation is incorporated in "German Monograph 903–400."

[22] These broadcasts were monitored and translated by Dr. Otto Zausmer of Boston University and the Boston *Globe*.

age, of persistence as well as practice; and, in the final analysis, of man over the sea. The amazing ability of young Americans to learn the unwelcome and unsought-for profession of fighting U-boats, their fortitude in meeting the wartime perils of the deep and of the air, their skill in operating ships and planes, surprised their friends and confounded their foes.

CHAPTER XIV

Within the Mediterranean

June 1943–August 1944

1. *The Mediterranean Convoy System* [1]

IN FEBRUARY 1944 Grossadmiral Doenitz decided to abandon attacks on Atlantic convoys west of Great Britain until he was provided with a sufficient number of the new Type XXI U-boats, which never happened. He issued an order that "the boats must continue to operate," but "in the present phase of the campaign it is not victory, but the *survival* of boats and their crews, that must take priority." Owing to the unexpectedly numerous "bugs" in the Type XXI boats, that phase lasted to the end of the war. Offensive submarine operations were, to be sure, put on in the Mediterranean, the Arctic and Indian Oceans; and in 1944 began a secondary blitz with snorkel-equipped submarines. But, for the most part, U-boat skippers in this concluding phase of the Atlantic war showed that they were only too glad to play for survival rather than for sinkings.

For the history of convoys and antisubmarine warfare in the Mediterranean, we shall have to go back to mid-1943.

The pattern of convoys from the United States to the Mediterranean was clearly woven in May of that year. Fast convoys of transports and tankers, designated UGF outbound and GUF homeward bound, sailed from or to New York or Norfolk at 25-day in-

---

[1] United States Naval Administrative History "Convoy and Routing" chap. iii pp. 77-87 and Appendices. For establishment and early record of these convoys see Vol. I 352-8; and, for details on the oceanic part of them, see this Volume Chapters VIII, X. Times in this chapter are either Zone A (minus 1) or B (minus 2).

tervals until September 1943, when they were discontinued because the Joint Chiefs of Staff had decided to commit no more American troops to Italy. In May 1944, when Operation DRAGOON (invasion of Southern France) was being prepared, these fast convoys were revived; and from 1 July 1944 they departed Norfolk at 27-day intervals until Germany was defeated. There were no losses in these fast convoys. Between December 1942 and March 1945, twenty-four UGF convoys transported 536,134 troops from the United States to the Mediterranean. Thirty "Oil Torch" (OT and TO) fast-tanker convoys from the Caribbean to the Mediterranean, with an average of seven tankers each, sailed at 32-day intervals between February 1943 and June 1944 with no loss or damage.

This impressive record was overshadowed in volume and importance, though not in safety, by that of the slow convoys, designated UGS when bound from the United States to Gibraltar and the Mediterranean and GUS homeward bound. Between November 1942 and VE day, 11,119 ships were convoyed in 189 UGS and GUS convoys, with the loss of only nine ships sunk while under United States naval escort. The routing of convoys from the western Mediterranean to Suez was made possible by a major minesweeping operation carried out by Royal Navy minesweepers between 9 and 21 May 1943. A channel 200 miles long and two miles wide was cleared between Galita Island and Tripoli, including the Sicilian Narrows, and made available for shipping. Within a week of the fall of Tunis the first through convoy left Gibraltar and on 26 May it reached Alexandria. This route saved 45 days each way between the United Kingdom and the Middle East, over the Cape route, and almost as much time between the United States and the Persian Gulf. Between May and September 1943 an average of 400 ships monthly sailed through the Tunisian War Channel; the numbers then increased so rapidly that in 1944 the figure was about 1200 a month. From all this press of shipping, only 25 vessels were sunk by U-boats. This remarkable record was not due to any lack of German opposition, but to the high quality of protection by the

British and American Navies and Air Forces, with some help from the Fighting French.

In July 1943, when the invasion of Sicily was under way, eastbound slow convoys began to sail at 10-day intervals from Norfolk. Convoys from the United Kingdom to the Mediterranean were timed to arrive between the UGSs in order to avoid congestion at terminal ports. Until March 1944, American ocean escorts were relieved at Gibraltar by other escort groups which carried UGS convoys to their destination. These were mostly British, but included ships of Vice Admiral H. Kent Hewitt's Eighth Fleet. Beginning with UGS–36, which passed Gibraltar 30 March 1944, Admirals King and Ingersoll arranged with the Admiralty to have the American ocean escort continue to Bizerta before being relieved. This had the additional advantage of not changing escorts at a time when the Luftwaffe was very active in the western Mediterranean.[2] By 23 October 1944, when the Allies had driven the Germans from Southern France and neither enemy planes nor submarines were operating within the Strait, UGS convoys were dispersed at Gibraltar and each vessel sailed independently to her desired haven.

The enemy knew well when a UGS convoy was coming. In order to avoid mine fields in the approaches to Gibraltar, convoys had to pass the Strait in daylight; and for 40 miles their course lay within sight of the Barbary Coast where Axis spies and coast watchers were thick as fleas. The stretch of 110 miles from Europa Point to Alborán Island was usually traversed at night, after which the convoys closed the Algerian coast about 25 miles west of Oran and hugged the shore for 180 miles to Algiers. Cape Bengut, 42 miles east of Algiers, was "Torpedo Junction" for the UGS convoys. Their progress along shore was signaled by bonfires on the beaches and in the hills, kindled by degenerate descendants of Barbary corsairs in Axis pay.

2 "Convoy and Routing" p. 80. Other reasons were the withdrawal of R.N. escort vessels for Operation NEPTUNE, and the increased number of U.S.N. escorts available.

2. U-Boats "Swamped," [3] July 1943–May 1944

Grossadmiral Doenitz planned to keep a dozen U-boats, based on Toulon, operating in the bottleneck between the Strait of Gibraltar and long. 3° W, together with nine in the Ægean and south of Crete; while the Italian Navy, which did not relish Teutonic intrusion into *mare nostrum*, took care of the Central Mediterranean. Just before the Allied landings in Sicily on 10 July 1943, the Axis partners agreed to concentrate south of Sicily the 16 submarines then available. These boats had moderate success against Allied shipping but were wiped out in the process. Destroyer *Nields* sank Italian submarine *Gorgo* off Oran 21 May 1943, and *PC–624* sank *U–375* on 30 July in the Sicilian Strait.[4] Doenitz then decided to commit more submarines. Twenty-seven U-boats attempted to pass the Strait between September 1943 and May 1944; 14 succeeded, 7 were lost in the attempt and the rest turned back. The largest number present at any one time was 18, in February 1944.

The Allied antisubmarine war in the Mediterranean stemmed from Cincmed, who was Admiral of the Fleet Sir Andrew B. Cunningham RN to 1 January 1944, when he was relieved by Admiral Sir John Cunningham RN. Vice Admiral H. Kent Hewitt commanded all United States Naval Forces in the Mediterranean and off Morocco, and Air Vice Marshal Hugh P. Lloyd RAF headed the Northwest African Coastal Command, including most of the land-based planes, British, American or French, which engaged in antisubmarine warfare.[5] Staff officers of these commands devised the so-called "Swamp operation," designed to keep the U-boat submerged to the point of exhaustion and overwhelm it when it surfaced.

On 12–13 December 1943 occurred a good example of Swamp tactics. At 0710 on the 12th, *U–593* sank H.M.S. *Tynedale*, escorting an eastbound convoy north of Djidjelli. U.S.S. *Niblack* and H.M.S. *Holcombe*, using as reference point the spot where the de-

[3] F.d.U. Italy (Kapt. Leo Kreisch) War Diary.
[4] See Vol. IX 40–42 for submarine sinkings by the R.N.
[5] See Vol. IX 13, 14, 323, for brief biographies and command relationships.

stroyer had sunk, began a sonar search, aided by three Wellington bombers from Bône. After several hours, no contact having been established, the area was enlarged, the number of planes doubled, and destroyers *Wainwright, Benson* and H.M.S. *Calpe* were added to the surface group. But *U–593* scored again, torpedoing H.M.S. *Holcombe* at 1445. The Swamp operation then shifted to a new center, the ships searching in pairs. After ten hours' methodical air-surface hunt, at 0035 December 13 one of the Wellingtons made a radar contact and closed for the attack, but was hit by the U-boat's antiaircraft fire and driven away. For twelve more weary hours the search went on. At 1408 *Wainwright* obtained sound contact and, with assistance of H.M.S. *Calpe*, started to drop depth charges. Three quarters of an hour later, *U–593* broke surface and was taken under brisk gunfire. The exhausted submariners promptly abandoned and scuttled their boat. This stubborn, persistent search had lasted almost 32 hours from the torpedoing of *Tynedale.*

A few days later, *Woolsey* and *Trippe* sank *U–73* ten miles off the coast near Oran, after a similar search. It started on the after-noon of 16 December 1943, when a ship was torpedoed out of a convoy. Two destroyers of the screen, *Niblack* and *Ludlow,* were detailed to hunt the assailant. A signal to Oran brought out two SOC float planes from U.S.S. *Brooklyn* (then lying in that port), which later were relieved by R.A.F. Wellingtons. Next, at 1715, *Woolsey, Trippe* and *Edison* arrived on the scene to relieve the two destroyers so that they could return to escort duty. An hour later, *Woolsey* made a sound contact, lost it, picked it up again at 1837, and attacked with depth charges. Another hour later, in pitch-darkness, both *Woolsey* and *Trippe* made radar contact dead ahead at less than a mile. They illuminated the boat with star shell and opened fire with all batteries. *U–73* replied with a few 20-mm bursts which wounded two men in *Woolsey;* but it failed to dive quickly enough to escape 5-inch hits, which dispatched it at 1935. Thirty-five survivors were recovered. This attack "developed as nicely and readily as one on the attack trainer," reported Com-mander Henry R. Wier, skipper of *Woolsey.*

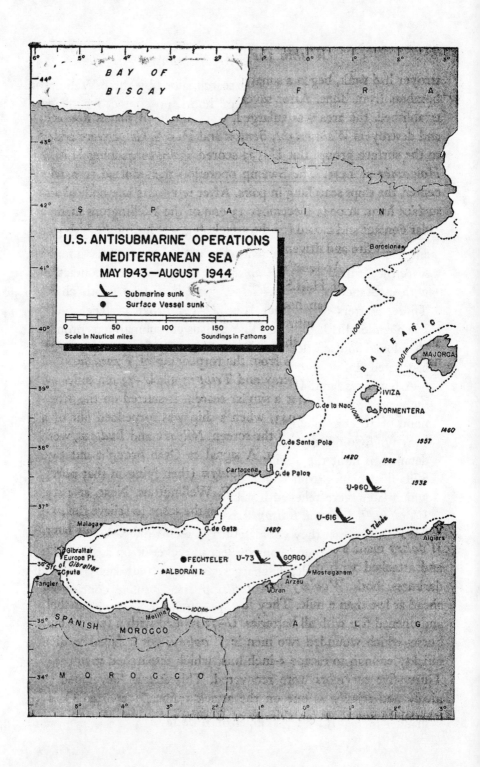

**U.S. ANTISUBMARINE OPERATIONS
MEDITERRANEAN SEA
MAY 1943 — AUGUST 1944**

↘ Submarine sunk
● Surface Vessel sunk

0   50   100   150   200
Scale in Nautical miles   Soundings in Fathoms

BAY OF BISCAY

FRA

SPAIN

Barcelona

BALEARIC

MAJORCA

IVIZA

FORMENTERA

C. de la Nao

1460

C. de Santa Pola

1420   1562   1357

Cartagena   C. de Palos

U-960   1532

Malaga   C. de Gata   1420   U-616

C. Ténès   Algiers

Gibraltar
Europa Pt.   ●FECHTELER U-73 ↘ ↘ GORGO
Ceuta   ▲ALBORAN I.   ● Mostaganem
Tangier   Arzeu
                                 Oran

SPANISH   MOROCCO

Melilla

M O R O C C O

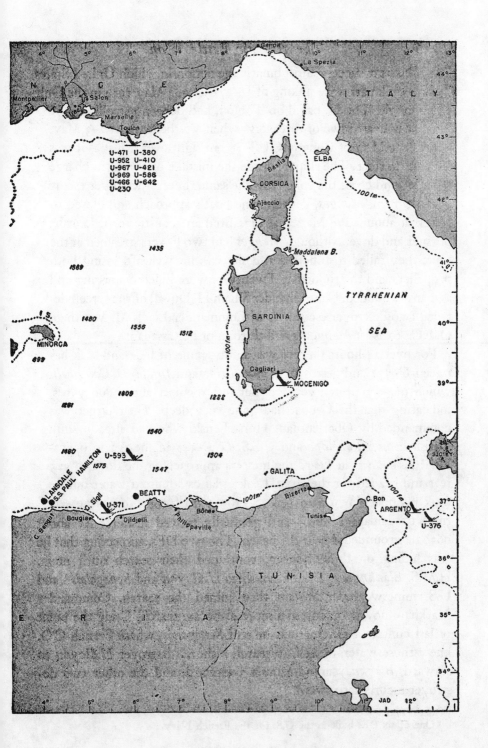

The next successful antisubmarine action in which United States ships took part was the sinking of *U-371* on 4 May 1944 in the Gulf of Bougie. This boat, based on Toulon, had been patrolling off the African coast for two or three days when, on the night of 2-3 May, the 80-odd ships of Convoy GUS-38 ran right over it just as it was about to surface. The skipper made the mistake of trying to charge batteries and chase the convoy at the same time. A destroyer escort of the screen, *Menges*, detected the boat's approach and closed to attack at about 0110 May 3; *U-371* fired an acoustic torpedo at its pursuer and dove. Although *Menges* had two Foxers streamed at the time, they failed to function and she was hit well aft, losing both propellers and the rudder. Twenty men were killed or missing and as many wounded. Commander William H. Duvall of the screen detailed two destroyer escorts, with Commander Lewis M. Markham O.T.C., to assist *Menges* and then to hunt her assailant.

For over 24 hours there was a deadly game of hide-and-seek between *U-371* and destroyer escorts *Pride* and *Joseph E. Campbell*, which made repeated contacts but lost them at about 800 yards, indicating that the U-boat had gone very deep. Their target was commanded by Oberleutnant Horst Fenski who had already sunk British cruiser *Penelope* and U.S.S. *LST-348* in the Anzio operation.[6] As soon as he heard the hunters approaching, he dove to 525 feet and headed for the coast. Leaky glands admitted water but he took his boat down to 656 feet — too deep for depth-charge settings to damage him — and gradually moved inshore. At about 0630 he grounded near the beach. The two DEs, suspecting that he was hiding on the bottom, continued their search until noon. H.M.S. *Blankney*, French warships *L'Alcyon* and *Senegalais*[7] and U.S. minesweeper *Sustain* then joined the search. Commander Markham now organized a more elaborate search. Using the point of last contact as reference, he sent *Senegalais*, whose French C.O. knew those waters well, to search inshore, destroyer *L'Alcyon* to seaward, *Blankney* and *Sustain* westward, and the other two destroyer escorts eastward.

[6] See Vol. IX 366.
[7] One of six DEs built in the U.S. for the French Navy.

U-371 lay on the bottom for some 21 hours, until 0300 May 4. With air very foul and batteries low, Fenski then decided that his only chance to escape was to surface and run for it on his diesels, first loading an acoustic torpedo in the stern tube. *Senegalais*, right on the job, hit the U-boat with gunfire as it surfaced. Fenski decided that the jig was up and gave the order to scuttle and abandon ship. At the same time he defiantly fired the acoustic torpedo at *Senegalais* and hit her, but the French DE was taken in tow and salvaged. The successful hunt had lasted 26 hours, and 49 German survivors out of a complement of 53 were recovered near the shore.

The very next day *U-967* reversed the pattern and became the hunter. Convoy GUS-38, by now grown to 107 merchant vessels by accessions from Algiers, was steaming westward in 16 columns along the Spanish coast about 120 miles east of Gibraltar, at 0225 May 5, when its screen made a radar contact 16 miles ahead. Destroyer escort *Laning*, detailed to investigate, reported that the blip disappeared from her radar at 6000 yards, indicating that the target was a submarine. Commander Duvall now sent destroyer escorts *Lowe*, *Fessenden* and *Fechteler* to assist *Laning*. At 0310 and again at 0345 heavy explosions, probably of acoustic torpedoes, were felt astern. In the meantime Duvall had ordered and the convoy commodore executed an emergency right turn of the big convoy. *Fechteler*, maneuvering during the turn, was torpedoed in the engine room so severely that her skipper had to order Abandon Ship almost immediately; and as *Laning* and British tug *Hengist* stood by to rescue survivors the unfortunate DE broke in two and sank.[8]

The next submarine to be put down for good, *U-616*, was the victim of a Swamp operation which well rated its code name MON-STROUS, because it set a record for the war, lasting three entire days and parts of two others. It began at 1400 May 13, 1944, when Commander George C. Wright of Desdiv 21 was ordered to take *Gleaves*, *Nields* and *Macomb* out of Oran and hunt for a submarine which had torpedoed two merchant vessels and was being held down by two British escorts about a hundred miles west of the

[8] F.d.U. Med. War Diary 7 May; CTF 66 (Cdr. Duvall) Action Report; *Laning* Action Report. She and H.M.S. *Hengist* rescued 188 of the crew.

harbor. Before Wright could reach the spot and commence searching, the British ships had lost contact and rejoined Convoy
GUS–39.

During the following night, 13–14 May, two more merchant
ships were torpedoed out of this convoy about 85 miles northeast
of the area being searched by Commander Wright. Cincmed (Admiral Sir John Cunningham RN) then ordered Captain Adelbert F.
Converse to take four destroyers (*Ellyson, Rodman, Hambleton*
and *Emmons*) of his Squadron 10 out of Oran to the scene of action
and put on a Swamp operation, in coördination with Coastal Command Air Squadron 500 (whose signal officer embarked in *Ellyson*
with Captain Converse) and with Commander Wright's three
destroyers.

Captain Converse departed Oran at 0330 May 14, arrived on the
scene at 0836, and there found destroyer *Hilary P. Jones* and two
DEs of the convoy screen already searching. *Jones* delivered the
first depth-charge attack, which damaged *U–616*. Commander
Wright turned up shortly after. All eight United States destroyers
searched until an airplane reported a disappearing radar contact 30
miles westward, whereupon ships and planes transferred activity to
that new point of reference and searched all day long. At nightfall
a Coastal plane made radar contact well north of the searching
destroyers and signaled to them with flares. Captain Converse
moved his surface group thither at high speed and was rewarded
by a sound contact at 2138 May 14. He attacked with depth
charges, then lost contact. At daylight 15 May a ten-mile slick of
diesel oil appeared on the surface, indicating that the U-boat had
been damaged and was trying to escape.

For two more days and nights air-surface search continued in the
vicinity of Cape Santa Pola. Not until 2226 May 16 did a searching
Wellington once more catch *U–616* on the surface. It was then 30
to 40 miles from the destroyers, and going fast. All ships closed at
top speed, and at four minutes before midnight *Macomb* made contact at 4600 yards. Three minutes later she illuminated the submarine and managed to get off six rounds of gunfire before it sub-

merged. Sound contact was regained at 0014 May 17; *Macomb*, *Hambleton*, *Gleaves* and *Nields* began a series of depth-charge attacks which lasted all night. They were rewarded at 0807 May 17, 1944, when *U-616* surfaced 3400 yards away. As five destroyers showered them with gunfire, the submariners rushed out of the conning tower and into the water; and five minutes later *U-616* went down.[9] Almost the entire crew, 53 in number, were rescued.

This lengthy hunt was marked by excellent communications between United States ships and British aircraft, for which Captain Converse was responsible; he had worked out the system shortly after arriving in the Mediterranean. For instance, when the plane sighted *U-616* on 16 May, the *Ellyson* group was 40 miles and the *Gleaves* group 30 miles distant; but less than an hour and a half elapsed before all destroyers made contact and the final action began. Operation MONSTROUS also served to refute the charge that United States escorts were not persistent enough when searching for a submarine. The search lasted almost exactly 72 hours from the first depth-charge attack to the final scuttling, or 90 hours from the time Commander Wright departed Oran to relieve the British escorts of Convoy GUS-39.[10]

Commander Robert B. Ellis of Desdiv 25 (*Woolsey*, *Ludlow*, *Niblack*, *Benson*), which was about to relieve Captain Converse's destroyers when *U-616* sank, did not have to wait long to start a Swamp of his own. In the forenoon of 17 May, torpedo tracks were reported by a plane about halfway between Oran and Cartagena. They came from *U-960*, which had just arrived in the Mediterranean from La Pallice. Cincmed sent Ellis's ships to the spot and ordered Coastal planes to coöperate. At 1252 the new Swamp began. Aircraft made a fresh contact at 2100, and the destroyers shifted their activities to that reference point. This search continued all that night, throughout 18 May and well into the second night. The searchers then divided into two groups 20 miles apart, each hunting along a possible track of the U-boat; but it was a plane that

[9] Position lat. 37°52' N, long. 0°11' E. Yellow Book is wrong on position and date.
[10] Com Destroyers Eighth Fleet (Capt. J. P. Clay) Report 22 May 1944; Com Desrons 10 and 21 and *Macomb* Action Reports.

at 0140 May 19 made radar contact about ten miles ahead of *Niblack* and *Ludlow*. It dropped a float light as a marker; both ships closed at flank speed, and within an hour had a sound contact. Eleven depth-charge attacks followed. Almost four hours later, at 0609, the brace of destroyers caught sight of *U-960* surfacing about a mile away and opened gunfire. At this juncture *Woolsey* and *Benson*, together with *Madison* which had joined, arrived on the scene; and a British Wellington, eager to be in at the kill, glided through their gunfire and that of the U-boat to drop depth bombs, miraculously escaping damage. After numerous five-inch hits had been scored the U-boat submerged. *Niblack* tossed out a depth-charge pattern which blew it to the surface long enough for the crew to abandon ship, and at 0715 *U-960* went down for good. The skipper and 21 members of the crew were rescued. This hunt lasted 42 hours and 18 minutes.[11]

U-960 was the last U-boat to threaten Allied convoys in the western part of the sea. The number of German submarines there dropped from 18 in February to 11 in May 1944, and at the end of that month Doenitz decided to send no more into the Mediterranean.

Strategic bombers of the United States Army Air Force had already destroyed *U-421* in the harbor of Toulon on 29 April, and destroyed five more in the same port by 6 August.[12] Operation DRAGOON, the invasion of Southern France, wiped out the main U-boat base at Toulon by the 19th, when all U-boats still there were scuttled by their crews. Only three enemy submarines were then left in the entire Mediterranean. Two British destroyers and one of Poland sank *U-407* south of Thera in the Ægean on 19 September; and on the 24th the remaining pair, *U-565* and *U-596*, was destroyed by an A.A.F. bomber raid on Salamis, the scene of Xerxes' defeat by Themistocles exactly 2424 years earlier. To paraphrase Byron, "Fritz counted them at break of day — and when the sun set, where were they?"

---

[11] Com Desdiv 25 (Cdr. Ellis) and *Niblack* Action Reports.
[12] Craven & Cate *Army Air Forces* III 381, 420. See Appendix II, below.

3. *Air Attacks on Convoys,*[13] *September–November 1943*

Even before the United States Navy ocean-escort groups regularly accompanied central transatlantic convoys all the way to Bizerta, a few did so when there were not enough British warships available. One of these groups, escorting Convoy UGF–10, commanded by Captain Charles C. Hartman in *Mervine*, was subjected to a spectacular dawn-and-dusk attack by the Luftwaffe between Oran and Algiers on 3 September 1943. Not one merchant vessel was hit in this attack; and although destroyer *Kendrick* took a Zaunkönig in the fantail, she made port under her own power.

Following two more successful escort missions, Captain Hartman's group was given the unusual assignment of escorting a United Kingdom–Mediterranean troop convoy, KMF–25A, destined for Palermo and Naples. In the late afternoon of 6 November the 26 transports were re-formed in three columns preparatory to entering the Tunisian War Channel. Captain Hartman had a strong screen: eight United States destroyers, antiaircraft cruiser H.M.S. *Colombo*, three British "Hunt"-class destroyers and two destroyer escorts manned by the Royal Hellenic Navy. In addition, destroyer *Laub* acted as radar picket five miles in the lead, *Beatty* and *Tillman* patrolled astern. The sky was overcast, ceiling at about one thousand feet. H.M.S. *Haydon* had picked up a shadower bearing north early in the afternoon; since it showed friendly "Identification, Friend or Foe" signals, it was not tracked. But the destroyer commanders, who by this time had become highly air-conscious, ordered General Quarters at sunset (1736), alerted their C.I.C.s, and prepared for a dusk visit from the Luftwaffe. And at sunset all Allied fighter planes retired to their land bases.

First inkling of a possible attack came within ten minutes of sun-

[13] Cominch Information Bulletin No. 24 *Antiaircraft Action Summary* June 1944; Convoy & Routing Files; information obtained by the writer when crossing in escort flagship of a UGS convoy Nov. 1944 and from British Naval Intelligence Center Gibraltar; files of the R.A.F. monthly *Coastal Command Review*.

set when *Laub's* radar picked up six planes ten miles distant bearing northerly. Since they too gave out friendly I.F.F. signals, they were not tracked. Shortly after 1800 *Tillman*, on the port quarter of the convoy, made a radar contact northwesterly at 8000 yards and almost simultaneously sighted the planes. The range was too great for accurate firing but Commander C. S. Hutchings opened up with automatic weapons as a warning to other ships, and Captain Hartman promptly ordered all destroyers to make smoke.

For the next twenty minutes, action was fast and furious. Torpedo planes and Do–217s with glide-bombs closed each angle and flank of the convoy; screening destroyers concentrated gunfire on every aircraft within range, using both timed and proximity fuzes on 5-inch shells, and firing automatic weapons as well; glide-bombs, glowing orange-red as they were released, were easily visible in the fading light.

Tillman, which the Germans selected as their special target, escaped damage owing to expert handling by her skipper and accurate gunnery by her crew. The plane first sighted, a Do–217, although taken under heavy fire by the main battery, managed to release its bomb before turning away. Port automatic weapons poured their maximum rate of fire at the glide-bomb at a range of about one thousand yards; hits on it were observed as it headed directly for the ship. When only 600 yards away the bomb went into a steep dive and exploded in the water about 150 yards from the destroyer's port bow. Immediately afterward, as Commander Hutchings turned to regain position in the screen, a second plane was reported releasing a glide-bomb on his port beam. He turned *Tillman's* bow directly toward it, automatic weapons concentrating on the bomb and main battery on the aircraft. The bomb glided ahead of the ship, then turned back and splashed about 150 yards on her starboard quarter; its mother plane was hit by a full salvo of 5-inch shell and disintegrated. And a third glide-bomb, launched by another plane at the same target, splashed about 500 yards on the starboard beam.

Although *Tillman* escaped a hit, her fire-control radar was knocked out by concussion and she had to use optical ranging on torpedo planes coming in low on the port side of the convoy. One group launched torpedoes at her but she turned toward the attackers and combed the wakes; two torpedoes were observed passing along her starboard side at about 1818, and one exploded in her wake and shook her up, cracking a few plates in the fantail. Commander Hutchings, justly proud of his crew in this hot and heavy action, believed that the Germans concentrated their glide-bomb attacks on the screen in order to clear the way for torpedo planes to get at the convoy.

Beatty, opposite number to *Tillman* on the convoy's starboard quarter, was not so fortunate as her sister ship. At about 1805 two planes showing friendly I.F.F. were picked up 16,000 yards astern; but as one of them was visually identified as a Ju–88, Lieutenant Commander William Outerson, skipper of *Beatty*, rightly concluded that I.F.F. was being faked. Protective smoke which drifted over the ship partially obscured her observation so that two Ju–88s surprised her by springing out of the smoke on the starboard quarter. Taken under fire promptly by automatic weapons, they turned away and disappeared; but half a minute later *Beatty* was hit by a torpedo in the after engine room. Her back was broken by the explosion, all electric power was lost, the engine room and fire room were flooded, and her situation looked very bad. All hands were ordered on deck to prepare to abandon ship; but as she was not settling they were set to work helping the damage control party and jettisoning topside weights. *Beatty* kept well afloat until about 2100, when she began to settle slowly. *Laub* took over a part of her crew and was just preparing to rig a towline when it became clear that she could not be salvaged; and at 2230 when the list had increased to 45 degrees, the rest of the crew abandoned ship, and she broke in two and sank. *Beatty* was a great loss to the Eighth Fleet. Since midsummer 1942 she had safely escorted numerous convoys across the Atlantic, and had taken an active part in the North African and Sicilian operations.[14]

About three enemy planes managed to get through the screen

[14] Comdeslant (Admiral Deyo) endorsement on *Beatty* Action Reports; see Vol. II and IX indices.

and torpedo two transports, American *Santa Elena* and Netherlands *Marnix van St. Aldegonde*. Captain Hartman directed Comdesron 16, Captain C. J. Cater, to take charge of rescue operations with five destroyers, transport *Monterey* and Dutch S.S. *Ruyz*. While the destroyers patrolled around them, the transports transferred passengers from the stricken ships, in a fairly heavy swell. Admiral Cunningham now ordered four more U.S. destroyers from Algiers and tugs from Philippeville to assist. The tugs, arriving about 0150 November 7, took the damaged transports in tow but did not quite make Philippeville. *Santa Elena* sank in the outer harbor and *Marnix* grounded while efforts were being made to beach her. The rescue ships recovered 6228 men, including the survivors of *Beatty*; loss of life was amazingly slight in this battle of 6 November off the Algerian coast.

4. *Intense Air-Surface Battles, April–August 1944*

During the rest of 1943 and the first three months of 1944, Mediterranean convoys had more to fear from submarine than from air attack; and most of them got through with few enemy contacts. But during the next four months there occurred in the Mediterranean some of the toughest air vs. surface battles of the entire war.

In April 1944, a month before Doenitz decided to send no more U-boats into the Mediterranean, the German air offensive grew more intense. It was aimed at the big UGS convoys, principal means of supplying Allied armies in the Italian campaign, of building up for the invasion of Southern France, and of carrying matériel to India and Russia. Destruction or diminution of these convoys was of such vital importance that Marshal Goering used all resources that he could spare from the Italian and Russian fronts and all the tactical ingenuity he could muster. These efforts long persisted, despite heavy losses and lack of success.

The planes used in these attacks, based on airfields in Southern France and on Bordeaux, were not numerous, amounting to about ten Ju–88 long-range reconnaissance planes, about 30 He–111 torpedo-bombers, 30 Ju–88s similarly fitted, about 20 Ju–88s fitted as long-range fighters, and some 50 Do–217s and He–111s carrying radio-controlled glide-bombs. Owing to the recent improvement in antiaircraft fire of Allied escorts and of the Naval Armed Guards in merchant ships, the Luftwaffe attacked only at night or in twilight.

For that purpose, elaborate — too elaborate — tactics were worked out. Each convoy, from the time it passed Alborán Island, was shadowed by long-range planes, who reported its course, speed and strength. Next step was to dispatch the *Gefechtsaufklärer* (tactical reconnaissance); two planes, flying low, laid the *Ablaufpunkt* (launch pointer), a line of acetylene float lights some 60 miles long, pointing toward the spot where the convoy was to meet its death. These float lights were laid with the aid of navigators' fixes obtained from Rennes and Seville radio beams. After the *Ablaufpunkt* had been laid, the reconnaissance planes orbited about 10,000 feet over the convoy to coach-in by radar the next performers to enter the stage. These were the *Verkandsführer* (master of ceremonies), a squadron commander who controlled the attack, and a few *Beleuchteren* (Pathfinders) carrying high-intensity flares, each burning seven minutes, to be dropped ahead of the convoy in order to drench it with light. If the flares were not dropped accurately, the *Verkandsführer* let off a red flare, upon which signal the *Gefechtsaufklärer* pin-pointed the convoy with a high-intensity magnesium flash-bomb, and the *Beleuchteren* made a fresh illumination. The bombing attack, delivered as soon as the convoy was well lighted, consisted of low-level torpedo attacks from as many angles as possible, assisted by the master of ceremonies, who amused himself by dropping a few 100-pound bombs in hopes of diverting the attention of ships' gunnery officers from the low-flying torpedo planes.

Defense consisted principally in giving each convoy a sufficient number of escorts well trained in antiaircraft fire, with main batteries under radar control, firing proximity-fuzed shells; and in providing both escorts and merchant ships with smoke-pots for covering the convoy with a dense white chemical smoke. The ocean escort was augmented by at least one British antiaircraft cruiser and one American destroyer, which joined the convoy around Alborán Island.

Search-radar beacons, at Oran and Beghaia on the Algerian coast, picked up approaching planes 60 or more miles off shore; and there were plenty of Beaufighters based at Oran and Algiers which could be vectored out to intercept the German bombers. These Beaufighters, belonging to Coastal Command of the Mediterranean Allied Air Forces, were manned not only by British pilots but also by members of the United States Army and Fighting French Air Forces.

An early example of this elaborate air attack occurred on 1 April 1944.[15] Eastbound Convoy UGS–36 comprised 72 merchant vessels and 18 LSTs in 13 columns. The ocean escort commander, Captain Harold S. Berdine USCG in *Decatur*, had under him seven Coast Guard-manned DEs and three old destroyers. At Gibraltar he was joined by two seagoing tugs and antiaircraft cruiser H.M.S. *Colombo* with a fighter-director team embarked. In addition, two Dutch and four British patrol craft formed antisubmarine screen six miles ahead of the convoy. On the afternoon of 31 March, Cincmed warned Berdine that as German reconnaissance planes had been sighted he had better prepare for a dusk or dawn attack.

At 0400 April 1 a string of flares was dropped on the convoy's starboard bow. The sky was clear and a gentle wind was blowing, with swells from the southwest; moon had set. Reaction was immediate; within half a minute the entire convoy was lighted up by tracers streaming from every gun. A score of planes, mostly low-flying twin-engined Do–217s (three of which were seen to splash), attacked over a period of twenty minutes. S.S. *Jared Ingersoll*, hit by a torpedo in the forward hold, was the only ship damaged. Destroyer escort *Mills*, assigned to stand by, helped the ship's crew to

[15] Capt. Berdine Action Report; Cincmed to Admiralty 9 June 1944, forwarding reports of UGS–36 and later convoys.

quench the fire, and *Jared Ingersoll* was towed into Algiers by a British tug.

Next convoy to be subjected to fancy Luftwaffe tactics was UGS–37 consisting of 60 merchant ships and six LSTs escorted by five United States destroyers, eight DEs, two British PCs, two tugs and antiaircraft cruiser H.M.S. *Delhi*. Commander William R. Headden in destroyer escort *Stanton* handled the escort. The convoy was shadowed all day 10 and 11 April 1944, and two snoopers were shot down by shore-based fighters. Attack developed shortly before midnight of the 11th. Shore radar stations gave prompt warning, so that Commander Headden had time to deploy his screen for added protection astern and on the seaward flank, and even to have the guns pointed. The convoy was in close formation, 400 yards' distance between ships, 600-yard intervals between columns, making 7½ knots over a calm sea under a cloudless sky, steering due east about 60 miles north of Cape Tenès. At 2252, ten minutes before moonrise, five to ten planes were orbiting near the convoy, and at 2318 a white flare was observed ahead. Four minutes later Commander Headden signaled, "They are coming in. Open up on them if they come close enough." Parachutes carrying gigantic magnesium flares were being dropped, and it soon became light as day. Escorts commenced making smoke at 2335, and at the same moment *Stanton* opened up on a plane crossing her bow from port to starboard. The plane nevertheless made a torpedo hit on destroyer escort *Holder*. H.M.S. *Delhi* and all escorts threw up a heavy barrage as well as aimed fire, which seemed to disconcert the German planes. Although at 2351, twenty to twenty-five more came in, low enough to elude radar, two Junkers and one Dornier were shot down, and the rest failed to press this second attack. *Holder* was able to make port under tow, and no other damage was done. Alertness and readiness, quick and concentrated fire on any and all targets, and the smoke screen, had won.[16]

[16] Smoke screen is useful not only to conceal the merchant ships but also to obscure the horizon and the moon's sheen on the water. Low-flying planes must have one or the other to maintain their level.

UGS-38, next eastbound convoy to be attacked, encountered superior Luftwaffe technique and was very roughly handled. Commander William H. Duvall in U.S.C.G.C. *Taney* had an escort group of twelve DEs, two fast minesweepers, destroyer *Lansdale* and Netherlands flak cruiser *Heemskerck*. Although this convoy was attacked at a point only three miles off Cape Bengut, it had no warning from shore, because the 25 to 30 attacking planes made their southing well east of the Balearics and approached the coast near Djidjelli, flying very low and evading both shore-based radar and a section of Airacobras (P-39) patrolling north of the convoy. The first news that the planes were headed for UGS-38 came from a coastwatcher on Cape Sigli, 42 miles east of Cape Bengut.

The Luftwaffe attacked in three waves on 20 April, flying between the convoy and the coast so that ships' radar was largely useless; and two escorts reported that their radar was jammed during the attack. The first wave of nine torpedo planes, attacking 25 minutes after sunset, damaged three merchant ships and sank American S.S. *Paul Hamilton* which was carrying 498 men of the Army Air Force. Since she was also carrying high explosives, *Paul Hamilton* was blown into bits, and every person on board, to the number of 580, was killed.[17] A frightful warning indeed against transporting troops and high explosives in the same ship, and a slow ship at that.

The second wave of this successful attack, consisting of seven Ju-88s, flew down the inboard flank of the convoy, sank one more merchantman, and damaged a third. Then came five He-111s, which concentrated on the port bow, the "coffin corner" of the convoy. Destroyer *Lansdale* bore the brunt. Torpedoed at 2105, she sank within 30 minutes, carrying down 47 officers and men out of her total complement of 282. This attack on UGS-38 marked high water for the Luftwaffe in the history of Mediterranean convoys.

UGS-39 got through without incident, and rôles were completely reversed in the next eastbound Mediterranean convoy,

[17] Casualties included 154 members of 831st Bombing Squadron, 317 of 32nd Photo Reconnaissance Squadron, 29 Naval Armed Guards, and 47 merchant mariners. Data from Office of Chief of Military History.

UGS–40, which inflicted heavy loss on the attacking German air-craft and got through with hardly a scratch.[18] Both escorts and merchantmen put on such a superb performance that an effort has been made to preserve this convoy's composition.[19]

Commander Jesse C. Sowell, escort commander in the veteran Coast Guard cutter *Campbell*, had given the subject of repelling air attacks a great deal of thought. At Norfolk, after consulting with Captain Thomas H. Taylor, the convoy commodore, he worked out an air defense plan. Four rehearsals of this plan were conducted; these and other training exercises occurred almost every day during the ocean passage.

At Gibraltar and off Alborán Island the escort received a wel-come accession of strength in antiaircraft cruiser H.M.S. *Caledon*, U.S.S. *Wilhoite* and *Benson*, salvage tug H.M.S. *Hengist*, and American minecraft *Steady* and *Sustain* which were fitted with ap-paratus for jamming the radio-controlled glide-bombs that had been very troublesome when first used against shipping.

Convoy UGS–40 passed through the Strait 9 May 1944. For two days it was shadowed by German planes; and, although shore-based aircraft were scrambled ten times and Beaufighters flew out to in-tercept, the snoopers escaped. Such persistent shadowing indicated that the Germans intended to put on something very special.

At 1950 May 11, as the convoy was steaming about 50 miles east of Algiers, the eight columns spaced 1000 yards and ships 500 yards apart, the screen assumed air-defense stations about 3000 yards out. Four minutes later, Commander Sowell warned his skippers over voice radio to expect an attack at dusk. When shore-based radar warning of approaching planes reached him at 2025, he informed Captain Taylor, "It is Red from now on." General Quarters sounded, and the convoy plunged into one of the most tense situa-tions in naval warfare — awaiting air attack. At 2044, shore-based

[18] CTF 61 (Cdr. Sowell) Action Report 15 May; reports from individual ships, both of escort and convoy, seen on board U.S.C.G.C. *Campbell*; conversations with Cdr. Samuel F. Gray uscg and other officers of *Campbell*; information from a captured German pilot, seen at Gibraltar, and from the monthly Luftwaffe Re-port for May 1944.
[19] See Appendix V.

radar picked up the bombers 70 miles north of Cape Corbelin. One minute later, the sun set. The convoy had just passed Cape Bengut and was steering due east. No moon, sky more than three-quarters overcast, light airs from the east, and a smooth sea — ideal for making smoke. As the sun dipped under the horizon, Commander Sowell gave the order to light smoke pots. Escorts stationed ahead of the convoy steered north for ten minutes and then southeast until back on station, in order to cover the van; and this white chemical smoke, laid on three sides of the convoy, produced a heavy and persistent haze which proved to be an important factor in thwarting the attack, while it offered no obstruction to the planned barrage — for the Germans sent no *Beleuchteren* on this attack, since it was timed for twilight.

At that moment, when evening twilight was fading, German torpedo planes were forming up for the attack at a point 10 to 20 miles north of the convoy. As two bells struck the van passed the bold headland of Cape Tedlès, about six miles off shore. The inevitable Arab spy was signaling from the cape with a blinker.

H.M.S. *Caledon*, on the northeast corner of the screen, kept an excellent radar plot of the oncoming "bandits," including their altitude; so that at 2106, when Commander Sowell gave the word for the planned barrage to begin, a curtain of fire from the screen was thrown up between convoy and planes, tracers making a fantastic and beautiful basket pattern in the sky. The Junkers planes, the Heinkels and the Dorniers planned to make a "pile-driving" attack in four waves of about seven planes each, spaced a few minutes apart, on the port and starboard bows, port quarter and port beam of the convoy. As soon as it became evident from radar plot that the first wave was coming in on the usual "coffin corner," the port bow, Sowell ordered an emergency 45-degree turn in that direction. Neatly and promptly executed, it presented the vessels' bows to the attack.

A large proportion of the torpedo-bombers got through or under the barrage. They were then taken under fire from escorts and Naval Armed Guard crews on the merchantmen, who had been ordered to hold gunfire until sighting definite targets. By 2110 there was a general mêlée. At least one merchant vessel was firing simultaneously with her 5-inch 38 at bombers over the center of the convoy, with her 3-inch 50 on planes coming from ahead, and with her 20-mm machine guns at torpedo-bombers passing down between her column and the next. These planes came down as low as 40 feet from the water with engines cut, but the chemical smoke put them off, so that they found it difficult to find a target. Some were skimming across the bows of the leading line of ships, some across the center; a second wave came in on the starboard bow; some slipped down the columns, harassed by gunfire and unable to launch torpedoes; a few exploded with bright flashes and loud roars which gave the erroneous impression that merchant ships were catching it. A large number of torpedoes were released, so ineptly that they were easily evaded. High-level Dorniers contributed to the sound and fury by dropping bombs, none of which hit a ship; and two radio-controlled glide-bombs were sighted but evaded.

All this time the escorts were maneuvering radically at top speed — 19 to 20 knots for the DEs — while the merchantmen maintained regular convoy speed of eight knots.

As the attack faded and surviving planes were making their getaway, destroyer escort *Wilhoite* signaled a new wave coming in on the port quarter. Accordingly, at 2122, Commander Sowell ordered an emergency 45-degree turn to starboard, which brought the convoy back to its column formation, heading east. This final stroke of the Luftwaffe met the same fate as the first two. Torpedo-bombers horsed around in the gathering darkness, looking for targets through the white smoke, and red flares were sighted in the water. At 2140 all was over, and at 2203 Algiers signaled "All Clear!" Many ships remained at General Quarters throughout the night, expecting a fourth attack which never came.

By the time the battle was over it was completely dark, and Convoy UGS–40 continued its course to Naples without further let or hindrance.

Although almost everyone present, especially the Germans,

thought that aircraft explosions were torpedoed merchantmen, not a single ship of the escort or convoy had suffered a hit. The only casualties in the entire formation were the wounding of one vessel's "Chips" and four Army passengers, by 20-mm fire from another ship.[20] This result testified to the excellent training, preparation and gunnery of convoy and escorts. Messages were transmitted quickly and accurately by shore and ship communication staffs. Credit is due also to the intercepting Beaufighters, two of which were lost. They not only forced the German fighter cover to turn back, but knocked down a couple of Junkers planes. Commander Sowell, after a careful collation of reports from screen and merchant ships, plotted 19 planes shot down and splashed over or near the convoy, out of 62 that started.[21] Admiral Ingersoll signaled, "Performance your Task Force in successfully opposing heavy air attack without loss is outstanding."

Having failed in twilight, the enemy next tried a midnight attack. Convoy UGS–42 was the intended victim, very near the same position as UGS–40, at 0100 May 31. One small merchant ship was sunk and one other damaged; three Junkers planes were shot down.

On 11 July 1944 Convoy UGS–46, consisting of 73 ships in 13 columns, under a predominantly American escort, was steaming at six knots east of Oran while waiting for some LSTs to join. The weather was clear and a gentle breeze was blowing from the east. Shortly after midnight H.M.S. *Caledon* gave warning of the approach of aircraft from the north, and, inconveniently, the moon rose; but the escort commander countered moonlight by ordering all ships to make smoke. For two hours the planes orbited, apparently trying to find the convoy through the smoke screen, and making only sporadic attacks (12 July) which were completely un-

[20] One of the torpedo planes was brought down by a merchantman's 20-mm manned by "Lt. G. B. Nicholson USA infantry and Pvt. Solomon Kenefsky USA, both passengers." Report of master of British S.S. *Samgallion*.
[21] Also, one crashed near Alicante on its way home, and one was shot down by R.A.F. Spitfires orbiting for that very purpose over its home base. Number starting checked from German Naval Staff War Diary. Berlin claimed sinking 7 M/V and 1 DD, and hitting 19 other ships.

successful.[22] A similar midnight attack was delivered on Convoy UGS–48 on 1 August 1944, six miles off Cape Corbelin. Heavy smoke was laid over the convoy, and the escorts again drove off the planes with no damage to any ship.[23]

By this time the German airfields in Southern France were under heavy Allied attack in preparation for the landings of 15 August, and after that event the Germans could no longer operate planes against Mediterranean convoys. The sea became so peaceful that, beginning with UGS–60, which passed Gibraltar 27 November 1944, convoys were dispersed at Point Europa and the ships proceeded independently to their terminal ports.

All in all, there was no more brilliant defense of convoys from air attack, unsupported by escort carriers, than these Mediterranean battles in the spring and early summer of 1944. Escorts, Naval Armed Guards in merchant ships, and intercepting land-based fighters all played their parts; careful planning by escort commanders, intelligent use of smoke, and excellent communications were jointly responsible for this series of defeats administered to the Luftwaffe.

[22] CTF 60 (Capt. Roger B. Nickerson in U.S.C.G.C. *Bibb*) Action Report.
[23] Comcortdiv 66 (Cdr. George F. Adams USNR) Action Report.

CHAPTER XV

Southern and Far Eastern Waters[1]

1943–1945

1. Passage to Penang, February 1943–March 1944

ALTHOUGH the Indian Ocean can by no definition be considered a part of the Atlantic, the U-boat operations therein were actually an extension of the Atlantic war, and so closely integrated with those in the South Atlantic that we must consider them here. And from June 1943 to the end, the Indian Ocean was the most profitable operating area in the "tonnage war" on Allied merchantmen.

Throughout the war the Indian Ocean and the Cape and Suez routes thither were areas of British responsibility on the one side, and joint German-Japanese on the other. An agreement signed December 1941 between Germany and Japan set up a "chop" line between them. But the Japanese Navy accomplished so little in the Indian Ocean after its Easter carrier raid of 1942 [2] that the Germans came to regard the Eastern sea as their bailiwick, and only a few Japanese submarines participated.

In February 1943 Doenitz sent four 740-ton U-boats to operate off Capetown where they did very well, sinking 24 ships of 165,709 tons (only five of them in convoy) in about three months. One of this pack, *U–182*, homeward bound on 16 May, encountered Con-

[1] Kap.-zur-See Kurt Freiwald "German U-boats in the Indian Ocean," O.N.I. *Review* Aug. 1953 pp. 362–70, is a useful review of these operations. Details in two reports after the war by Vizeadmiral Paul W. Wenneker, German naval attaché at Tokyo, to 44th Counter-Intelligence Corps Detachment U.S. Army, on German-Japanese relations, 3 May 1946; Doenitz "The War at Sea" sec. 103.
[2] See Vol. III 381–86.

voy UGS–8 about 200 miles WNW of Funchal and was sunk by its escorts, *MacKenzie* and *Laub*, after two depth-charge attacks. A second pack of six boats, which relieved the first four, rounded the Cape and sank 137,357 tons of shipping, mostly off Madagascar, between 1 June and 30 August. Four unescorted American merchantmen were among their victims.[3] Doenitz called this group "Monsun" because he intended it to operate during the southwest monsoon in the summer of 1943. Numbering nine boats initially, it lost two in the Bay of Biscay, including one of its milch cows, *U–462;* the other intended refueler, *U–160*, together with *U–509*, was sunk by the *Santee* escort carrier group in July.[4]

When the second pack returned home, one of its number, *U–178*, was detained to help establish a German submarine operating base at Penang, that island off the Malay Peninsula familiar to readers of Joseph Conrad. Although the German-Japanese "chop" line was long. 70° E and Penang lies in long. 100° E, the Japanese apparently acquiesced; and this base, already used by the Japanese, proved a boon to U-boats in the southern ocean. Of the five "Monsun" boats that got through, three had to head for Penang in October for repairs; *U–533* was sunk by planes of the 244th Squadron R.A.F. in the Gulf of Oman. These five, with the assistance of several Japanese submarines, sank 21 vessels of 125,625 tons, including two Liberty ships, in the Indian Ocean during the last four months of 1943. Only two of the 21 ships were in convoy, and those convoys had no air support.

United States submarine *Tarpon* (Commander Thomas L. Wogan) operating in the North Pacific at this time, made an important contribution to the defeat of Germany. When patrolling 120 miles south of Tokyo Bay in the small hours of 17 October 1943, *Tarpon* sighted an unescorted ship in bright moonlight, distant six miles. It was the disguised and heavily armed German commerce raider *Michel*, heading for a Japanese port. Feeling perfectly se-

[3] Also, S.S. *Henry Knox* was sunk by a Japanese I-boat 19 June 1943 off the Maldives.
[4] See Chapter VI.

cure, she was steaming at 16 knots without zigzagging and without proper lookout. *Tarpon* made a deliberate approach and sent the raider to the bottom at 0230 with four hits from eight torpedoes. *Michel* fought back vigorously but scored no hits. She was the last of the commerce raiders that had taken a substantial toll of Allied shipping in the earlier years of the war. When her loss was reported to Doenitz he demanded information as to why she had not been under Japanese escort; and, when Konteradmiral Godt learned details from the German naval attaché at Tokyo, he noted in his war diary that such laxity was "unbelievable" and "extraordinary." [5] He even suspected that *Michel* had been mistakenly sunk by a Japanese submarine.

Late in 1943 a number of Japanese I-boats entered the Indian Ocean and conducted a blitz against Allied shipping which was marked by instances of sadistic cruelty. British S.S. *Daisy Moller*, torpedoed by one of them on 14 December 1943 in mid-ocean, lost 55 men out of 127 passengers and crew by the ramming and machine-gunning of rafts and lifeboats. The crew of S.S. *British Chivalry* met the same fate.[6]

Dockage and repair facilities were being improved at Penang, and three Italian submarines which were seized by the Japanese when Italy surrendered in September, were there refitted and manned by German officers and mixed crews. At the turn of the year, these and the "Monsun" boats started to leave Penang. Six of them did a great deal of damage to Allied merchantmen and "country ships" along the Aden-Bombay route and elsewhere in the Indian Ocean, assisting the Japanese I-boats to sink 184,122 tons of Allied and neutral shipping in the first three months of 1944. Several victims were Liberty ships, one of which, S.S. *Richard Hovey*, had a most devastating experience on 29 March 1944. The Japanese

[5] *Tarpon* Report of Ninth War Patrol; War Diary Op. Div. German Naval Staff 20 Oct. 1943.

[6] O.N.I. Summary of Statements of *Daisy Moller* Survivors 15 Feb. 1944 and of *British Chivalry* 30 March; statements in Judge Advocate General Case No. 67-24 at Statistical Analysis Office. On the other hand, the crews of S.S. *José Navarro*, *Robert F. Hoke* and *Albert Gallatin*, all sunk by I-boats, were not molested. These Japanese submarines have not been identified.

submarine, after fatally torpedoing the vessel, moved to within a thousand yards of its lifeboats and, as the Naval Armed Guard officer recalled, opened fire on the survivors: —

Just as soon as it was evident that they were shooting at the lifeboats and rafts all hands that were visible jumped overboard into the water and did everything possible to avoid being struck by shells from what appeared to be 20-mms and bullets from automatic high-velocity rifles which were carried by the Japs as they ran back and forth on the submarine spraying the water with bullets. The submarine approached No. 2 lifeboat first, firing on it, and, then, rammed it, causing it to overturn and partially sink. . . . Many of us swam underwater and under the raft for protection. As the submarine was within a few feet of us we could definitely determine that the men, who were lined up on its deck as though they were on parade, were Japanese. They were all dressed the same, in khaki uniforms and khaki caps. They were laughing and seemed to get quite a bit of sport out of our predicament. One of them, with a motion picture camera, took pictures of what transpired.[7]

The vessel's master, Hans Thorsen, was taken on board the I-boat as prisoner and was never heard of again. Most of the survivors climbed back into their lifeboats after the submarine departed. Thanks to a water distillery rigged by a junior engineer, they managed to survive until rescued by British merchant ships 16 days later.

Richard Hovey was the last merchantman to be sunk in the Indian Ocean for several months. Local defense forces of the Royal Indian Navy and the R.A.F. were steadily improving and more convoys were being organized. An escort team of one Indian gunboat and two Australian minesweepers sank Japanese *RO–110* on 11 February 1944 about 200 miles NE of Madras. H.M.S. *Paladin*, also escorting a convoy, sank *I–27* next day, south of the Maldives. On the 14th, one of the converted Italian boats under German command, *UIT–23*, was sunk by a British submarine, *Tally Ho*, in Malacca Strait.

[7] Lt. (jg) Harry C. Goudy USNR, N.A.G. officer S.S. *Richard Hovey* Report to V.C.N.O. 11 July 1944, Enclosure A. Position lat. 16°40′ N, long. 64°30′ E.

About this time the "Monsun" group started its homeward passage to France. Two German supply ships, which had been servicing raiders since early in the war, were sent out by Doenitz to refuel and provision the group before rounding the Cape. One, *Charlotte Schliemann*, was scuttled by her crew southeast of Mauritius on 12 February 1944 when about to be attacked by H.M.S. *Relentless*. The other, *Brake*, fell victim a month later to a neat operation by a British task force comprising two cruisers, two destroyers and H.M.S. *Battler*. At a point about 900 miles SE of Mauritius a carrier plane sighted *Brake*, accompanied by U-boats, steaming southwesterly in a heavy sea. Estimating correctly that they were seeking smoother water for fueling, the task force commander sent destroyer H.M.S. *Roebuck* on their track. She made contact at noon 12 March and opened fire. *Brake's* captain promptly set scuttling charges and abandoned ship. Three U-boats at that moment were still around, about two-thirds replenished. They submerged when the destroyer hove in sight, sat out her battle with *Brake*, and surfaced to find nothing but oil, wreckage and boatloads of survivors. These were taken on board by two of the U-boats, which made for Batavia and Singapore as they had insufficient fuel to reach the next "filling station" off the Cape Verdes; the third, *U–188*, reached home on schedule — the only "Monsun" boat to do so.

2. *Escort Carriers off Cape Verdes and Madeira,* *March–April 1944*

Admiralty and Tenth Fleet alike decided that to prevent more Indian Ocean submarine operations they must scour around the Cape Verde Islands to catch outbound boats at fueling rendezvous. A group of them was actually heading thither in early March 1944. One was suspected to be the new 1200-ton IX–D type. These, we learned subsequently, had a standard cruising range of 20,000 miles and could make the round voyage to Penang without refueling.

American escort carrier groups which had made a cleanup in the Azorean fueling area were chosen for this assignment.

First to be sent into these waters was *Block Island* (Captain Logan C. Ramsey), screened by a destroyer, *Corry*, and four destroyer escorts, *Thomas, Breeman, Bronstein* and *Bostwick.* Departing Chesapeake Bay 16 February 1944, this group fueled off Fayal on the 26th and was then dispatched northward in wide support of convoys that were coming through. On the evening of the 29th, about 600 miles north of Terceira, *U–709* steamed right into its embrace and returned an echo to *Thomas's* pinging. While *Thomas* and *Bostwick* were searching for it, *Block Island's* radarman at 2139 [8] picked up what looked like a second U-boat about five miles westward. *Bronstein* (Lieutenant Sheldon H. Kinney) was sent to run down this second target, but her star shell revealed the first contact, *U–709*, on the surface and moving in to attack her two fellows. *Bronstein* made several gunfire hits; *U–709* dove, and *Thomas* (Lieutenant Commander D. M. Kellogg USNR) made nine depth-charge attacks lasting until 0549 March 1, which finished the career of *U–709*.

Nevertheless there was a second U-boat, *U–603*, which shortly after midnight began moving in for a shot at the carrier. Kinney drove it away with a "scare" attack, pursued, and sank the boat at about 0122 March 1 some 600 miles north of Terceira.

The *Block Island* group entered Casablanca 8 March [9] for urgent repairs. Departing 11 March with a new skipper, Captain Francis M. Hughes, but the same screen, it made radar contact four days later on *U–801* about 300 miles west of Santo Antão in the Cape Verdes group. As often happens off these islands, a heavy haze formed of dust particles from the Sahara lay over the water, shielding the U-boat from searching aircraft. But when *U–801* surfaced on the evening of 16 March it had the bad luck to find overhead an Avenger-Wildcat team from the carrier. Their attack killed or

[8] Zone O (plus 2).
[9] On the next day DE *Leopold*, escorting tanker convoy CU–16, at lat. 57°36′ N, long. 26°30′ W, was sunk by an acoustic torpedo from *U–255*. She lost 171 of her crew of 199 coastguardsmen.

wounded ten submariners, but the boat dove and evaded a sonobuoy search. In the small hours of the 17th, the German skipper
made the mistake of calling Berlin to get the course for his milch
cow. *Corry* ran down the bearing of his transmission and made a
radar contact late in the midwatch. That proved to be on an Aphrodite radar decoy. *U–801*, still on the surface, was sighted shortly
before dawn 17 March by an Avenger pilot, who dropped a 500-
pound depth bomb close aboard, which holed the engine room.
The U-boat then submerged to great depth, leaking enough oil to
reveal its position. *Corry* and *Bronstein* methodically searched, and
in two and a half hours delivered eight depth-charge attacks which
forced *U–801* to surface at 1118. The crew abandoned and scuttled their boat; only the engineer officer went down with it.

Throughout 17 and 18 March 1944 the *Block Island* group
searched for the inevitable milch cow, and was rewarded at 0726
March 19 by the dawn patrol's sighting something else — 1100-ton
U–1059. Some of its crew were then swimming, but all save one
got on board before a Wildcat, piloted by Lieutenant (jg) William H. Cole USNR, strafed the conning tower; and guns were
manned so promptly that the next attacker, Lieutenant (jg) Norman T. Dowty's Avenger, was hit in a vital spot. Dowty, before
he splashed, managed to drop two depth bombs, one right into the
boat's ammunition locker; the explosions raised it high in the air,
and down it went, bow first. Seven submariners of *U–1059*, including the skipper, and one crewman of the Avenger were recovered; but Lieutenant Dowty was lost.

In the course of this cruise, on 23 March 1944, two of *Block Island's* escorts, *Breeman* and *Bronstein*, were detached and reported
next day at Dakar to perform a traditional duty of the old sailing
Navy: the transport of gold. About $60,000,000 in gold ingots be-
longing to the Bank of Poland had reached French West Africa
after numerous transfers and hairbreadth escapes, and the French
were as anxious to be rid of them as the Polish Government in Ex-
ile was to set the gold to work, which could best be done in America. The DEs had to clear sundry magazines and lockers near their

keels to accommodate this heavy metal. After the wooden boxes, containing four large ingots each, had been shouldered on board by Senegalese sailors of the French Navy and struck below by American bluejackets, *Breeman* and *Bronstein* departed for New York with orders not to deviate from the great-circle course, nor to run down submarine contacts. Met at Brooklyn 3 April by a fleet of armored trucks, and a small army of civilian police, F.B.I. men and Marines, the DEs delivered the gold and returned to their normal duties. Unfortunately for their skippers, the unkind person in Washington who wrote their orders specified that the ancient Navy regulation granting commanding officers a "cut" on gold transported would not apply in this instance.[10]

The *Bogue* escort carrier group, which relieved *Block Island's*, drew a blank off the Cape Verdes during the first week of April 1944, then headed for Trinidad. Thus those islands were unguarded by Allied forces when the next group of nine U-boats started the passage to Penang; and Doenitz, by that time, had shifted his fueling area to a point west of Madeira. These nine, together with *U-123* of a previous group that had got through, and five which had started in April, made 15 boats — five of which were sunk by escort carrier groups in the Atlantic, and two in the Indian Ocean.

Next group to score in these waters was Captain Daniel V. Gallery's, built around *Guadalcanal* of the first pair of Kaiser-built CVEs that entered the Atlantic war. "Can Do," as the crew nicknamed her,[11] had a screen composed of destroyer *Forrest* and four DEs. Admiral Ingersoll's orders to Captain Gallery were typical: "Operate against enemy submarines in the North Atlantic." And the skipper had a good "bull session" with his classmate Captain Isbell of *Card*, before he left Norfolk in early January 1944. On the 16th three of his planes were flying patrol about 300 miles W by N of Flores, when they sighted three submarines fueling. The aircraft

[10] Lt. Cdr. Sheldon Kinney (C.O. of *Bronstein*) "Tin Can Gold Rush" in U.S. Naval Inst. *Proceedings* LXXIV (Feb. 1948) 169–72; dates corrected from *Breeman* War Diary.
[11] Rear Admiral Daniel V. Gallery *Clear the Decks!* (1951) describes his experiences as skipper of "Can Do," including a vivid account of teaching his aviators to fly night patrols, and of the hazards of night takeoffs and landings.

made a highly unconventional attack, firing rockets and dropping bombs on the same run; and that finished *U-544*.

After a second and uneventful passage, *Guadalcanal* departed Casablanca 30 March in support of Convoy GUS–37. The carrier group peeled off 8 April to run down a U-boat transmission. It proved to be 740-ton *U-515*, whose skipper, Kapitänleutnant Werner Henke, surfaced again at dusk to find himself being stalked by aircraft. He dove, surfaced once more before midnight, and was promptly pounced on by two "night owl" Avengers. Shortly after dawn 9 April, an oil slick and sonobuoy echoes enabled the hunters to pick up the scent, and at 0645 a fighter pilot straddled *U-515* with a brace of depth bombs. Henke survived this attack, but at 1030 destroyer escort *Pope* made sound contact within two miles of the carrier and delivered several vigorous hedgehog and depth-charge attacks, one of which badly damaged the boat's pressure hull. Contact was constantly maintained. Around 1300, when big oil bubbles began to break the surface, Commander Frederick S. Hall, Captain Gallery's screen commander in *Pope*, signaled over TBS, "We want to get this baby before dark. Don't miss any bets!" He set up a scouting line of four escort vessels. Henke was already in desperate straits, sinking to 600 feet before he could blow enough tanks to surface. When he was on the way up at 1403, destroyer escort *Chatelain* made contact; and, just as her second brace of depth charges exploded, *U-515* broached with water streaming off its black decks, barely 75 yards on the DE's starboard beam and within plain sight of the carrier. *Chatelain* and *Flaherty* overwhelmed *U-515* with gunfire at point-blank range while *Pillsbury* rang up flank speed to get into the fight; an Avenger fired rockets and two Wildcats not only strafed the boat but exploded an acoustic torpedo that seemed to be chasing *Pillsbury* around.

Henke could not take any more, ordered Abandon Ship, and at 1412 *U-515* went down, 175 miles northwest of Funchal. The skipper, who was rated as one of the U-boat "aces," and 43 of his crew, were rescued.[12]

---

[12] Times of this action are Zone N (plus 1). Interesting details on interrogation of these survivors in *Clear the Decks!* pp. 196–204.

Doenitz had warned his southward-steaming group on 6 April that a "12,000-ton carrier" and four escorts were looking for them; but he did not know, nor did they, that *Guadalcanal* was flying patrols around the clock. *U-214* evaded a depth-bomb attack and escaped; but 900-ton *U-68* was caught on the surface in broad moonlight 10 April, and sunk by depth bombs, strafing and rocket fire from two "Can Do" Avengers and a Wildcat. This happened about 300 miles south of Horta. "Captain Dan" and his merry men got an "Exceptionally well done!" from Admiral Ingersoll.

Doenitz now set up a new fueling rendezvous in mid-Atlantic, a good 700 miles west of the Cape Verdes. There, on 16–17 April, 1600-ton *U-488* fueled *U-129*, outward-bound for Brazil, and *U-537*, en route to the Indian Ocean. Three other customers were expected but failed to show up, owing to the activities of two other escort carrier groups which Admiral Ingersoll had sent to this mid-ocean area: one built around *Tripoli*, and the other around *Croatan*. The former had poor luck; her one contact, *U-543* on 19 April, got away. But "Old Crow," with a new skipper, Captain John P. W. Vest, and a new screen of five destroyer escorts under Commander Frank D. Giambattista, did very well.

In the night of 19–20 April *Croatan's* HF/DF picked up a transmission from 900-ton *U-66* but obtained no bearing on it. That U-boat, its fuel and provisions depleted after a long patrol in the Gulf of Guinea, badly wanted a refill before turning homeward, and Doenitz ordered it to be serviced by *U-488* on the 26th. As *Croatan* turned in the same direction as the U-boats, her Avenger pilots on the night of the 25th obtained a fleeting glimpse of *U-66* in the moonlight. Sonobuoys and sound gear of two escorts failed to establish contact. Captain Vest then set up a retiring sweep which was rewarded at 0442 April 26 when *Frost* made a sound contact on *U-488* at 1000 yards. *Inch* delivered two hedgehog attacks, as did another destroyer escort; but the sea was so calm that turbulence lingered indefinitely and thwarted the sound gear. The search continued until into the morning watch when, guided by a patch of oil, *Snowden*, *Frost* and *Barber* dropped maximum-depth patterns over a motionless target which registered 560 feet on the fathometer. No debris appeared, but *U–488* was never heard from again.[13]

"Refueling even in mid-Atlantic will scarcely be possible in future," remarked the official War Diary after Doenitz had given up *U–488* for lost. "This situation will continue until the introduction of submerged fueling. Until then, refueling will be carried out only in urgent cases from combatant boats. All boats have received instructions to begin homeward passage in good time so they can reach port without refueling."

3. BUCKLEY's *Battle; Loss of* BLOCK ISLAND,
May 1944

Just before the *Croatan* group disposed of *U–488*, Admiral Ingersoll sent the *Bogue* and *Block Island* groups south to relieve it, and to close the Cape Verdes passage to Brazil and the Indian Ocean.

Block Island (Captain Francis M. Hughes), equipped with "night owl" Avengers whose pilots kept continuous patrol, and a screen of four new destroyer escorts, departed Norfolk 22 April for the latest mid-ocean fueling area. On 1 May Hughes received a Tenth Fleet HF/DF fix indicating a boat about 550 miles west of Santo Antão. It turned out to be *U–66*, which we have already encountered more than once. It was looking for *U–188*, to obtain much-needed fuel and provisions before going home.

Captain Hughes promptly sent DEs *Ahrens* and *Eugene E. Elmore* some 60 miles ahead of *Block Island* to search. After four days of systematic stalking, he was rewarded on the night of 5 May by the unexpected and somewhat disconcerting surfacing of *U–66* only three miles ahead of his carrier. The skipper, Oberleutnant Seehausen, at the end of his submerged endurance, reported by radio to Doenitz that refueling was impossible under constant stalking. "Mid-Atlantic worse than Bay of Biscay!" he concluded.

[13] Position about 720 miles W of Santo Antão. *U–66* was in the neighborhood and observed the attack.

Almost simultaneously, the carrier's radar registered the surfaced submarine at 5000 yards and the U-boat detected the presence of *Block Island*. Then began the contest — who would sink what?

While the carrier hot-footed out of the area, *Buckley* (Lieutenant Commander Brent M. Abel USNR) headed down the radar bearing at 2120 May 5,[14] but was unable to obtain contact during a search lasting several hours. A "night owl" pilot, Lieutenant (jg) Jimmie J. Sellars USNR, at 0216 May 6 reported to Abel a radar contact estimated to be 20 miles almost due north of him, and 66 miles north of *Block Island's* position. Sellars, who was armed with nothing heavier than a pistol,[15] stalked the German for three quarters of an hour, coaching Abel to the spot. It was a calm, clear night with light airs from the NE and moon two days short of full; but Seehausen, on observing Sellars's Avenger, figured that it would not attempt to bomb his boat until he submerged; and, ignorant that he was being hunted by a ship too, stayed on the surface, charging his batteries and hoping to locate his milch cow.

At 0246, after obtaining a radar contact on the U-boat, distant less than seven miles, Lieutenant Commander Abel called his crew to General Quarters and closed the target in such wise that it would be between him and the moon. Sound gear was secured, depth charges set for shallow burst, and at 9000 yards Foxer was streamed; but gunfire was withheld in the hope that *Buckley* would either escape detection or be mistaken by the U-boat for its expected refueler. The ruse worked. At 0308 Seehausen sent up three red flares to guide the milch cow to him, and by 0317 his boat was in plain sight two miles away, a black silhouette against moonlight reflected in the calm waters. Abel promptly turned to unmask his main battery and to expose the Foxer to any acoustic torpedo that might be aimed at him. At 0320, distant 2100 yards from the target, he opened up with his 3-inch guns and with the first salvo scored a direct hit just forward of the conning tower. Rapid fire followed

---

[14] Times of this action are Zone N (plus 1).

[15] "Night owl" Avengers had had all machine guns and bombs removed to permit the installation of extra gasoline tanks so that they could stay aloft for as long as 14 hours.

with all guns that could bear, Jimmie Sellars spotting for him by voice radio. *U–66* replied briefly and inaccurately.

Lieutenant Commander Abel, matching every turn of the U-boat, dodged a "fish" that crossed his bow at 0324 and closed until his ship and *U–66* were steaming board-and-board, both firing furiously across the scant twenty yards of clear water that separated them. Planes from *Block Island* arrived on the scene but dared not bomb or strafe for fear of hitting the wrong ship. Faithful Jimmie Sellars was still overhead, giving both *Buckley* and his carrier a play-by-play report over TBS.[16] At 0329 Abel ordered Hard Right Rudder to ram. Seehausen ordered Abandon Ship just as the destroyer escort's bow crashed across his fore deck.

Then ensued a hand-to-hand battle recalling the close-in fighting in days of sail. German submariners came boiling out of the conning tower and deck hatches, some brandishing small arms but others with hands up in token of surrender. Several scrambled up onto *Buckley's* forecastle; others dodged tommy-gun and pistol fire, shell cases, and even coffee mugs hurled by the Americans; a few would-be boarders were even repelled by bare fists. After this brawl had lasted little more than a minute, *Buckley* backed off to clear the U-boat, with five Germans still clustered about her anchor windlass, yelling for quarter.[17] A gunner's mate armed with a hammer took their surrender and they were led below.

[16] Extracts from *Buckley's* TBS log: —
0316, Sellars to Abel: "The s.o.b is taking a few shots at me and I wish I had something to throw back at him!"
0317, same to same: "Sub is turning towards you — sub is now turning away from you — sub's course is parallel to you."
0318, same to same: "He is moving across from port to starboard at a 40-degree angle at 3 o'clock on the watch."
0320, Sellars to Capt. Hughes: "*Buckley* has opened fire — sub is returning fire. Boy! I have never before seen such concentration! *Buckley* is cutting hell out of the conning tower." Sellars to Abel: "Turn your sights up a little."
[17] "Ammunition expended at this time included several general mess coffee cups which were on hand at ready gun station. Two of the enemy were hit in the head with these. Empty shell cases were also used by crew of three-inch gun No. 2, to repel boarders. Three-inch guns could not bear. *Buckley* suffered its only casualty of the engagement when a man bruised his fist knocking one of the enemy over the side. Several men, apparently dead, could be seen hanging over the side of the sub's bridge at this time. One German attempting to board was killed with a .45 pistol by the boatswain's mate in charge of the forward ammunition

Not all Germans had abandoned ship. There were enough below to run the engines, apparently still undamaged. *U–66* drew ahead so rapidly that Abel feared for a moment that it was escaping. He rang up flank speed, drew abreast, and was just about to smother the boat with depth charges from his side-throwing K-guns when the submarine — probably out of control — lunged into a course to ram. At 0335 May 6 it struck *Buckley* a glancing blow on her starboard side aft, sliding under her keel and heeling to such an angle that bluejackets had a clear view of the burning conning tower; one of them even tossed a hand grenade down the hatch into the control room. Scraping clear a minute later, the boat again made off at high speed, but it was now out of control and wreathed in flames. The rest of the crew abandoned ship and *U–66* went down sizzling with open hatches revealing fierce fires below.

The entire action lasted only 16 minutes from start to finish, and three minutes later the breaking-up noises were heard. *Buckley* had fired 105 rounds of 3-inch 50-caliber, over 3000 rounds from her machine guns and 360 pistol bullets — no exact record kept of shell cases and coffee mugs! And her crew had suffered no other casualties than one bruised fist. *Buckley* roved about the scene of the sinking until the sun was well up, searching for survivors; and 36 men, half the total complement, were recovered.[18] They were bearded, pallid as ghosts, and suffering from vitamin deficiency after their long patrol.

That afternoon, 6 May 1944, a somewhat battered *Buckley* rejoined her task group, received a rousing welcome, and transferred her prisoners to *Block Island*. Although holed in her after engine

party. Man fell back over the side. Midships repair party equipped with rifles manned the lifelines on the starboard side abaft light lock, and picked off several men on the deck of the submarine. Chief Fire Controlman used a tommy gun from the bridge with excellent results." – *U.S. Fleet A/S Bulletin* June 1944 p. 25. It has been assumed, in the "popular" accounts of this action that have appeared hitherto, that the Germans were trying to capture *Buckley* by boarding. Actually they were merely trying to save their skins; but since it was dark and neither side spoke or understood the other's language, their intentions were not understood. One German even got below and tried to enter the wardroom, whence he was expelled by a steward's mate armed with a coffee pot.

[18] Two British prisoners, taken from a sunken merchantman, were lost. The position of the sinking was 400 miles west of S. Antão, Cape Verdes.

room, sheared of her starboard propeller shaft, and with her stem twisted, she was able after temporary repairs to steam to Boston under her own power. "The commanding officer," concluded Abel, "is proud of the fighting spirit, coolness in action, and thorough-going teamwork of all hands. It was these characteristics, rather than individual brilliance or heroism of any one officer or man, which concluded the action successfully." [19]

U-188, from which *U-66* had intended to fuel and replenish, was actually near enough to witness the gun flashes and hear the rumble of this battle. It hastily cleared the area and, by dint of running submerged almost continuously, reached Bordeaux 19 June 1944.

Only *U-843* and *U-1062* of the nine boats sent forth during January and February 1944 were still on their way to Penang. But Doenitz made one more try in the same direction which was more successful. In March he dispatched 14 U-boats from European ports, with orders to hunt in either the South Atlantic or the Indian Ocean. The Grossadmiral felt that, with an Allied invasion of France imminent, the tropics offered the best opportunities for his long-range raiders. He was right.

Hunting would not be so easy now for the American escort carrier groups, because U-boats were more wary, having learned that night surfacings were apt to be sighted by "night owl" Avengers.

Bogue had departed Hampton Roads 5 May 1944 with a screen of five destroyer escorts, Commander T. S. Lank in *Haverfield* commanding. The C.O. of the carrier and of the group was Captain "Abe" Vosseller, lately relieved from a year's duty as Comasdevlant. He welcomed this opportunity to put into practice the tactics and devices that he had worked out at Quonset. His first success was scored at dusk 13 May when *Francis M. Robinson* (Lieutenant

---

[19] *Buckley* Action Report 8 May; Capt. Hughes "Report on Surviving Prisoners from *U-66*" to Cominch 18 May; War History Composite Squadron 55; data from Lt. Cdr. Abel and three other officers, received in 1955. *U-66*, on its 9th war patrol, was the boat that had mined the harbor of St. Lucia in 1942 (See Vol. I Appendix IV) when Lt. Cdr. Abel, then in command of *PC-490*, was one of its hunters; fate had brought them together again.

John E. Johansen usnr) sank Japanese *RO-501* (ex-German *U-1224*) with one hedgehog and two depth-charge attacks in the space of ten minutes. For a completely green crew, this was most encouraging. On 29 May Captain Vosseller's *Bogue* group put in at Casablanca.

Block Island departed Casablanca 23 May after spending only two days in port, to relieve *Bogue* in patrolling the waters around Madeira and the Cape Verdes. *U-549*, and possibly another unidentified submarine, escaped a plane's bombing attack on 28 May and an Avenger attack next day. Captain Hughes was running down the estimated track of his target at 1955 May 29, screened by four destroyer escorts. Light airs were blowing over a calm sea, a first-quarter moon was up, visibility was low. Without warning, at 2013 *Block Island* was blasted by a torpedo from *U-549* which had managed to slip undetected inside the screen. Then a second torpedo struck. All propulsion was lost and the rudder jammed. Captain Hughes called all hands topside except men in damage control parties. Presently a third torpedo struck and the carrier settled rapidly by the stern. *Eugene E. Elmore* (Lieutenant Commander G. L. Conkey) sighted the U-boat's periscope and attacked; result negative. *U-549* promptly launched an acoustic torpedo which wrecked the stern of *Barr*, but quick work at damage control saved that destroyer escort from sinking. At 2040 Captain Hughes, mindful of 65,000 gallons of aviation gas on board *Block Island*, ordered Abandon Ship; and while the men were going over the side another torpedo missed *Elmore*. Commander Henry Mullins, screen commander in *Ahrens*, now assumed tactical command, ordered the two remaining escorts tó hunt the submarine, and closed the carrier to recover survivors. En route his sound operator made contact on the U-boat 1800 yards distant, and he ordered *Elmore* to attack. She made three hedgehog patterns after which, at 2120, "two short 'booms' and one big 'wham' " were heard; and then "another heavy, crawling explosion," that marked the breaking up of *U-549*, about 320 miles WSW of Funchal.

Ahrens and *Robert I. Paine* recovered 951 survivors from *Block*

Island's crew.[20] Sadly they watched their carrier's bow rise until her hull was perpendicular to the water and she slowly disappeared from sight. She was the only United States carrier lost in the Atlantic during the entire war. The rest of the task group, with *Barr* in tow, made Casablanca 2 June.

By this time, five of the eight U-boats that Doenitz had sent out for his summer blitz in the Indian Ocean had run the Madeira-Cape Verdes gantlet. But before following their fortunes we must relate a celebrated exploit by Captain Dan Gallery and his "Can Do" team.

4. *The Capture of U–505, June 4*[21]

Mulling over his recent experience with *U–515*, Captain Gallery felt that he might well have captured that submarine if only he had had a boarding party trained and alerted. At the departure conference at Norfolk with his senior task group officers and representatives of Admiral Ingersoll's and Admiral Bellinger's staffs, he announced a plan to capture the next U-boat that he encountered. It was well received; and accordingly he instructed each ship under his command to organize a boarding party.[22]

The *Guadalcanal* group departed Hampton Roads 15 May 1944 with a new composite air squadron (VC–8) on board, and the same screen — five destroyer escorts under Commander Frederick S. Hall, who flew his pennant in *Pillsbury*. For two weeks they drew

[20] *Barr* lost 12 killed or missing and 16 wounded; and 4 out of 6 pilots whose planes were caught aloft when the carrier was torpedoed were lost.

[21] CTG 22.3 Action Report 19 June 1944 with statements by skipper of *U–505* and other prisoners; Comcortdiv 4 (Cdr. F. S. Hall) Action Report 8 June; Compron 8 War History. Gallery *Clear the Decks!* chap. x gives additional details about the towing, but is somewhat inaccurate about the capture. His Interview recorded in the Navy Department 25 May 1945 is a better source. Times for this action are Greenwich.

[22] Four submarines had already been captured in World War II: mine-damaged H.M.S. *Seal* by the Germans in 1940, Italian *Galilei* by H.M.S. *Moonstone* the same year, and *U–570*, which surrendered to a Hudson of the R.A.F. in 1941. *U–570*, as H.M.S. *Graph*, had provided useful information on the actions and capabilities of German submarines. *U–110* was captured by H.M.S. *Bulldog*, 1940.

a blank, for the good reason that U-boats were now steaming near the African coast around Capes Blanco and Verde, inside the islands. Upon being so informed from HF/DF fixes, Captain Gallery swung south down the same channel and put into effect an air search plan to scour the waters 100 miles on either beam, 125 miles ahead, and 125 miles astern of the carrier.

For four days the search was unsuccessful; and the task group's fuel supply was becoming dangerously low. So, at 1100 June 4 — a beautiful sunny day with NE wind force 4, and a heaving sea but no whitecaps — Captain Gallery reluctantly reversed course and headed for Casablanca. Ten minutes later, as the screen was re-forming for the northward run, Lieutenant Commander Dudley S. Knox USNR, skipper of *Chatelain*, reported "possible sound contact"; and at 1112, "Contact evaluated as sub. Am starting attack."

Then, plenty of action! The two DEs nearest *Chatelain* broke off to assist. Wildcats circled overhead like hawks, and *Guadalcanal* swung clear at top speed since, as Captain Gallery wrote, "A carrier right smack at the scene of a sound contact is like an old lady in a barroom brawl. She has no business there, and can do nothing but get out of the way of those who are going to need elbow room for the work at hand."

Chatelain's hedgehogs had barely hit the water, and she was standing out to obtain sea room for a second run, when two Wildcat pilots [23] sighted the shadowy shape of a submarine gliding under the unruffled sea like a great fish. They signaled over TBS "You're going in wrong direction, come back!" and fired machine-gun bullets into the water to indicate the position of the U-boat.[24]

It was 740-ton *U-505*, one of three boats that had been patrolling the Gold Coast, now homeward bound. Oberleutnant Harald Lange brought his boat to periscope depth for a brief look-around and then, dismayed by the array of enemies, took it down. *Chate-*

[23] Ens. J. W. Cadle USNR and Lt. W. W. Roberts USNR.
[24] Position about 130 miles off Cape Blanco. Cdr. Knox, in letter of 21 Jan. 1953 to Rear Admiral Gallery, states that his attack was based entirely on information from *Chatelain's* sound operators, and that the Wildcats' action merely confirmed and accelerated decisions already made.

lain, too quick for him, delivered a full depth-charge pattern which caught the submariners just as lunch was being served.[25] This attack holed the outer hull and rolled the boat on its beam ends, dumping crockery, food and sailors into the bilges. Some of the men, panic-stricken, rushed up to the conning tower shouting that the boat was sinking; the inexperienced skipper, taking their word for it, blew his tanks and surfaced.

Lieutenant Commander Knox has just sent the words "We struck oil!" over TBS when the black hull of *U-505* breaks water at 1122½, barely 700 yards away. Three destroyer escorts open fire with all their guns. Two Wildcats spray the U-boat with machine-gun fire. *Chatelain* fires one torpedo,[26] which fortunately, in the light of what will presently happen, misses. When Germans begin to raise their hands and jump overboard, Commander Hall orders Cease Firing; Away Boarding Parties! The boarding party — machinists, torpedomen and other picked men, commanded by Lieutenant (jg) Albert L. David USNR — shoves off in a whaleboat from *Pillsbury* with salvage gear stowed and ready. The U-boat is circling, with rudder jammed, at 3 to 4 knots; but Lieutenant David finally manages to leap on board.

Although there was good reason to assume that Germans were still engaged in opening sea-cocks and setting demolition charges, Lieutenant David and two petty officers, Arthur W. Knispel and Stanley E. Wdowiak, boldly scrambled below and were relieved to find that the boat was completely abandoned. First they bundled up all important-looking papers, charts and code books, and sent them away in a whaleboat; next they disconnected demolition charges, closed valves, and stopped an 8-inch stream from a bilge strainer. It took them half an hour to secure the engines; during that time *Pillsbury*, endeavoring to close the circling boat to rig a towline, was herself rammed, but not severely. From the carrier's

[25] An odd occasion to serve lunch; but that is what the survivors said.

[26] Cdr. Knox explains this in a letter of 18 Feb. 1953. The sub was heading for him, a lookout thought he saw torpedo tracks, and *Chatelain*, only 500 yards away with engines stopped and broadside to *U-505*, was very vulnerable to torpedo attack.

bridge the efforts of the DE to close looked absurdly like a rodeo cowboy trying to rope a steer.

At 1230 a salvage party from the carrier, led by Commander Earl Trosino USNR, an old merchant service engineer, helped Lieutenant David's men to rig handy-billy pumps to improve the boat's buoyancy, which had dropped dangerously low. A 1¼-inch wire hawser passed from *Guadalcanal* was secured to the sub's bullnose and the carrier took *U-505* in tow, a big American ensign flying from its conning tower. Forty rescued German submariners were transferred to the carrier.

Course was shaped for Bermuda, by Admiral Ingersoll's orders. Cinclant also ordered out from Casablanca oiler *Kennebec*, which fueled the entire group on 7 June, fleet tug *Abnaki* which took over the tow, and seaplane tender *Humboldt*, which put an experienced submarine officer, Commander C. G. Rucker, on board the captured boat. By the evening of 8 June his crew had it fully surfaced and on an even keel. After a slow but uneventful passage, this strange procession entered Port Royal Bay, Bermuda, on 19 June; and so excellent were security measures at Bermuda as well as in Captain Gallery's task group that the capture of *U-505* was long kept secret from the enemy. This enabled Naval Intelligence to make full use of the captured code books and other material.[27]

5. *Fourth Fleet Interlude, February–September 1944*

We broke off air-surface operations under Fourth Fleet in January 1944. Naturally some of the boats destined for the Indian Ocean were encountered by Admiral Ingram's forces. On 6 February an Ascension-based Liberator, piloted by Lieutenant (jg) C. I. Pinnell, sank outward-bound *U-177* about 480 miles WSW of its

[27] Including three acoustic torpedoes. Salvaged from Oblt. Lange's cabin was a book entitled *Roosevelt's Kampf*, which attempted to prove that F.D.R. had started the war and was out to conquer the world. This, with an appropriate inscription was sent to President Roosevelt who added it to the Hyde Park library. *U-505*, after serving as a "tame submarine" during the remainder of the war, has found a final resting place in the Chicago Museum of Science and Industry.

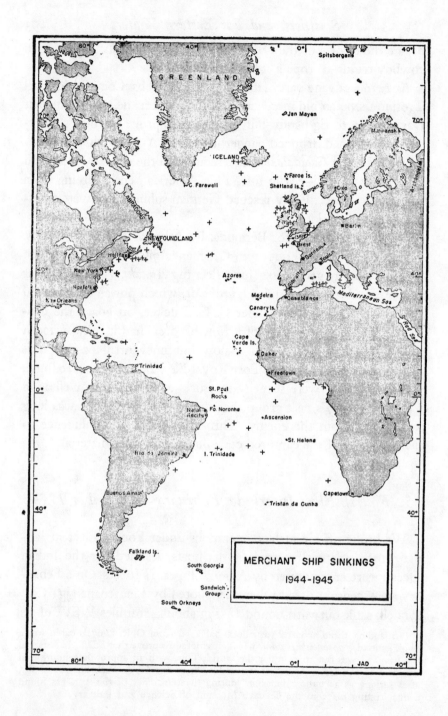

MERCHANT SHIP SINKINGS
1944-1945

island field. C. in C. Fourth Fleet, who had not had an escort carrier group under his command for over a year,[28] was delighted when *Solomons* (Captain Marion E. Crist), sister ship to *Guadalcanal*, came south to help. With a screen of four DEs, she departed Recife 14 April to sweep the Atlantic Narrows. On the 23rd, *Gustafson* of her screen made an unsuccessful hedgehog attack on a target that was probably *U-196. Solomons's* cruise was a disappointment. She had VC-9, a veteran air group, on board, but for two months sighted nothing but whales and wreckage.

On 15 June, things began to happen. At a point estimated 575 miles due south of St. Helena HF/DF indicated a U-boat. Ensign George E. Edwards USNR, piloting a *Solomons* Avenger, flushed it. The boat, *U-860*, shot him down even before he could radio his position to the carrier; but a vigorous air-surface search put on by Captain Crist was rewarded shortly before sunset when the VC-9 commander, Lieutenant Commander Howard M. Avery, caught *U-860* on the surface. Knowing that he had small chance of sinking the "long-legged" 1200-tonner unassisted, Avery teased it with long-range strafing for 20 minutes while homing-in three more planes, one of which mounted rockets. *U-860* fought back vigorously but was sunk, as darkness fell on 15 June, by Lieutenant (jg) William F. Chamberlain; but he too was lost. The bombs were dropped from so low an altitude that his Avenger was engulfed by the explosion.

Since Doenitz continued to send U-boats into the Fourth Fleet bailiwick at long intervals, Admiral Ingram in August borrowed the *Tripoli* escort carrier group commanded by Captain Thayer T. Tucker, to try for a clean-up. For three weeks in August–September 1944 it searched unsuccessfully, then put in at Recife. It had not been there two days when HF/DF indicated a U-boat transmitting off Sierra Leone, and Admiral Ingram sent Captain Tucker across to get it. Tracked by Tenth Fleet HF/DF operators, this boat was reported to *Tripoli* on 18 September as apparently about to rendezvous with a second boat west of the Cape Verdes.

[28] *Santee* in March 1943; see Vol. I 384.

That was correct. Doenitz had ordered the big cargo submarine *U–1062* from Penang, laden with a valuable cargo for Germany, to fuel *U–219*, outward bound for Japan, about 600 miles WSW of Fogo.

The *Mission Bay* escort carrier group (Captain John R. Ruhsenberger), which put in at Dakar 20 September after a sweep across the North Atlantic, was now ordered by Admiral Ingersoll to join *Tripoli* and break up this meeting. Rendezvous effected on 28 September, the two carriers alternated in maintaining round-the-clock air search for two days. Almost immediately, Lieutenant W. R. Gillespie USNR of the *Tripoli* air squadron made a contact and radioed, "I've got him! He's shooting at me, I'm going in to make a run!" The rest was silence; that plane was shot down with loss of all hands. Two other aircraft attacked the boat — probably *U–219* — but without success. There were no further contacts on the 28th, and none on the 29th.

Finally, early in the first dog watch of 30 September, three destroyer escorts of *Mission Bay's* screen were detached to investigate a sonobuoy indication of a submarine. One of them, *Fessenden* (Lieutenant Commander W. A. Dobby USNR), fired a hedgehog pattern, heard four explosions, and threw out depth charges as a clincher. Gurgling and cracking noises were heard; German evidence proves that this was the end of the blockade runner, 1080-ton *U–1062*.[29]

U–219 had better luck. In the small hours of 30 October an Avenger from *Tripoli* attacked it on propeller indications heard through a sonobuoy. Four minutes later, strange underwater noises were heard, followed by a series of explosions which sounded like a sure kill; but Tenth Fleet assessors were right in estimating "no damage." *U–219* reached Batavia on 12 December.[30]

[29] This happened within 15 miles of the position indicated by Tenth Fleet's estimate of the U-boat rendezvous.

[30] There is a possibility that the object of this attack, and of Lt. Gillespie's, was *U–195*, which is known to have been in the area and which also escaped.

6. *Caribbean Conclusion, March–July 1944*

During the first two months of 1944 the Caribbean was completely free of U-boats. Then began a series of nuisance raids that checked an impending reduction of Sea Frontier forces. In early March, *U-518* entered by the Mona Passage and *U-154* by the Windward Passage west of Hispaniola. Shortly after, the floating bow of an abandoned tanker, reported to Panama Sea Frontier Headquarters, touched off an intensive air-surface hunt. Neither of the above-mentioned U-boats was the cause — the tanker had succumbed to an internal explosion — but owing to the belief that they were responsible, a hot reception for them was prepared. *U-154* was attacked intermittently for five hours by *PC-469* on 15 March off Point Manzanillo, and damaged; the same night, *U-518* had a battle with two Mariners. Both German skippers decided that Panama waters were now too hot for them, and, excusing themselves on the ground that there was "no traffic" (!) in the Caribbean, pulled out and headed for home.

U-218, loaded with mines to plant off Trinidad, also entered the Caribbean in March. Driven away from the Bocas by Trinidad Sector aircraft, it compromised by sowing two mines off St. Lucia and, on 1 April, 15 mines off San Juan de Puerto Rico. Like all other attempts to mine American waters after 1942, these were completely ineffective; and *U-218*, hotly but vainly pursued by local defense forces, headed for Europe.

Vice Admiral R. C. ("Ike") Giffen, who relieved Admiral Cook at San Juan in May 1944, began at once to fold up Caribbean Sea Frontier air and naval forces. This process was interrupted on 2 June when a Mariner pilot sighted a surfaced U-boat off Puerto Rico. It was *U-539*, heading for the Spanish Main. It sank a small Panamanian freighter on 5 June; and after being shaken up though not seriously damaged by several air and surface attacks, made for the Dutch islands. *U-539* missed shots at two big tankers but celebrated the Fourth of July by torpedoing a third, S.S. *Kittaninny*.

When the fireworks subsided, the stubborn and resourceful master of that vessel, R. S. Shambus, refused to give up his ship, and with assistance from a Coast Guard cutter got her safely into port. *U–539* called it a cruise and headed for Norway.

Next U-boat to appear in the Caribbean in early July was none other than *U–516*, still commanded by Tillessen, the skipper who had given Panama Sea Frontier the runaround in 1943. It sank American *Esso Harrisburg* on 6 July, 95 miles NW of Aruba; and a smaller one, *Point Breeze*, on the 7th.

Admiral Ingersoll was so disturbed by the ease with which these raiders sported around the Caribbean that on 10 July 1944 he sent two escort carrier groups to show flyers and sailors down there how to hunt submarines. The negative results afforded the frontier forces a certain consolation. *U–539* happened to surface in the Mona Passage just as the *Card* group was entering; the unwonted sight of a flattop gave the German skipper such a fright that he missed a good opportunity to torpedo an easy target. Next he encountered the second escort carrier, *Guadalcanal*, fresh from the capture of *U–505* and roaring south. Captain Gallery's planes spotted *U–539*, but that boat seems to have had a charmed life; it reached Europe safely.

Doenitz sent no more into the Caribbean.

7. *South Atlantic and Indian Ocean, June 1944– May 1945*

On 15 June 1944 Admiral Ingersoll diverted the *Bogue* escort carrier group from covering a convoy to a spot some 850 miles west of the Cape Verdes, where HF/DF indicated U-boat activity. Actually, Japanese submarine blockade runner *I–52* was looking for *U–530* to take on board a German pilot for Bordeaux. After it had done so, on 23 June, *I–52* registered on the radar of one of Captain Vosseller's Avengers.

The first watch that night was a lively one for the *Bogue* group.

The commander of VC–69, Lieutenant Commander Jesse D. Taylor, made a second radar contact, illuminated the Japanese boat with a flare, drove it down with a bombing attack, homed in other planes, heard propeller noises through a sonobuoy that he had dropped, and planted a 500-pound depth bomb. *I–52* escaped that time; but at 0054 June 24 a third Avenger made a bombing attack, guided by sonobuoy indications, and presently heard a series of breaking-up noises. Next morning the escorts recovered such evidence as human remains, a Japanese sandal and 65 bales of crude rubber.

The next kill in these waters was made on 2 July by the *Wake Island* carrier group, Captain James R. Tague. *U–543*, homeward bound after a fruitless patrol of the Gulf of Guinea, was intercepted by a 19-year-old Avenger pilot, Ensign Frederick L. Moore usnr, about 220 miles SW of Ferro. Although met by heavy antiaircraft fire, Moore made two bombing attacks which finished *U–543*. No "evidence" of it was gathered, so the *Wake Island* group, aided by Azores-based B–17s of Coastal Command, stalked the ghost of *U–543* for two weeks, breaking off on 16 July to cover an eastbound Mediterranean convoy.

Antisubmarine operations in the spring and early summer of 1944 had disposed of 14 U-boats and one I-boat along the transit lanes between France and the Far East. This took a good deal of fire out of Doenitz's planned Indian Ocean blitz that summer, but enough snorkel-equipped boats got through to make a spirited final effort.

Japanese I-boats continued their sadistic tactics. The 1950-ton *I–8*, Commander Tatsunosuke Ariizumi, had massacred 98 survivors of Dutch merchantman *Tjisalak* south of Colombo on 26 March, but for three months had enjoyed rather thin diet. On 2 July it torpedoed American freighter *Jean Nicolet*, steaming unescorted between the Chagos and Maldive Island groups. Ariizumi's crew, after several hours' intensive search, collected about 96 members of the merchant crew and Naval Armed Guard. First to be brought on board, a 17-year-old mess boy, was shot and thrown overboard. The rest had their hands tightly bound with cords or

wire and were then kicked and beaten, and harangued by Ariizumi in broken English on the iniquities of President Roosevelt.
Around midnight began the real fun, from the Japanese point of
view. Each American was forced to run the gantlet on the submarine's deck, Red Indian fashion, between laughing Japanese sailors armed with clubs, swords, and bayonets; at the end of the line,
whether dead or alive, the victim was shoved overboard. After
about 60 Americans had been tortured in this fashion and 35 were
still awaiting their turn, the diving alarm bell rang. All Japanese
sailors bolted down the hatch and quickly submerged their boat,
leaving the Americans on deck to swim or be sucked down by the
swirl. Twenty-three of them, nevertheless, managed to survive by
treading water while gradually working out of their bonds, and
by clinging to wreckage from their sunken ship. Sighted by aircraft the following morning, they were rescued on 4 July by a
vessel of the Indian Navy.[31]

Fortunately such atrocities were not common. Another of this
period that has come to light was committed by Kapitänleutnant
Heinz Eck and other officers of *U–852*. On 13 March 1944, outward bound to the Indian Ocean, this boat torpedoed the 4700-ton
Greek freighter *Peleus* about 400 miles south of Liberia. The ship
went down in three minutes, leaving a handful of her crew afloat on
life rafts. Two survivors were brought on board the U-boat for interrogation, after which their life jackets were taken away and
they were returned to the raft. Eck then sought out all the rafts
in the darkness and riddled them with machine-gun fire and hand
grenades. No man escaped injury, but five Greeks were still alive
when Eck broke off his gruesome sport and *U–852* resumed its
southward course. Thirty-five days later a Portuguese freighter
rescued four out of five; the other had died.

U–852 rounded the Cape of Good Hope successfully but was

[31] Statements of survivors in Naval Armed Guard files, especially by Radioman
C. C. Stone, Lt. (jg) Gerald V. Deal USNR, and Charles E. Pyle, asst. engineer
officer of *Jean Nicolet*. In Reports of Investigation Div. Legal Sec. GHQ Supreme
Commander Allied Powers, Tokyo, 1946–47, former members of his crew state
that as the submarine entered Tokyo Bay in August 1945 Ariizumi committed
suicide.

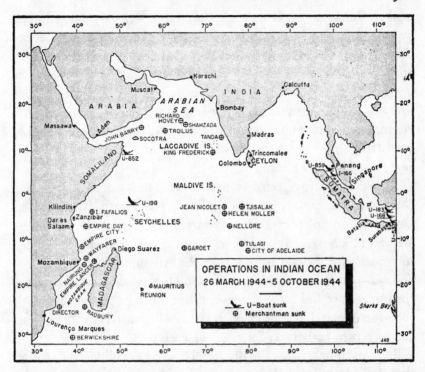

OPERATIONS IN INDIAN OCEAN
26 MARCH 1944 - 5 OCTOBER 1944

🛩 U-Boat sunk
⊕ Merchantman sunk

forced by British bomber planes to beach itself on the coast of Somaliland on 3 May 1944. The skipper and the entire crew were captured and taken to London. After the war Eck and four other members of his crew were arraigned before a War Crimes Court and charged with willful murder of defenseless men, "in violation of the laws and usages of war." Eck argued in defense that he had to do it in self-protection because a plane might have spotted the rafts, or they might have signaled to enemy ships. The court found all five defendants guilty. Eck and two of the others were shot, one was sentenced to life imprisonment and the other to fifteen years.[32]

Another Far Eastern boat, *U-862* (Kapitänleutnant Timm), sank three merchantmen and an ammunition ship in the Mozambique Channel, shot down a Catalina and reached Penang on 9 Sep-

[32] R. M. Langdon "Live Men Do Tell Tales," U.S. Naval Inst. *Proceedings* LXXVIII 17-21 (Jan. 1952); B.d.U. War Diary Jan.-Mar. 1944.

tember. But 1200-ton *U–198* fell victim to a well-coördinated hunt by a killer group built around H.M.S. *Begum* and *Shah* — Kaiser-class CVEs. Two of their escorts sank that boat near the Seychelles on 12 August. During the same month, *U–861* and *U–859*, between them, sank four unescorted freighters including Liberty ship *John Barry*. *U–859* in turn was sunk by British submarine *Trenchant* off Penang on 23 September, and Netherlands submarine *Zwaardvisch*, on patrol from Fremantle, Australia, disposed of *U–168*, another new arrival in the Indian Ocean.

Tropical lethargy seems to have overcome veterans of the old "Monsun" group; six remained in Far Eastern ports from July to October, enjoying protracted upkeep and overhaul. When the summer monsoon season was over, Doenitz ordered all boats not equipped with snorkel to return to the Atlantic. With that intention, *U–181* departed Batavia 19 October, sank American merchantman *Fort Lee* on 2 November, but missed a rendezvous with 1600-ton fueler *U–219*, which had already passed the Cape, and had to return to Batavia for want of fuel.

By November 1944, British and Dutch submarines and Allied aircraft had rendered Penang so vulnerable to the enemy that the I-boats shifted their bases to Surabaya and the U-boats to Batavia. *U–537* was caught off Bali by United States submarine *Flounder* (Commander James E. Stevens) of the Southwest Pacific Command. After passing north through Lombok Strait, he sighted on 9 November an object that looked like a native sail but which turned out to be the conning tower of a submarine. Commander Stevens approached cautiously and fired a spread of four torpedoes. At least one of them hit with a tremendous explosion, and 900-ton *U–537* completely disintegrated, leaving no survivors.

U–862 made the last successful cruise of a German submarine in the Indian Ocean, along the coast of Australia. On the day before Christmas 1944, off Sydney, it encountered Liberty ship *Robert J. Walker*. The master, crew and Naval Armed Guard put up a long and spirited fight which they thought might have been successful if air support had been sent promptly. They lost their vessel but were picked up by an Australian warship. On 6 February 1945, *U–862* sank American S.S. *Peter Silvester*, bound from Melbourne to Colombo with over a hundred troops embarked; Timm made no attempt to repeat the *Peleus* tactics and almost every man was saved.

In April 1945 six U-boats were still supposed to be operating in the Indian Ocean, but they were unable to add a single merchantman to the bag. When Germany surrendered in May, the Japanese took possession of four German and two former Italian submarines, but accomplished nothing with them. Even before this, U-boats were disguising themselves as Japanese, judging by the experience of United States submarine *Besugo* (Lieutenant Commander Herman E. Miller) on 23 April. When patrolling the Java Sea, Miller sighted a surfaced submarine with a Japanese emblem painted on it, and flying a huge Rising Sun flag. He fired a spread of six torpedoes at a range of 1500 yards, one of which caused the boat to sink "in one second," as the only survivor, the navigator, informed Miller. He identified this boat as 900-ton *U–183*.

Despite this lame conclusion to the Germans' Indian Ocean campaign, it had been, in terms of tonnage sunk, the most profitable during the period covered by this volume. For ten consecutive months, June 1943 through March 1944, and again in July and August 1944, this ocean surpassed all Atlantic areas in number of ships and amount of tonnage destroyed. The 15 vessels sunk there in July 1943, and the 11 sunk in March 1944, were the largest monthly scores for any area subsequent to the North Atlantic convoy attacks of April–May 1943; and the total Indian Ocean score from 1 May 1943 to the end of the war was 102 ships of 615,791 gross tons.[33] This was doubtless a pleasing compensation to Doenitz for his lack of success elsewhere; but half a million tons sunk in the Indian Ocean had less influence on the outcome

[33] See Appendix I sec. 3, to which I have added the score for months not there mentioned. These figures include sinkings by Japanese submarines.

of the war than 100,000 tons' loss would have had on an Atlantic convoy route or in the Mediterranean. The great majority of sinkings in the Indian Ocean were of unescorted vessels, since the Allied Navies were unable to spare many escorts from the Atlantic. Unlike Doenitz, they had the wisdom to concentrate their strength on the strategic routes.

The Germans paid heavily for their score. Out of 45 boats intended for the Indian Ocean during the entire war, only 16 made Penang or other Malayan ports; and of these, only five returned home.[34] In all, 34 were sunk, many of them before reaching the Cape of Good Hope. Passage to Penang proved to be mainly a one-way affair.

[34] *U-178, U-188, U-843, U-861, U-181.* The last named made the round voyage Bordeaux to Bordeaux in 198 days (23 Mar.–14 Oct. 1943) and sank 8 ships of 39,155 tons. Frank *Sea Wolves* p. 190 states that this was the longest U-boat patrol of the war, but adds 22 days to its actual duration. *U-181* returned to the Indian Ocean for a second patrol in Oct. 1944 and was scuttled at Singapore after the defeat of Japan.

CHAPTER XVI

In Arctic Waters

1944–1945

1. *Renewed German Activity, January 1944*

WITHIN twenty-four hours of the sinking of *Scharnhorst* on 26 December 1943, Grossadmiral Doenitz, feeling that something must be done to stop the flow of lend-lease goods to Russia, ordered his Norwegian submarine flotilla increased to 24 boats. These had a measure of success against the first northbound convoy of 1944.

JW–56A, known as the "hard luck convoy," was so battered by foul weather that it had to put in at a port in Iceland and make a fresh start on 21 January. Several submarines of the ten-boat Group "Isegrimm," which Kapitän Peters was beginning to deploy east of Jan Mayen, attacked this convoy on 25 January. They damaged the stern of escort H.M.S. *Obdurate* with an acoustic torpedo, and sank U.S. freighters *Penelope Barker* and *Andrew G. Curtin*, and the convoy commodore's flagship *Fort Bellingham*.[1] Despite vigorous counterattacks by the British escort, none of the U-boats were damaged. On 28 January, as JW–56A entered Kola Inlet, Group "Isegrimm" broke off to intercept the next northbound convoy,

---

[1] While *Barker* was being abandoned, Ens. Paul O. Woods USNR, Naval Armed Guard officer, went below with a British naval surgeon (there to treat an appendicitis case) to assist trapped seamen; both were lost. Most of the crew, as well as that of *Curtin*, were saved. Abandonment of these Liberty ships was orderly, except in the case of one master who leaped into the first lifeboat. On the other hand, Commo. I. W. Whitehorn RNR reported that a "panic party" of about 40 men abandoned *Fort Bellingham* without orders, and all were lost except two who were picked up by *U-957* and who gave the Germans valuable information on the routing of North Russia convoys. *U-957* War Diary 26 Jan. and F.d.U. Norway War Diary 1 Feb. 1944.

JW–56B, which was already passing Bear Island. Strengthened by the arrival of eight destroyers from the screen of JW–56A, the escort beat off repeated submarine attacks on 30 January but lost H.M.S. *Hardy* to an acoustic torpedo attack by *U–597*. That happened in the midwatch; before noon *Hardy* was avenged by H.M.S. *Whitehall* and *Meteor*, who sank *U–314*, first U-boat killed in the Arctic since 6 April 1943. JW–56B arrived at Murmansk 1 February without losing a single merchant ship, although no fewer than 14 U-boats had been deployed against it.

Pessimistic Peters, Captain U-boats Norway, felt that his boats had performed very ill against those two convoys — as indeed they had. Owing to numerous "depth-charge pursuits," he recorded, they were "forced so far back that they were no longer able to reach their patrol lines in time." [2] He could not blame this on the Luftwaffe, which had persistently shadowed the convoys.

Murmansk was well described at this time by a British convoy commodore as "a bombed city filled with black ghosts moving in the twilight over the snow in deathly silence, broken only by tinny music broadcast during certain intervals by the State." In some respects, however, it was improving. Captain S. B. Frankel, U. S. Navy representative since 1942, reported that the former Russian officials had been replaced by people of more drive and experience,[3] and that, following the arrival of Convoy JW–56B, their stevedore gangs were discharging over 7000 tons of cargo daily. As the Luftwaffe had been virtually driven from nearby airfields by the R.A.F., flying from United Kingdom and Russian bases, unloading was no longer interrupted by bomber raids. The Soviet authorities had not changed their suspicious attitude toward British sailors and American merchant mariners who were maintaining this lifeline at vast expense and great personal danger; conditions ashore were still lugubrious. As a colored steward of S.S. *Will Rogers* summed it up on departure, "I'd sure like to go any place else — just any place at all!"

[2] F.d.U. Norway War Diary 31 Jan. 1944.
[3] Capt. Frankel to Rear Admiral C. E. Olsen of U.S. military mission to U.S.S.R., 21 Dec. 1943 and 9 Feb. 1944. For Capt. Frankel's earlier reports see Vol. I 372–75.

2. *British CVEs on the North Russia Run,*
February–December 1944

Between 3 and 11 February 1944 the first southbound convoy of the new year, 37 merchant ships and 23 escorts, got through without an attack. Kapitän Peters blamed this on the Luftwaffe's failure at reconnaissance. And before the end of the month the Admiralty introduced a new defense for the North Russian convoys in the shape of escort carrier groups.[4]

Hitherto the performance of American-built escort carriers under the White Ensign had been something short of spectacular, and their lengthy "reconversion" and long delays in port between cruises had been the subject of animadversion by the Allied Antisubmarine Survey Committee and even the Combined Chiefs of Staff.[5] Acting on a hint from the Admiralty, Admiral King in October 1943 sent to England Captain Marshall R. Greer, successful skipper of the *Core* group, to give the Admiralty the benefit of his experience in CVE hunter killer operations. The Royal Navy reacted to Captain Greer's mission with more politeness than enthusiasm; but the Fifth Sea Lord, who was responsible for naval aviation, listened to him and was persuaded to countermand one structural change in CVEs being delivered, which would have made another delay. *Post hoc*, if not *propter hoc*, the Admiralty, after supplying several CVEs with American-built fighter planes and an improved Swordfish equipped with rocket launchers, decided to try them in Arctic waters. These northward-plying CVEs of the Royal Navy covered themselves with glory.

H.M.S. *Chaser*, first to be so employed in February 1944, helped notably to protect the 42-ship Convoy JW–57 from a patrol of 15 U-boats. Her Swordfish pilots, in open cockpits, were unable

---

[4] H.M.S. *Avenger* had accompanied Convoys PQ–18 and QP–14 in Sept. 1942 (see Vol. I 360–65) but she was sunk off Gibraltar that fall. H.M.S. *Dasher* tried it in Feb. 1943 but had to return to port with split seams.

[5] See Chapter III sec. 2.

to press attacks very far in the Arctic winter, but kept the U-boats beyond torpedo range. Two boats were sunk on 24–25 February; one by H.M.S. *Keppel* of the screen, and the other by a Catalina based on the Faroes or Iceland. Unfortunately a third U-boat countered by sinking H.M.S. *Mahratta* with an acoustic torpedo. *Chaser* more than evened the score on her return passage, as escort to Convoy RA–57: her rocket-equipped Swordfish sank no fewer than three submarines in as many days — 4–6 March.

For the next northbound convoy, JW–58, the Admiralty provided two escort carriers, H.M.S. *Tracker* and *Activity*, together with cruiser *Diadem*, U.S.S. *Milwaukee* (being transferred to the Russian Navy), a close screen of nine ships, and two support groups, including Captain Walker's. In addition, this convoy of 48 merchantmen (40 of them American) was covered by two battle forces of the Home Fleet, including two fleet carriers and four CVEs, under Vice Admiral Sir Henry Moore in H.M.S. *Anson*.[6]

Kapitän-zur-See Peters, no cheery character at best, was so depressed over the sinking of three U-boats by *Chaser's* aircraft that he decided to limit his boats to night attacks on Convoy JW–58. He had some consolation in the fact that his boats had just been rearmed for "fight back" tactics; but he did not know that H.M.S. *Tracker* was equipped with 12 Avenger torpedo-bombers and 7 fighters, while *Activity* had 7 fighters and 2 Swordfish, trained to use the tactics of American fighter-bomber teams.

U–961, first submarine to challenge Convoy JW–58, fell victim on 29 March to two depth-chargings by Captain Walker's famous flagship *Starling*. The U-boat sank before it had a chance to send a contact report to Narvik; but next morning a Luftwaffe pilot sighted the convoy and notified Peters, who at once ordered a patrol of 17 U-boats set up to block the Bear Island Passage. The convoy broke through this barrier with great success. Aircraft from the two carriers, aided by the destroyers, disposed of three more

---

[6] The main objective of these two forces was *Tirpitz*, now lying in Kaafjord. They peeled off from the convoy when a couple of days out, and aircraft from the carriers obtained eight hits on the German battleship on 3 April, just after she had been repaired and was about to get under way.

U-boats on the first three days of April. Incidentally, they shot down so many German planes that the Luftwaffe's local wing commander refused to continue daytime reconnaissance. Convoy JW-58 arrived Murmansk 4 April without losing a ship.

The next two convoys, one northbound and the other southbound, made the passage without being subjected to air or submarine attack. Southbound RA-59 of 45 merchantmen lost one. A contact report by one German plane enabled Peters to home-in a group of nine U-boats on 30 April 1944; one of these sank American Liberty ship *William S. Thayer*.[7] H.M.S. *Fencer's* air squadron more than squared accounts by sinking no fewer than three U-boats on the first two days of May; and these were not victims of Avengers but of the new-type Swordfish equipped with rockets. *Thayer* was the only merchantman in North Russia convoys sunk in two months — a small exchange for eight U-boats.

From 6 May 1944, when RA-59 entered Loch Ewe, to August, no North Russia convoys were run; owing in part to the long days, and in part to the employment of merchant shipping in the build-up for Operation OVERLORD. But northern waters were not left to the submarines. British, Canadian and Norwegian bombers under Coastal Command got right after Group "Mitte," which Doenitz had set up to counter a possible invasion of Norway, and in two months sank some 15 U-boats. That was the most effective air offensive in the antisubmarine war, relative to the means employed; better, even, than that of the Bay of Biscay.

Swordfish from H.M.S. *Vindex*, one of two British CVEs escorting the next North Russia convoy on 22 August 1944, sank *U-354* off Bear Island,[8] and two days later the 20th Escort Group (Commander I. J. Tyson RN) disposed of *U-344* when escorting the returning southbound convoy. On 2 September the same group, assisted by aircraft from *Vindex*, sank *U-394*.

Fregattenkapitän Suhren, who by this time had relieved Peters

[7] Lt. (jg) W. E. Clark USNR, N.A.G. officer, Report of 7 Aug. 1944. H.M.S. *Whitehall* rescued all but 33 of her large complement of passengers and crew.
[8] *U-354* had just torpedoed but not sunk H.M.S. *Nabob*, which was launching air strikes against *Tirpitz*.

as F.d.U. Norway, continued to probe. He deployed no fewer than 17 boats against Convoy JW–60 in mid-September, and they managed to sink two merchantmen, American freighter *Edward H. Crockett* and British S.S. *Samsuva*. Swordfish from the attached escort carrier, H.M.S. *Campania*, sank *U–921* on 30 September. The same afternoon *U–425*, moving in on the convoy, was spotted by lookouts in American S.S. *Warren Delano* and driven away by her Naval Armed Guard. H.M.S. *Bamborough Castle*, a corvette equipped with the Royal Navy's newest ahead-throwing weapon, "squid," sank *U–387* on 9 December when helping to escort Convoy RA–62. That convoy experienced some trouble from a squadron of Ju–88s which had recently been fleeted up to northern fields from France, where they were no longer of any use to Germany. Two Ju–88s were shot down by the Naval Armed Guards of American freighters *William Wheelwright* and *Harold L. Winslow* on 12 December; and Swordfish of *Campania* sank *U–365* next day.

The arrival of Convoy RA–62 in Scotland 19 December virtually ends North Russia convoy history for 1944. Seven convoys had got through since 2 September, with the loss of only two merchantmen out of 215; and their escorts had added two more U-boats to the large bag made earlier in the year.

In the meantime much-battered *Tirpitz* had received her death blow. Twenty-five Lancasters, which the Soviet government, with unusual coöperation, had permitted to stage through North Russian airfields, attacked her near Tromsö on 12 November with 6-ton bombs. After two direct hits and four near-misses the big battleship rolled over and sank, taking down over a thousand members of her crew.

3. *Concluding North Russia, February–May 1945*

The Germans seldom let the North Russia convoys alone. Now that their principal submarine bases were in Norway, the Bear

Island Passage was the nearest place where they could hope to score. As the war in Europe mounted to its climax, Russian demands for munitions and matériel became more and more insistent.[9] So the convoys continued to run through the winter of 1944-45 and the following spring, each heavily escorted and accompanied by two British CVEs.

By this time the Admiralty had decided to appoint a flag officer to handle these convoys. The first was Rear Admiral Roderick McGrigor RN, flying his flag in H.M.S. *Campania*. One of the best of the British rear admirals, he handled these convoys in a masterly manner, and the work of escorting, of maneuvering of merchant ships, and of shooting by Naval Armed Guards was of the highest order. Two torpedo planes were shot down by the bluejackets of American S.S. *Nathan Towson* and *Edwin L. Drake* on 10 February 1945. The convoy of which they were a part, JW-64, lost a Norwegian tanker and H.M. corvette *Denbigh Castle* to a U-boat on the 13th. The same or another boat torpedoed American freighter *Horace Gray*, which was towed into Kola Inlet by a Russian tug.

Since for the Germans the Bear Island Passage had by this time proved to be dangerous and unproductive, U-boats now awaited convoys near the Russian terminus. Two were on hand to attack RA-64 as it sortied from Kola Inlet. During the midwatch 17 February, *U-425* was sunk by H.M.S. *Lark* and *Alnwick Castle*, which made an offensive sweep before the convoy sailed. Later in the morning *Lark's* stern was blasted by a torpedo from *U-968*, which then proceeded to torpedo American S.S. *Thomas Scott*. This Liberty ship was carrying a large number of Norwegian refugees, mostly women and children, as passengers; but the master effected an orderly abandonment in ten minutes, and the entire ship's company was rescued by a British destroyer.

[9] See *Fleet Admiral King* p. 593 for the attempt to get more out of him at Yalta. On the other side it should be said that the Russian Air Force now gave good coverage to the North Russia convoys between Fisher Peninsula and the White Sea, and that occasionally a task group composed of *Arkhangelsk* (ex-H.M.S. *Royal Sovereign*) and 10 destroyers supported convoys in the same general area.

Next victim of U-boats was H.M.S. *Bluebell* of the screen. A torpedo exploded in her magazine and she sank in four minutes, losing almost all hands. That night (17–18 February) a southerly gale made up, scattering Convoy RA–64 but also baffling the stalkers. On the 20th, when the gale had abated and all but 4 of the 33 merchant ships were back on station, they were jumped by over 25 Ju–88s. These were greeted by such intensive gunfire from the Naval Armed Guards, including those in Liberty ships *Caesar Rodney* and *John La Farge*, that after repeated attacks over a period of three and a half hours they jettisoned bombs and retired.

On 23 February, hard on the heels of a 75-knot head gale and snowstorm, 23 Ju–88s attacked RA–64. The German flight commander decided to warm up by picking on Liberty ship *Henry Bacon*, Alfred Carini master, which had suffered an engine breakdown and was straggling at low speed about 50 miles astern. The gallant fight put up by the Naval Armed Guard of this vessel (Lieutenant (jg) John C. Sippola USNR commander), and by her merchant seamen, was one of the most memorable events of the North Russia run.

At 1415, 23 torpedo-bombers approached *Henry Bacon* in close formation, 20 to 30 feet above the water. They then formed a circle around the ship and attacked in pairs, one on the port and the other on the starboard side, dropping two torpedoes apiece from point-blank range and then banking away. For 65 minutes the Navy gunners, helped by merchant mariners, beat off repeated attacks. They spoiled the aim of those that approached near enough to drop, shot down five planes and damaged three others. In one instance the 20-mm naval guns hit a torpedo hanging from the releasing hook of a plane and it exploded in midair. Finally, at 1520, the enemy scored. A torpedo detonated in *Bacon's* magazine, blowing off hatch covers, splitting seams and bulkheads, smashing the steering gear. As the ship began to settle, the Ju–88s, apparently satisfied, flew away; but the convoy escaped, as it was too dark for them to locate it.

Lieutenant Sippola, after directing this gallant defense of the freighter, was lost when helping wounded members of his Naval Armed Guard. The 19 Norwegian passengers (16 of them women and children) got off in the first lifeboat, whose assigned crew unselfishly gave up their places; but Captain Carini and one other of the ship's officers went down with the ship. Escort vessels of the convoy, attracted by the radio operator's S O S, saved 64 out of the total complement of 86. Convoy RA–64 steamed on, through more heavy weather, to a safe haven in Gourock.[10] There is no finer instance of merchant-ship defense in the history of North Russia convoys than this battle of 23 February 1945.

Northbound Convoy JW–65, which departed Gourock 11 March, enjoyed fair weather but ran into two or more snorkel-equipped submarines off Kola Inlet. American S.S. *Horace Bushnell* was torpedoed 21 March 24 miles off North Kildin Light and had to be beached; H.M.S. *Lapwing* of the escort was broken in two by a torpedo hit and went down with heavy loss of life; American S.S. *Thomas Donaldson* was torpedoed and sunk 20 miles from the mouth of Kola Inlet.[11] Although this convoy had two British escort carriers in its screen, their aviators' efforts to cope with the submarines were frustrated by the snorkel, as were those of other aircraft elsewhere.

Next month, however, accounts were evened with the snorkelers lying off Kola Inlet. On 29 April the escort commander of Convoy RA–66 sent ahead of his main body a vanguard composed of H.M.S. *Loch Insh*, *Cygnet*, *Cotton* and *Goodall*. The quartet stole up on *U–307* and *U–286* in a dense fog and sank both by "squid" attacks, yet not before the latter had lashed back at frigate *Goodall* and had sunk her with heavy loss of life.

From the time these North Russia convoys began, in August 1941, to the end of the war, there were 40 northbound and 35 southbound. The former delivered 720 merchant ships and lost

[10] Gunner's Mate J. F. Gerold (senior Armed Guard survivor *Henry Bacon*) Disaster Report to C.N.O. 28 Apr. 1945 in Armed Guard Files; by U.S. Naval Port Officer, Gourock, Letter to Admiral Stark 17 June 1945.

[11] *Horace Bushnell* was laden with lend-lease trucks, ammunition and locomotives, which the Soviet authorities salvaged, although they reported that ship and cargo were a total loss.

63; [12] the latter brought back 707 ships and lost 27. The total supplies from the Western Hemisphere shipped to Russia by this route amounted to 3,964,231 long tons; [13] and of this about some 3,700,-000 tons (2,700,000 from U.S.; the rest from U.K.) actually reached Russia.[14] Merchant ships lost heavily in the earlier PQ–QP convoys; but the JW–RA series which started in November 1942, and in which American freighters predominated, lost only five merchant vessels, and their surface and air escorts sank 27 U-boats. This notable record was achieved at a vastly heavier cost than that of any other convoy route during the war. Not only did an escort strength approximately fivefold that of the northern transatlantic convoys have to be employed, but the Home Fleet had to support them, and losses were very heavy. The Royal Navy lost 2 cruisers, 6 destroyers and 10 smaller warships in the course of protecting the North Russia run.[15]

In almost every respect North Russia convoys were exceptional. Occasionally a bigger U-boat group was hurled against a northern transatlantic convoy; but the pressure by enemy submarines and aircraft on the PQs and QPs, the JWs and the RAs, was heavy and unremitting. Weather conditions were worse than on any other route in the world. These convoys steamed through continual

[12] Including 5 sunk in Kola Inlet by air bombing after arrival.

[13] The following table is from T. H. Vail Motter *The Persian Corridor and Aid to Russia* (U.S. Army in World War II series, 1952) pp. 481–83:—

CARGOES SHIPPED FROM WESTERN HEMISPHERE TO U.S.S.R.
22 JUNE 1941–20 SEPTEMBER 1945

Route	Long Tons	Per cent of Total
North Russia	3,964,231	22.7
Persian Gulf	4,159,117	23.8
Soviet Far East	8,243,397	47.1
Black Sea	680,723	3.9
Soviet Arctic	452,393	2.5
Total	17,499,861	100.

According to 80th Congress 2nd Session House Doc. 568 (Report to Congress on Lend-lease Operations 1941–47) the total value of U.S. defense aid to Russia was, in round numbers, $10,982 million, as compared with $31,384 million to the British Empire. According to Admiralty figures, the value of cargoes to Russia from the U.K. was £428 million, carried in 811 ships, by all routes.

[14] Data from British Ministry of Transport in Aug. 1955.

[15] Also, the Polish Navy lost one submarine.

darkness during the winter months and under the revealing light of the midnight sun in the summer solstice. They encountered heavy gales up to force 12, 80 knots' velocity; snow and sleet storms were frequent from September to May; the seas were heavy and tumultuous at almost every season; ice offered an additional menace to navigation; the thick fog frequently encountered was welcome as a protection, but produced serious hazards and made convoy control exceedingly difficult. Sailors here were in greater danger than on any other route, because survival in Arctic waters was unlikely after more than a few minutes' immersion. Engines broke down under the strain of keeping formation in rough weather; heavy vehicles broke loose from their deck lashings and crushed men who tried to secure them. The task of the screen was extremely wearing. Merchant vessels could at least plod along at low speed; but the destroyers, sloops and corvettes on patrol had to crash through high seas, their exposed bridges drenched with spray that often froze to their upper works. As reported by Maitland Boucher, the veteran British convoy commodore, after one hard-pressed winter convoy under his charge had got through almost intact, escorts "faced conditions which can fairly be described as appalling for small ships, with a devotion to duty, care of the convoy and desire to find the enemy that could not have been surpassed." The conduct and discipline of the merchant ships, he said, despite a "succession of almost unimaginable perplexities and trials," reflected "the very greatest credit on the masters and officers concerned, some of whom have made repeated voyages to the Arctic carrying fabulous quantities of munitions without which it would have been impossible for our Russian allies to have gained their spectacular victories in the field."

The faint hope that these efforts on Russia's behalf would produce a change of attitude on the part of the Soviet Government was not destined to be realized, even in the first flush of victory. But there was something comic as well as pitiful about the celebration of VE-day at Murmansk. The American and British ships in port got the news first and at once started to celebrate. The Russian captain of the port, who had not been told by his own government and refused to believe the B.B.C. announcement, informed Colonel J. M. Maury usmc, the senior assistant naval attaché present, that the joy was premature and the celebration should be called off. However, once the Russians had the news confirmed from Moscow, they spontaneously welcomed all Allied sailors as brothers, and plenty of vodka was shared. They also started the firing of antiaircraft guns; Americans and British gladly added theirs to the din, and in the course of this phase of the celebration some Russian barrage balloons with pictures of Stalin painted on them were shot down. The local Russian authorities blamed this on the Americans and had the effrontery to demand reparation! [16]

But it should in fairness be recorded that, subsequently, the Soviet Government conferred 127 orders and 70 medals on American sailors "for outstanding military activities aiding the delivery to northern ports of the Soviet Union during the war . . . of transports with military cargo and for valor and courage displayed while performing this duty." [17]

[16] Conversation with Col. Maury, June 1955.
[17] Complete list in U.S. Naval Institute *Proceedings* LXXX (April 1954) 413–17.

CHAPTER XVII

Snorkels in the Atlantic

March–December 1944

1. Doenitz Springs the Snorkel

THE FEW U-boats that managed to slip past the Cape Verdes
in 1944 did so by grace of the snorkel, which enabled them
to cruise continuously submerged and escape the attentions of escort carrier groups and land-based planes. But the chief theater
of activity for snorkel-equipped submarines was the North Atlantic.

This device the Germans called *Schnorchel*, a dialect word for
"nose"; we abbreviated it to "snorkel," and the British to "snort."
It was a combined air-intake and gas-outlet that allowed submarines to run their diesels submerged, charging batteries if needed.
It took the shape of a streamlined steel cylinder 26 feet long which
could be folded back when not in use, and was provided with an
automatic float-valve, to keep out slopping sea-water, and with a
small radar grid. When the snorkel was in use, it made a "feather"
on the water scarcely bigger than that of a periscope head, and
almost impossible to pick up by the radar sets in use in 1944.[1]

[1] Simon Lake *The Submarine in War and Peace* (1918) p. 286 envisaged the
snorkel principle as early as 1900; but the first to use it practically was the Royal
Netherlands Navy before World War II. The Germans got the idea from two
captured Dutch submarines but, hoping to win the war in a blitz, did not
trouble to experiment with it until late in 1942. An operational snorkel reached
mass production only at the end of 1943. The installations were made at St.
Nazaire, and, as special operational training was required, all boats so equipped
had to spend weeks in the Baltic, based on the Polish port of Hela. No snorkel-
equipped subs were on war patrols before 1944; probably the first to be sunk in
action was *U-264*, by the killer group of Capt. Frederick J. Walker RN on 19
Feb. 1944. *U-575*, the weather reporter sunk by *Bogue* group 13 Mar. 1944, also
had a snorkel.

U-boat skippers were none too happy about the snorkel. If a wave caused the float-valve to close, the diesel engines quickly exhausted the oxygen below; and if the boat turned to leeward in a strong breeze the wind was apt to make exhaust gases back up. Engineer officers had to be ready to make instant switch from diesel engines to batteries in order to prevent their crews from being asphyxiated.

Doenitz, who regarded the snorkel as a mere stopgap until he had Type XXI in operation, used it fairly effectively. Early in the spring of 1944 he began to send snorkel-equipped boats on nuisance raids to the east coast of America, in hope of sinking strategic cargoes destined for the invasion of *Festung Europa,* and of pinning down American antisubmarine forces three thousand miles from the English Channel.

Prior to that rather dim blitz, three independent U-boats of the older type had a small success against convoys between New York and the United Kingdom. *U–311* departed Brest 9 March 1944 and ran afoul of Convoy CU–17 on the 18th. Destroyer escort *Daniel T. Griffin* picked it up and the convoy made an emergency turn, but *U–311* penetrated the screen, torpedoed and sank 10,000-ton tanker *Seakay,* and escaped. *U–302* cut two Norwegian merchantmen out of slow convoy SC–156 on 6 April about 375 miles NW of Flores. *U–550* departed Kiel 6 February 1944 on its first and only patrol. The skipper, choosing the convoy bottleneck off Nantucket Lightship as the most likely spot for easy targets, lay in wait for several days until fast tanker convoy CU–21, New York to the United Kingdom, came along. At 0806 April 16, just as the ships were re-forming after picking up some tankers from a feeder convoy, *U–550* torpedoed and sank tanker *Pan Pennsylvania,* laden with 140,000 barrels of 80-octane gasoline and seven planes. She burst into flames and had to be abandoned. While destroyer escorts *Joyce, Gandy* and *Peterson* of the screen were recovering survivors, the first-named made a sound contact at 0950 and delivered a pattern of eleven depth charges. When *U–550* surfaced about a mile away on his starboard quarter, Lieutenant Commander W. A.

Sessions USNR gave the order to open gunfire and to stand by to ram. *Gandy* headed for the submarine's "bandstand" but the boat maneuvered so briskly that she hit it 30 feet from the stern, then hauled clear to engage in a short-range gunfire duel. *Peterson* and *Joyce* bore in to assist. At 1015 a muffled explosion on board *U–550* was heard, and 29 minutes later it sank, within sight of the burning tanker. Twelve of the crew were recovered. *Gandy* had lost about 3½ feet of her bow strake and had had several plates buckled, but she and the other DEs resumed their escort duty.

First snorkeler to reach American shores was 740-ton *U–107*, which, after one false start owing to snorkel trouble, departed Lorient 10 May 1944, missed several targets off Nova Scotia, and turned back 7 July with an empty bag. The next raider, not snorkel-equipped, was 1500-ton *U–233*, sent to mine the approaches to Halifax. Before it could close the Nova Scotia coast, this boat was detected by a plane from escort carrier *Card* and became the target of an intensive hunt by her group. *Baker* and *Thomas*, destroyer escorts of the screen, flushed it south of Sable Island on the afternoon of 5 July, drove the Germans from their guns by intensive gunfire, and sank it with a vigorous ramming by *Thomas* (Lieutenant Commander D. M. Kellogg USNR), which recovered 29 survivors.[2]

2. *The U-boats and* OVERLORD,[3] *June–August*

Grossadmiral Doenitz's major efforts to embarrass the great cross-channel operation (D-day 6 June 1944) were confined to weather reporters and attempted assaults on the thousands of Allied ships and small craft in the English Channel.

In order to provide the Luftwaffe with accurate weather fore-

[2] *Card*, which had been engaged in plane ferrying and pilot training for 5 months, was now commanded by Capt. Rufus C. Young.

[3] B.d.U. War Diary Mar.–Aug. 1944; German Naval Group Command, West, War Diary June 1944; Vice Admiral Eberhard Weichold "German Naval Defense against Allied Invasion of Normandy," prepared for O.N.I. after the war.

casts and German Intelligence with guesses as to Allied D-day, Doenitz set up a weather picket patrol of five U-boats in mid-Atlantic waters between Newfoundland and the Azores, each with a trained meteorologist on board. On 4 June the *Croatan* group, still under command of Captain Vest but carrying VC–95, *Bogue's* old air squadron, headed toward the Azores to break up this group. It first encountered, however, 1600-ton (Type XIV) supply boat *U–490*, outward bound for Penang with supplies for the Indian Ocean raiders. Destroyer escorts *Frost* and *Huse* of the screen attacked it at a point midway between Flores and Flemish Cap at 0600 June 11. Muffled explosions raised false hopes that the boat was done for; but Oberleutnant Wilhelm Gerlach took his fat cow down to a great depth,[4] where he moved slowly and silently while depth charges set at maximum burst overhead. The *Croatan* group maintained contact all day, using sonobuoys and the latest mathematical search technique. Milch cow submariners' morale seldom equaled that of the fighting U-boat crews, and *U–490's* became depressed by foul air, repeated explosions of depth charges, continual pinging of sonar on their hull, and a mysterious buzzing noise which they called the "singing saw," the sound made by the escorts' Foxer gear. Adding to their dismay, a dozen guinea pigs which the surgeon had on board for experimental purposes squealed so loud and shrill that the skipper feared lest they be overheard by enemy sound gear and had them killed.

Commander F. D. Giambattista, Captain Vest's screen commander in *Frost*, made several shrewd estimates of the situation: that the boat lay deeper than depth charges could reach, that its endurance was fast diminishing, and that if given a fair chance the skipper would try to escape that night. So the gambit of pretending to give up the hunt was tried, with success. Two DEs retired in one direction, and another in the opposite direction, at decreasing speed. They then crept back toward the spot where Giambattista estimated the boat would surface. He had guessed right; *U–490* sur-

[4] He claimed 300 meters — 164 fathoms. U.S. submariners believe that this was impossible, and actually the boat's depth gauge had been knocked out.

faced at 2147 about 8000 yards from *Frost* and the same distance
from *Snowden*. Oberleutnant Gerlach, coming on deck, realized
that he was trapped; and, just as the two DEs opened fire, he sent
the blinker signal, "S O S. Please save us." Captain Vest in *Croatan*,
informed of this, signaled to Giambattista, "Don't take any of that
guff. Illuminate and let him have it!" The screen commander had
already done just that. Before many shots had been fired, the German engineer officer opened his Kingston valves and, at 2253
June 11, down went *U-490*, stern first.[5] Although it was a dark
night, the DEs rescued every last member of *U-490's* demoralized
crew of sixty.

Captain Vest now resumed his search for the weather pickets.
Early on 15 June his HF/DF obtained three bearings on *U-853*
(Kapitänleutnant Helmut Sommer), which had been transmitting
weather reports for almost a month. Sommer had already repelled
a rocket attack by three Swordfish from H.M.S. *Ancylus* and
MacKendrick [6] on 25 May, and was feeling very cocky. *Croatan's*
planes searched continuously night and day for 72 hours. *U-853*
was so hard to locate that the carrier's crew nicknamed it "Moby
Dick," and Captain Vest was beginning to feel like Captain Ahab
by 1307 June 17 when *Croatan* picked up a weather report from
the boat, then 30 miles to the southward. Within eleven minutes
two fighter planes were strafing *U-853*. They killed two men and
wounded eleven, including the skipper, but the boat submerged
before Avengers could reach the spot with bombs. Contact was
maintained with sonobuoys and three escorts took up the hunt; but
"Moby Dick" worked out of the area and (according to Doenitz's
War Diary) "commenced return passage on account of a large
number of the crew being unfit for duty." Later, most appropri-
ately, it succumbed not far from the original Captain Ahab's home
port.

Croatan broke off her ten-day hunt on 24 June and entered

[5] Times for this attack are Zone O (plus 2). It cost 239 depth charges to sink
U-490.
[6] These were M.A.C. (merchant aircraft catapult) ships fitted with a short flight
deck and catapult and capable of carrying up to five aircraft each.

Casablanca. On the 30th Admiral Ingersoll ordered the group out to hunt a U-boat that was supposed to be heading for the South Atlantic. Actually this boat, *U–154,* had been ordered to strike shipping off Cape Hatteras, but it never got very far. Escorts *Inch* and *Frost* made a perfectly coördinated series of attacks for an hour and a half on the morning of 3 July, which disposed of it at a point 140 miles NW of Funchal. Captain Vest combed the waters north of the Madeiras for the next ten days, fueled his escorts on 13 July, and returned to Chesapeake Bay.

Although these snorkel-equipped weather boats seem to have done the Germans no good in forecasting weather conditions at the time of the Normandy landings,[7] three of them continued to transmit from off Flemish Cap during July; and efforts to catch them gave Admiral Ingersoll and his escort carrier groups some bad moments.

After *U–853* had been chased out with a decimated crew, Admiral Ingersoll sent the *Wake Island* group to sweep the weather-picket area. Departing Casablanca 24 July, Captain Tague's first real contact came about 480 miles east of Flemish Cap and the same distance north of Flores at 1056 August 2, when the conning tower of *U–804* broke surface eight miles from destroyer escort *Douglas L. Howard.* The bow quickly submerged. While *Howard* and *Fiske* were making a cautious sonar approach, *U–804* fired three torpedoes at them from periscope depth; the third hit *Fiske* square on her starboard side amidships, virtually breaking her in two. The skipper, Lieutenant John A. Comly usnr, ordered Abandon Ship, which was done in orderly and seamanlike fashion. The other escorts concentrated on the rescue of survivors, which they calmly performed under constant threat of torpedoes.[8] *U–804* got away, claiming two destroyers sunk.

Early in 1944 the German high command intensified preparations to meet the Allied invasion of *Festung Europa.* Since Hitler

[7] So I infer from Harry C. Butcher *My Three Years with Eisenhower* pp. 646–47.

[8] Of her crew of 213 officers and men, 30 were killed and 50 badly wounded by the explosion; but all who survived it were rescued. Times of this action are Zone O.

was still convinced that Norway would be the first target, Doenitz on 16 February set up a group of ten U-boats, called "Mitte," to counter any invasion of that country or of Jutland. These, as we have seen, were flung at the North Russia convoys. Next, on 22 March, he established Group "Landwirt," 15 boats, in Biscayan ports, to repel a possible attack on France. By D-day, 6 June 1944, these groups had been built up to 22 and 36 boats respectively. Although Doenitz hoped to have snorkels on all "Landwirt" boats, only 7 of the 36 were so equipped by D-day, and those were at Brest.

First reports of Allied paratroop landings in Normandy reached Doenitz's headquarters at 0005 June 6, and within a few minutes Groups "Landwirt" and "Mitte" were alerted. By 0500, when it became apparent that OVERLORD was a major landing, the seven snorkel boats at Brest, together with eight not so equipped, were ordered into the English Channel. The Grossadmiral also set up a 14-boat patrol along the 100-fathom line across the Bay of Biscay, anticipating possible Allied landings in the Bay. All 36 of the "Landwirt" group were at sea by the close of D-day.

"For those boats without snorkel this means the last operation," records Doenitz in B.d.U. War Diary. His ominous prediction was almost completely fulfilled. General Eisenhower's staff planners, well aware of the "Landwirt" boats, also expected invasion forces to be attacked by German motor torpedo boats and other light craft. Since the right (west) flank of the cross-channel invasion was deemed the more vulnerable, a surface force called West Wall, consisting of eight British destroyers, 36 MTBs and various coastal craft, was set up under the command of Admiral Sir Ralph Leatham RN, C. in C. Plymouth. In addition, two patrol lines of destroyers were established, one west of the Channel Islands, the other about 50 miles northwest of Ushant, to cope with E-boats, U-boats and German destroyers known to be in Biscayan ports; and three British escort carriers were stationed 130 miles west of Land's End to cover sea approaches to the Channel. In expectation that submarines would hug the French shore to gain the protection of coastal batteries, Admiral Leatham had a series of mine fields laid along the Brittany coast.

For air defense, the 19th Group R.A.F. Coastal Command, under which Commodore Hamilton's Fairwing Seven, together with six R.A.F. squadrons of Liberators, was operating, maintained a round-the-clock patrol over the southwestern approaches to the Channel and Bay of Biscay. As Air Chief Marshal Sir Sholto Douglas described it, there was "a solid wall of air patrols," so wide that no U-boat could get through without surfacing, and so dense that no U-boat which surfaced could escape detection. Other R.A.F. groups covered the North Sea and Norwegian coastal waters.

For several days after 6 June the German command had no definite news of its U-boats. Coastal Command's planes made 14 contacts on D-day, delivered eight attacks and forced three U-boats to return to base. On the three days 7–9 June, the Germans lost five boats sunk by British aircraft, and seven driven off station by damage; Group "Landwirt" was reduced 40 per cent. Eight more boats were sunk by Coastal Command or by West Wall ships in the Channel or its approaches during the month. U-boat skippers who made port reported that intense antisubmarine measures made it very difficult to attack any of the abundant and attractive targets. They made plentiful claims of sure sinkings, but their first real success came on 15 June when they sank two frigates, H.M.S. *Mourne* 50 miles north of Ushant, and H.M.S. *Blackwood* 20 miles NW of Cape de la Hague. On 27 June the veteran corvette H.M.S. *Pink* was torpedoed and sunk 20 miles NE of Cape Barfleur. The big day for the U-boats was 29 June when an empty troopship was sunk in mid-Channel, and four Liberty ships and another merchant ship were torpedoed nearby, but all of these made port.

By the time the assault phase of the Normandy invasion was concluded in early July 1944, U-boat efforts against the immense stream of shipping crossing the Channel could be written off as almost complete failures. Thirteen submarines had been sacrificed to sink two frigates, one corvette and one transport. Nevertheless, the Grossadmiral continued to order boats into the Channel until 23 August. By that time his losses in the Channel and its approaches had amounted to 25 boats, with at least seven more sunk in the Bay of Biscay.

On 7 August, three days after the Allied break-through isolated the Brittany peninsula, Doenitz directed U-boats departing on patrol, and all then at sea, to put in at Norwegian ports; those without fuel enough to reach Norway were sent to Bordeaux. General Eisenhower's armies actually broke through at Avranches on 4 August. All boats then at Brest, Lorient and St. Nazaire were ordered to Bordeaux or La Pallice. The command of Captain U-boats, West, was dissolved on 25 August; and all survivors of the "Landwirt" group were in Norway by 18 September.[9]

3. *Snorkel Nuisances, August–December*

On 2 August 1944 when the *Wake Island* group attacked weather-picket *U–804*, the *Bogue* group was already en route from Bermuda to help. Captain Vosseller began a round-the-clock hunt with his searchlight-equipped Avengers on the 4th, about 475 miles east of Flemish Cap. By that time *U–804* and two other snorkel-equipped pickets, *U–858* and *U–855*, had moved northeastward, out of reach. After scouring the area of the recent action for a week, *Bogue* swept west to within 100 miles of Cape Race, and on 13 August, on orders from Admiral Ingersoll, turned southeasterly to intercept another submarine that had been located by HF/DF off the Grand Bank of Newfoundland. By this time the pilots and crewmen of *Bogue's* air squadron (VC–42) were exceedingly weary from almost continuous patrols; and one of them, Lieutenant (jg) Wayne A. Dixon USNR, after signaling a radar contact

---

[9] Admiral Stark informed the writer at London in Dec. 1944 that he had made efforts to induce the R.A.F. and A.A.F. to bomb the new Norwegian bases of the U-boats before they could be made impregnable like the French ones; but that the Allied Air Forces could not spare units from their strategic bombing of Germany.

38 miles north of the carrier and dropping sonobuoys in the early hours of 15 August, must have splashed, as no trace of him and his crew was ever found.

Dixon had, however, made a real contact on *U–802*, which had been sent to raid the Gulf of St. Lawrence. Owing to the August fogs common in those waters, *Bogue's* flight operations were interrupted, and it was not until 2130 August 18 that another "night owl" Avenger made a radar contact 65 miles north of the carrier and about 70 miles south of the Grand Bank. The pilot, Lieutenant Carl E. Lair USNR, flew down the bearing, illuminated fully surfaced *U–802* at 1500 yards, and dropped three 250-pound depth bombs. But the boat managed to continue its snorkel cruise undamaged, passed through Cabot Strait on 2 September, and spent the rest of the month in completely unfruitful operations. On 24 October it reported "no shipping" (!) in the Gulf of St. Lawrence and returned to Norway on 12 November empty-handed. *U–802* must have spent most of its time on the bottom doing nothing.

In the meantime the *Bogue* group had made contact on a much more interesting target, *U–1229*, which had departed Trondheim 26 July for the special purpose of landing a spy in Maine. Although his boat was equipped with snorkel, the skipper preferred fresh air and cruised on the surface, plunging for protection into the midst of an equinoctial storm that was making up off the Grand Bank. Captain Vosseller, with his destroyer escorts and six Canadian frigates, lay across the intended course of this boat. At 1100 August 20 one of *Bogue's* Avenger pilots, Lieutenant (jg) A. X. Brokas USNR, sighted *U–1229* on the surface about 300 miles S by E of Cape Race. The Avenger attacked promptly, blasting five German gunners overboard and cracking so many battery cells that the skipper went to snorkel depth in hope of venting the escaping chlorine gas. Unable to get sufficient power from his batteries, and feeling his situation to be hopeless, he blew tanks and ordered all hands to abandon ship. On surfacing, the boat was severely rocket-strafed and bombed by no fewer than five Avengers. While the crew was struggling to release life rafts, *U–1229* kicked its stern high in the air at 1313 August 20 and plunged, hastened by a 500-pound bomb planted by an Avenger.[10] *U–1229* was the twelfth submarine sunk by the *Bogue* group, and it was not the last.

The only snorkel-equipped raider to become a menace in the summer of 1944 was 740-ton *U–518*, a veteran of Caribbean operations that departed Lorient 4 July. Off the Carolina coast in early September it became the object of several organized hunts by DEs, and three different escort carrier groups. Eastern Sea Frontier, believing that this boat had retired, called off the hunt on 9 July; but three days later, during the midwatch, *U–518* torpedoed S.S. *George Ade* at a point about 125 miles off Wilmington, North Carolina. Before it could deliver a second and lethal shot, it was driven away by the ship's Naval Armed Guard under Lieutenant (jg) M. A. Schadewald USNR, and by minesweeper *Project*. Salvage vessel *Escape* then towed the Liberty ship to an anchorage. A few hours later, a hurricane struck the Carolina coast, *George Ade* was swamped, and four other United States ships went down.[11] But *U–518* reached Norway 22 October.

Snorkel submarines proved hard to catch. Asworg scientists and Comasdevlant were endeavoring to find some method to counter them, as well as to meet the new Type XXI whose appearance (so prisoners from *U–1229* informed us) could be expected shortly. On the other hand, Allied escort-of-convoy and air cover had been so much improved by the summer of 1944 that the snorkel skippers were extremely wary, took few chances, and fired torpedoes only at easy setups. They avoided transatlantic convoys, as these statistics for 1944 indicate:

[10] Times are Zone P (plus 3). Among the 42 survivors was Oskar Mantel, a former barkeep of Yorkville, N.Y. This individual was to have been set ashore at Winter Harbor, Maine, to act as spy with the not very generous sum of $2000 in American currency, of which he was promptly relieved. At the end of the war, Mantel's Yorkville friends had the impudence to threaten Capt. Vosseller with a lawsuit for recovery of the money, claiming that it belonged to an aged mother in Germany. Director F.B.I. memo to Director of Naval Intelligence 25 Oct. 1944.

[11] Destroyer *Warrington*, escorting "beef boat" *Hyades*, foundered off the Bahamas in the midwatch 13 Sept., losing all but 66 of her crew. *YMS–409* was lost with all hands; U.S.C.G.C. *Jackson* went down with a loss of 21 officers and men including the C.O.; U.S.C.G.C. *Bedloe* sank with 26 men.

NORTH ATLANTIC CONVOYS, 1944 [12]

Designation	Convoys	Ships	Escorts	Sunk in Convoy	Sunk Straggling
HX–272–326	55	4,169	421	2	0
SC–150–163	14	690	101	2	1
ON–216–271	57	4,083	407	1	2
ONS–25–37	13	512	87	0	0
UT–6–11	6	164	78	0	0
TU–6–11	6	122	74	0	0
CU–10–51	43	1,402	363	4	0
UC–8–37, 38A–49B	54	1,440	332	0	0
Special Convoys	18	325	82	1	0
Totals	266	12,907	1,945	10	3

In other words, the ship losses were about one tenth of one per cent.

Snorkel patrols took the form of isolated raids, which produced flurries of antisubmarine activity. Most successful of the snorkel-equipped boats was *U–482*, which sailed northabout from Kiel and operated in the Western Approaches in August, in order to divert attention from the movement of U-boats to Norway. *U–482* sank a British corvette and four merchantmen, including American tanker *Jacksonville*, not fifty miles from Londonderry. Across the Atlantic, *U–541* on 3 September torpedoed and sank unescorted British tanker *Livingston* off Sydney, N.S., and then cruised around the Gulf of St. Lawrence with no more success than *U–802* had enjoyed.

The following week, 8–15 September, was probably the most frustrating time of the war for Captain Vosseller and the *Bogue* group. They swept the approaches to Cabot Strait and the southern part of the Grand Bank, with the assistance of the Royal Canadian Air Force and three destroyer escorts of the *Core* group, searching for submarines that were not there,[13] but obtaining frequent sound

[12] *U.S. Fleet A/S Bulletin* Jan. 1945. See Appendix I for total ship losses in Atlantic.

[13] B.d.U. War Diary 8 Sept. indicates that the nearest boat, *U–541*, was then about 500 miles from *Bogue's* position.

contacts on the remains of ships wrecked over a period of three centuries in those shoal waters. A supposed snorkel, upon which repeated radar and sonar contacts were made, turned out to be a derelict telephone pole floating upright.

In addition to the snorkel, Doenitz's raiders were now equipped with radar intercept gear which gave them warning of planes using microwave radar. Good use of these devices enabled two boats, *U–1221* and *U–1223*, to thread their way safely through the air patrol of *Core* and under MAD-equipped planes from Argentia to the Gulf of St. Lawrence, where they relieved the two boats that were spending an idle summer in those waters. Off Pointe des Monts, on 14 October, *U–1223* blasted the fantail of Canadian frigate *Magog* with an acoustic torpedo, but failed to sink her; [14] and in early November it knocked the bow off an unescorted tanker. Hardly a brilliant score; but by this time the Germans were grateful for small change.

From September to a few days before Christmas 1944, naval warfare virtually ceased in the Western Atlantic. In November, on an average, only 41 U-boats were operating in the entire ocean, the smallest number since 1941. British and Canadian air and surface forces sank about 24 of them between 1 September and Christmas, and an unusually large number were lost by collision or marine· casualty. United States forces in the same period added only five boats to the bag; and those, in distant waters; but that was because so few were operating off the Eastern Sea Frontier, and none in the Caribbean or along the Central Atlantic convoy route.[15]

[14] Joseph Schull *The Far Distant Ships* p. 380. On 4 Oct. *Magog's* sister ship H.M.C.S. *Chebague* was torpedoed by an unidentified U-boat in mid-Atlantic while on convoy duty, but was towed to port despite terrible weather. They were avenged by H.M.C.S. *Annan*, which sank *U–1006* north of the Shetlands 16 October.

[15] The two sunk at Salamis by A.A.F. raid 24 Sept., *U–863* sunk by VB–107 off Brazil 29 Sept., *U–1062* sunk 30 Sept. by *Fessenden*, and *U–537* sunk by *Flounder* off Bali 9 Nov.

CHAPTER XVIII

Snorkel Blitz in European Waters

December 1944–April 1945

1. U-boats Help Battle of the Bulge

THE STATE of "all quiet on the Eastern Sea Frontier" which had existed since July was interrupted by several incidents in the fall of the year. *U–1230* succeeded in the mission in which *U–1229* had failed, of landing spies and saboteurs on the Maine coast; the spies, when captured, made disturbing revelations; and attempts of hunter-killer groups to catch snorkel submarines proved that new tactics were needed.

U–1230 carried as passengers a German subject and a renegade American who had been given a thorough course of training in Nazi spy sabotage schools.[1] The big snorkel-equipped submarine raised Cape Cod 27 November and shaped a course for Mount Desert Rock, where it observed numerous fishermen, escaped the notice of coastal pickets and air patrol, steamed into Frenchman's Bay on the calm night of the 29th, and off Egg Rock debarked the spies in a rubber boat. Rowing undetected past the small district naval base at Bar Harbor, they landed at Hancock Point, but were observed by a smart lad who notified the police.

The two men, well heeled with $30,000 apiece, were trailed by F.B.I. agents to New York City and there picked up and questioned. They asserted that U-boats were being fitted out with a rocket-firing device for guided missiles, which would enable them to bomb the coast from positions well under the horizon. *U–1230*

[1] O.N.I. "Report on Interrogation of German Agents Gimpel and Colepaugh"; A.B.C. Whipple "The Education of Willie," *Life* Magazine 22 Jan. 1945 pp. 11–12.

hung about Mount Desert Rock for a few days and on 3 December sank Canadian S.S. *Cornwallis;* only 5 members of her crew of 49 survived. Cinclant and Eastern Sea Frontier put on an intensive search by two CVE groups and surface craft, but the boat got away. In view of this incident, frontier authorities were apprehensive of the possible effect of a fleet of snorkelers, equipped to launch against American seaboard cities robot bombs such as were then being rained on London.

At the same time, a northern transatlantic convoy suffered damage for almost the first time in 1944. A task group composed of 21 vessels, some of which had been damaged in the Normandy invasion and were under tow, escorted by four DEs under Commander Allen B. Adams in *Fogg,* departed Plymouth 11 December. On the morning of the 22nd, when this very slow convoy was about 370 miles northeast of São Miguel, and after two Azores-based patrol planes had failed to discourage a shadowing snorkeler, *U–870* torpedoed *LST–359.* It then blasted the fantail of *Fogg,* killing 14 men. Thanks to an efficient damage-control party, which restored a part of his power plant, Adams was able to direct the escorts on retiring searches that kept *U–870* from doing further damage.

Unwittingly, this convoy had stumbled on the southernmost of a picket line of three weather-reporting U-boats which succeeded in giving the word to Hitler to start the Battle of the Bulge. The other two were *U–1053,* which began transmitting daily weather reports 5 December from a point 150 miles off Rockall; and *U–1232,* which started her reports on the same date from a point between the Faroes and Greenland.[2] It was possibly owing to the data transmitted by these boats that Hitler's meteorologists were able to predict the periods of foul weather on the Western Front which grounded Allied planes and enabled Field Marshal von Rundstedt to make his thrust toward the Meuse. In any case, they got the credit. Doenitz radioed to these boats on 20 December, "Your weather reports in this last period carried decision for estab-

[2] Data from Dr. Jürgen Rohwer. *U–870* also started reporting 5 December. There was also a weather-reporting trawler near Jan Mayen.

lishing the start of our major offensive in the West, begun 16 December." [3]

Tenth Fleet, and probably Admiralty too, knew about the presence of these boats but did not appreciate their significance. *U-870* had already finished its weather mission when it attacked *Fogg*, and it was en route to the Strait of Gibraltar — off which, in early January 1945, it sank a Liberty ship, a British freighter and a French patrol craft. *U-1053* was the only one of the two still reporting weather on Christmas Day when Cinclant — now Admiral Jonas Ingram,[4] — sent a hunter-killer surface group to track it down. That method of hunting submarines had been proved very successful in the South Pacific by Commander Hamilton Hains in destroyer escort *England*.[5] No escort carriers were then available; they were doing plane-ferry service to keep the R.A.F. and A.A.F. supplied with replacements.

Commander Jack F. Bowling in destroyer escort *Otter* with two other destroyer escorts, *Hubbard* and *Varian*, departed Casco Bay 26 December 1944. All three were equipped with a new, improved type of HF/DF called the "DAQ." After fueling at Fayal in the Azores 3 January 1945, they began to search for the weather reporter. Since U-boats in that service commonly transmitted several times daily, Commander Bowling set up a 24-hour watch and opened out his search line to ten miles, steaming toward the last point of HF/DF contact. During the evening of the 4th, *Hubbard* made a radar contact and the group hunted all night; the contact must have been on *U-248*, which had recently relieved *U-1053*. On the morning of the 5th Bowling's group turned north to run down a new Tenth Fleet estimate of the enemy's position, which turned out to be inaccurate by 150 miles. Reversing course, the DEs had to enter Pico Channel on the 10th for replenishment.

[3] Noted in *U-1053* War Diary 20 Dec. Confirmed by Konteradmiral Godt in 1955.

[4] See Vol. I 382*n* for Admiral Ingram's earlier career and above, chap. xii, for his service as C. in C. Fourth Fleet, from which he was relieved in Nov. 1944. He served as Cinclant 15 Nov. 1944–Sept. 1945, retired in 1947 and died 9 Sept. 1952.

[5] See Vol. VIII 224–30.

On the same day, Commander Bowling received by radio a sharp reproof from Admiral Ingram to the effect that he should take "drastic steps" to improve the quality of his group's searching. The three reservist skippers [6] promptly buckled down to a "skull session" in Horta harbor with their group commander. As a result, they set up three search formations of their own devising: a 180-mile line of advance, a "delta" formation of three ships in an equilateral triangle (16 miles to each leg) to fix transmissions with the DAQs; and a smaller "half delta," 9 miles to each leg with one ship ahead of the apex, for sonar search. These innovations were based on the knowledge that HF/DF fixes made from the coastal stations could not be depended on for accuracy, and that the snorkel-equipped U-boats moved so much faster than their predecessors as to make existing box-search plans ineffective.

Strengthened by the arrival of a fourth destroyer escort, *Hayter*, Bowling's group departed Terceira in the midwatch 12 January and formed its 180-mile line of advance. Next afternoon, when about 500 miles north of Fayal, the delta formation with *Varian* in the center was set up to sweep the latest Tenth Fleet estimate of the target's position. Actually Admiral Low was directing them to *U-1230*, which had taken up weather reporting duties after its Maine spy mission. But even this latest fix was inaccurate. After searching all 14 and 15 January, with no contact, Commander Bowling decided to head southwest. He was rewarded by three of his ships obtaining bearings on a target ten miles distant, at 0550 January 16.[7] Quickly squeezing themselves into the "half delta," the DEs began sound search; and at the end of 80 minutes obtained contacts on the target, weather reporter *U-248*.

While *Hayter* acted as tracker and coach, *Varian* and *Otter* closed to make deliberate depth-charge and hedgehog attacks. *U-248* maneuvered briskly at a depth of 500 feet. At 1012, after several patterns had been dropped, a boil of water on the surface indicated that the boat was blowing tanks. A moment later it sur-

[6] *Otter*, Lt. Cdr. J. M. Irvine USNR; *Hubbard*, Cdr. L. C. Mabley USNR; *Varian*, Lt. Cdr. L. A. Myhre USNR. *Hayter*, Lt. Cdr. Frederick Huey USNR, joined later.
[7] Zone N (plus 1) time.

faced. *Otter* gave it the final punch. Ships' boats recovered human remains and a copy of the official songbook *Morgen Marschieren Wir*. There were no survivors.

Commander Bowling scoured neighboring waters for 24 hours and then headed for Horta. News of his success produced a handsome amends from Admiral Ingram: "My first scalp as Cinclant deeply appreciated. Well done!" [8]

Sending weather reports was not the only way in which submarines helped the Battle of the Bulge. In December the boats began to leave their new Norwegian bases, as well as those in the Baltic, in large numbers, to discover that with snorkel they could operate successfully in coastal waters. They appeared off the East Coast of Britain, in the Western Approaches and in the Irish Sea. Taking advantage of currents and unfavorable sound conditions in shallow waters, they often eluded the antisubmarine vessels and did a good deal of damage. Just before Christmas 1944, snorkeler activity was renewed in the English Channel. On 23 December a coasting vessel was sunk in the approaches to Cherbourg Harbor. And on Christmas Eve occurred a serious sinking.

Leopoldville, an 11,500-ton Belgian steamer formerly in the Congo service, with a Belgian master and crew and a British Naval Armed Guard, had been under charter to the Admiralty since early in the war. She was chosen for lifting from England to France 2235 troops of the 66th Division United States Army, intended as reinforcements in the Battle of the Bulge.[9] Departing Southampton at 0915 December 24, she joined a small convoy which was escorted by destroyer H.M.S. *Brilliant* and three other escort vessels. No lifeboat, fire or abandon ship drills were held during the Channel passage; the soldiers were not even instructed what to do in an

[8] CTG 22.8 Cruise Report 29 Jan. 1945; War Diaries and Action Reports of the DEs; interview with Cdr. Bowling in 1951.
[9] It had been intended to land them at Antwerp, but that city was being so intensively bombed by the Luftwaffe that the destination was changed to Cherbourg.

emergency, or how to fasten life belts, although three sonar contacts and depth-charge attacks were made by the screen. *Leopoldville* was still in this convoy, and only 5½ miles from the entrance to Cherbourg Harbor, when at 1754 she was hit in No. 4 hold by a torpedo from *U–486*. The after parts of two decks collapsed, trapping the troops in certain compartments. The other ships in the convoy, and the rest of the screen (H.M.S. *Anthony* searching for the submarine), moved away at 1820, leaving *Brilliant* standing by. Her C.O. then ordered the transport to anchor.[10] At 1756 he had reported the incident to C. in C., Portsmouth; but not until 1820 or 1835 did he signal to anyone ashore. (He then swung *Brilliant* close to the jetties and blinked, "Want assistance." [11]) Nor did C. in C. Portsmouth, who only received *Brilliant's* signal at 1845, repeat it to Cherbourg.

American officers ashore, in the meantime, were watching *Leopoldville* and wondering what was wrong. Since no explosion had been heard, her mishap looked like a mere engine breakdown and they naturally assumed that the four British escort vessels could take care of her. Upon receiving *Brilliant's* blinker message, they sent out rescue tug *ATR–3*, thinking that the ship needed a tow; and some time later a United States Army officer, on his own responsibility, dispatched a motor torpedo boat, then lying at the harbor entrance, to report what had happened. When the PT drew near the ship, the United States naval lieutenant commanding saw at once that she was sinking, and radioed ashore for more small craft to come out. *Brilliant* had already closed *Leopoldville* between 1830 and 1840 when it was growing dark, and had begun to take off troops. A fairly heavy sea was running in the roadstead,

[10] She had by that time drifted a mile inshore, and was 900 yards from Fort de L'Ouest, or 3 miles 264° from buoy H–10.

[11] Discrepancy here in the evidence. American officers ashore state that the blinker message "Want assistance" was received at 1835. *Brilliant's* C.O.'s report states that visual signal to Cherbourg saying "*Leopoldville* torpedoed or mined. Send tugs," was sent at 1820, and that he closed the ship at 1830. But his report admits that his signals were "logged hurriedly or not at all, and are subject to textual errors."

which made it difficult to embark troops, and it was not until 1929, when the C.O. considered that he had taken on board the maximum number consistent with safety,[12] that he cast off and steamed into harbor.

At 1930 – whether or not on the master's orders is in dispute– the word Abandon Ship was passed, but only to the crew. All but a few, who stood by the master, abandoned. They made no effort, except for taking 30 stretcher cases with them, to help the soldiers to get off in the remaining lifeboats, or to cut the lashing of life rafts and floater nets secured on deck. Most of the lifeboats were left hanging in their davits.

Brilliant made only one trip ashore with survivors, and she was uncommonly slow about it; she took 38 minutes, after entering harbor, to moor alongside Avant Port, and 45 minutes more to land the troops. Her commanding officer, who was still Officer in Tactical Command, did not allow other vessels of his screen to close *Leopoldville* and take on troops, because he wanted them to hunt the submarine; and, believing that the ship was in no immediate danger, he thought that the large number of small craft coming out could complete the work of rescue.

The small craft did what they could. When they began to come alongside at 1940 it was already dark. The troops remaining on deck were mustered in perfect order at the rail, dressed in overcoats and with full packs. They were being taken off the ship as quickly as possible when, at 2030, a second explosion was heard, probably marking the collapse of a bulkhead. *Leopoldville* settled fast and sank within ten minutes. There was no confusion or panic among the troops, but over a thousand [13] were left afloat (water temperature 48° F) and without life-jacket lights, which were on board but had not been issued. Small craft combed the area all night and succeeded in picking up several hundred men; but 802 were killed or missing out of a total of 2235. Of the Belgian crew and

[12] No exact count was made; the U.S. Army Report says 500 were taken ashore by *Brilliant;* her C.O. estimated 700 to 800.

[13] The exact number of floating survivors is not known: a hundred or more were killed by the initial explosion or trapped below.

British Armed Guard of 237, only 17, including the master, were lost.[14]

Everyone who observed the sinking or took part in the rescue remarked on the perfect discipline and exemplary courage of the American infantrymen.

U–486 got away safely and sank H.M.S. *Affleck* and *Capel* when they were patrolling off Cherbourg on 26 December. In mid-channel, *U–772* sank S.S. *Empire Javelin*, also crowded with troops, on the 28th. Her crew were well disciplined and her escorts displayed good seamanship, so that she lost only six men.

On 9 January 1945, Convoy ON–277, attacked in the narrows of St. George's Channel, lost one ship. The snorkelers then moved to the Irish Sea, where they had a field day, torpedoing nine unescorted merchantmen and escort carrier H.M.S. *Thane*. These waters were combed by the British 22nd Escort Group with no success until the last ten days of January when C. in C. Western Approaches assigned this and all other groups to convoy support. On the afternoon of the 21st a ship was torpedoed in a westbound convoy four miles south of Longships Lightship. One of the escorts, H.M.S. *Mignonette*, soon had contact, attacked, and sank *U–1199*. On 25 January H.M.S. *Manners* was torpedoed about 20 miles west of the Skerries. Two surface escort groups closed in and forced *U–1172* to the surface, where it was rammed and sunk by H.M.S. *Aylmer*. On the 27th, Convoy HX–322 had two ships torpedoed about 30 miles southwest of Bardsey Island. Fifth Escort Group (H.M.S. *Tyler* flag) searched, attacked, and was rewarded by large quantities of wreckage from *U–1051*.

[14] Lt. Col. Milton W. Witt "Report of Investigation by Inspector General's office Normandy Base Section U.S. Army" 3 Jan. 1945; Report of Naval Investigation by Capt. M. C. Jackson USNR 6 Jan. 1945; Report of Admiralty to Admiral Stark 9 April 1945, subsequent to its own Board of Inquiry; Report of C.O. H.M.S. *Brilliant* to Capt. 1st Destroyer Flotilla 1 Jan. 1945; additional details told to the writer in 1955 by Col. Richard H. Lee USA, who witnessed the affair from the U.S. Navy command post, Cherbourg.

2. *Snorkels in British Coastal Waters, February–April*

At the beginning of 1945 the high command, both British and American, was seriously concerned over enemy submarine capabilities. The subject was discussed both at the Combined Chiefs of Staff conference at Malta in the last week of January, and at the Yalta conference of the C.C.S. with the three Chiefs of State, in early February.

Snorkel submarines were the most immediate problem. By 1 February at least 25 of them were in or moving into British coastal waters; a most disturbing fact, as this was the first time since 1941 that shipping in the narrow seas had been troubled by U-boats. Snorkelers could approach the coast undetected, both because of their greater underwater endurance, and because they had been equipped with a radar detection device which offset the ASV radar in Allied aircraft and enabled them to dive before a plane could attack; Coastal Command was baffled. Once arrived in shoal water, the boats were able to lie on the bottom where the snorkelers were most difficult to detect by sonar, owing to the confusing echoes from wrecks and rocks near the shore; and, if the skipper used his hydrophone cleverly, he could emerge to take a pot shot at a passing ship, then return to his chosen lair like some prehistoric sea monster.

Even more of a menace were the new Types XXI and XXIII U-boats. The Allies knew that the Germans had dozens of them ready [15] and could not imagine why none had yet been encountered on war patrols. The reason, we now know, was this: the new types were so full of "bugs" and built of such inferior materials that they had to be recalled after their training cruises or even during their initial war patrols, for extensive repairs and alterations. But, for aught the Allies knew then, Doenitz was merely saving the new boats for one colossal blitz on Atlantic shipping which might well

[15] See table of U-boats commissioned monthly, in Appendix I, sec. 2. All except 34 of those commissioned after May 1944 were of these new types.

prejudice logistic supply to the Allied armies in Europe and prolong the war into 1946.

No new tactics were devised or new measures adopted to cope with these threats. Air bombing of submarine assembly points in Germany, and air patrol of the English Channel and the North Sea, continued, together with a constant and intensive search by support and escort groups of the Royal Navy.

In February–April 1945 snorkel-equipped U-boats of the older types were active in the Narrow Seas, and one or two got away into blue water. On 4 February, 23rd Escort Group R.N. located and destroyed *U–1014*, hiding on the bottom of Lough Foyle near Londonderry. On the 16th H.M.C.S. *St. John*, escorting a convoy, sank *U–309* in Moray Firth — first U-boat reported there in five years. On the 20th, H.M.S. *Vervain*, veteran of 32 Atlantic crossings, was torpedoed when escorting Convoy HX–337 about 20 miles south of Waterford. Two other vessels of the screen made sound contact on *U–1208* five minutes later and H.M.S. *Amethyst* sank it. On the 24th a merchantman in a convoy steaming past Land's End was torpedoed by *U–480*. The 3rd Escort Group then sank that boat. On the 27th H.M.S. *Loch Fada* sank *U–1018* about six miles west of the Lizard. A few hours later, a United States Navy Liberator of the 112th Squadron sighted a moving oil-slick twelve miles south of Wolf Rock and homed-in the 2nd Escort Group, which disposed of *U–327*. This was one of the few occasions when aircraft were able to help ships to sink a snorkeler. *U–869* was sunk off the Strait of Gibraltar by destroyer escort *Fowler* (Lieutenant Commander S. F. Morris USNR) and French *L'Indiscret* of the screen of Convoy GUS–74, on the 28th.

During March, as had been feared, the snorkel blitz became more intense. Tonnage of shipping sunk rose to over 65,000, highest for any month since July 1943; and in April the figures almost reached 73,000 tons. The Wehrmacht was collapsing under Russian and Allied advances into Germany, but Doenitz was trying to do as much damage as possible before he and the gods of Nazidom passed into the twilight.

On 7 March the 25th Escort Group R.N. sank *U–1302* off the North Pembrokeshire coast. Early on the 11th, *U–681* hit a rock off the Scilly Isles and damaged its hull and propellers. When trying to escape on the surface it was spotted and sunk by a United States Navy Liberator of Squadron VPB-103, three miles WNW of "Long John" (Bishop Rock). On 20 March the usual rôles were reversed; *U–1003* rammed H.M.C.S. *New Glasgow* which was patrolling off Lough Foyle. The German skipper took his damaged boat down and was held down by an intensive hunt until the early hours of the 23rd, when he surfaced and abandoned ship. The 3rd Escort Group on 26 March sank *U–399* only 15 minutes after it had attacked a convoy five miles southwest of the Lizard. Between the 27th and 30th three kills were made by the 21st Escort Group, and that cleared the enemy from approaches to the Minches.

Even in April 1945 the scale of U-boat operations around the British Isles gave no indication that the end of the war was near. On the 6th, *U–1195* torpedoed a ship in convoy seven miles off the Nab outside Portsmouth Harbor. H.M.S. *Watchman*, after helping to escort the convoy into harbor, searched for, attacked and sank the boat. On the 12th there was a similar affair about 16 miles south of Chicken Rock in the Irish Sea; *U–1024* was captured by H.M.S. *Loch Glendhu*, but sank under tow. Three days later *U–1063* was sunk near Land's End by the 17th Escort Group. On 16 April a tanker in convoy was sunk off the Northumberland coast by *U–1274*, which was promptly disposed of by H.M.S. *Viceroy*, in an action memorable for the salvage of six cases of good brandy from the U-boat's wreckage. On the 21st, another U-boat was sunk off Northern Ireland by the 4th Escort Group; and on the 30th a combined attack by a Sunderland and 14th Escort Group sank *U–325* in the Irish Sea.

All in all, the Royal Navy reaction to this snorkeler blitz was exemplary. And its efforts were augmented by American and British bomber planes, which vigorously attacked German ports where U-boats were waiting to go to sea. Powerful raids of the United

States Army Air Force on Bremen, Hamburg and Wilhelmshaven on 30 March destroyed no fewer than eleven boats, and three more were similarly disposed of at Hamburg the same month. Early in April, Bomber Command R.A.F. joined with the A.A.F. in attacking Kiel, Hamburg and Baltic ports, destroying ten more.

CHAPTER XIX

Victory in the Atlantic

February–May 1945

1. *Snorkels in the Eastern Sea Frontier, February–April*

WE NOW turn to happenings on the American side of the Atlantic, where the snorkelers were few, and less enterprising than those in British coastal waters.

During the first week of February, the only two U-boats that were active in the Western Atlantic accomplished nothing. Their first reinforcement, *U–866*, was hunted between 6 and 18 March by a killer group of four DEs, *Pride, Mosley, Menges*, and *Lowe*,[1] under Commander Reginald H. French USCG, from Cape Sable eastward. *U–866* had been damaged in an Allied air raid on Bremen, and its snorkel did not work well. It tried to escape attention by lying on the bottom off Sable Island, but was rooted out and destroyed through persistent hedgehog attacks by all four of the named ships.

U–857 moved into the Gulf of Maine in late March and announced its presence on 5 April by torpedoing an empty American tanker, *Atlantic States*, off Highland Light. A salvage crew brought the tanker safely into port, and within a few hours a task group under Commander Ralph R. Curry USCG, consisting of two frigates and two DEs, began hunting for the boat. *U–857* also tried "doggo" tactics, lying on the bottom off Cape Cod; but DE *Gus-*

---

[1] These were all U.S.N. ships but had Coast Guard officers and crews. Their search was aided by Canadian 16th Escort Group.

tafson destroyed it by repeated hedgehog attacks in the early hours of 7 April.

A third snorkeler, *U–879*, fell victim to a surface hunter-killer group under Commander Edward H. Headland, who flew his pennant in the redoubtable *Buckley*, now skippered by Lieutenant R. R. Crutchfield USNR. In the midwatch of the 19th, as the group was zigzagging through fog 120 miles southwest of Sable Island, *Buckley* made a sound contact with the help of *Reuben James*, and at 0329 planted 24 hedgehogs which finished *U–879*. Admiral Ingram congratulated the group on their "donation of one swastika to the collection."

Eastern Sea Frontier was harried for the last time by the 740-ton snorkeler *U–548* with a veteran skipper, Kapitänleutnant Gunther Pfeffer, who proved to be as hot as his name. He first made his number off Cape Henry on 14 April 1945 by torpedoing and sinking unescorted freighter *Belgian Airman*, bound from Houston to New York; all but one of her crew were rescued by another merchantman.

Cinclant, with the full coöperation of Admiral Herbert F. Leary,[2] now Commander Eastern Sea Frontier, promptly put on an intensive air and surface hunt. Six DEs under Captain G. A. Parkinson USNR steamed out of Hampton Roads; a mixed group of destroyers, frigates and gunboats came down from Narragansett Bay; Mariners and Venturas roared out from the Norfolk and Elizabeth City airfields; several blimps bobbed overhead. Foggy weather foiled them all. *U–548* worked north with impunity, and on 18 April torpedoed and sank an unescorted tanker, *Swiftscout*, off the Delaware Capes. Again Pfeffer eluded his pursuers, and on

[2] Herbert Fairfax Leary, b. Washington 1885, Naval Academy '05, made the world-wide cruise with the Battle Fleet in 1908. C.O. *Lamson* 1912; liaison officer with the French and British Navies early in World War I and gunnery officer in Battle Force One from Oct. 1917. Duty in Buord 1919, fleet gunnery officer Atlantic Fleet 1922, exec. of *New York* 1923, and quasi-diplomatic duties, 1924–26. Inspector of ordnance and War College course 1928–32; C.O. *Portland* 1933; chief of staff to Com. DDs Battle Force 1934. Staff of C. in C. U.S. Fleet in *Pennsylvania* 1938. Director of Fleet Training division C.N.O. 1936–37 and 1939–41; Com Cruisers Battle Force Feb. 1941; Com Anzac Force and Allied Naval Forces SW Pacific 1942–43; Com Eastern S. F. Nov. 1943 to 1946, when he retired.

23 April torpedoed Norwegian tanker *Katy* some 75 miles south-east of Cape Henry; but her crew managed to bring her safely into Lynnhaven Bay. On 27 April *U–548* was sighted by a freighter's lookouts. Signals were sent to Captain Parkinson's hunters, and on the night of 29–30 April the boat was detected by the escort of Convoy KN–382, which it was about to attack. *Natchez*, a frigate of the screen, drove it off with a "scare" barrage, and before midnight three of Captain Parkinson's DEs arrived and began a series of creeping attacks. *U–548* tried every trick, "turning in circles, fishtailing, changing speeds, backing down, and . . . firing *Pillenwerfers*," but the DEs hung on and *Bostwick* at 0115 April 30 delivered a heavy barrage that forced the boat down to 100 fathoms. Three hours and a half later, DEs *Coffman* and *Thomas* delivered a creeping attack which ended the career of *U–548* and the lives of all its crew.

With these four sinkings under its belt, Atlantic Fleet was well prepared in morale and training to meet Doenitz's final effort in the Western Atlantic.

2. TEARDROP *vs.* "SEEWOLF," *March–May*

While sea frontier forces were grappling with individual U-boats, there was taking place in mid-ocean a battle royal, penultimate round to the war in the Western Atlantic.

Early in 1945, exaggerated tales of captured German spies, and various items of intelligence coming from Europe, created a certain apprehension in the military high command that U-boats might attempt to launch attacks on East Coast cities with robot rocket bombs such as were then falling on London. Admiral Ingram, who felt that the public on the Eastern seaboard was becoming too complacent, announced this dire possibility at a press conference on 8 January and created a sensation. Doenitz was indeed planning a final blitz on the Eastern Sea Frontier, but the six 740-ton snorkel U-boats which made up Group "Seewolf" carried no secret or unconventional weapons. In fact he had none; and in late March 1945, when he dispatched these six boats from their Norwegian bases, the Nazi régime was on its last legs; armies under General Eisenhower and General Zhukov were battering their way into the heart of the Reich. Group "Seewolf" for Doenitz was a means of employing part of his large submarine fleet in a manner to annoy and defy the United States.

Tenth Fleet, whose new chief of staff was Rear Admiral A. R. McCann,[3] furnished Cinclant with a plot of the progress of Group "Seewolf" in good time for him to set up a formidable defense in the form of two so-called Barrier Forces, of which the Second was to relieve the First. Each was built around two escort carriers; their mission was given the frivolous designation Operation TEARDROP. Admiral Ingram was an old hand at erecting ocean barriers in the South Atlantic; but this problem was different — to bar off the entire Eastern Seaboard of Canada and the United States to a phalanx of snorkel boats. Admiral Leary already had a plan for Eastern Sea Frontier craft "to search for, discover, attack and destroy enemy seaborne platforms for launching robot bombs";[4] while the Army Air Force and Army antiaircraft batteries prepared to cope with bombs in flight.

The First Barrier was set up in this fashion: —

NORTHERN FORCE — of which the nucleus was escort carrier *Mission Bay* (Captain John R. Ruhsenberger [5]) — took care of the approaches north of latitude 48° 30′ (that of St. John's, Newfoundland).

SOUTHERN FORCE — of which the nucleus was escort carrier *Croatan* (Captain Kenneth Craig) — operated south of that latitude.

Twenty destroyer escorts, under Commander Morgan H. Harris

[3] Allan R. McCann, b. Mass. 1896, Naval Academy '17, a submarine specialist, served in *Kansas* in World War I; C.O. of various submarines 1920–34, and in *Indianapolis* and *Chicago* 1935–38; C.O. *Iowa* 1944; chief of staff Tenth Fleet Jan.–June 1945; CTF 68 in *Philadelphia* and Com Sub. Force Pacific Fleet 1945. Retired 1950.

[4] Eastern Sea Frontier Op Plan 2–44 in "History of the Eastern Sea Frontier" (Administration Series) p. 43.

[5] Also O.T.C. of the entire First Barrier Force.

USNR, initially maintained a 120-mile picket line along the 30th meridian, which passes between Fayal and Flores, steaming alternately north and south.

Each carrier, retaining a screen of four DEs, cruised in support, 40 to 50 miles in the rear.

Croatan departed Hampton Roads 26 March. Western Ocean weather was then at its worst; on one occasion, planes could not be recovered and had to fly 360 miles to land at Argentia.[6] Wind and sea continued very heavy; one lurch at dinner hour on 5 April rolled tables, benches, mess furniture and food in *Croatan's* mess halls into a heap on the port side, then hurled the whole conglomeration to starboard, injuring over a hundred men. But all ships were in position on the morning of 11 April.

That was President Roosevelt's last day but one on this earth. One regrets that he could not have been spared at least another week to hear about the brilliant fight that followed, where a type of naval vessel in which he had taken particular interest, the destroyer escort, broke up the last German threat to the United States. When the news of his death came through to the Barrier Force, it was intended to hold memorial services on board every ship; but the weather was so rough and the hunting so tense that most ships had to content themselves with a minute's silence.

No accurate fixes or contacts on the approaching "sea wolves" were obtained until 15 April, after *Croatan* had refueled the escorts of the Southern Force. Forty-knot winds, bad visibility and wildly pitching flight decks were still making air operations very hazardous.

On the evening of the 15th a heavy sea was still running and fog lay on the water. At 2135[7] destroyer escort *Stanton* (Lieutenant Commander John C. Kiley USNR), in *Croatan's* screen, made radar contact at 3500 yards; closed to 1000 yards; and turned on a search-

[6] *Croatan* War History. One of the pilots so dispatched was Lt. (jg) J. G. McDaniel USNR who had been in the air when *Block Island* was torpedoed and had to fly to the Canaries. He inquired plaintively over voice radio, "Why does this always have to happen to me?"
[7] Zone O (plus 2) time.

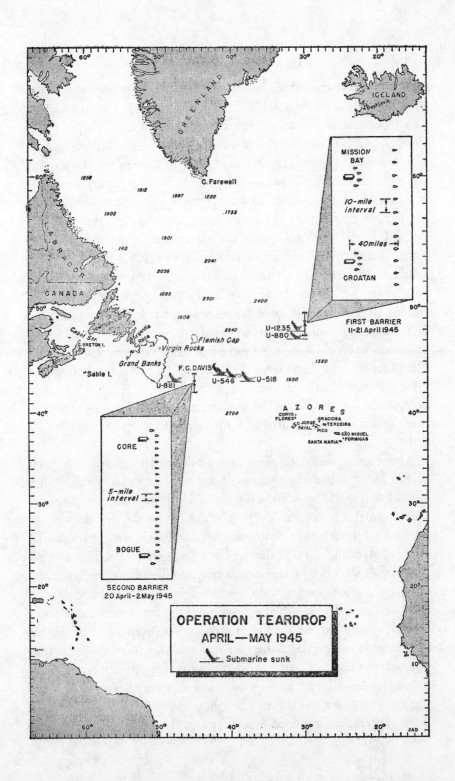

light which so penetrated the fog that a white wake and an obscure dark hull could be seen from the bridge. *U–1235*, which had surfaced because the weather was too rough for snorkel, promptly dove. As *Croatan* scuttled out of the way, Commander Giambattista brought in *Frost* (Lieutenant Commander Andrew E. Ritchie USNR) to assist, while *Stanton* dropped a hedgehog pattern on sound contact. Six minutes later an underwater explosion was heard, of such force that *Stanton* thought for a moment that she was torpedoed. Kiley and Ritchie now played a sleuthing game in the fog, under Giambattista's direction, continually exchanging information although invisible to one another. *Stanton's* third attack produced four more explosions; hedgehogs continued to plummet through the fog-mull as the boat dove deeper, and at 2302 April 15 there was an underwater explosion so terrific that *Croatan*, twelve miles distant, was shaken. A moment later the calm voice of Commander Giambattista was heard over TBS saying, "That is the end of the attack. I think that is the end of the sub. The explosions jarred us completely off the deck." It was, indeed, the end of *U–1235* at a point about 500 miles north of Flores and 520 miles east of Flemish Cap.

About 40 minutes later, and only a mile and a half from the spot where *U–1235* had disappeared, *Frost* made a radar contact on a second "Seewolf," *U–880*, which was trying to escape on the surface from this hot area. Very ill-advisedly its skipper decided to close the hunters, who naturally assumed that they had missed *U–1235* after all, and that this was it. The fog had closed in so thick that *Frost's* star shell at 1450 yards failed to illuminate the boat. She tried again at 650 yards, with a searchlight which revealed *U–880* fully surfaced. Ritchie then opened with gunfire, but the seas were too heavy for him to alter course to ram or even to bring all his 3-inch guns to bear; and the German took his boat down. Sound contact was regained, and *Frost* moved in for a deliberate attack. *Stanton* followed with a hedgehog pattern. Every wave broke over the escorts' bows, where the hedghog crews were loading; they were repeatedly drenched with very cold water, but they were ready at every order to fire. And at 0153 April 16 a blast was heard, even more violent than the breaking-up of *U–1235*, followed by several smaller explosions. That was the end of *U–880*.

The exceptionally violent effects when these two boats broke up strengthened the impression at Tenth Fleet headquarters, as in the Barrier Force, that the sea wolves were carrying something very powerful and nasty to throw at Eastern cities. Although this estimate was mistaken, it stimulated everyone from Cinclant down to make special efforts to mop up the rest of the group.

As Admiral Ingram moved the Barrier Force southwesterly to conform to his HF/DF plot of the U-boats' estimated track, carrier-plane pilots searched these rough waters through high winds and heavy rain squalls, but in vain.

The next contact was obtained by a Leigh-light-equipped Coastal Command Catalina based at Terceira, at a point 420 miles north of Flores in the early hours of 18 April. That area was then in the Northern Force (*Mission Bay*) bailiwick, so it was destroyer escort *Mosley* of this group that searched the area. The detected submarine, *U–805*, had a cautious skipper who noticed so much radio activity that he turned north before shaping his course for Long Island.

First Barrier Force was now due to be relieved by the Second. As a final gesture on 21 April before heading for Argentia, *Croatan* put on an air-surface sweep. That night, with heavy seas still prevailing, four of her escorts hunted a boat which was probably *U–805*. There were underwater explosions, but the U-boat was subsequently heard throwing out knuckles, backing into its own wake and performing various evasive tactics. It escaped a second time. At about 2200, Captain Craig's Southern Force broke off its share of Operation TEARDROP and headed for Argentia. Within an hour (it was still 21 April and the seas were described as "mountainous"), destroyer escort *Carter* obtained sound contact on a boat that proved to be a third "Seewolf," *U–518*. Commander Harris, in *Carter*, first coached in *Neal A. Scott* for a "creeper" attack on the almost motionless target, then got a depth indication himself; and, finding the target to be only 150 feet down, moved in for a methodical attack under a light fog dimly illuminated by a first-quarter moon. One pattern of hedgehog, at 2309, finished *U-518*, which was on its second snorkel patrol.

Three of the six wolves were now sunk, and by surface action alone. The escort carriers and their planes might as well not have been present. It was not that they didn't try — "No squadron in our experience had ever tried any harder," as the chronicler of *Croatan* recorded — but that aircraft had not yet learned how to deal with the snorkelers. Until they did, these boats could be destroyed only by the deliberate, prolonged "rooting out" tactics that Giambattista and other escort commanders had devised, with the help of Asdevlant.

On 23 April Admiral Doenitz, ignorant that he had already lost half of this group, dissolved it and ordered each unit to proceed to a patrol station off the East Coast. By that time Captain Ruhsenberger's First Barrier Force had been relieved by the Second, commanded by Captain George J. Dufek in *Bogue*. This Second Force was organized in fashion similar to the first. TG 22.3, built around *Bogue*, had as screen commander Jack Bowling, with ten DEs; and TG 22.4, built around *Core* (Captain R. S. Purvis), had twelve DEs under Commander F. S. Hall. Drawn from widely separated bases, the *Bogue* group departed Quonset 16 April. The *Core* Group, in part starting from Bermuda, joined it at a mid-ocean rendezvous.

Rendezvous effected, Captain Dufek (to whom Cinclant had given full discretion) formed a different and more attenuated disposition than Ruhsenberger's, along the 45th meridian. Fourteen destroyer escorts under Commander Hall were stationed at five-mile intervals to form a long patrol line; the CVEs, each with a screen of four DEs, instead of lurking in the rear, were at either end of the line: *Core* 25 miles north of the left flank, and *Bogue* 25 miles south of the right flank. And on the evening of 20 April this formidable barrier, 120 miles long with air patrol flying 80 miles east and 80 miles west, moved eastward. By the 21st it had reached the 41st meridian,[8] close to which the first profitable contact was made at 0645 April 23 by DE *Pillsbury*, near the center of the line.[9] While six DEs developed this contact there came in an excited report from one of *Core's* Avenger pilots. He had sighted a feathery wake such as snorkels make, attacked with depth bombs, and reported a subsequent explosion and "motor noises." But when two DEs reached the scene they found only a very dead whale and a life raft which the pilot had generously dropped for "survivors."

At 1307, however, Lieutenant Commander William W. South, skipper of *Bogue's* VC-19, sighted *U-546* breaking surface about 74 miles northeast of the carrier, not far from the center of the search line. This was the first real contact made by any pilot in the course of the entire TEARDROP operation. Commander South attacked, without result. Captain Dufek launched another flight of Avengers and ordered Commander Hall to the scene. The screen commander organized a southern group of escorts in a retiring search clockwise, and a northern group in a retiring search counterclockwise. There was no positive result until 0829 April 24, when *Frederick C. Davis* of the northern group made a sharp, clear sound contact at 2000 yards, at a point 275 miles southwest of Flemish Cap.

Frederick C. Davis (Lieutenant James R. Crosby USNR) had joined the Atlantic Fleet in 1943 and had seen rugged service off Anzio as "jam ship" for glide-bombs.[10] "Fightin' Freddy," as the crew called her, claimed to have shot down 13 planes in the Mediterranean, and had made a good reputation for skill and alertness.

As the target picked up by her sonar passed down her starboard side the contact was lost, drowned out by the Foxer gear. Lieutenant (jg) John F. McWhorter USNR, officer of the deck, imme-

[8] New datum point in accordance with orders from Cinclant 20 April. *Bogue* War Diary.

[9] Zone O (plus 2) time. This battle is related in greater detail than others of equal importance in this volume, in order to give the reader some idea of the hazards of antisubmarine warfare even during this closing phase of the war.

[10] See Vol. IX 347, 355.

diately ordered hard right rudder, notified the C.O. and signaled over TBS to other escorts nearby. C.I.C., guns and hedgehog and depth-charge throwers were quickly manned. The target upon which sound contact was regained had been plotted for about five minutes at 0835 when a tremendous explosion blasted the ship on the port side, abreast of her forward engine room. *U–546*, detected as it was trying to slip through and get a carrier, had loosed a torpedo from a range of only 650 yards.

In a matter of seconds the engine space and several large living compartments were flooded, and within five minutes "Fightin' Freddy" was breaking in two. Fires fed by ruptured fuel lines roared through the lower bridge area. The gunnery officer and his hedgehog crew managed to rescue several men from the forward living compartments, including a hardy chief gunner's mate who climbed up a red-hot ladder. The wardroom deck had been blown up to the level of the portholes, killing all the officers who were eating breakfast and the steward's mates who were serving them. Almost everyone on the flying bridge had been catapulted overboard. While the gunnery officer endeavored to flood the forward magazines, a few uninjured bluejackets ran up to the bridge, found the officer of the deck dead within a gun tub into which his body had been hurled, the starboard lookout hanging dead from a belaying pin on the signal bridge, and the body of the skipper cut in two by a wire shroud when the mast snapped off. The only survivor from C.I.C., Ensign R. E. Minerd USNR, broke open the jammed door of the pilothouse, where he found the helmsman lying on the deck with both legs broken; he picked the injured man up and struggled to the signal bridge, where both were swept into the sea.

Three junior officers not on watch tumbled out of their bunks aft and attempted to establish order. Ensign Philip K. Lundeberg USNR, assistant damage control officer, organized a repair party which passed rapidly through the after compartments, dogging down hatches and securing the few valves that were still open. Topside, they joined the division radar officer, Lieutenant (jg) R. F. Kip USNR, and several gunner's mates, in checking the safe setting of depth charges — but two charges had had their caps and forks removed and could not be set safe. Life rafts and floater nets were set free, and about nine minutes after the explosion Ensign Lundeberg, senior officer aft, ordered Abandon Ship. The afterdeck was already awash. About one hundred men, most of whom had been sleeping aft when the torpedo exploded, were able to abandon. Conditions were unfavorable for survival. The sea was rough and cold; some men had no life jackets; the two unsecured depth charges exploded; and sharks were about. In the end, only 77 officers and men, some already dead, were picked up by the other escorts.

When Commander Hall witnessed the explosion he sent *Hayter* and *Neunzer* to hunt the U-boat and ordered *Flaherty* to rescue survivors. The last-named closed within 15 minutes of the explosion, and at the very moment when the floating remains of *Frederick C. Davis* went down. *Flaherty's* skipper, Lieutenant Commander Howard C. Duff USNR, not inclined to make his ship a second target, moved gingerly through the groups of survivors, picked up some men on the fly and tossed rafts and empty depth-charge cases to others. At 0917 his sonar man detected the U-boat lurking under the wreckage. He then moved in for a creeping attack while *Hayter* (Lieutenant Commander Frederick Huey USNR) took over rescue operations, aided by carrier aircraft which spotted several men hidden in pools of oil. Hospital Corps men and the division medical officer on board *Hayter* gave their best, but several men died after rescue. The net number of survivors was only 66 (including 3 officers) out of a total of 13 officers and 179 men.

A hunt lasting almost twelve hours followed the torpedoing of "Fightin' Freddy." Every known type of surface antisubmarine attack, and several not found in the book, were tried; but it was too foggy for aircraft to help. Commander Hall may have spoiled *Flaherty's* first creeping attack by charging in with *Pillsbury*, her Foxer whacking; but it was *Pillsbury* that relocated *U-546*. She coached *Flaherty* in, at 0951, for a hedgehog attack which did not connect. Shortly after regaining contact, *Flaherty's* soundman mistook the release of a *Pillenwerfer* for the launching of an acoustic torpedo, and her skipper threw consternation into adjacent ships by shouting, "Stand by for torpedo!" *Hayter,* slowly drifting down on groups of survivors with several members of her crew swimming to assist the dazed and wounded, had to get under way and leave them afloat for a time.

At 1025 *Flaherty* made a hedgehog and then a depth-charge attack yet only jarred *U–546,* which nearly escaped at this point, but the DE picked up contact again at 1156. *Varian* (Lieutenant Commander L. A. Myhre USNR) followed with a series of creeping attacks which kept the boat down and exhausted its crew. *Janssen* and *Hubbard* made a couple of runs. *Neunzer* and *Flaherty* returned to action at 1341, joining *Hubbard* in a three-ship creeping attack which again failed to score.

Commander Hall, realizing that the U-boat must be nearing the end of its endurance submerged, at 1350 passed the word to his skippers that the enemy "must be pretty worried. . . . We will just keep hounding him." The escort commander then directed his ships to determine the German's depth as well as his exact position. At 1513 *Varian* reported the boat to be about 600 feet down. She and *Neunzer,* coached by *Chatelain,* made a three-ship attack at 1556. Contact was lost and the search line was re-formed for an eastward sweep. *Varian* located the slippery German again at 1728 and directed *Keith* on a depth-measuring run which showed that the boat had come up to a depth of 160 feet.

After nearly ten hours of depth-charging, *U–546* could hold out no longer. The noise of its main pumps — which had to be used to check flooding — blanked out the hydrophone and made it impossible to gauge the position of the hunters. At 1810 hedgehog from *Flaherty* wrecked the submarine's bridge, and blasted a 15-inch hole in the pressure hull; it ruptured batteries and released chlorine gas. After receiving another hedgehog attack, the German skipper blew tanks to bring his boat up for a last-ditch surface fight.

At 1836 *Flaherty* warned her neighbors, "Sub is coming to surface, stand by guns!" Two minutes later *U–546* broached nearly a mile from the last contact and promptly launched a torpedo, which missed, at its latest tormentor. Lieutenant Commander Duff of *Flaherty*, after reporting "That stinker fired a torpedo at me!" countered with two of his own; they, too, missed. *Pillsbury*, *Keith*, *Neunzer*, and *Varian* banged away at the submarine's conning tower. At 1845 April 24, when Commander Hall ordered "Cease Fire, sub sinking," *U-546* up-ended almost perpendicularly and slid down into the depths.

Rescue operations, carried out by five DEs and continuing for one hour and 40 minutes, saved the skipper and 32 of his crew. They were a bitter and truculent group of Nazis, who refused to talk until after they had been landed at Argentia and had enjoyed a little "hospitality" in the Marine Corps brig. As a result of interrogations it became clear to Tenth Fleet that group "Seewolf" was making no robot-bomb offensive — merely a final gesture against American coastal shipping.

Two sea wolves, *U-858* and *U-805*, were still unaccounted for. Captain Dufek at 1925 April 24 re-formed his barrier along long. 41° W and began to sweep southwesterly at 5 knots, hoping that this inordinately low speed would prove a tempting wolf-bait. But no boats were in that area. On 2 May, Admiral Ingram split Second Barrier Force in two, one to patrol long. 50° and the other, long. 50°30′ W. At the same time he ordered the *Mission Bay* group, then in Argentia, to patrol along lat. 43°05′ N, starting at long. 47° W.

None of these new dispositions encountered the two surviving boats but the *Mission Bay* group disposed of *U-881*, which Doenitz had dispatched from Norway 8 April to strengthen his nuisance operation off the East Coast. This boat was maneuvering to attack the carrier when *Farquhar* (Lieutenant Commander D. E. Walter USNR) made a sound contact at 0413 May 6 and sank *U-881* with one depth-charge attack. There were no survivors. And a final sweep along the 60th meridian made no contacts.

Thus, Admiral Ingram's well planned and executed barrier operations broke up the "Seewolf" group and sank five of the six U-boats that it encountered, with the loss of one destroyer escort. These results caused no great jubilation at Tenth Fleet headquarters, because the air aspects of Operation TEARDROP had been anything but brilliant. It is true that the carrier planes had been hampered by the spring fog, but except for making a couple of contacts they might as well have stayed ashore. Snorkel had not turned the tide of victory for Germany, but it had proved baffling to aircraft on both sides of the Atlantic. It was the surface ships' sound gear and radar that made and kept contacts and led to attacks; and it was hedgehog, assisted by a few depth charges, that sank the U-boats.

3. *Battle off Block Island, 5–6 May*

Before the war ended in the Western Atlantic there was to be one brief battle, the only action within sight of the New England coast, against a shore-hopping snorkeler of the type then numerous around the British Isles.

At 1740 May 5, only 28 hours before Germany surrendered,[11] Boston-bound collier *Black Point* was torpedoed and sunk off Narragansett Bay, losing a dozen men from her crew and Naval Armed Guard. *U–853*, Captain Vest's "Moby Dick," which had been prowling undetected about those waters for days at snorkel depth, had sprung this surprise. A passing merchantman, Yugoslav S.S. *Kamen*, sighted *U–853* briefly and reported to shore. Eastern Sea Frontier and Cinclant promptly organized a hunter-killer group under Commander Francis C. B. McCune in destroyer *Ericsson*. His ship was then off Boston, having just escorted a convoy thither; but the rest of the group was available, south of Cape Cod. Numerous SCs, PTs, PCs and other small craft in Narragansett Bay could have been used, but the Navy had learned that something bigger, faster and more powerful than a subchaser was needed to kill a snorkel submarine.

[11] General Jodl and General Bedell Smith signed the unconditional surrender papers at Rheims at 0241 May 7 Central European Time; this was 2141 May 6 Eastern Standard Time, which forces in Narragansett Bay were using. May 8, however, when Russia signed, is the officially recognized VE-day.

At 1920 May 5, one hour and 40 minutes after the torpedoing, and before Commander McCune had had time to traverse the Cape Cod Canal, Lieutenant Commander L. B. Tollaksen USCG in frigate *Moberly* of the newly set-up group arrived at the scene of the sinking and assumed tactical command of destroyer escorts *Atherton* and *Amick*. Promptly forming a scouting line, they swept seaward. Within fifteen minutes *Atherton* (Lieutenant Commander Lewis Iselin USNR) obtained a sound contact five miles east of Grove Point, Block Island. At 2028 a full pattern of depth charges was dropped, followed by two hedgehog attacks. In a depth of 18 fathoms it was impossible to determine whether explosions heard on shipboard were inside the submarine or on the ocean floor. Contact was lost; but the skipper of *U-853* had decided to sit it out on the bottom rather than make a dash for blue water. *Atherton* regained contact at 2337 and delivered a hedgehog attack which proved to be lethal — although it was long before the hunters were certain of their kill.

Commander McCune, having arrived in *Ericsson*, assumed tactical command and ordered searchlights turned on to illuminate the scene. Oil geysers and various debris were then seen; but, uncertain whether these were from the U-boat or relics of some wreck, the group continued to search all night and resumed attacks at daylight 6 May. The opportunity to work over a bottomed U-boat and to shoot off ammunition at the end of the war was so welcome that the group made repeated attacks, breaking off at noon after recovering such convincing evidence as the German skipper's cap and his chart table. Admiral King gave credit for this kill, almost the last of the Atlantic war, to DE *Atherton*, frigate *Moberly* assisting.[12]

"Captain Ahab" Vest was avenged; his "Moby Dick" went down not far from the old whaling port of New Bedford.

One cannot help contrasting this methodical and successful attack with those of three years earlier, in May 1942, when mer-

[12] King *U.S. Navy at War 1941–1945* p. 205. Naval divers subsequently identified the remains of *U-853*. Farquhar's kill of *U-881* took place a few hours later. There were two kills by R.A.F. Squadron 86 the same day in the Kattegat, and one on the 7th by R.A.F. Squadron 210 between the Shetlands and Norway.

chant ships were torpedoed almost daily off Cape Cod and New York, and U-boats escaped to kill, and kill again.

4. *Surrender and Conclusion* [18]

On 30 April 1945, before *U-853* and *U-881* had fought their last and fatal fights — even before Operation TEARDROP was over — Adolph Hitler committed suicide. Grossadmiral Doenitz heard the news that evening in the garbled form that Hitler had died fighting, and at the same time learned that he had been designated the new Fuehrer. He had obeyed orders and done his best, but he had a higher duty now, to stop the fighting for the sake of his country. "I will hear no more of this 'heroes death' business," he said.[14] "It is now my responsibility to finish." He did, however, spend the better part of a week trying to arrange that all German forces surrender to the Western Allies rather than to Russia. General Eisenhower firmly refused.

Advanced detachments of the American and Russian armies had already met at the River Elbe; British troops made contact with the Russians at Lübeck on 2 May. By noon on the 4th, Doenitz had his first partial surrender offer in the hands of Field Marshal Montgomery. General Eisenhower, in accordance with his instructions from the C.C.S., required an unconditional surrender to all three Allies. This meant, among other things, that all German warships must be handed over. Doenitz still hedged on surrendering to Russia; but on the evening of 4 May, as evidence of his peaceful intentions, he ordered every German warship at sea to cease hostilities and return to port.

Even before Hitler's death, Doenitz had dispatched everything

[18] Details in F. C. Pogue *The Supreme Command* (U.S. Army in World War II Series, 1954) chap. xxv, and C. D. Bekker *Swastika at Sea* (1953) chap. xv. Stories of U-boats that surrendered to U.S. forces are in American newspapers for 11-20 May 1945.
[14] "*Ich will jetzt nichts mehr von Helden Tot hören.*" Told to me by Konteradmiral Godt, who was with Doenitz, in 1955.

that could float up the Baltic to rescue Germans fleeing before the Russian armies. "Monty" informally gave permission for this operation to continue, which it did until the complete surrender became effective 9 May. It amounted to the greatest mass evacuation of the war. Dozens of submarines, small craft, torpedo boats and merchant vessels made repeated shuttle trips and rescued over two million men, women and children from Russian clutches, losing about 20,000 in the sinking of three large steamers by Russian submarines and aircraft.

On 8 May Admiral Harold M. Burrough RN, acting for the Supreme Commander, ordered all U-boats at sea to surface, fly a black flag or pennant, report position to nearest Allied radio station and proceed to such port as directed.[15] *U–249*, first to comply with this order of the 8th, was spotted off the Scilly Islands flying the black flag of surrender by a Navy Liberator of Fleet Air Wing Seven, piloted by Lieutenant Frederick L. Schaum USNR. Schaum signaled ashore and two Royal Navy sloops came out to escort the boat into Portland Bight.

Doenitz's surrender order characterized the long and bitter battle of his U-boats against the freedom of the seas as "a heroic fight which knows no equal." Perhaps not, in the short annals of the German Navy; but to an American or British naval historian there is bathos in the claim. Whatever heroics there were in the U-boats' war may be more than matched by the deeds of Allied sailors and airmen, to whose skill and endurance, and dogged determination in fighting the underwater enemy, victory came as a crown well deserved.

There was to be no spectacular surrender of the German Fleet, as at Scapa Flow in 1918. As the end neared, remnants of the German high seas fleet were lying in Danish or Baltic ports where they were destroyed by Allied bombers or scuttled by their crews. Numerous small naval craft were scuttled or captured when the Allies took possession of German, Danish, Norwegian and Polish harbors. When Doenitz ordered the U-boats to surrender, 49 were still at

[15] New York *Times* 9 May 1945.

sea, and most of these obeyed his order. The total number that surrendered was 181, but 217 were destroyed by their own crews.[16] Most of the completed Type XXI and XXIII boats were scuttled, but several were acquired intact by the Allies.

Few submarines surrendered to United States forces, because at the time few were on the western side of the Atlantic. *U–853* and *U–881*, most recent victims of the United States Navy, probably never got the word because they were cruising at snorkel depth or wholly submerged. Most of the skippers who received the surrender order in western waters, obeyed. Kapitänleutnant Bernardelli of *U–805*, one of the sea wolves that had eluded the Barrier, broadcast his position on the morning of 9 May, rendezvoused with *Varian*, one of his recent hunters, off Cape Race on the 13th, and there gave himself up. Next morning *U–858*, the one "Seewolf" still afloat, flying a couple of drab blankets in lieu of a black flag, surrendered to Commander F. S. Hall, off the Delaware Capes. By 19 May five more U-boats had given up in the Western Atlantic. *U–234*, a 1600-ton cargo submarine en route to Tokyo with a German technical mission that expected to help the Japanese,[17] surrendered 14 May to destroyer escort *Sutton*, which took it in to the Portsmouth Navy Yard at Kittery, Maine. Three other U-boats were already there.[18]

Two diehard skippers, of *U–530* and *U–977*, ignored their new Fuehrer's orders and kept the sea for more than two months before reaching a neutral port. Embittered Nazis, they had absorbed the spirit of a slogan posted at Christiansand at their last departure: "The enemy shall find nothing but rats and mice in Germany. We

---

[16] Admiral Sir Frederic C. Dreyer RN *The Sea Heritage* (London 1955) p. 372. Sir Frederic was on the Admiralty Assessment Committee of U-boat Losses which, in conjunction with the U.S.N. Tenth Fleet Assessment Committee, made such accurate assessments of U-boat losses that their total score was correct within a few units. The actual total score was 1179 U-boats employed, 699 sunk by Allied action, 82 lost by marine casualty or from unknown causes.

[17] The skipper of *U–234* gave permission to two Japanese officer passengers to commit suicide before he surrendered; but to his disgust they dosed themselves with Luminal instead of performing the traditional *seppuku* and died slowly and ignobly.

[18] *U–805, U–873, U–1228.*

will never capitulate. Better death than slavery!" *U–530* reached a patrol station off Long Island in early May, made several unsuccessful attacks on convoys both before and after the German surrender, then shaped a course for the River Plate where the skipper hoped for a friendly reception from Argentine Fascists. He reached Mar del Plata on 9 July, and a month later was joined by *U–977*, which had crossed the Atlantic at snorkel depth.[19] To the chagrin of both skippers, they and their crews were interned by the Argentine government, and their boats surrendered to United States Naval representatives at Buenos Aires.

On the afternoon of 28 May 1945, the United States Navy and British Admiralty issued this joint announcement: —

"Effective at 2001 this date, Eastern Standard Time, (0001 May 29 Greenwich Mean Time), no further trade convoys will be sailed.

"Merchant ships by night will burn navigation lights at full brilliancy and need not darken ship."

Certain conclusions on the Battle of the Atlantic are appropriate before we leave this vital aspect of the war to describe the Navy's part in the liberation of France. First and most obvious is that, without victory over the U-boat, the American men and matériel who contributed to the defeat of Germany could never have reached the theater of conflict, and in all probability the British Isles would have been blockaded and starved into submission. Second, that Grossadmiral Doenitz's "tonnage warfare" strategy failed completely. Although Germany actually built more submarines in 1944 than in 1943 or 1942, merchant ship sinkings fell off after mid-1943, and only rose briefly during the snorkel blitz in British waters.

Next, we must candidly admit that the Royal Navy, the Royal Canadian Navy and the Coastal Command of the Royal Air Force, acting under Admiralty supervision, contributed more to the destruction of the enemy submarine fleet than did the United States

[19] Heinz Schaeffer, C.O. of *U–977*, has an inaccurate article on this cruise in *Sat. Eve. Post* 22 Nov. 1952, and published an unreliable book, *U–977*, the same year. It is he who was falsely accused of having transported Hitler to Argentina.

Navy and the United States Army Air Force. Several explanations may be given for this undoubted fact. The United States had a second major war to fight, virtually unaided, in the Pacific. The United Kingdom lay so much nearer the sources of U-boat activity that British forces encountered by far the greater number of targets.[20] It is probable, though not susceptible of proof, that the Royal Navy down to late 1942 excelled in escort-of-convoy work; that the Anglo-Canadian escort groups were then better trained than those of the U.S. Navy, partly because every effort was made to keep them intact and partly because they had had more experience and constant practice. Subsequent to 1942 it would be difficult to say which nation excelled; certainly the Germans saw no difference between the relative antisubmarine skills of their two principal enemies.[21]

No one can deny that American escort commanders such as Captain Paul R. Heineman, Captain Charles C. Hartman, Commander Jesse C. Sowell, Captain Adelbert F. Converse and Commander F. D. Giambattista were among the best in either Navy. By any standard, the American escort carrier groups were superior to those which flew the White Ensign; and here comparison is valid, because after 1942 all CVEs in the Atlantic came off the same assembly lines. These escort carrier groups were probably the greatest

[20] Statistical evaluations made shortly after the war by Asworg scientists indicate that the proportion of kills of U-boats to contacts was approximately the same for both navies; but since there was no uniform method of establishing what constituted a contact, these statistics have little value.

[21] So Konteradmiral Godt informed me in 1955, and followed it up with a written statement which may be translated as follows: —

"No fundamental distinction in the capability of British and American U-boat hunting was established during the war. Naturally the British units into 1942 were ahead of the Americans on account of their longer war experience. Until mid-1942 the German U-boats off the American East Coast had throughout a feeling of superiority over the American defense. Later, throughout 1943 and 1944, the distinction between American and English combatant skill was always harder for the U-boats to establish because possibilities of observation were always less, and countless lend-lease ships and aircraft were plying under British flags so that identification of the ships by the U-boats was impossible. In general, a U-boat defense in the 'center of gravity areas' was much more dangerous than in the remoter areas. Therein the nationality of the ships made no difference, only the lack of practice and experience in the Allied vessels in the remote areas."

single contribution of the United States Navy to victory over enemy submarines.

It was a very costly war to both sides. The Germans reckon that they lost 32,000 submariners from 781 U-boats.[22] They and the Italian submarines sank 2828 Allied and neutral merchant ships of 14,687,231 tons,[23] together with 158 British Commonwealth and 29 American warships,[24] several warships of other nations, and a very large number of aircraft. The loss of life at sea that the U-boats and Luftwaffe inflicted on the Allies has only been computed for the British merchant marine, which alone lost 29,994 men to enemy action. Hardly less than 40,000 men, and several hundred women and children, went down into the depths as a result of enemy submarine and aircraft attacks. The Atlantic, which since the dawn of history has been taking the lives of brave and adventurous men, must have received more human bodies into its ocean graveyard during the years 1939–1945 than in all other naval wars since the fleets of Blake and Van Tromp grappled in the Narrow Seas.

Sailormen all, and passengers too, we salute you!

During the war and after there have been many debates, supported by statistics, as to whether aircraft or naval vessels contributed most to the defeat of the submarine. The controversy is futile and the announced results are misleading, since each arm contributed its part in close coöperation with the other. For instance, the sinkings by an escort carrier group, whether made by an Avenger dropping a depth bomb or by a destroyer escort with guns and hedgehog, cannot justly be scored to "air" alone, or "surface" alone, but to both. Carrier-borne aircraft depended on a ship as a roving base; surface hunters were frequently led to their

[22] Konteradmiral Godt, speech at Hamburg war memorial 16 May 1954 (trans. by Cdr. H. T. Hardenburg USNR).

[23] Admiralty figures. Of these, 94 ships of 532,393 tons were sunk by Italian submarines, the rest by U-boats. Admiralty analysts find that 63 per cent of the merchant ships sunk were unescorted, 29 per cent in convoy and 8 per cent stragglers or rompers from convoys.

[24] Ops. Evaluation Gp. File "U.S. and Foreign Naval Casualties"; O.N.I. Statistical Section "Naval Losses of All Nations," 1946.

quarries by air reconnaissance. Ships acted as U-boat bait for land-based aircraft as well as warships. Even in the northern transatlantic convoys where a large proportion of the kills were made by sur-face escorts, aircraft helped to frustrate the attacks on merchant-men. Except in the Bay of Biscay, off the coast of Norway, and in the attacks on German harbors in 1945, it would be difficult to find kills that can be attributed exclusively to aircraft. And only in dis-tant waters not reached by air cover did warships operate without assistance from the air.

Still less may it be said that any one weapon or gadget led to vic-tory in the Atlantic; not even the plane-mounted microwave radar which the Germans frequently name as the cause of their defeat. ASV certainly contributed, as did the Leigh light, the rocket, im-proved depth charges, hedgehog, Fido, and, perhaps most of all, old "Huff-Duff," the high-frequency direction-finder, pointer for the Fleet. So many vessels and types of ships, such a variety of air-craft, such an array of training and other commands (Cinclant, Cotclant, Cincwa, and so on), so much latent valor and inge-nuity — that vast reservoir possessed by the American and British people — combined to defeat the underwater menace of the Ger-man Navy that it would be invidious to single out a few for special commendation. Nor am I forgetting the Coast Guard and amateur auxiliaries of 1942–43, or the merchantmen and Naval Armed Guards who faced "the battle and the breeze" from the opening of the war to the German surrender. This was, above all, a battle fought by men.

To one and all, then, of the British, Canadian and United States Navies, Air Forces and Merchant Marines, and to the gallant ships and squadrons of other Allied nations operating under their com-mand, and to the scientists, shipbuilders and builders of aircraft — this historian, who has followed them from the humiliating winter of 1941–1942 to the glorious summer of 1945, can only say: —

"Well done; aye, magnificently done; and the free world is your debtor!"

APPENDIX I

Losses of Merchant Shipping and of Enemy Submarines

May 1943–May 1945

1. *Monthly Losses of Allied and Neutral Merchant Vessels to Submarine Attack* [1]

	Atlantic & Arctic		Indian Ocean		Mediterranean	
	NUMBER	GROSS TONS	NUMBER	GROSS TONS	NUMBER	GROSS TONS
1943						
May	41	211,929	3	13,472	1	5,979
June	7	37,825	7	34,208	6	23,720
July	24	136,106	15	82,404	5	25,977
August	4	27,941	6	37,944	5	20,673
September	8	46,892	6	39,471	6	32,478
October	11	53,886	6	25,833	3	17,688
November	6	29,917	4	29,148	3	7,481
December	7	47,785	5	31,173	1	8,009
1944						
January	5	36,065	8	56,213	0	0
February	2	7,048	10	64,169	6	21,706
March	8	41,562	11	67,658	4	33,724
April	7	47,763	0	0	2	14,386
May	3	17,277	0	0	1	7,147
June	8	38,556	3	19,319	[None after May 1944]	
July	7	33,175	5	30,176		
August	8	40,944	9	57,732		
September	6	37,698	1	5,670		
October	0	0	0	0		
November	5	15,567	2	14,025		
December	8	51,338	0	0		
1945						
January	11	56,988	0	0		
February	14	58,057	1	7,176		
			[Rest of 1945, zero]			
March	13	65,077				
April	13	72,957				
May	3	10,022				

[1] Fleet Operations Statistical Analysis Office, Navy Department.

2. *U-Boats Built, Operating, and Sunk Monthly* [2]

It. = Italian submarines; J. = Japanese submarines. All others are German. Losses include boats sunk in port, or so badly damaged that they were unserviceable.

	NEW BOATS BUILT	AVERAGE OPERATING DAILY [3]	LOSSES *Atlantic*	LOSSES *Arctic* [4]	LOSSES *Medit.*	LOSSES *Baltic* [5]	LOSSES *Other Areas*
1943							
May	26	108	38(+ 2 It.)	0	3(+ 2 It.)	0	0
June	25	79	14(+ 1 It.)	2	1(+ 1 It.)	0	0
July	26	73	33	1	3(+ 8 It.)	0	0
August	21	51	21	2	1(+ 1 It.)	1	0
September	21	57	7	0	1(+ 2 It.)	2	0
October	26	76	24	0	1	0	1 Indian Ocean
November	25	70	17	0	0	2	1 J., Ind. O.
December	28	60	5	0	2	1	0
1944							
January	21	61	13	1	0	0	1 Adriatic
February	19	60	14	2	0	3	1 Malacca Str. (+ 2 J., Ind. O.)
March	23	62	14	4	5	2	0
April	23	52	13	3	2	3	0
May	20	38	6(+ 1 J.)	10	4	1	1 Indian Ocean
June	12	57	16(+ 1 J.)	9	0	0	0
July	15	34	15	3	2	4	1 J., Ind. O.
August	15	42	22	2	6	1	1 Ind. O., 3 Black Sea
September	20	58	6	8	3	0	1 Ind. O., 3 Black Sea
October	17	38	4	6	0	1	1 Indian Ocean
November	22	31	2	2	0	2	1 Indian Ocean
December	30	38	8	2	0	3	0
1945							
January	29	36	8	0	0	4	0
February	25	48	12	5	0	5	0
March	25	48	33	1	0	2	0
April	7	50	37	4	0	14	1 Java Sea
May	1	43	3	2	0	5	26 Skagerrak to Belts

[2] Data in first 2 columns from Dr. Rohwer. By "built" he means completed and ready for sea.

[3] Including those in or in passage to Indian Ocean, but *not* those operating in Arctic, Baltic, Black or Mediterranean Seas.

[4] Here defined as waters north of the line from lat. 60°30′ N, long. 5° E, to lat. 65°30′ N, long. 37° W.

[5] Including Kiel.

3. *Monthly Losses of Allied and Neutral Vessels by All Causes*

World-Wide

DATE	BY SUBMARINE		BY ALL OTHER CAUSES (AIR ATTACK, MARINE CASUALTIES, ETC.)		TOTAL	
	ATLANTIC-ARCTIC	OTHER AREAS			SHIPS	TONNAGE
1943						
May	211,929	52,923	64,079		72	328,931
June	37,825	57,928	62,223		44	157,976
July	136,106	108,381	144,735		75	389,222
August	27,941	58,617	89,865		38	176,423
September	46,892	71,949	60,004		43	178,845
October	53,886	43,521	70,932		53	168,339
November	29,917	36,629	118,367		56	184,913
December	47,785	39,182	122,897		47	209,864
				(May–Dec. 1943)	428	1,794,513
1944						
January	36,065	56,213	92,454		51	184,732
February	7,048	85,875	74,479		46	167,402
March	41,562	101,382	55,320		56	198,264
April	47,763	14,386	98,623		39	160,772
May	17,277	7,147	16,003		12	40,427
June	38,556	19,319	65,925		46	123,800
July	33,175	30,176	39,452		28	102,803
August	40,944	57,785	55,503		44	154,232
September	37,698	5,670	44,284		34	87,652
October	0	7,176	33,768		22	40,944
November	15,567	14,025	38,343		28	67,935
December	51,338	7,180	107,642		44	166,160
				(1944)	450	1,495,123
1945						
January	56,988	0	63,878		37	120,866
February	58,057	7,176	47,719		36	112,952
March	65,077	0	77,681		44	142,758
April	72,957	0	63,808		33	136,765
May	10,022	0	13,897		9	23,919
				(Jan.–May 1945)	159	537,260

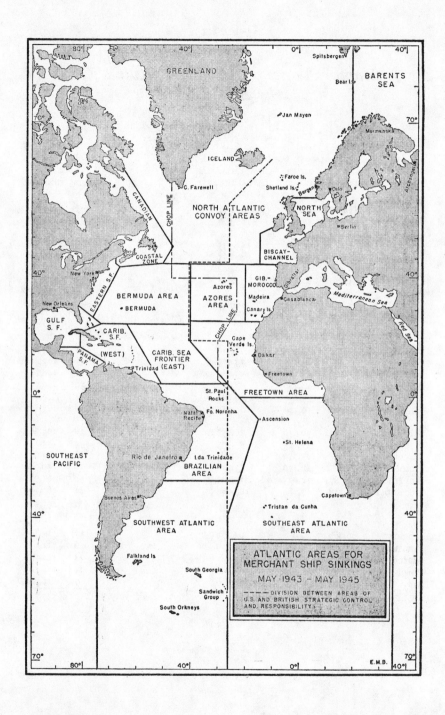

ATLANTIC AREAS FOR
MERCHANT SHIP SINKINGS
MAY 1943 — MAY 1945
----- DIVISION BETWEEN AREAS OF
U.S. AND BRITISH STRATEGIC CONTROL
AND RESPONSIBILITY

4. *Ocean Areas*[5] *of Heaviest Monthly Merchant Shipping Losses by Submarine Attack*

(Only Areas with 4 or more sinkings per month included)

DATE	AREA	SHIPS	GROSS TONS
1943			
May	North Atlantic Convoy	17	87,935
	Freetown	8	45,691
	Southeast Atlantic	7	41,105
June	Indian Ocean	7	34,208
	Mediterranean	6	23,720
July	Indian Ocean	15	82,404
	Brazilian	11	64,478
	Caribbean West	8	35,096
	Mediterranean	5	25,977
August	Indian Ocean	6	37,944
	Mediterranean	5	20,673
September	Indian Ocean	6	39,471
	North Atlantic Convoy	6	36,422
	Mediterranean	6	32,478
October	Indian Ocean	6	25,833
November	Indian Ocean	4	29,148
December	Indian Ocean	5	31,173
1944			
January	Indian Ocean	8	56,213
February	Indian Ocean	10	64,169
	Mediterranean	6	21,706
March	Indian Ocean	11	67,658
	Mediterranean	4	33,724
June	English Channel	5	30,994
July	Indian Ocean	5	30,176
August	Indian Ocean	9	57,732
	English Channel	6	24,811
December	English Channel	7	45,880
1945			
January	Northeast Atlantic	6	27,820
	Canadian Sea Frontier	4	24,531
February	English Channel	6	15,524
March	English Channel	7	34,402
April	North Sea	5	21,369
	English Channel	4	33,848

[5] See appended chart for limits of these areas.

APPENDIX II

Sinkings of German, Italian and Japanese Submarines by U.S. Forces in Arctic, Atlantic and Mediterranean[1]

(Sinkings by CVE Groups credited to the Carrier, in SMALL CAPS*)*

DATE	BOAT	AGENT	AREA
1943			
May 13	*Mocenigo*	A.A.F.	Cagliari, Sardinia
14	*U–657*	VP–84	E of Cape Farewell
15	*U–176*	VS–62 and Cuban *CS–13*	Old Bahama Channel
16	*U–182*	*MacKenzie*	Madeira
17	*U–128*	VP–74, *Moffett, Jouett*	Brazil
21	*Gorgo*	*Nields*	N of Oran
22	*U–569*	BOGUE	NE of Flemish Cap
25	*U–467*	VP–84	Iceland
June 2	*U–521*	*PC–565*	Eastern Sea Frontier
5	*U–217*	BOGUE	SW of Azores
12	*U–118*	BOGUE	SW of Azores
20	*U–388*	VP–84	SE of Cape Farewell
24	*U–200*	VP–84	E of Cape Farewell
July 7	*U–951*	A.A.F.	W of Lisbon
8	*U–232*	A.A.F.	NW of Lisbon
9	*U–590*	VP–94	Brazil
12	*U–506*	A.A.F.	W of Cape Finisterre
13	*U–487*	CORE	NW of Cape Verdes
14	*U–160*	SANTEE	S of Azores
15	*U–159*	VP–32	N of Barranquilla
15	*U–509*	SANTEE	S of Azores
15	*U–135*	VP–92 and H.M.S. *Balsam*	NE of Cape Juby
16	*U–67*	CORE	SW of Azores
19	*U–513*	VP–74	E of Florianapolis, Brazil
20	*U–558*	A.A.F. and R.A.F.	N of Cape Finisterre
21	*U–662*	VP–94	SE of Cayenne
23	*U–527*	BOGUE	S of Azores

[1] Including those in which U.S. Forces are credited with an "assist."

DATE		BOAT	AGENT	AREA
	23	U–613	BOGUE	S of Azores
	23	U–598	VB–107	NE of Cape San Roque
	24	U–622	A.A.F.	Trondheim
	26	U–759	VP–32	Port au Prince
	28	U–359	VP–32	SE of Ciudad Trujillo
	28	U–404	A.A.F. and R.A.F.	N of Cape Finisterre
	30	U–461	A.A.F., R.A.F., R.A.A.F.	NW of Cape Ortegal
	30	U–591	VB–127	Recife
	30	U–43	SANTEE	SW of Azores
	30	U–375	PC–624	W of Malta
	31	U–199	VP–74 and Brazilian A/C	Rio de Janeiro
Aug.	2	U–706	A.A.F	NNW of Cape Finisterre
	3	*Argento*	*Buck*	S of Pantelleria
	3	U–572	VP–205	N of Cayenne
	7	U–615	VP–204, 205, VB–130, A.A.F.	SW of Martinique
	7	U–117	CARD	W of Azores
	9	U–664	CARD	NW of Azores
	11	U–604	VB–129, –107, *Moffett*	NW of Ascension
	11	U–525	CARD	WNW of Corvo
	24	U–185	CORE	SW of Azores
	24	U–84	CORE	SW of Azores
	27	U–847	CARD	SW of Azores
Sept.	27	U–161	VP–74	Brazil
Oct.	4	U–336	VB–128	E of Cape Farewell
	4	U–422	CARD	N of Azores
	4	U–460	CARD	N of Azores
	13	U–402	CARD	N of Azores
	20	U–378	CORE	N of Azores
	28	U–220	BLOCK ISLAND	NE of Flemish Cap
	31	U–584	CARD	NE of Flemish Cap
Nov.	1	U–405	CARD	NE of Flemish Cap
	5	U–848	VB–107, A.A.F.	W of Ascension
	10	U–966	VB–103, –110, Czech. Sqdn.	Off Cape Finisterre
	12	U–508	VB–103	Bay of Biscay
	25	U–849	VB–107	E of Ascension
	29	U–86	BOGUE	E of Azores
Dec.	13	U–593	*Wainwright*, H.M.S. *Calpe*	NE of Algiers
	13	U–172	BOGUE	NW of Cape Verdes
	16	U–73	*Woolsey, Trippe*	NE of Oran
	20	U–850	BOGUE	SW of Azores
	24	U–645	CARD	NE of Azores
1944 Jan.	9	U–81	A.A.F.	Adriatic
	16	U–544	GUADALCANAL	W of Azores
	28	U–271	VB–103	W of Ireland

DATE		BOAT	AGENT	AREA
Feb.	6	U–177	VB–107	WSW of Ascension
	24	U–761	VP–63, VB–127, R.A.F., H.M.S. *Anthony*, *Wishart*	Strait of Gibraltar
March	1	U–709	BLOCK ISLAND	N of Azores
	1	U–603	BLOCK ISLAND	N of Azores
	11	U–380	A.A.F.	Toulon
	11	U–410	A.A.F.	Toulon
	13	U–575	BOGUE, R.A.F., H.M.C.S. *Prince Rupert*	N of Azores
	16	U–392	VP–63, H.M.S. *Affleck*, H.M.S. *Vanoc*	Strait of Gibraltar
	17	U–801	BLOCK ISLAND	W of Cape Verdes
	19	U–1059	BLOCK ISLAND	SW of Cape Verdes
April	7	U–856	*Champlin, Huse*	Eastern Sea Frontier
	9	U–515	GUADALCANAL	NW of Madeira
	10	U–68	GUADALCANAL	Madeira
	11	U–108	A.A.F. and R.A.F.	Stettin
	16	U–550	*Gandy, Joyce, Peterson*	Eastern Sea Frontier
	17	U–986	*Swift*, PC–619	W of Land's End
	26	U–488	CROATAN	W of Cape Verdes
	29	U–421	A.A.F.	Toulon
May	4	U–371	*Pride, Jos. E. Campbell*, F.S. *Senegalais*, H.M.S. *Blankney*	NE of Bougie
	6	U–66	BLOCK ISLAND	W of Cape Verdes
	13	RO–501(U–1224)	BOGUE	W of Cape Verdes
	15	U–731	VP–63, H.M.S. *Kilmarnock*, *Blackfly*	Strait of Gibraltar
	17	U–616	*Nields, Gleaves*, H. P. *Jones, Macomb, Hambleton, Rodman, Emmons* and Brit. Sqdn. 36	W of Algiers
	19	U–960	*Niblack, Ludlow*, Brit. Sqdns. 36 and 500	NW of Algiers
	29	U–549	BLOCK ISLAND	WSW of Funchal
June	4	U–505	GUADALCANAL	Capt'd SW of Port Etienne
	11	U–490	CROATAN	NW of Azores
	15	U–860	SOLOMONS	S of St. Helena
	24	I–52	BOGUE	W of Cape Verdes
July	2	U–543	WAKE ISLAND	W of Cape Bojador
	3	U–154	CROATAN	NW of Madeira
	5	U–233	CARD	Eastern Sea Frontier
	5	U–586	A.A.F.	Toulon
	5	U–642	A.A.F.	Toulon
	29	U–2323	A.A.F.	Bremen
	29	U–872	A.A.F.	Bremen

Appendix II

373

DATA		BOAT	AGENT	AREA
Aug.	6	U–952	A.A.F.	Toulon
	6	U–471	A.A.F.	Toulon
	6	U–969	A.A.F.	Toulon
	19	U–466	Scuttled before capture	Toulon
	19	U–967	U.S. troops	Toulon
	20	U–1229	BOGUE	SW of Cape Race
	21	U–230	Scuttled	Toulon
Sept.	24	U–565	A.A.F.	Salamis
	24	U–596	A.A.F.	Salamis
	29	U–863	VB–107	Brazil
	30	U–1062	MISSION BAY	SW of Cape Verdes
1945				
Jan.	16	U–248	Hayter, Otter, Varian, Hubbard	N of Azores
	17	U–2523	A.A.F. and R.A.F.	Hamburg
Feb.	24	U–3007	A.A.F.	Bremen
	27	U–327	VPB–112, H.M.S. Labuan, Loch Fada, Wildgoose	Land's End
	28	U–869	Fowler, F.S. L'Indiscret	SW of Gibraltar
March	11	U–681	VPB–103	Land's End
	11	U–2515	A.A.F.	Hamburg
	11	U–2530	A.A.F.	Hamburg
	18	U–866	Lowe, Menges, Pride, Mosley	Eastern Sea Frontier

[On 30 March 12 U-boats were destroyed by A.A.F. bombers in raids on Bremen, Hamburg and Wilhelmshaven, and three others were sunk at Hamburg in March, exact day unknown.]

[On 3 and 4 April 6 U-boats were destroyed by A.A.F. bombers in raids on Kiel.]

April	7	U–857	Gustafson	Eastern Sea Frontier
	15	U–1235	CROATAN	N of Azores
	16	U–880	CROATAN	N of Azores
	19	U–879	Buckley, Reuben James	Eastern Sea Frontier
	21	U–518	CROATAN	SE of Flemish Cap
	24	U–546	BOGUE, CORE	SE of Flemish Cap
	25	U–1107	VPB–103	Bay of Biscay
	28	U–56	A.A.F. and R.A.F.	Baltic
	30	U–548	Natchez, Coffman, Bostwick, Thomas	Eastern Sea Frontier
	30	U–1055	VPB–103	W of Brest

[Ten U-boats were destroyed by A.A.F. and R.A.F. bombers at Kiel and Hamburg and in Baltic ports during April, exact day unknown.]

May	6	U–853	Atherton, Moberly	Block Island
	6	U–881	MISSION BAY	S of Flemish Cap

APPENDIX III

Mine Fields Laid by U-boats in Western Atlantic from 1 May 1943

DATE LAID		LOCATION	LAID BY	NO. LAID	NO. DE-TECTED	DISCOVERED BY	CASUALTIES
1943							
June	1	Halifax	*U–119*	66	55	Ship	S.S. *Halma*
July	30	Chesapeake	*U–566*	12		Undiscov-ered	None
July	31	Chesapeake	*U–230*	8		Undiscov-ered	None
Aug.	26–27	Charleston	*U–107*	12	1	Sweeper	None
Oct.	8	Panama	*U–214*	15	10	Floater	None
Oct.	9–10	St. Johns	*U–220*	66	34	Floater	S.S. *Delisle,* S.S. *Penolver*
Oct.	27	Trinidad	*U–218*	14		Undiscov-ered	None
1944							
March	23	St. Lucia	*U–218*	2	1	Ship	None
April	1	San Juan	*U–218*	15	1	Premature	None

APPENDIX IV

Task Organization of U.S. Navy Escort Carrier Groups Operating in the Atlantic, 1943-45

(Dates in parentheses indicate when a new ship or air squadron, or a new commanding officer, joined. Missions in which no important events occurred are omitted.)

BOGUE, Captain Giles E. Short

(I) *5 Mar.–18 June 1943*: 5 missions

VC–9: 12 F4F–4 (Wildcat); 8 (12 *after 23 Apr.*) TBF–1 (Avenger), Lt. Cdr. W. McC. Drane

Screen Commander, Lt. Cdr. Doyle M. Coffee (Cortdiv 1)

Destroyers

BELKNAP, Lt. Cdr. Coffee; GEORGE E. BADGER,[1] Cdr. W. H. Johnsen; (*15 May*) Lt. T. H. Byrd USNR; (*23 Apr.*) GREENE, Lt. Cdr. L. J. Bellis; (*13 May*) Lt. Cdr. J. S. Lewis; OSMOND INGRAM, Lt. Cdr. N. J. Sampson; (*23 Apr.–2 May*) LEA, Lt. Cdr. D. I. Thomas; (*30 May*) CLEMSON, Lt. Cdr. E. W. Yancey.

BOGUE, Captain Joseph B. Dunn

(II) *12 July–25 Dec. 1943*: 6 missions

VC–9: Same types of planes, Lt. Cdr. Drane
(*5 Sept.*) VC–19: 9 FM–1 (Wildcat), 13 TBF–1C, Lt. Cdr. C. W. Stewart

Screen Commander, Lt. Cdr. E. W. Yancey (Cortdiv 1)

Destroyers

GEORGE E. BADGER, Lt. Byrd; CLEMSON [2] Lt. W. F. Moran USNR; OSMOND INGRAM, Lt. Cdr. N. J. Sampson; (*14 Nov.*) Lt. Cdr. R. F. Miller USNR; (*29 Sept.*) DUPONT, Cdr. J. G. Marshall; (*14 Nov.*) Lt. E. M. Higgins USNR.

(III) *26 Feb.–12 Apr. 1944*: 2 missions

VC–19: Same types of planes, Lt. Cdr. J. F. Adams USNR

Screen Commander, Cdr. T. S. Lank (Cortdiv 51)

---

[1] Not in 23 Apr.–2 May crossing.
[2] Detached 30 Sept., back 15 Nov.

Destroyer Escorts

HAVERFIELD, Lt. Cdr. J. A. Mathews USNR; JANSSEN, Lt. Cdr. H. E. Cross USNR, WILLIS, Lt. Cdr. G. R. Atterbury USNR; SWENNING, Lt. R. E. Peek USNR; HOBSON, Lt. Cdr. Kenneth Loveland.

BOGUE, Captain Aurelius B. Vosseller

(IV) *5 May–24 Sept. 1944:* 4 missions

VC–69: 9 FM–2, 12 TBM–1C (Avenger), Lt. Cdr. Jesse D. Taylor USNR (*1 Aug.*) VC–42: 9 FM–2, 14 TBM–1C, Lt. Cdr. J. T. Yavorsky

Screen Commander, Cdr. Lank

Destroyer Escorts

HAVERFIELD, JANSSEN, WILLIS, as above; (*to 30 June*) FRANCIS M. ROBINSON, Lt. J. E. Johansen USNR; (*1 Aug.*) WILHOITE, Lt. Cdr. E. B. Roth.

BOGUE, Captain George J. Dufek

(V) *15 Apr.–11 May 1945:* Barrier Force Mission

VC–19: 3 FM–2, 16 TBM–3, Lt. Cdr. W. W. South

Screen Commander, Cdr. Lank

Destroyer Escorts

HAVERFIELD, Lt. Cdr. R. W. Dudley USNR; JANSSEN, Lt. Cdr. S. G. Rubinow USNR; WILLIS, Lt. Cdr. J. M. Gunn USNR; WILHOITE, Lt. R. C. Moore USNR; SWENNING, Lt. Cdr. R. E. Peek USNR; COCKRILL, Lt. Cdr. J. H. Castle USNR; OTTER, Lt. Cdr. J. M. Irvine USNR with Cdr. J. F. Bowling (Cortdiv 62) embarked; HUBBARD, Cdr. L. C. Mabley USNR; VARIAN, Lt. Cdr. L. A. Myhre USNR; HAYTER, Lt. Cdr. Frederick Huey USNR.

CARD, Captain Arnold J. Isbell

(I) *30 July–9 Nov. 1943:* 4 missions

VC–1: 6 F4F–4, 11 TBF–1, Lt. Cdr. Carl E. Jones USNR (*25 Sept.*) VC–9: 6 F4F–4, 12 TBF–1, Lt. Cdr. H. M. Avery

Screen Commander, Lt. Cdr. J. E. Flynn

Destroyers

BARRY, Lt. Cdr. Flynn; (*27 Sept.*) Lt. Cdr. H. D. Hill USNR; * BORIE, Lt. C. H. Hutchins USNR; GOFF, Lt. Cdr. H. I. Smith USNR; (*27 Sept.–18 Oct.*), DUPONT Cdr. J. G. Marshall.

(II) *23 Nov. 1943–2 Jan. 1944:* 2 missions

VC–55: 9 FM–1, 12 TBF–1C, Lt. B. A. Miles USNR

Screen Commander, Cdr. B. S. Copping (Desdiv 53)

Destroyers

LEARY, Cdr. James E. Kyes; SCHENCK, Lt. Cdr. E. W. Logsdon; DECATUR, Cdr. J. B. Williams.

* Sunk 1 Nov. 1943.

CARD, Captain Rufus C. Young

(III) *10–18 July 1944*

VC–12: 9 FM–2, 12 TBM–1C, Lt. Cdr. J. H. McCurtain USNR

Screen Commander, Cdr. G. A. Parkinson USNR (Cortdiv 48)

Destroyer Escorts

THOMAS, Lt. Cdr. D. M. Kellogg USNR; BRONSTEIN, Lt. Cdr. S. H. Kinney; BREEMAN, Lt. Cdr. E. N. W. Hunter USNR; BOSTWICK, Lt. C. G. Hall USNR; BAKER, Lt. Cdr. N. C. Hoffman USNR.

BLOCK ISLAND, Captain Logan C. Ramsey

(I) *15 Dec 1943–3 Feb. 1944:* 2 missions

VC–58: 9 FM–1, 12 TBF–1, Lt. Cdr. C. H. McCroskey

Screen Commander, Cdr. R. B. Ellis (Desdiv 58)

Destroyers

PAUL JONES, Lt. Cdr. G. P. Unmacht; PARROTT, Cdr. J. N. Hughes; BULMER, Lt. Cdr. G. T. Baker; BARKER, Lt. Cdr. R. G. Colbert.

BLOCK ISLAND, Capt. Ramsey; (*11 Mar.*) Capt. Francis M. Hughes

(II) *16 Feb.–31 Mar. 1944:* 2 missions

VC–6: 9 FM–2, 12 TBF–1C, Lt. R. M. Payne USNR

Screen Commander, Cdr. G. A. Parkinson USNR

Destroyer Escorts

THOMAS, Lt. Cdr. D. M. Kellogg USNR; BREEMAN, Lt. Cdr. E. N. W. Hunter USNR; BRONSTEIN, Lt. Cdr. S. H. Kinney; BOSTWICK, Lt. Cdr. J. H. Church; CORRY, Lt. Cdr. G. D. Hoffman.

* BLOCK ISLAND, Captain Hughes

(III) *22 Apr.–29 May 1944:* 2 missions

(*to 15 May*) VC–58: 9 FM–1, 12 TBF–1, Lt. Cdr. R. K. Gould
(*23–29 May*) VC–55: 9 FM–1, 12 TBF–1, Lt. Cdr. B. A. Miles USNR

Screen Commander, Cdr. Henry Mullins (Cortdiv 60)

Destroyer Escorts

AHRENS, Cdr. Morgan H. Harris USNR; EUGENE E. ELMORE, Lt. Cdr. G. L. Conkey; BARR, Lt. Cdr. H. H. Love USNR; (*to 15 May*) BUCKLEY, Lt. Cdr. B. M. Abel USNR; (*33–29 May*) ROBERT I. PAINE, Lt. Cdr. Drayton Cochran USNR.

CORE, Captain Marshall R. Greer

(I) *27 June–2 Sept. 1943:* 3 missions

VC–13: 6 F4F–4, 12 TBF–1, Lt. Cdr. C. W. Brewer

Screen Commander, Lt. Cdr. R. G. Colbert (Desdiv 58)

Destroyers

BARKER, Lt. Cdr. A. J. Miller; BULMER, Lt. Cdr. L. F. Volk; BADGER, Lt. Cdr. R. A. Wolverton.

* Sunk 29 May 1944.

CORE, Captain James R. Dudley

(II) *5 Oct.–19 Nov. 1943:* 2 missions

VC–13: Same types of planes, Lt. Cdr. Brewer

Screen Commander, Cdr. E. W. Yancey (Cortdiv 1)

Destroyers

GREENE, Lt. Cdr. J. S. Lewis; BELKNAP, Lt. B. T. Brooks USNR; GOLDSBOROUGH, Lt. W. J. Meehan USNR.

CORE, Captain Robert S. Purvis

(III) *13 Apr.–11 May 1945:* Barrier Force Mission

VC–12: 3 FM–2, 16 TBM–3, Lt. Cdr. McCurtain

Screen Commander, Capt. T. S. Dunstan USNR (Cortdiv 7)

Destroyer Escorts

MOORE, Lt. Cdr. H. R. Jones USNR; SLOAT, Lt. Cdr. W. A. Cashman USNR; TOMICH, Lt. Cdr. C. B. Brown USNR; J. RICHARD WARD, Lt. Cdr. E. B. Seeley USNR; OTTERSTETTER, Lt. Cdr. L. E. Whitmore USNR; KEITH, Lt. Cdr. W. W. Patrick USNR; PILLSBURY, Lt. Cdr. G. W. Cassleman USNR with Cdr. F. S. Hall (Cortdiv 4) embarked; POPE, Lt. Cdr. R. J. Montgomery USNR; FLAHERTY, Lt. Cdr. H. C. Duff USNR; * FREDERICK C. DAVIS, Lt. James R. Crosby USNR; CHATELAIN, Lt. Cdr. D. S. Knox USNR; NEUNZER, Lt. Cdr. V. E. Gex USNR.

CROATAN, Captain John P. W. Vest

(I) *12 Apr.–26 June 1944:* 2 missions

(*to 12 May*) VC–42: 9 FM–2, 11 TBM–1C, Lt. Cdr. J. T. Yavorsky
(*2 June*) VC–95: 9 FM–2, 10 TBF–1C, Lt. Cdr. J. F. Adams USNR

Screen Commander, Cdr. Frank D. Giambattista (Cortdiv 13)

Destroyer Escorts

FROST, Lt. Cdr. J. H. McWhorter USNR; BARBER, Lt. Cdr. E.T.B. Sullivan; SWASEY, Lt. Cdr. H. M. Godsey USNR; SNOWDEN, Lt. Cdr. N. W. Swanson USNR; HUSE, Lt. Cdr. R. H. Wanless USNR; INCH, Lt. Cdr. C. W. Frey USNR.

CROATAN, Captain Kenneth Craig

(II) *25 Mar.–25 Apr. 1945:* Barrier Force Mission

VC–55: 3 FM–2, 16 TBM–3, Lt. Cdr. Clark W. Johnson

Screen Commander, Cdr. Giambattista

Destroyer Escorts

FROST, Lt. Cdr. A. E. Ritchie USNR; HUSE, Lt. Cdr. J. H. Batcheller; INCH, Lt. Cdr. D. A. Tufts USNR; STANTON, Lt. Cdr. J. C. Kiley USNR; SWASEY, Lt. Cdr. H. A. White USNR; CARTER, Lt. Cdr. F. J. T. Baker USNR with Cdr. M. H. Harris (Cortdiv 79) embarked; NEAL A. SCOTT, Lt. Cdr. P. D. Holden USNR; MUIR, Lt. Cdr. T. A. O'Gorman USNR; SUTTON, Lt. T. W. Nazro USNR.

* Sunk 24 Apr. 1945.

Appendix IV

GUADALCANAL, Captain Daniel V. Gallery

(I) *30 Mar.–17 Apr. 1944*

VC–58: 9 FM–2, 3 TBF–1C, 9 TBM–1C, Lt. Cdr. R. K. Gould

Screen Commander, Cdr. F. S. Hall (Cortdiv 4)

Destroyer Escorts

PILLSBURY, Lt. Cdr. G. W. Cassleman USNR; POPE, Lt. Cdr. E. H. Headland; FLAHERTY, Lt. Cdr. Means Johnston; CHATELAIN, Lt. Cdr. D. S. Knox USNR; FORREST, Cdr. K. P. Letts.

(II) *14 May–19 June 1944*

VC–8: 12 TBM–1C, 9 FM–2, Lt. N. D. Hodson

Screen Commander, Cdr. Hall

CHATELAIN, PILLSBURY, POPE, FLAHERTY, as above; JENKS, Lt. Cdr. J. F. Way.

MISSION BAY, Captain John R. Ruhsenberger

(I) *21 Sept.–16 Oct. 1944*

VC–36: 9 FM–2, 12 TBM–1, Lt. Cdr. F. M. Welch

Screen Commander, Cdr. E. W. Yancey (Cortdiv 9)

Destroyer Escorts

DOUGLAS L. HOWARD, Lt. J. T. Pratt USNR; FARQUHAR, Lt. Cdr. D. E. Walter USNR; J. R. Y. BLAKELY, Lt. A. S. Archie USNR; HILL, Lt. Cdr. P. A. Bane USNR; FESSENDEN, Lt. Cdr. W. A. Dobbs USNR.

MISSION BAY, Capt. Ruhsenberger

(II) *27 Mar.–25 Apr. 1945*, Barrier Force Mission

VC–95: 9 FM–2, 10 TBF–1C, Lt. Cdr. John F. Adams USNR

Screen Commander, Cdr. Yancey

Destroyer Escorts

DOUGLAS L. HOWARD, Lt. Pratt; J. R. Y. BLAKELY, Lt. Cdr. A. S. Archie USNR; HILL, Lt. A. G. Borden USNR; FESSENDEN, Lt. Cdr. Dobbs; FARQUHAR, Lt. Cdr. Walter; PRIDE, Lt. Cdr. W. H. Buxton USCG with Cdr. R. H. French USCG (Cortdiv 46) embarked; MENGES, Lt. Cdr. F. M. McCabe USCG; MOSLEY, Lt. Cdr. E. P. MacBryde USCGR.

SANTEE, Captain Harold F. Fick

(I) *13 June–6 Aug. 1943:* 2 missions

VC–29: 13 TBF–1, 9 SBD–5 (Dauntless), Lt. Cdr. W. R. Staggs USNR
VF–29: 12 F4F–4, Lt. H. B. Bass

Destroyers

BAINBRIDGE, Lt. Cdr. A. M. Boyd; OVERTON, Lt. Cdr. R. O. Lucier; MACLEISH, Lt. Cdr. G. E. T. Parsons.

SOLOMONS, Captain Marion E. Crist

30 May–23 June 1944

VC–9: 9 FM–2, 6 TBM–1, 6 TBF–1, Lt. Cdr. H. M. Avery

Screen Commander, Cdr. C. G. McKinney USNR (Cortdiv 24)

Destroyer Escorts
STRAUB, Cdr. McKinney; GUSTAFSON, Lt. Cdr. A. E. Chambers USNR; TRUMPETER, Lt. G. B. Buck USNR; HERZOG, Lt. J. B. Fyffe USNR

TRIPOLI, Captain Thayer T. Tucker

22 Aug.–12 Oct. 1944: 2 missions

VC–6: 13 FM–2, 17 TBM–1, Lt. R. M. Payne USNR

Screen Commander, Cdr. C. G. McKinney USNR

Destroyer Escorts
STRAUB, Lt. J. E. Coie USNR; ALGER, Lt. Cdr. W. J. Barney USNR; MARTS, Lt. Cdr. N. M. Goodhue USNR; GUSTAFSON, Lt. Cdr. Chambers.

WAKE ISLAND, Captain James R. Tague

17 June–15 Aug. 1944: 2 missions

VC–58: 9 FM–2, 12 TBM–1C, Lt. Cdr. R. K. Gould

Screen Commander, Cdr. J. H. Forshew USNR (Cortdiv 9)

Destroyer Escorts
DOUGLAS L. HOWARD, Lt. Cdr. W. F. Stokey USNR; * FISKE, Lt. John A. Comly USNR; FARQUHAR, Lt. Cdr. D. E. Walter USNR; J. R. Y. BLAKELY, Lt. A. S. Archie USNR; HILL, Lt. Cdr. P. A. Bane USNR.

* Sunk 2 Aug. 1944.

APPENDIX V

Composition of Convoy UGS-40 under Air Attack in the Mediterranean

11 May 1944

Convoy Commodore: Capt. T. H. Taylor in *Abangarez*
Escort Commander: Cdr. Jesse C. Sowell (CTF 61) in *Campbell*

Screen

U.S.C.G.C. CAMPBELL, Cdr. Sam F. Gray USCG; destroyers DALLAS, Lt. Cdr. J. W. Coolidge USNR with Cdr. N. C. Barker (Desdiv 60) embarked; BERNADOU, Lt. W. C. Meredith USNR; ELLIS, Lt. P. Cutler USNR; BENSON, Cdr. J. B. Williams; destroyer escorts EVARTS, Lt. Cdr. T. G. Bremer USNR with Cdr. R. A. Fitch (Cortdiv 5) embarked; DOBLER, Lt. E. F. Butler USNR; DECKER, Lt. H. S. Cody USNR; SMARTT, Lt. E. R. Wepman USNR; WYFFELS, Lt. S. N. Gleis USNR; WALTER S. BROWN, Lt. L. C. Burdett USNR; WILHOITE, Lt. Cdr. E. B. Roth; H.M.S. CALEDON, Capt. R. F. Nichols RN; French Ships TUNISIEN, Capt. de Corv. de Roziers; CIMETERRE, Lt. G. Cagger; fleet tug H.M.S. HENGIST, Lt. A. E. Purves RNR; minesweepers SUSTAIN, Lt. J. E. Lindeman USNR; STEADY, Lt. Cdr. B. Orella USNR.

Partial List of Merchant Ships [1]

NAME	MASTER	NAVAL ARMED GUARD COMMANDER [2]
Samgallion (Br)	G. Y. Dobeson	F. L. Rowden
Ben H. Miller (Br)	R. S. Kearon	
Sampenn (Br)	Thomas W. Ellis	
Samkansa (Br)	C. K. Blake	
Peter Zenger	F. A. Toro	Ens. Thomas C. Babylon USNR
Fort Michipicoten (Can)	W. H. Alexander	
Samuel Moody	S. S. Vendsen	Lt. Carl S. Meister USNR
William H. Moody	William McDonald	Lt. (jg) Jess K. Wells USNR
Samlea (Br)	W. A. Owen	
James W. Fannin	B. O. Scott	Lt. (jg) I. O. Nelson USNR
Empire Alliance	F. G. Vine	
Abraham Lincoln	Christian Dietz	Lt. (jg) P. A. Kinsey USNR
Van Lear Black	H. E. Callis	Lt. (jg) G. A. Greer USNR

[1] Escort Commander's file of Masters' and Naval Armed Guard Commanders' reports made after the action; those not reporting are not listed. There were 65 merchant ships present at the time of the attack.

[2] On British ships the 2nd Officer commanded the Naval Armed Guard.

John Stevens	Nils P. Johansson	Lt. L. G. Davidson USNR
Grenville M. Dodge	Thomas Kennedy	Lt. C. Edwin Johnson USNR
George H. Dern	J. Kramer	Lt. (jg) M. D. Synhorst USNR
Port Melbourne (Br)	P. S. Ball	
John W. Griffiths	P. H. Johnson	Ens. H. R. Kratky USNR
Colin P. Kelly Jr.	T. R. Sorrensen	Lt. J. A. Harvey USNR
John Dickinson	A. L. Holderman	Lt. W. L. Martin USNR
Zachary Taylor	J. S. Hulings	Ens. M. L. Kelly USNR
Salamis (Nor)	K. Henriksen	T. Berggren
James Whitcomb Riley	A. J. Vandegeer	Lt. John A. Watts USNR
Thomas W. Bickett	Andrew Anderson	Lt. (jg) D. F. Nash USNR
Odysseus	R. Paer	
Abangarez	A. Gray	Ens. Ward E. Bakken USNR
Thomas L. Clingman	Hans Bentsen	Lt. (jg) R. E. Stephens USNR
Conrad Weiser	R. J. Dexter	Ens. H. M. Marshall USNR
Benjamin Huntington	E. R. Hornquist	Lt. C. W. Comfort USNR
John Banvard	T. E. Evans	Lt. W. C. Medford USNR
Cornelius Gilliam	R. S. Blood	
Carter Braxton	L. W. Knudsen	Lt. (jg) T. L. Sullivan USNR
William Mulholland	Ernest Mountain	Lt. H. H. Chisman USNR
James J. Pettigrew	C. E. Foltz	Lt. (jg) H. W. Hickey USNR
Clement Clay	Frank G. Roys	Lt. (jg) E. L. Stanley USNR
Fernbrook (Nor)	F. Weibust	S. Larsen
Francis M. Smith	F. D. Carpenter	Lt. (jg) P. K. Likes USNR
Janet L. Roper	W. J. Coveney	Lt. (jg) V. E. Lentz USNR
Stephen A. Douglas	A. R. Mawdsley	Lt. Daniel Witt USNR
Magdala (Dutch)	J. Sohler	
Ben F. Dixon	Bruce B. Rawding	Ens. F. W. House USNR
Albino Perez	W. P. Magann	Lt. (jg) G. F. Reed USNR
Samharle (Br)	E. C. Radford	
Thomas Nuttall	E. L. Randall	Ens. W. M. Sadler USNR
John F. Myers	A. P. Pedersen	Lt. D. E. Anderson USNR
William B. Giles	C. C. Murray	Lt. (jg) B. Bigelow USNR
Samfairy (Br)	J. Nicolson	
Samspelga (Br)	R. Linaker	
Neocardia (Br)	G. Birkett	J. L. Charlton
Samdaring (Br)	C. Blakey	
William H. Aspinwall	E. P. Thayne	Ens. George Spink USNR
Laurentide Park (Can)	J. A. T. Llewellyn	
Empire Stalwart (Br)	W. Laidler	
William Patterson	H. C. Bergen	Lt. (jg) L. W. Scott USNR
Junecrest (Br)	F. J. Anderson	
James M. Gillis	John Metsall	Lt. (jg) Carl C. Cook USNR

Index

Index

Names of warships, and code names of operations and
conferences, in SMALL CAPITALS
Names of merchant ships, and lettered and numbered
combatant ships, in *Italics*
Ships and officers appearing in the Appendices only are not indexed

Abbreviations:

A/S = Antisubmarine; T.O. = Task Organization

A

Abel, Lt. Cdr. B. M., 285–8
Abel-Smith, Capt. E. M. C., 78
ABNAKI, 293
Achilles, Kaptlt. Albrecht ("Ajax"), 180, 224
ACTIVITY, 308
Adams, Cdr. A. B., 331
Adams, Cdr. G. F., 273n
ADMIRAL HIPPER, 57
AFFLECK, 337
AHRENS, 284, 289
Air A/S Patrol and Convoy Cover, land-based, 7, 20; mid-Atlantic, 44–6, 144; Europe, 85–107, 129–32; So. Atl. and Ascension, 209–28; Med., 252, 259–60, 266
Aircraft, carrier-based, 231–3. *See also* Escort Carriers
Aircraft in A/S warfare, 245; types, 43; list, 44; So. Atl. strength, 209, 212
Aircraft, Navy, 42–4, 245; Liberator, 43–4, 91n, 99–104, 227–8; "Madcat," 93–103; Catalina, 131, 216; Ventura, 146, 206, 219; Mariner, 195–7, 226; "Nightowls," 285n
Aircraft types, Army, Liberator, 69, 88–94, 129–32; Bolo, 196, 216; Mitchell, 225–7. *See also* Army Air Force
Aircraft types, British, Swordfish, 39n, 78, 82, 307–10; Wellington, 53, 89; Halifax and Sunderland, 92; Beaufighter, 266; Lancaster, 310

Aircraft types, Canadian, Canso, 71; Liberator, 151; Sunderland, 148
Aircraft types, German. *See* Luftwaffe
ALABAMA, 230
Albert Gallatin, 187
Alexander, Lt. (jg) J. H., 101
ALNWICK CASTLE, 311
ALSTERUFER, 104, 227
ALTAIR, 50
AMETHYST, 339
AMICK, 357
ANCYLUS, 321
Anderson, Rear Adm. Bern, x
ANDRES, 49
Andrew G. Curtin, 305
Andrews, Vice Adm. Adolphus, 178–80, 188
ANNAMITE, 157
ANNAN, 329n
ANSON, 231, 308
ANTHONY, 335
Antisubmarine. *See* A/S
A/S Commands, 12–31
A/S Development Det. (Asdevlant), 50–51
A/S Measures and Warfare Units, 22n, 48
A/S Survey Board, 16–17, 39n
A/S Training, 8–9, 47–51
A/S Warfare, summary for 1943, 244–8; for the war, 361–4
A/S Warfare Op. Research Group (Asworg), 22n, 24, 146, 208–10
"Aphrodite," 138, 180, 205, 221